WOMEN IN THE CHARTIST MOVEMENT

STUDIES IN GENDER HISTORY

Recent years have shown that the study of gender has proved to be of too great an importance to be ignored. By challenging long-accepted approaches, categories and priorities, gender history has necessitated nothing less than a change in the historical terrain. This series seeks to publish the latest and best research, which not only continues to restore women to history and history to women, but also to encourage the development of a new channel of scholarship.

Published titles

Jutta Schwarzkopf
WOMEN IN THE CHARTIST MOVEMENT

Cornelie Usborne
THE POLITICS OF THE BODY IN WEIMAR GERMANY

Women in the Chartist Movement

Jutta Schwarzkopf

MACMILLAN

First published 1991

Published by
MACMILLAN ACADEMIC AND PROFESSIONAL LTD
Houndmills, Basingstoke, Hampshire RG21 2XS
and London
Companies and representatives
throughout the world

Typeset by Nick Allen/Longworth Editorial Services
Longworth, Oxon.

Printed in Hong Kong

British Library Cataloguing in Publication Data
Schwarzkopf, Jutta
Women in the Chartist Movement.—(Studies in gender history).
1. Chartism
I. Title II. Series
322.440941
ISBN 0–333–53915–X

Contents

Chps 3 4 6 8

Acknowledgements

This book has evolved from a Ph.D. thesis, and my thanks are due, foremost of all, to Logie Barrow, who has seen this work through from beginning to end over a period lasting for more than nine years. In the process, he proved to be stimulatingly critical while an unfailing source of support. His manner of supervising foreshadowed a time when differences of gender and status would no longer imply hierarchical relationships: it was always highly sensitive to the unequal distribution of power between a male supervisor and a female researcher and, moreover, one who was researching into women's history.

I am also greatly indebted to Eileen Yeo, who, from the very beginning, guided me through the maze of mid-nineteenth-century English social history. She particularly helped me to reach an understanding of Chartist women's political aspirations by drawing my attention to the forces constraining these women's choices.

Barbara Taylor gave me a great deal of encouragement, especially at the early stages of my work, while her *Eve and the New Jerusalem* proved to be a profuse source of inspiration. Angela John generously shared with me her knowledge about the women of the period, and I owe a great deal to the interest she has shown in my project. Earlier drafts have greatly profited from critical comments by Nancy Grey Osterud, Dagmar Herzog and Vibeke Jensen, who became a close friend in the process.

This book would, however, not have come into being without Rachel Magowan, who made me very welcome on the many occasions when my research required lengthy stays in London. Her interest in my work never flagged, and the language, not to say the contents, of many a chapter, painstakingly combed through for linguistic inaccuracies and clarity, benefited from her sharp comments.

In the final stages, when time was at a premium and a manuscript needed to be turned into a typescript ready for the public gaze, Christine Weber's commitment easily matched my own.

The research for this book was made possible by grants from the Studienstiftung des deutschen Volkes, the British Council, the

German Historical Institute and Bremen University.

My particular thanks are due to Ruth and Eddie Frow, who welcomed me into their Salford home and let me see the Chartist material they had collected over the years, including one of their greatest treasures, the only copy of R. J. Richardson's *The Rights of Woman* extant in the UK.

Finally, I would like to thank the staff of the many libraries I visited, particularly of the British Museum, Bloomsbury and Colindale, who made available to me the rich materials of their archives.

List of Abbreviations

ELFPA	East London Female Patriotic Association
FCA	literally: Female Chartist Association, used here to denote the female Chartist association of any given locality
FPU	Female Political Union
LFDA	London Female Democratic Association
LWMA	London Working Men's Association
NCA	National Charter Association
WMA	literally: Working Men's Association, used here to denote the male Chartist association of any given locality

Introduction

When, towards the end of the 1830s, working people merged their grievances in the People's Charter, a struggle that had lasted for decades reached its climax. The movement that evolved around the Charter fought for universal male suffrage. It saw this as the precondition for improving working people's situation by ensuring their representation in parliament. The movement was important at the time – and still is as the subject of historical reflection – not only in the intensity of its struggles, in the large numbers it involved, in the national coherence it achieved despite the pronounced variability of local conditions, but also as a relevant factor in constituting British workers as a class. Chartism was the first instance of a political movement initiated and sustained by working people relying on their own resources alone. According to E. P. Thompson,[1] in Chartism, the working class was 'no longer in the making . . . but already made'. The struggles immediately following the movement's petering out after 1848 lacked its radical challenge of the social system.

This conventional account of Chartism is seriously flawed due to its exclusive focus on class, which is, moreover, conceived of as an ungendered social category. Traditional historiography has always assumed men and women to have been affected equally, in both manner and extent, by the socio-economic changes that occurred in the course of industrialisation. Consequently – as traditional history would have it – they hoped to achieve identical results, by recourse to identical means, through their involvement in Chartism. This approach has presumed men and women to be equivalent with reference to their way of acting politically, or has subsumed women, as political actors, under men.

The resulting blindness to the interaction of women and Chartism afflicts the bulk of the movement's historiography. Despite marked differences of approach, studies of Chartism have all focused on the class-based issues the movement pursued. Although the presence of women in Chartism has been noted right from the beginning,[2] reference to them has remained accidental and limited to more or less anecdotal evidence throughout.

1

It is Dorothy Thompson's merit to have paved the way for filling this gap. In her seminal article,[3] she has placed women's involvement in Chartism in the tradition of female participation in radical politics since around the end of the eighteenth century and has tentatively accounted for their subsequent dropping out of working-class politics. Meanwhile, other historians, and Dorothy Thompson herself, have brought to light additional features of female participation in the movement.[4] Yet all of these studies have been confined merely to adding evidence of women's presence in the movement to that of men.

The Chartist movement, like anything historical, occurred in social conditions that were characterised not only by divisions of class but also by those of gender. The term 'gender' denotes the fundamentally social quality of all distinctions based on sex. Like class, therefore, gender is not a natural given, but is constantly constructed and reconstructed in the battle of power between women and men, both within the same class and across class lines.

Women, unlike men, experience suppressive conditions of power and domination not only according to their position in the productive process: for them, power and domination also become concrete in their relations with men. These relations can be classified as patriarchal. They represent a particular male-dominated organisation of relations between men and women, in the process of which gender differences are produced and defined. These living processes are common to all people, and the unfolding of historically specific forms of masculinity and femininity is influenced, however variably, by class position. Relations of gender, in their historically specific forms, have been similar to relations of class in that they have conferred radically unequal chances for the development and satisfaction of human needs. They have therefore necessarily involved struggle wherever women have become aware of the forms of male control and the unequal exchanges that most transactions on the base of gender imply. The construction of gender is thus the result of men and women's interdependent efforts. This is because women, just like men, interact with their environment, and in this sense they are the agents of their own history (rather than victims passively enduring the onslaught either of allegedly determinative im-personal structures or of the personal whims of men who are imagined to be incessantly seeking gratification at women's expense).

In the wake of the Industrial Revolution, traditional demarcations of social status and customary ways of life were being eroded. Thus, adjustment to the changing conditions involved the renegotiation of the relations of both class and gender throughout large sections of British society.

By the time Chartism emerged, the middle class had established its own class-based identity and had, through the 1832 Reform Act, won political recognition of its success in trade and manufacture. Ruthless competition in the economic sphere was counterbalanced by a domestic realm that was sentimentally cast as a haven of purity, offering refuge from the impurities and adversities of the world outside. This rigid division of the world into a public and a private sphere served at the same time to define masculinity and femininity respectively. In the public sphere of the economy and politics, men wielded power, while in the private one of home and family, women exerted moral influence, this vestige of their power. Davidoff and Hall have recently shown in great detail[5] how this division of the world along gender lines operated at every level of middle-class life, and what tensions it created for women who wished, or were forced, to live the prescribed ideal in often adverse circumstances. The redefinition of masculinity and femininity were constitutive elements in the formation of the middle class and rose to social dominance along with its proponents.

Among plebeian people, too, the socio-economic upheaval of the early nineteenth century produced a response that, though less unified, equally encompassed all types of social relations, those of gender and family as well as those of production. The small vanguard movement of the Owenites, inspired by the wish to make a clean break with the 'old immoral world', strove to build a completely new society from the fragments of the old one. In the realm of productive relations, they attempted to replace competition by co-operation, while in the field of gender relations, they made a bid for sexual equality and collectivised family life.[6]

The vast number of people who rallied round the Charter, though lacking the Owenites' visionary impetus to remould social relations entirely, were as preoccupied with preserving the status of their various trades as with what they saw as men's and women's proper station in society and as healthy family life. These concerns were shared by men and women alike. For women, participation in Chartism was to represent the high, and at the same time final, point of their involvement in radical politics. With the waning of the Chartist movement, women almost entirely disappeared from working-class campaigns for the next three decades. In the Chartist era, men and women were brought together in an unprecedented swirl of political activities; yet subsequently, they took divergent routes.

Women's conspicuous absence from working-class politics in the third quarter of the nineteenth century is an important pointer to the differential impact of Chartism's defeat on its male and female adherents. When the political struggle against the impact of industrialisation by means of the Charter was definitely lost, working-class men increasingly turned to trade unions as a way of improving their lot. Though an immediate failure, the campaign for the Charter had bolstered male working-class stamina, enabling men to come to terms with industrial capitalism and to fight for improvements from within. By the same token, the definite defeat of Chartism left women doubly disempowered. Not only had their Chartist aspirations been foiled, but in the course of campaigning for them, women had also lost out with regard to their scope of action and their ability to bring pressure to bear in public. The class that came into its own in Chartism was one in which women's needs and requirements were submerged in those of men and in which unquestioned male authority and female subservience, its counterpart, became the proclaimed hallmarks of working-class masculinity and femininity respectively. In the Chartist struggle, in the course of which working people confirmed their class identity, issues of class closely intermingled with those of gender. In this process, working men staked out their claim to a place within the pale of the constitution. This claim partly rested upon, and reinforced, the standards of man- and womanhood that working people hammered out in the Chartist era.

It is the impact of Chartism on the construction of gender and on gender relations as an integral part of the formation of the working class that are traced in the following chapters.

*   *   *

Chartism was, despite marked regional variations, a British movement. Thus its impact on gender relations has to be evaluated, first, on an all-British scale. There are good reasons to assume that what was true for England in this respect applied equally to Scotland and Wales. However, consideration of Scottish and Welsh national specificities has been omitted for reasons of manageability.

Furthermore it should be noted that the term 'feminism' – a creation of the late nineteenth century – and its derivatives have here been applied, however anachronistically, to those ideas that focused, more or less critically, on women's gender-specific condition. Such ideas existed in various forms long before the label was invented.

1
Changes in Plebeian Women's Living Conditions

From around the middle of the seventeenth century, the guild-dominated urban industries increasingly failed to provide for the growing demands of expanding markets, whether at home or abroad. Merchant capital therefore began to extend into the countryside, putting out to rural dwellers the raw material for the production of a great number of consumer goods, and textiles in particular. This development centred on rural districts with poor soils and a marked seasonality of agricultural activity, where there existed a workforce who, though living off the land, depended upon supplementing their income by non-agricultural labour. Their consequent ability to survive on less than subsistence wages rendered their employment particularly profitable. As a result of growing demand, earnings obtainable from handicraft production increased, and what had started off as a source of supplementary income gradually became a full-time employment. In the course of this process, peasants turned into fully fledged waged labourers, who went about their trades in their own homes.

In this domestic industry, the whole family functioned as the unit of production, with all its members, regardless of sex and age, contributing to the family income. Rural domestic workers thus lived in a 'family economy', which, according to Tilly and Scott,[1] was constituted by 'The interdependence of work and residence, of household labor needs, subsistence requirements and family relationships.' Non-upper-class women had customarily been expected to work for their own upkeep even in marriage.

Obviously, no changes took place in a historical vacuum. In the peasant household of the previous period, men and women had not only carried out different tasks, but had also occupied different spaces. While men had performed public functions for

6

the family and the farm, women had taken care of all matters domestic, including the household as well as the private affairs of family life. As long as the agrarian basis of domestic industry remained intact, men continued to carry out most of the labour outside the home.

As a result of the increasing subjection of those families involved in domestic industry to the fluctuations of a market economy, this rigid division of labour was eroded. In order to maintain a given level of income in times of trade decline, the family had to expand its output. One way of achieving this consisted in reallocating the family's entire labour resources to income-generating activities. In weaving, for example, it became common for both husband and wife to work a loom, and the same was true for other textile trades, such as lace making and framework knitting.

Despite this flexibility of work roles, supervisory functions, expressive of social status as they were, remained a male domain. The husband/father was normally responsible for the execution of the work obtained from the putter-out and accordingly assigned to the members of his family the various tasks involved in the productive process. In weaving, for instance, small children and old people would help by winding the weft for those family members working a loom. Furthermore, the father trained his children in his trade. On account of his ability to devote himself full time to producing goods for sale, which combined with supervision as a male prerogative, the husband/father counted as the chief earner within the family economy.

Women's labour, on the other hand, had become devalued following the expansion of domestic industry, which brought increasing competitive pressure to bear upon traditional workshop production. Refusal to take on female apprentices was one means of counteracting this pressure. Conversely, the availability of work for women within domestic industry reduced parents' motivation to put their daughters out to apprenticeships. Female labour in domestic industry, thus deprived of formal qualification, was cheaper than in workshops. In the context of the family economy, women's cash earnings, regardless of the necessity and actual extent of female contributions, came to be associated with household duties and thus to be regarded as supplementary to the income provided by the husband/father. These developments were rooted in the sexual division of labour, within which housework and childcare were women's responsibility. The ensuing differential value conferred upon male and female labour helped create the male figure of the chief earner or 'breadwinner'.

Apart from sharing in the family's productive process, the wife/mother had to fulfil all reproductive tasks. The flexible integration of housekeeping and childcare with producing goods for sale was feasible because, in domestic industry, the production of both goods and people took place in the home. Although reproduction was defined as women's primary responsibility, time spent on productive tasks might take precedence over reproductive ones according to economic requirements, possibly even leading to a temporary role reversal with regard to household chores.[2]

In peasant society, deferred marriage had been common, for the young men had had to wait for an economic opening before starting a family. Older brides were given preference, because they were more useful as work partners and had fewer childbearing years before them. These prudential factors shaped the norms of rural communities, governing the rules of courtship and premarital sex.

In a waged-labour relationship, on the other hand, the labourer, freed from these economic constraints, tended to reach a maximum income relatively early. In such an economy, marriage and children could be a positive asset as sources of domestic labour and thus of increased income. Inherited property as a determinant of family and household formation therefore gave way to the overwhelming importance of family size in domestic production. Consequently, the age at which sexual activity commenced decreased, along with the age at which marriages were contracted.

In the pre-industrial period, premarital intercourse was almost universal in rural districts. In Lancashire, for instance, premarital intercourse was common among couples intending to marry[3] and was looked upon as something young men were entitled to. According to the Poor Law Commissioners, it was commonly believed that if a girl refused to have intercourse, she would be abandoned and never acquire a husband.[4] Such behaviour did not arouse concern, occurring as it did between parties who had agreed to marry anyway. If the man defaulted, the close-knit community was able to exert sufficient pressure on him to marry the woman or to form a stable common-law union with her, which, in public consciousness, was as valid as marriage proper.

Not only did premarital intercourse frequently result in premarital pregnancy, but, in view of the premium on children, in many parts of Britain marriage was commonly delayed until signs of pregnancy proved the woman's fertility. Accordingly, the technical legitimacy of children was not held to be essential. Neither did sexual experience nor even an illegitimate child spoil a woman's marriage prospects altogether. Children, future wage-earners as they were, counted as positive assets, whether legitimate or not. Gandy has found with regard to Culcheth, a Lancashire handloom-weaving community, that in the early decades of the nineteenth century marrying a single mother, even if she had more than one child, was socially quite acceptable.[5] Acceptance of illegitimacy, however, was subject to economic considerations. During times of crisis, men grew reluctant to saddle themselves with another man's offspring.

From 1680 to 1800, the proportion of prenuptial pregnancies rose in England from 15 to 35 per cent, while, during the same period, the illegitimacy ratio increased from 1.5 to 5 per cent.[6] Around the middle of the eighteenth century, illegitimacy rates began to rise significantly all over Europe until, by the mid-nineteenth century, the trend began to reverse. A close study of Culcheth has revealed the interdependence of rising illegitimacy rates and employment structure. Between 1780 and 1860, it was normal for women in this village to conceive their first child out of wedlock, which resulted in 80 per cent of first children being technically illegitimate. The rate of premarital conception rose by approximately 10 per cent between the 1780s and the 1800s, reached its peak in the 1830s and subsequently declined. During the same period, over half of the total number of first conceptions resulted in the child actually being born illegitimate. A comparatively low incidence of illegitimacy in the eighteenth century was followed by a period of very rapid growth between 1790 and the 1810s, which continued thereafter, but at a slower rate. From the 1840s onwards, the incidence of illegitimacy rapidly reverted to a level similar to that of the 1780s. The rise in the illegitimacy rate was the result of a trend among women to marry later so that the age below which pregnancy usually implied a spell as a single mother increased.

When the illegitimacy rate peaked, the vast majority of

unmarried Culcheth mothers were handloom weavers. It is the
fluctuations and eventual decline of this trade – and possibly of
other branches of domestic industry as well – that account for the
development of local illegitimacy rates. In times of declining trade,
people restricted entry to marriage, only to relax their controls
when prospects improved. From perhaps as early as the 1790s
onwards, and stretching over a period of about forty years, the
secular pressure on piece-rates in weaving meant longer hours of
work if weavers were to maintain a given level of income. During
that period, illegitimacy rates rose, for unmarried mothers residing
with their parents were able to rear their children more cheaply
than they could have done had they married. The parental
household not only contained more potential child-minders, but
illegitimate grandchildren may also have been substituted for
elder children who had left the parental household. Furthermore,
courtships became more protracted, presumably as a result of the
reluctance of unmarried mothers to expose themselves to the high
rate of childbirth associated with marriage before their earlier
children began to earn. Being free of the legal ties and obligations
inherent in church marriage, common-law unions provided
another means of flexibly responding to the vicissitudes of the
trade. Whenever depression set in and the man–woman dyad
became economically unviable, both partners would be able to
return to their respective parental household.[7]

If, during the eighteenth century, a single woman declared
herself to be pregnant and charged a man with being the father of
the child-to-be, he would, under 6 George II, c. 31 and 49 George
III, c. 68, be made to pay for the child's maintenance under threat
of prison, unless he married the woman. If he absconded, mother
and child would be cared for by the parish. If the settlement of the
putative father was in another parish, the overseers would take
action to shift the expense of providing for the child by forcing the
couple to marry. As the Poor Law Commissioners discovered,
women considered it their right to swear their child on any man
they had had intercourse with, because they felt he had done
enough to be a father, and it was only by accident that he was not.
He was also likely to be the father in other cases where he had got
off.[8]

In domestic industry, male familial authority rested on the
father's/husband's economic superiority as the chief earner, while
women's contribution to the family income was recognised as

indispensable and valued accordingly. Sharing in the family's productive process was considered to be as important as bearing and rearing children, who, by their work, would increase the family's income. Especially under worsening economic conditions, the adult worker employed in domestic industry was decreasingly able to exist as an individual, and depended to a growing extent on the co-operation of a large family. The material inter-dependence of husband and wife may have been conducive to at least a 'rough equality' between them. This is indicated, for instance, by the absence from plebeian weddings of inauguration rituals typical of peasant society. These had marked both the advance in status within the community that marriage involved and the subjugation of the wife under her husband. Furthermore, community pressure, commonly expressed through charivari or 'rough music', was no longer aimed at reinforcing the rigid submission of wives, but was geared instead towards moderating domestic violence and restoring the desired degree of reciprocity within marriage.[9] In addition, men ceased invariably to be privileged consumers as compared to women, as did the rigid gender separation of pastimes.[10] In the public arena, women also assumed an active role when they instigated and participated in food riots aimed at setting a 'fair' price for articles of daily consumption. This was in accordance with women managing all monetary exchanges of the family and with allocating its few resources. Women's familial status derived from competent hand-ling of these responsibilities.

The specific conditions of production in domestic industry, then, were associated with a whole way of life that grew out of and was organised around rural cottage industry. This pattern of life came under attack in all its aspects from the changes wrought by the Industrial Revolution in the conditions of production. These changes were not confined to domestic workers alone. Those engaged in workshop trades also suffered from a decline that, though varying in pattern from one trade to another, had the same general effect. Wage levels came down, while unemployment went up, or rather, for many urban workers at least, periods of unemployment alternated with intense overwork. Overall living standards deteriorated markedly.

This decline in living standards was the result of the concentration of capital in a trade, which strengthened its bargaining power against skilled workmen by undermining the

exclusiveness of the latters' skill. Manufacturers introduced
technological innovations that enabled them to dispense with
skilled craftsmen and to employ cheap, unskilled labour instead.
This process was further accelerated by the erosion of
apprenticeship restrictions. The ranks of women and children
streaming into occupations hitherto closed to them were swelled
by immigrants from agricultural districts and from across the Irish
Sea. The cheapness of their labour and of the goods they produced
posed a serious threat even to the ever-dwindling number of those
craftsmen who managed to preserve the exclusiveness of their skill
along with the privileged status attached to it.

Those who had already lost the battle had to rely on their wages
being substantially supplemented by the earnings of their wives
and children in order for their families to survive. The loss of
status this implied was at least as keenly felt as the gnawing pain
of hunger.

While countless men, women and children thus suffered from
overwork and underpay in the isolation of their garrets, the
spinners and weavers engaged in the cotton textile industry,
which was centred in Lancashire and the adjoining part of
Cheshire, were the first to make the transition into factories.

From around the mid-eighteenth century onwards, the
production of cotton textiles gradually moved from rural dwellers'
cottages to factories as a result of the increasing mechanisation of
the production process. The invention of quicker methods of
spinning was motivated by the discrepancy between the amount
of work turned out by spinners and the amount of yarn needed
by the weavers. The large spinning jennies required workshops or
factories for their operation, while, at this stage, weaving still
remained at home.

The mechanisation of spinning increased in turn the demand for
handloom weavers, who enjoyed a golden age of good wages and
decent living standards. This led to an enormous influx of
unskilled immigrant labour into the trade and to the consequent
collapse of customary rights and craft protection, so that weaving
as a trade was opened up to women and children. Despite this
expansion of handloom weaving, productivity did not increase
sufficiently to absorb the output of mechanised spinning. This led
to the large-scale introduction of powerlooms in the 1830s and
1840s.

In the course of the nineteenth century, there evolved in

Lancashire an increasingly rigid geographical separation between spinning and weaving. The north of the county, in continuation of its tradition of weaving plain, coarse goods by hand, became the centre of the weaving industry. The southern part of the county, on the other hand, where handloom weaving had been less common, came to specialise in spinning.

The introduction of factories brought in its wake a crucial change in the sexual division of labour involved in textile production. Spinning had traditionally been a female occupation, and in the early factories the spinning jennies continued to be operated by women and children without the assistance of any auxiliaries. The introduction of the more complex mule spinner, however, required the employment of piecers, who were directly placed under the spinner's authority and were paid out of the latter's gross wages. Spinning thus came to involve supervisory functions, and at this juncture male spinners established their paternal authority, derived from their social position in the family. It was common for the spinner's entire family to exchange their rural cottage for the factory as the locus of production, where wives and children, or other close relatives, worked as the spinners' helpers. In this manner, spinners attempted to maintain their social status both within their families and the community at large, despite their relinquishing the independence of un-supervised handicraft production and their submission to factory discipline and to a pace of work set by machinery.

In the weaving branch of the industry, the powerlooms were initially almost exclusively operated by women and children. These were given preference in employment over men due to their willingness to submit to factory discipline and to accept lower wages. The tradition of low wages, established within the family economy of domestic industry, contributed to the subsequent low pay offered to factory women. True, wages of men and women fluctuated; but the point is that women's wages remained stubbornly below 50 per cent of those of men. Around 1840, when the cotton industry was hit by a severe crisis, the average weekly earnings of the male operatives amounted to only 88 per cent of those of 1833, while the average female wage had merely gone down to 96.9 per cent. The wages of the lowest-paid female workers had even remained stationary. These figures show that women's wages, seen as merely supplementary earnings, were so close to subsistence level that in time of crisis there was not much leeway for diminution.[11]

Male handloom weavers strongly resisted factory employment. Their resistance fed upon their tradition of independence in determining the rhythm and pace of work, which domestic industry still afforded them despite the pressure under which it had come from technologically advanced production. In Marxian parlance, they tried as long as possible to delay their transition from formal to real subordination under capital because of their awareness of the radically different behavioural dispositions demanded of a workforce that operated as mere appendages of machinery. It required the pressure exerted by the impossibility of surviving any longer on handicraft production for handloom weavers' resistance to crumble and for them to become ready to adapt to factory work.

Women, on the other hand, due to the traditional subordination of female jobs in the sexual division of labour, which in turn was closely associated with women's inferior social position, were accustomed to flexibly allocating their labour power to that work-domain likely to benefit their families most. In that sense, factories simply added another dimension to women's shifting back and forth between an emphasis on domestic chores and on production for the market. Women's tradition of flexibility rendered them more adaptable to the new conditions involved in factory work, and this in turn formed the material base of that female submissiveness so highly esteemed by factory owners. Moreover, even after the transition, women's subordinate position at work remained the same: they exchanged supervision by husbands/fathers for that by overseers.

Due to competition from technological improvements, the condition of the handloom weavers deteriorated steadily. The periods of the most acute decline in handloom weaving were the years 1825–35 in the early mechanised south of Lancashire, and the subsequent decade in the north of the county, particularly after 1842, when weaving began to expand in the north on a massive scale.

In this situation, the handloom-weaving family was faced with the choice of remaining as a unit of production at a level of abject poverty, or of sending more and more of its members, mostly children, into the factories to help eke out a living. A growing number of families had to adopt the latter course, which ultimately eroded the traditional familial functions. The Children's Employment Commissioners found in 1834 that over the previous twelve years, weavers had sent almost all their children into mills. Before the introduction of protective legislation, children were able to work in factories at an earlier age than working a loom.[12] In Oldham, if two weaver's children aged fourteen and eleven were employed in factories, the family would certainly not require relief, and probably neither with only one child in employment.[13] Weavers with children working in factories were able to cling to their trade as late as 1849.[14] Yet by the end of the 1840s, the resistance of male handloom weavers to factory employment had finally crumbled, their number having declined from 240,000 to 40,000 or to one-sixth.[15]

While the handloom-weaving family was torn apart by the impact of mechanisation, the spinning family had carried its traditional roles and functions over into the factory. Family employment, recruitment and training of labour persisted in spinning factories throughout the nineteenth century,[16] although between 1820 and 1840, there may have been an increasing tendency for the master rather than the spinner to employ piecers.

Even after the massive influx of men into cotton factories, however, women not only remained predominant within the cotton workforce, but their proportion even expanded. The increase, though varying from region to region, extended to married female workers.[17]

The proportion of married female factory workers varied not only according to particular local conditions such as the demand for female labour, but also to the husband's trade and to the income he derived from it. A much larger proportion of the wives of cotton weavers than of the wives of cotton spinners continued to work in mills after marriage.[18] This fact acted as an incentive for men to strive for spinning jobs.[19]

Every working-class family went through a 'poverty cycle', which governed the changes in the form and extent of women's workforce participation in the course of a life-time. The ranks of female wage-earners were dominated by single women. Once a woman got married, the composition of the family came to bear upon its prosperity. Subsequent to marriage, couples prospered, for both husband and wife received wages. But after the births of several children, who needed supervision, the cost of living increased, while the wife's contribution to the family income decreased. At this juncture, that is, married women would give up factory employment for irregular and casual labour, improvising cash-producing activities to substitute for full-scale labour participation. As children grew up and started earning themselves, the situation improved until they set up on their own. This usually coincided with the onset of sickness and old age of the parents. Then the wife (unless she herself were ailing) was the only earning substitute for an infirm husband. If he died first, she had to become self-supporting. The desperate condition of old, single women was equalled by that of young widows with children to support.

In Lancashire, the family economy persisted under the factory system and continued to be governed by the poverty cycle, which underwent certain modifications as a result of people's adaptation to the conditions of factory work.

In the cotton district; the wife's contribution to the family income was absolutely vital.[20] The answers received by the factory inspectors interviewing female cotton-mill workers about their attitude towards the ten-hour day revealed that the overwhelming majority welcomed the reduction in hours. The only way of making up for the concomitant cut in wages, however, was in many cases a reduction in the number of daily meals for the family. Those married women who did come out in support of the twelve-hour day were their families' chief earners. Women doing piecework managed to retain almost the former level of wages by working faster.

Children's wages were also important. The Children's Employment Commissioners were repeatedly told that parents could not keep their children without finding them employment, regardless of the physical effects the work might have. This was also why parents with large families were prone to falsify age certificates so as to obtain employment for children to whom protective legislation applied.[21] The economic constraints operating on parents' care of their children also had negative repercussions on paternal functions. With the introduction of the factory system, the father's significance in providing economic security by training his children in a prospering trade was undermined. Meanwhile, children had to work harder than ever before, and received even less security in return. If parents were unable to find their children employment, they would eventually have to send some or all of them into the workhouse, at least temporarily[22] and often reluctantly.

The intricacies of a family economy are demonstrated by the case of a handloom weaver who earned 4s. a week with his wife winding for him. He also received relief from the parish. His daughter worked in a cotton mill, and her children lived with them. She fed herself and her children and paid her parents a small sum per week for lodging and childminding. A reporter who had visited them commented: 'I tried to get at the literal particulars, but there were so many charges and countercharges, and deductions and sets off, of pennies and twopences, that I gave up.'[23]

Normally wives were able to leave work only when children started earning, at which time a period of comparative family prosperity might ensue.[24] This was certainly the case in Stockport, where working wives were the most important contributors of secondary income shortly after marriage and when all children were small. As children started work at a later age, so women remained working longer, normally leaving the mills in their thirties. The same was true in Oldham, where over one-third of the women with children aged eleven and under went out to work.[25] In Preston, on the other hand, wives who were also mothers worked away from home only if forced to do so.[26] In general,

> The extent of married women's work was . . . determined . . . by economic criteria and size of family and household, industrial structure and local custom, and perhaps above all while children were young, by the level and regularity of the male wage (if there was one) in the family.[27]

Not even the onset of old age gave women respite in the daily struggle for survival. When old age was coupled with inability to work, application for poor relief became inevitable. Otherwise even old women would perform odd jobs such as selling coal.[28]

As a result of the relocation of productive labour outside the home in conditions of a persisting sexual division of labour, women's flexible integration of productive and reproductive tasks ceased to be possible. Factory women had to spend a large part of the day away from home. The working day in cotton mills was extremely long, the maximum working week being fixed at sixty hours in 1850.

The majority of factory women would delegate household chores, such as cleaning, washing and cooking,[29] as well as sometimes dress-making, to another woman, thus providing those unable to work in factories with opportunities of earning. In the early days of mechanisation, women seem to have been able to make their own clothes in their working hours, work-speed permitting.[30] After the passing of the Ten Hours Bill, a considerable number began to do their own sewing again.[31] Only a few operatives lived sufficiently close to the factory in which they worked to have their dinner at home. Many would eat at a cook-shop near the factory or have a midday meal brought to them at the mill.[32] This meal may have been prepared by the woman hired to clean the house.[33]

The payment for these services proved to be a considerable drain on women's scanty wages, which was why women welcomed the Ten Hours Bill, when the reduction in wages could be compensated for by saving the expense for hired labour in the home. But this saving, in turn, deprived other women of casual employment.[34] The Children's Employment Commissioners, however, jumped to conclusions by attributing female factory work to the need for women to pay hired labour.[35] What life was like for a woman who could not afford to pay for services is shown in the case of a mother of three who sometimes had to stay up twenty hours to complete her housework after working in the factory. She preferred working ten hours quite simply because it enabled her to go to bed earlier.[36] The double shifts many factory women had to work took their toll. Around 1850, the people worst affected by tuberculosis, the classic disease of overwork, were women between twenty-five and thirty-four, the group supplying the greatest share of millworkers.[37]

One of the major objections against female factory work put forward by middle-class observers was their conviction that factory women lacked even the most basic domestic skills. With both mothers and daughters working in the mills, the standard argument ran, girls had no opportunity to receive training, so that ignorance in domestic matters was passed on over the generations. This was why, ignorant themselves of the living conditions of the women in question, the commissioners attributed the latter's delegation of household tasks to an ignorance as to how to do these themselves.[38] The preoccupation with domestic skills also accounts for the commissioners' persistent enquiries as to whether male factory workers would consider their female counterparts fit housewives and therefore marry them. Not all the male workers interviewed were ready to concur with the commissioners' denunciation of the female workers' housewifery. It was maintained that factory women did their housework just as well as others, and that some did it even better than some servant women, who were regarded by the commissioners as more suitable wives, from having come into contact with middle-class household arrangements during their service. Some interviewees also claimed that slovenliness in factory women was a personal trait, and could not be attributed to them as a group.[39] And one woman, whose reply expressed her annoyance at the interviewer's prejudiced attitude, explained that operatives liked to marry factory women because they were neater and because, despite opinions to the contrary held by the commissioners, they were quite capable of housekeeping.[40] However, in order to preserve improvements in working conditions, working people were ready to pander to their superiors' prejudices. Thus, when petitioning in favour of the Ten Hours Act, workers pointed to the opportunity to acquire domestic skills that the reduction in hours gave to young women.[41]

The women themselves were quite often unhappy about having to delegate their housekeeping to others. This was why, after the passing of the Ten Hours Bill, they explained that now they could manage their houses with greater satisfaction to themselves[42] and could keep their homes tidier and more comfortable. This difference was also noticed by husbands.[43]

Under the factory system, women continued to bear the chief responsibility for housekeeping and could not expect much help from male members of the family. Saturday, the customary pay-day and half-day in factories, was the universal cleaning day with women being principally involved. While the children were sent to fetch water from the nearest pump, men might be seen performing tasks that could be considered within the masculine realm, such as blackleading stoves.[44] The distinction between manly and womanly tasks about the house seems to have become more marked as time went by. By the beginning of the twentieth century, no working-class man would put his virility into jeopardy by performing traditionally female tasks. And those more kindly disposed – or sensitive to their wives' exhaustion – would only help substantially on condition that news of their assistance would not spread in the neighbourhood.[45]

Even though housekeeping could, albeit reluctantly, be delegated to other women, childcare posed more difficult problems. Often there was no alternative but to hire a nurse to look after a child. This would normally be an older woman unable to perform any other work, who would take in between two and four infants depending on the amount of money mothers were willing and able to pay. Some nurses also worked as washerwomen to supplement their income, and would then depute a little girl to tend to their charges. A child would normally be nursed out until about the age of three, or a nurse-girl aged around ten might be hired to look after the infant in its home. Although this saved mothers two journeys before and after their workday at the mill, they seem to have preferred leaving their children in the care of an older person, presumably because she was more likely to possess experience and circumspection.[46]

In Preston, however, Anderson has found that only a minority of children of mothers working away from home were left with hired nurses. In 17 per cent of the cases where a mother was employed at a factory, the household contained an otherwise unemployed grandmother, and in 28 per cent of these cases there was some other unemployed person available in the house, usually a co-lodger, a sibling or a relative. Many more children were presumably cared for by close relatives living next door or up the street. Twenty-nine per cent of the women with a grandmother in the house and children under ten worked, and 58 per cent of those with no grandmother or other unemployed person in the house did not work at all. Women, then, tended to give up work when a grandmother or other non-professional childminder was no longer available.[47]

A similar pattern was found by Cooke Taylor to prevail in Stockport. As in Preston, attention to children was combined with a system of providing for the old. Aged women would keep house and take care of a family's youngest children, thus enabling the mother to go to the mill. Even non-kin women were taken in for that purpose,[48] thus maybe becoming the co-lodgers mentioned by Anderson above. Having a trustworthy female relative as a household member was held to be a great asset by factory women.[49]

It is not surprising, therefore, that on the whole only a very small proportion – less than 2 per cent – of all infant children in industrial Lancashire were cared for by professional childminders.[50] Even assuming the worst about these minders, this figure stands in stark contrast to the outcry of moral indignation at the indifference towards children that middle-class observers believed to be detectable in female cotton operatives.

Contemporary concern focused upon the high rate of infant mortality in the factory districts. This was ascribed to the practice of putting children out to nurse, the extent of which was grossly exaggerated, and to the drugging of children to keep them quiet while their mothers were at work.[51] Infant mortality in England and Wales ranged between 142 and 164 per 1000 live births between 1839 and 1861.[52] In Oldham, however, these figures were far surpassed. Here, 204 out of 1000 children died before their first birthday. This rate of infant mortality was higher than elsewhere and can clearly be attributed to the larger number of mothers working in factories.[53]

Opiates were indeed occasionally administered to children by mothers, but nurses did so regularly.[54] While parents who would rarely drug their children during the day might well administer 'sleeping stuff' to obtain an undisturbed night's rest to gather enough strength for another strenuous working day, nurses did this so as to be able to go about their own business, usually washing, which was another typical source of casual income. Very young girls, when left in charge of children, were also found to drug them, presumably to make them more manageable.

Nurses would administer drugs without the mother's knowledge or consent, but the unmistakable symptoms would soon give them away. Once having lost a child from putting out to nurse, parents seem not to have resorted to this practice afterwards. If they did persist, it was because they could trust the nurse. This seems to have been the case when a nurse did not depend on her nursing-income for survival and could therefore afford to take in fewer children to whom she could devote all her attention, without being distracted by having to do washing at the same time.

Given that the extent of children being put out to nurse was grossly exaggerated, and given mothers' reluctance to condone their children being drugged, other factors must be found to account for the high rate of infant mortality in the cotton district.

Hewitt has ascribed it to unsuitable diet and irregularity of feeding. Infants whose nurses lived near the mill were fed by their mothers during the dinner-break and would therefore be breastfed four times a day: before being taken to the nurse, during the mother's dinner-hour, in the evening, and once during the night. Others would be entirely spoon-fed.[55] Mothers did attempt to feed their infants more regularly by having them brought to them in the factory at particular hours. In many cases, however, they met with the resistance of the millowner, who thought this practice disruptive to the work.[56] Only at Ashton were children often put out to wet nurses.[57] This was made possible by three or four women clubbing together. Breastfeeding, however, did not guarantee a child's survival, for it was affected by women's deficient diet.[58]

As has been shown above, the availability of a grown-up woman in the working-class household considerably facilitated life for the married female operative. Such a person could be entrusted with the care of the children and would look after the household. Therefore it was common practice among factory operative couples to get one of their mothers to keep house for them while both husband and wife continued in the factory after marriage.[59] Lodgers, whether kin or not, would be welcomed for easing the strain on a family's financial resources.[60] All these considerations reflected the composition of the working-class household.

A feature of working-class family life commonly deplored by contemporary middle-class observers was the supposed early break-up of domestic ties, due to children earning their own wages. This was not normally the case until age sixteen or eighteen.[61] Previously children's wages would have been paid directly to their parents; or else they would have been expected to hand over virtually all their wages until about the age of fourteen, which seems to have been regarded within the working-class community as an intermediate coming of age, particularly for the son of the family, no matter whether or not it actually marked the taking up of an apprenticeship. From then on, children would be permitted to retain an increasing portion of their wages for their own use. Around the age of fifteen or sixteen, they would receive more wages than would cover their living. They would then pay their parents some money for board and lodging and pocket the rest.[62]

The reporter of *The Morning Chronicle*, visiting South Lancashire in 1849, found a great number of 'shades' of family disruption. Sometimes the scattered members of a family would remain in constant communication with each other. Sometimes only death and sickness would bring them together, and sometimes they would completely lose touch with one another, each member of the family having become part of a new circle of social relationships. The reporter found that an existence of constant labour and frequent privation tended to diminish the time during which the family remained a cohesive unit. Members of a family living in comparative comfort continued together much longer than a family struggling to live. In factory families, where children had to contribute to the family income, they withdrew and went into lodgings once they found their benefits less than their investments. He concluded that

> Nothing can be more warm and keen than the affections of parents throughout the cotton districts for children, so long as they continue children, and nothing more remarkable than the lukewarm carelessness of feeling which subsists between these parents and their children after the latter are grown and doing for themselves.[63]

The separation of parents and children was frequently precipitated by the second marriage of a parent. It was very rare for someone to live with a step-parent.

Contrary to this contemporary observer, Vincent has concluded from his analysis of working-class autobiographies that the material interdependence of the members of the family economy made for emotional as well as material cohesion. In return for their contributions to the family income, children received from their families what little emotional sustenance was to be had.[64] The bonds of affection were particularly strong between mothers and children, reflecting the greater importance of the mother in the life of a child and her role as chief sacrificer as well as protector from an occasionally drunken father.

The cohesion of families is further underlined by the findings of family historians. In Preston, according to one of these, young couples often shared accommodation with their parents.[65] In the life-cycle, the peak period for sharing with kin was not when family poverty was greatest, but when families had few children and were unlikely to be poor. This was mainly in order to avoid overcrowding, which would necessarily have resulted from two nuclear families sharing accommodation.

In Ashton – except in the case of lodging houses or during periods of economic depression – the typical dwelling, a two-storey tenement of four rooms, would be inhabited by six to eight persons.[66] Such relatively favourable housing conditions were clearly dependent on people's income.

In Oldham, on the other hand, one half of the working population lived in shared accommodation, which put considerable strains on family relations. This forming of a combined household with relatives, called 'huddling', was possible because most of the population was locally born, and because the combination of child labour with slightly higher wage levels as compared to other towns meant that the original child-poverty period was somewhat shorter. As a result, a young couple with children could be carried by relations for the worst three or four years, on the understanding that they would themselves help out when their own children were earning.[67] In Oldham, situated in the spinning region of Lancashire, co-residence would also help procure a job, given the pattern of family employment, recruitment and training common in spinning factories.

In Stockport, too, marriage was not always followed immediately by the establishment of an independent household. Lichfield therefore concludes that

> Judging from the long period of child-bearing and the age of parents when younger children began to work and when older children were likely to leave home, parents in their mid-to-late thirties began to experience a period of about twenty years when children contributed to family income. Indeed, even after marriage, working children tended to live at home with their parents into their mid-to-late twenties, an indication of a solidarity of family relationships that an established pattern of contribution of secondary wage earners to family budgets might create.[68]

It is this persistence of kinship ties and family solidarity on which most modern family historians agree. The patterns of co-residence show that assistance given and received was not necessarily mutual or characterised by immediate reciprocity. Relationships can instead be characterised along a spectrum, from support through mutuality to dependence.[69] A grandmother co-residing with young children and a mother employed outside the home suggests a relationship of mutual assistance. This could turn into dependence when old age was coupled with illness and inability to work. Then, co-residence with an earning child or grandchild was very welcome.[70]

Housing conditions, under strain from crowding through sharing with kin, were further exacerbated by the appalling standard of the accommodation that the cotton proletariat could afford. Conditions in lodging houses, the customary abode of migrant labourers, were notoriously bad with several families often crowded together in a single bedroom. Manchester's working-class districts were moreover notorious for their cellar dwellings.[71]

No wonder, then, that these dwellings held little charm for those forced to live in them. The latter preferred the street or nearest public house. Engels cogently analysed the interdependence of physical exhaustion and the impossibility of relaxation in surroundings hardly fit for human habitation in generating alcoholism.[72] Any form of indoor recreation was impossible, and the streets became the foci of a working-class neighbourhood. In the evening, when the weather was nice, they turned into scenes of enjoyment. People would laugh and gossip from door to door and from window to window. Women were apparently fond of sitting in groups on the threshold knitting and sewing, while for the young people it was an opportunity to meet and make friends.

On the rarer occasions when people were provided with better accommodation, they would take great pride in their houses and make them as comfortable as possible by furnishing them well and looking after them.[73]

So far, it has been shown how the working-class family operated as an institution providing support for its members. Solidarity and mutual help, however, extended well beyond kinship networks into the working-class community. The crucial distinction between neighbours and kin was that whereas the former would often supply invaluable short-term assistance, only kin would be

expected to take in one's household in time of crisis. Knowing the
people in one's neighbourhood, so that one would have someone
to fall back upon in case of need, was considered a great asset:[74]
the poor would not fail the poor. John James Bezer, the active
Chartist and Christian socialist, received vital support from his
poor neighbours as a little boy. When his badly rheumatic father
had been taken in by the naval college at Greenwich, his mother
fell dangerously ill. Besides working as an errand boy, he nursed
her at night, but would not have managed without his
neighbours' help, whom he praised thus:

> God bless the poor! *they* saved her life when parish doctor, and
> parish overseer had passed her by, and said that the workhouse
> would take me, after they had buried Mother; – the poor
> neighbours – not the rich ones – played the part, as they always
> do, of good Samaritans, by rushing to the rescue, and nursing
> her in turns night and day for weeks, without fee, or thinking of
> fee. God bless the poor! Amen![75]

Such assistance need not necessarily spring from kind hearts
alone, but could also serve as a sort of insurance against future
mishaps that might befall the current benefactor.

Community support networks were to persist as a feature of
working-class life into the twentieth century. From her analysis of
survival networks in London working-class districts before the
First World War, Ross has concluded that, apart from their
housekeeping skill, it was wives' neighbourhood activity that
provided the difference between mere subsistence and a
reasonable level of comfort for their families.[76]

Rathbone wrote of the poor women of Liverpool in the early
twentieth century:

> One unfailing source of help is that of neighbours and friends.
> They know the circumstances of the family as no outsider can
> hope to know them and time after time come to the rescue,
> helping with food and shelter, clothing, attendance as the case
> may require. It is to this source that application is made in any
> slight difficulty and it is only in the most serious pressure that
> help is asked either of the clergyman . . . or of one of the
> numerous charitable societies that distribute relief in food or
> clothing.[77]

Reluctance to apply to the latter may well have been due to the conditions imposed by middle-class charitable societies upon the distribution of relief. Only the 'deserving' poor were entitled to it. To qualify for relief one had not only to conform to middle-class moral standards, but also to submit to middle-class prying into one's home.

The individual wage income that factory work afforded young, single women – whose domestic responsibilities were still comparatively light – may have laid the foundation for a degree of, at least temporary, independence unknown to their counterparts in domestic industry, who were supported out of the family income, but had no right to the contribution they were making to it. The factory inspectors observed that single women on the whole resented the loss of wages resulting from the reduction of hours following the passing of the Ten Hours Act.[78] Single women with dependants to support were anyway unable to afford any wage cuts but, according to the factory inspectors, the reduced pay was even insufficient for the upkeep of a single woman on her own. It was the ensuing loss of independence that young, single women therefore seem to have resented most.

Older, married women, on the other hand, whose contribution to the family income could not be spared, or who might have been the only earners within their families, were driven by sheer economic necessity to accept the drudgery of factory work and the disruptive effects it had on family life. This is why, after the passing of the Ten Hours Act, female factory operatives from various parts of the country petitioned to be exempted from legislation framed particularly with a view to protecting women and children. The economic depression of the late 1840s and the lack of any alternative to factory employment at their place of residence deprived these women of the possibility 'to assist in honestly maintaining themselves and their families'.[79]

If it had been economically viable, older, married factory women would have preferred to have stayed at home. During the Preston cotton strike of 1853, for instance, women expressed their desire to relinquish factory labour. In its report on trades' societies and strikes, the National Association for the Promotion of Social Science, mentioned how

the agitation received a little variety from the appearance of female delegates, who travelled about and spoke at the public meetings with all the energy, and perhaps more than the loquacity of their male coadjutors. The theme upon which these women principally dilated was the obligation of the employers to pay such wages to the men as would enable them to keep their wives in comfort at home, without the necessity of sending them to work at the mills.[80]

By the last quarter of the nineteenth century, however, the majority of the women working in cotton mills had developed a tradition of skilled, well-paid work and enjoyed a limited independence not matched by working women elsewhere. By then, mill work had become a stage of their lives that most working-class women in the area could reasonably expect to pass through. The unique conditions mill-women enjoyed, combined with the inevitability of at least a spell at factory labour, both enabled and required women to develop some sense of identification with mill work. As Liddington and Norris have discovered in the course of their research into suffragists, 'Women in Lancashire took great pride in their work and were conscious of their vital importance to the national economy. England's bread [depended on the weaving done] by women in the mills around Blackburn, Preston and Burnley.'[81]

Apart from completely reorganising the production process – thereby forcing factory women to develop new ways of coping with their domestic workload – the Industrial Revolution also had repercussions on working-class sexual mores. Middle-class observers expressed great concern about what they perceived as a higher degree of interest in sexuality at an earlier age in the manufacturing districts as compared to rural areas.[82] In fact, however, the establishment of factories led at least to a decline of illegitimacy rates. In Culcheth (the Lancashire handloom-weaving village with the rocketing illegitimacy rate mentioned above), the number of illegitimate children declined dramatically when a local textile mill was opened. In Stockport, a typical cotton-mill town, the number of illegitimate children born to factory women in the early 1840s amounted to only one-third of those born to non-factory women.[83] Yet the factory system undoubtedly led to a decrease in the age of people getting married. The wages obtained by many men in Lancashire enabled them to support themselves and at least a small family while relatively young. This early independence, coupled with the expectation of wages falling with increasing age, resulted in most young people thinking it best and safest to marry young. The possibility of going into lodgings or sharing with parents made housing no obstacle to marriage. It was not uncommon for young people to get married at eighteen.

Under the factory system, the customary control over premarital sexual relationships weakened: in the context of increased mobility, the impulse to marry in the event of pregnancy was sapped or thwarted. As geographical and occupational mobility increased with the vicissitudes of the economy, men were more easily able to abandon women they had seduced, while traditional premarital sexual experiences were more precarious for women, given their unstable employment opportunities.

From court cases concerning 'neglect of family' and affiliation, as well as from observations made by charities, a picture emerges of the increasing economic pressure that acted on working-class sexual relationships in the cotton district. There were numerous cases in which a woman deserted by her husband was thrown into destitution.[84] Often a family was left behind, indicating how a woman's inability to earn on account of her child-rearing responsibilities coupled with increased family expenditure on children would induce a man to abscond. In common-law unions, even when these were long-standing and had resulted in several pregnancies, the man might have to be forced by the parish to pay for the upkeep of his children if unwilling to marry the mother.[85] His reluctance may have been due to his inability to maintain a family.[86] An order of payment for the support of a family could, of course, be evaded by leaving the parish.[87]

Machinery for tracking down defaulting husbands would only be set in motion on the wife's application to the parish for relief. Legally a wife had no guarantee of livelihood from her husband whether or not both were living together or whether they were separated, voluntarily or not. Redress could only be had through the parish, which could make the husband liable for the maintenance it had paid out to his family.

Search for work was the chief factor making for mobility in men's lives. Applications for relief by deserted wives increased in periods of high unemployment. Men might leave their families on the understanding that they would send for them once they had obtained employment elsewhere. Failing this, the financial burden thus entailed would make them reluctant to fulfil their promise. Some men tried to provide for their families during their absence, but no working man was able to lay by enough to compensate for a protracted absence of the chief earner.[88]

Resistance to legal marriage among the working class was strong. Many were quite simply unable to afford the necessary licence and, when that was not the case, were unwilling to pay the Church for it. It was only in 1837 that marriage according to religious rites other than those of the Church of England and civil marriage in the local registry office became available. Yet in its first phase, civil marriage was closely connected with the Poor Law machinery, which may well have deterred working-class people. Moreover, contracting a civil marriage was a highly complicated and costly affair, only surpassed by the intricacies involved in chapel marriage.[89]

As the evidence concerning the poverty cycle has revealed, being married and having children were essential in order to secure survival in the working class. Women depended on family even more than men due to their lower wage-levels and their reproductive capacity, which impeded their wage-earning ability at certain stages of their lives. For many women, however, marriage of any kind was unattainable due to the discrepancy in the number of men and women in the population.[90]

Lack of an earning husband, however, was not the only cause of poverty among women. In addition, they had a longer life expectancy than men at all ages. As this difference was most marked among the most badly off, poor women were more likely to be widowed with young children to support, and more likely to survive past work into old age and dependency. Due to women's economic disadvantage, marriage break-ups were also more likely to cause poverty for them than for men, especially when there were young children to support.[91] On account of the demographic disproportion between the sexes, women were less likely to remarry if widowed.

Poverty was not only reflected in women's housing conditions. The reporter of *The Morning Chronicle*, travelling the Lancashire factory districts in 1849, discovered that in Manchester, for instance, cellars would often be inhabited by poor, old, single women, and that garrets were frequently occupied by older single women making a precarious living as laundresses.[92] Poor women, whether married or not, also consistently had more deficient diets than men. Their health was further impaired by frequent child-bearing. This meant that women survived for long periods in poor health with such debilitating chronic ailments as anaemia, while men were more likely to die young from acute illness or occupational hazards to which they were more prone. Consequently, throughout the history of the New Poor Law, women formed the majority of adult recipients of relief both from the parish and charities.[93]

The New Poor Law, introduced in 1834, completely reorganised the parish relief system. It had been framed with the intention to render application for relief less attractive than even the most menial labour available. In principle, outdoor relief was abolished and replaced by reception of the needy into the workhouse. Inside it, husbands and wives as well as mothers and children over the age of two were separated in order to discourage procreation and to enforce the recognition among the poor of the value of family life by temporary withdrawal.

One of the most marked effects of the New Poor Law on women's lives was exerted by the Bastardy Clause it contained. It made the child's upkeep the sole responsibility of the mother. Affiliation procedures were rendered more complicated in order to prevent the kind of abuse that had supposedly been possible under the previous system. Formerly (as noted above), many women had allegedly sworn their child on the most well-off man who could conceivably have been the father. Under the new system, affiliation actions were transferred to Quarter Sessions, where the mother's evidence had to be corroborated independently in some material particular. The maintenance payments were not to exceed the actual cost to the parish of maintaining the child, and imprisonment of the man for failure to pay was abolished.

The punitive intentions embodied in the Bastardy Clause affected the outcome of affiliation cases. When a woman had more than one illegitimate child, the allowance would deliberately be kept small.[94] Moreover, when removed to the workhouse, unmarried mothers were treated more harshly than other women. They had to pick oakum rather than carry out domestic tasks, and for some years they were excluded from the privilege of attending church 'outside'.

When taking legal action against the father of her child, a woman would be subjected to severe questioning concerning the character of her relationship with the child's father, with a view to disproving her claim on the man involved. Alternatively, the counsel for the defendant would not deny the fatherhood but would try to protect his client against more than an ordinary order by making his income appear minimal.[95]

The new act led to an increase in the illegitimacy rate, because it removed so many of the incentives for men to marry. At the same time, the number of chargeable bastards decreased as a result of the complicated nature of the affiliation procedure. Few working-class women were likely, without the intervention of parish officers, to start their own action before the magistrates. The Bastardy Clause of the New Poor Law can therefore be seen as an expression of the ruling-class belief that the regulation of female sexuality was the key to solving what was perceived as the problem of public moral order.

By the 1830s and 1840s, there occurred decisive shifts in working-class women's sexual behaviour. The range of ways of living that were open to them narrowed markedly. Practices such as premarital pregnancy and free unions, which had hitherto been perfectly acceptable, became less desirable to women as their vulnerability in sexual matters increased. Economic disruption militated against the stability of sexual relationships, rendering the financial situation of unmarried mothers highly precarious. Their condition was exacerbated by the Bastardy Clause, the punitive intent of which was one instance of the manifold attempts, both from within the working class and from above, to impose rigid moral standards on the working population. As a result of a puritanism that fed on working-class Methodism and on middle-class Evangelicalism alike, the distinction between sexual respectability and 'irregular' behaviour became more clear-cut, and anti-erotic attitudes increasingly prevailed. Consequently, women became more prudent in indulging their sexual needs, while men faced no such constraints. By the end of the nineteenth century (and if, for once, London may serve as an example), according to Ross,[96] working-class women had come to classify sex somewhere between an experience akin to rape and an ordinary fact of life occurring without emotional intimacy. Unwilling and unable to marry on account of economic vicissitudes, men often met with female reluctance when seeking sexual pleasure. They seem to have come to regard sex as normally requiring the overcoming of women's resistance, rather than as mutually desired enjoyment. Consequently, 'seduction' frequently relied on the use of violence.[97]

This increase in violence against women outside the family was matched by a similar development within marriage. Gender relations can be inferred from court cases, and from material collected by middle-class observers – though this is tainted by their preconceptions with regard to gender roles and their ignorance of working-class life. This was why, regardless of the actual extent of this phenomenon, their attention focused on the men who, unable to find employment themselves, stood in as housekeepers for their wives, whose earnings in the mill alone maintained the family.[98] They found the men unfit and unwilling to carry out housework and highly resentful at being deprived of their role of breadwinner.

From an analysis of court cases dealing with husbands' assaults on their wives, Tomes has concluded that in the working-class marriage tensions centred around questions of privilege and allocation of resources. The husband had privileges because of his status as breadwinner. He would give his wife part of his wages to keep house and would spend the rest on himself.[99] In return for supporting her, he expected his wife to run errands for him, to prepare his food, and to keep house for him. The wife's wishes were subordinate to her husband's, and she could not exercise them without his permission. Where the husband's control of the family money was limited, tensions were likely to occur. When the wife worked and the husband did not, the usual pattern of expectations did not apply, and either person's use of the family money could be questioned.[100] That this analysis of London cases may apply to Lancashire as well is indicated by assault cases from that region, which disclose a similar background.[101]

Tomes has concluded that physical conflict between the sexes characterised situations of male insecurity rather than complete domination over women. A working-class man became violent when a woman challenged his authority rather than when she submitted to him. Disobedience could be expressed by nagging, taunting, insult or any form of wilful behaviour on the wife's part. The most provoking form of aggravating behaviour was felt to be the wife's use of 'bad language', which was perceived as an expression of insubordination.

The apparently high rates of assault in the 1840s and 1850s may have stemmed from the difficulties a working-class husband experienced in fulfilling his expected role in the family during economically unstable years. He would become more sensitive to challenges to his authority, and his wife would be less obedient since he did not fulfil her expectations of support.[102] As Vincent has found: 'The home was seen not as a refuge but as a cockpit, the arena in which the consequences of exploitation and inequality were experienced and battled with.'[103]

The effect of violent male behaviour was eased by the close-knit working-class neighbourhood. It afforded women some degree of protection from husbands who were judged by local opinion to have gone too far. Without interfering directly in violent quarrels, female neighbours would nurse a beaten wife and give her shelter. Underlying this behaviour was the belief that husbands had a right to beat their wives, especially when provoked by them, but only up to a point.

Unfortunately for such husbands, the structural base of their authority had in important parts of Britain been undermined. One aspect of the Chartist movement, as this book argues, involved an attempt by means of political action to shore up this authority.

Women, then, had to bear the brunt of the appalling conditions of working-class life in the Chartist era. In their dual role as wage-earners and mothers of families, they were equally affected by the changes occurring in the productive as well as the reproductive spheres of society. Women very often displayed great strength and ingenuity in their attempts to fend off the encroachments of the factory system on their families. In these efforts they were able to rely on the solidarity of the extended working-class family and of the community at large. .

2
The Chartist Prospect of Society

SOME REFLECTIONS ON THE USE OF CHARTIST NOVELS AS SOURCE MATERIAL

The argument put forward in this chapter relies in part on results gained from an analysis of Chartist novels. The question therefore arises of the specific use that can be made of fictional material for historiographical purposes. The term 'Chartist novel' denotes novels written by committed members of the Chartist movement. They afford important insights into Chartist thinking about women.

In a work of fiction, an author creates a world governed by coherence, a world in which each action and each incident make sense through being related to each other and to the whole of the plot. This 'world' of fiction is not a mirror image of the real world, but an ideological entity that has been created out of certain literary devices that the author has selected for the formation of a particular subject matter. Even though a literary text about Chartism may maintain empirical historical accuracy, the treatment remains fictive in that historical data operate according to the laws of textual production. Through this process, the work of fiction becomes an expression of its author's perception of social reality.

By being used as material expressive of Chartist ideology, these novels are considered in their own right as aesthetic creations, and are not abused as merely another kind of source from which socio-historical facts can be gleaned, an approach chosen by some Chartist historiographers.[1]

All novels here under consideration, as indeed all Chartist novels ever published, were written by male authors and have therefore been constituted by male thinking about women. Their analysis thus yields their authors' ideology concerning women –

the complex of ideas they held with regard to women's position in society in general and within the Chartist movement in particular. Consequently, the novels analysed have been chosen for their presentation of female characters who play an important part in the development of the plot.

The following is a brief summary of the novels selected: Thomas Martin Wheeler's *Sunshine and Shadow* was serialised in *The Northern Star* from 31 March 1849 to 5 January 1850 and deals with the lives of Arthur Morton and Walter North, two school-friends. The latter joins his father in his business, and, by ruthlessly pursuing his commercial interests, acquires great wealth so that he can marry an earl's granddaughter and eventually gains a title himself.

The orphaned Arthur Morton, on the other hand, learns the trade of printing, and his experiences as a working man, combined with his noble character and lofty ideals, make him turn to Chartism. To escape the government crackdown on the movement in 1839–40, he sails for the United States. Shipwrecked, he is rescued by the boat that is taking Julia North, his former friend's sister, to the West Indies. There she is to join her husband, whom she has been coerced into marrying by her brother. Julia and Arthur fall in love with each other, but, unable to live according to her inclination, Julia dies of a broken heart. Arthur returns to Britain, where he resumes his Chartist activities and marries a female supporter of the movement. Their initial marital happiness is blighted by a long period of unemployment and ensuing poverty. In the end, Arthur, having been involved in the events of 1848, has to go into exile and leave his family behind.

Thomas Frost's novel *The Secret* appeared in *The National Instructor* from 25 May 1850 to 19 October 1850. It deals with a working man's revenge on the family of the gentleman who seduced and then abandoned his daughter. The girl's father exchanges his grandchild for the gentleman's daughter. The novel also figures a Chartist class-leader, who falls in love with the old man's granddaughter, who is really of noble descent. This line of the plot, however, is not fully developed and seems to have been abandoned by Frost at some point.

Ernest Jones's *Woman's Wrongs. A novel. – In four Books*, which appeared in the second volume of the author's journal *Notes to the People* in 1852, was intended to depict the plight of women in all classes of society. The first book deals with *The Working-Man's*

Wife, whose life is marked by hardship caused by poverty and her husband's lack of consideration. In the end, she is hanged for a murder committed by her husband, who, following his loss of employment, has turned into a criminal. *The Young Milliner* of the second book also has to battle with poverty. For a while, she lives with a medical student, whom she genuinely loves. Unwilling to marry her due to their difference in social standing, he abandons her, and she consequently dies of a broken heart. In the third book, the eponymous tradesman's daughter is a dull being crippled by the strenuous clerical work she has to perform in her father's business. It is not until after her marriage of convenience to another tradesman that she discovers that her love for her literary-minded cousin is reciprocated. She withers away by the side of an unsympathetic husband, and, after a last meeting with the man she loves, she too eventually dies of a broken heart. The fourth book, called *The Lady of Title*, deals with what Jones considered the depravity of the aristocracy and was never completed.

CHARTIST GOALS FOR THE WORKING CLASS

The factory system that came to dominate the production of cotton in north-west England embodied, in working people's minds, the worst effects of what would one day be the lot of all. The only remedy was to put a halt to the erosion of customs and traditions of working and living observable everywhere. Thus it was that working people all over the country focused their attention on the cotton districts, without denying that in other parts of England, as yet unaffected by factory production, workers' existence was also becoming more precarious.

The Chartist project was not an exclusively economic one. At the centre of the struggle lay the concern with working people's dignity, seen as hinging on men's right to vote. The suffrage was to bring them within the pale of the constitution and to put them on a footing of civic equality with the other classes of society: the franchise was to be vested in the person and no longer in property.

Equality of citizenship would terminate 'class legislation', the powerful mechanism that enabled the ruling classes to frame laws to the detriment of the working people. To this political

oppression, itself the result of 'class legislation', Chartists traced
back working people's deprivation. Consequently it was in the
political sphere that they sought for redress of their grievances.

A very clear statement of the typical Chartist reasoning – one
that the present author arrived at independently via a reading of
Chartist petitions, but one that is also used by Stedman Jones in
his analysis of Chartism[2] – was made by Gammage. He had
himself been involved in Chartism and, in 1854–5, published not
only the first history of the movement, but also the only one ever
to be written by a veteran Chartist. Gammage maintained:

> It is the existence of great social wrongs which principally
> teaches the masses the value of political rights. . . . [In a period
> of adversity, the] masses look on the enfranchised classes, whom
> they behold reposing on their couch of opulence, and contrast
> that opulence with the misery of their own condition. Reasoning
> from effect to cause there is no marvel that they arrive at the
> conclusion – that their exclusion from political power is the
> cause of our social anomalies.[3]

This type of argument places Chartism firmly in the tradition
of radicalism, which had inspired a succession of movements
of 'the unrepresented', challenging their exclusion from political
power. The 1832 Reform Act had narrowed the social base
of 'the unrepresented' down to the working classes, rendering dispossession and disfranchisement co-terminous. Chartism's
significance, therefore, derives from its being the first self-initiated
and self-organised mass movement of the British working class.

The year 1837 saw the onset of what turned out to be one of the
worst and most prolonged periods of depression in the nineteenth
century. The economic crisis gave an edge to people's suffering
and made them look, once again, to a reform of parliament as a
means of alleviating their plight. The ensuing campaign for the
enactment of the Charter provided the national focus for struggles
that had been going on at a more regional level. There merged
into Chartism the northern campaigns for a reduction of hours in
the factories and against the New Poor Law as well as the
London-based fights against all forms of political oppression.

In Chartist parlance, the 'misery of the people' encompassed
economic deprivation and political oppression alike, which were
conceived of as two sides of the same coin, namely monopoly

political power. By fighting both, Chartism provided a comprehensive response to the Industrial Revolution, in the course of which both had become more marked, and each attempt at resisting exploitation had been quashed by either employers or the state, and frequently by both.

The identification of monopoly political power as the root of all evil, as Stedman Jones has argued,[4] made for the strength of Chartism in its initial stages. Yet as early as 1839, the government's failure to clamp down on the Convention proved difficult to accommodate to a radical frame of reference. This was even more true of the changing, less directly oppressive, character of the state that emerged as the 1840s wore on and several Factory Acts were passed. By clinging to a radical analysis of the state, Chartism sapped much of its credibility among the working classes, and the hold the movement had initially had on them dwindled away. Yet in its heyday Chartism had rallied hundreds of thousands of working people and given a focus to their hopes and aspirations by striving to bring them within the realm of respectable citizenship.

In his *Address to the Women of England*, John Watkins, the Whitby Chartist who later moved to London, fleshed out the notion of a respectable lifestyle. He drew 'the picture of a labouring man who can support himself, his wife and children, in a cottage of content, not necessitated to overtask his strength for half wages; but one, who can lay by something against a "rainy day"'.[5] Central to Watkins's picture is the 'cottage of content', which embodies his notion of sufficiency. It implies housing conditions under which each family enjoys the comfort of their own home, preferably in rural surroundings, where want and misery stay shut out. The 'cottage of content' thus stands for the extreme opposite of the living conditions obtaining in the factory districts, where people were crammed into unsanitary dwellings during the few hours of rest that a long day's toil in the factory afforded them, and where they struggled to survive on their scanty earnings.

The content prevailing in Watkins's cottage, however, is more than a function of mere material well-being. It is also the result of properly regulated familial relations, which hinge on the husband/father bringing home wages sufficient to maintain his wife and children in comfort without recourse to any supplementary income. The gender relations implied in Watkins's image provide a further contrast to the reality of contemporary working-class life and are an important pointer towards the social position Chartists wished to accord to women.

In Watkins's cottage, wife and children are maintained by the man going out to work, and indeed all Chartists were opposed to female waged labour. Although some may have envisaged women continuing to work, they all objected to women leaving their homes to perform waged labour. According to Vincent, 'We contend that home is the place for woman, and not the factory.'[6]

Chartist opposition to female waged labour outside the home was directed against the degradation it was supposed necessarily to entail, and which had many facets. The low wages paid to female workers in slop-shops and factories alike forced them allegedly to prostitute themselves in order to survive. Female servants who were unable to procure themselves a situation were also seen as often having to resort to prostitution.[7] The needlewoman was the stereotype of the poor female slaving away in a garret for a pittance. And it is this hackneyed image that Jones, the national Chartist leader and novelist, employed to denounce *Woman's Wrongs*, as his novel was called. His milliner, being an orphan, is forced to provide for herself. Her scanty wages, however, are insuffiiscient for her upkeep. Out of necessity, she accepts the offer of money from a man, who proceeds to presume on her obligation to him.[8]

The physical strain involved in the types of jobs available to women also received attention. Factory work was recognised as not so much requiring a great deal of muscular strength, but rather as wearisome by demanding unceasing attention and the endless repetition of the same movements.[9] The lot of domestic servants, on the other hand, was presented as a life of unremitting toil. According to Frost, their drudgery deprived them of all human dignity.[10] Female servants were considered to be completely at the mercy of their masters and mistresses, often to be overworked and underpaid, until finally dismissed due to exhaustion caused by overstrain. These women, unless virtually worked to death, were supposed commonly to end their lives as beggars or prostitutes. Alternatively, they were assumed to have to eke out a living from some sort of casual labour until finally dying in the street from exposure or in the dreaded workhouse.[11] Female slop-workers, finally, were depicted as suffering from excessive hours of work under unhealthy conditions for scanty pay. Their labour was held to generate illness and premature death, driving the most desperate among them to commit suicide.[12]

Chartists perceived waged work outside the home as contravening female nature. Vincent's denunciation of factory women having to carry out men's work, made in 1839,[13] was echoed as late as 1851 by a 'working man in Loughboro'' writing in to the *Notes to the People* and complaining that, in the hosiery industry, girls had to perform men's work.[14]

Jones, too, conceived of work as something alien to woman's nature, threatening her well-being. The tradesman's daughter of the third book of his novel, though not earning a salary, is indispensable to her father's business, yet at the price of being deprived of her looks and moral character. The author describes her as a being so completely void of any human characteristics as to resemble an automaton. Having been made subservient to her father's commercial interest, her body has been crippled, and the dullness and exertion of her job lead her to seek relaxation in trashy novels. Women, according to Jones, have some innate romantic yearning, which the systematic routine involved in all kinds of waged work cannot gratify.

Other Chartists went even further by denying women the physical capacity to perform any arduous work at all. The female working-class protagonist of Wheeler's novel *Sunshine and Shadow* does not carry out any waged labour until compelled to do so by her husband's prolonged unemployment. Yet her constitution cannot sustain the combined impact of poverty and exertion, and consequently her health fails.[15]

It was the condition of women working in coal-mines that, in Chartist opinion, highlighted the suffering that female waged labour generally entailed.[16] This had been brought to public attention by the reports of the Children's Employment Commission formed in 1840. The commissioners' first task involved the examination of children's work in mines and collieries, where the investigators were so horrified by the condition of female mineworkers that they included them in their reports on their own initiative. Chartists eagerly seized on the evidence collected by the middle-class inspectors, inserting extracts from it in their papers.[17] This was despite the fact that these observations were tainted by a marked class bias and ignorance of working-class life, which led the investigators to condemn outright anything that did not conform to their standards of morality. Female mineworkers were thus presented as the epitome of immorality and degradation. Due to the heat underground, it was pointed out, women dressed indecently. Swearing and filthy songs were found to be common among them, as were obscene conversations, and the early marriages common in colliery districts were attributed to boys and girls working together in seclusion.[18] Even statements concerning marriage customs were thus used to insinuate licentious behaviour.

The adverse impact of waged labour on women, Chartists feared, also imperilled future generations, as highlighted by the soaring rate of infant mortality. This was attributed to factory work impairing women's health and to the lack of consideration given to pregnant women, who had to carry on working until their confinement, some even giving birth on the shopfloor. Women's speedy return to their jobs was seen as preventing them from breast-feeding their babies. Consequently, the mothers fell ill, and their children were given opiates to keep them still.[19]

Again in the coal-mines, even worse conditions were supposed to prevail. There was no relief for pregnant women either, who had to continue working despite terrible physical conditions. Pit women, furthermore, brought their children down the mines as they had no one to mind them. As a result, very young girls had to carry out extremely arduous tasks and thus became used to working underground. Chartists concurred with middle-class observers in believing that habituation from infancy was the only means of overcoming innate female virtue and of breaking girls in for colliery work. Chartists thus chimed with middle-class opinion: these girls were unfit to become wives and mothers, and thus the cycle of degradation was perpetuated.[20]

The abhorrence Chartists evinced at women's working conditions was not directed at exposing the exploitation occurring at the workplace; rather it derived from the multifaceted degradation that waged labour outside the home was seen as entailing for women by definition. In the case of the female mineworkers, concern for the suffering female receded in the face of the outcry of moral indignation at the indecency and licentiousness supposed to prevail underground. Likewise, anxiety about the well-being of working mothers' offspring predominated over the plight of the toiling women. In Chartist novels, labour, once it has become habitual, is shown to have the most deplorable effects on the woman concerned. Yet this is not the result of the nature of the work performed – clerking of the kind described by Jones must be equally stupefying for the male mind – but is attributed to its incompatibility with female nature. Furthermore, waged labour was condemned for the sexual abuse it entailed. Thus, waged labour outside the home was primarily considered a sexual issue in that it was rejected for its pernicious effects specifically on women rather than for the economic exploitation it entailed for all waged labourers regardless of their sex.

Chartists were wary of the adverse effect on general wage levels caused by women competing with men in the labour market. As Vincent explained:

> And the system has not only a tendency to drive women and children to drudging toil, but the throwing [of] so many new hands into the labour-market has an immediate effect in reducing wages; so that after the workman has sent his wife and children to work, their very labour competes with his, and wages soon fall to the price at which the cheapest labour can be purchased.[21]

The supreme remedy Chartists advocated in view of this evil was 'universal representation', which would abolish the whole system 'generative of these abuses'. More to the point, Chartists endorsed the total prohibition of female labour in coal-mines and elsewhere. Publicising the abuse of women's work underground to ensure its abolition was recommended as a course also to be followed with regard to other branches of female employment.[22] J. R. Stephens of Stalybridge, familiar with the plight of factory workers from living among them, called on husbands to put an end to female factory work simply by resolving not to let it continue any longer:[23] women's chief employment was to be in the home.[24]

Tied up with the demand for women's withdrawal from waged labour was male resentment at losing control over their dependants' labour power. In the early nineteenth century (as noted in Chapter 1), at least in spinning, entire families had changed the location of their work by moving from domestic workshop to the factory, where the husband/father continued to supervise the labour of his family. The 1833 Factory Act, however, which limited the hours of children working in the textile industry, as well as attempts at introducing the self-acting spinning mule, which began around the same time and threatened the kinship-based staffing and training system, jeopardised the coherence of the family as a work unit. It is to these developments at the workplace, as Smelser has argued,[25] that Chartist opposition to female factory labour has to be related. For Chartists, the problem of child supervision created by the 1833 Act was to be solved by mothers staying at home, which would simultaneously have prevented the transfer of the control over their labour power to someone outside the family.

This had long been the case in weaving, where children and women had preceded men in the factories and where command over their labour power had shifted from the husband/father to the mill-owner. The Chartist denunciation of female factory labour as slavery is thus revealed as hinging on the person of the supervisor, and not on the amount of work actually performed. Women's contribution in domestic industry may have entailed the same amount of labour; the crucial difference was that it had taken place under the supervision of the male head of the family.

The factory system also threatened the working-class male's prerogative with regard to his dependants' sexuality: thence the preoccupation with female virtue, seen as jeopardised by the encroachments of men in authority. In the factories, where the employment of women was nearly exclusive, the absence of men able and willing to defend them was believed to render factory women fair game for masters and overseers. Likewise, female servants were considered liable to be seduced by their masters and consequently driven into prostitution.[26]

In a series of articles denouncing the evils of the factory system, Peter Murray McDouall, the Manchester Chartist, painted a lurid picture of textile factories as the site of working-class women's sexual degradation. Central to his scenario of large-scale seduction was a room set aside at the mill, 'decorated with the splendour which the profits of the master can easily bestow upon it, and adorned with the appliances of luxury and the convenience of vice'. The incident taking place in these purpose-built rooms was presented as an infringement on the (literally) patriarchal power of the victim's menfolk, who had to suffer 'the most promising flowers of the workman's home' being 'corrupted, debased, and withered by the biting poison of vice and immorality'.[27]

However, as early as 1844, Cooke Taylor, having investigated conditions in the cotton district of Lancashire, refuted as unfounded any allegations that sexual relationships between factory women and their superiors were commonplace.[28] True, Cooke Taylor was a fervent advocate of the factory system. Yet the correctness of his statement has recently been borne out by a modern study.[29] Furthermore, *The Northern Star* itself carried reports of sexual assaults which showed where sexual dangers for working women really lurked. In these cases, women had been attacked on their way home from work.[30]

In view of these observations, Chartist concern with sexual abuse by overseers in particular appears interestingly out of proportion. Overseers were indeed able to presume upon their position of authority over the workers in their charge. They had considerable control over the hiring and dismissal of the workforce and, from 1847, overseers in cotton weaving were paid a commission, which gave them a direct interest in the productivity of those in their charge. The Chartist preoccupation with sexual abuse by overseers can be interpreted as a largely male obsession resulting from the loss of control over working-class female labour power and sexuality. This had passed to other men who, despite their working-class origin, came to be identified with the mill-owners on account of their supervisory function and the power they wielded. Sexual abuse of mill girls was thus also an emotive metaphor for workers' oppression. It harked back to the image of the innocent but poor maiden seduced and abandoned by an aristocratic libertine, which had originated with the Jacobin novelists of the eighteenth century. This metaphorical class rape powerfully expressed the double loss of control sustained by working-class men in the course of industrialisation. As waged labourers, they were at the mercy of their employers, who used and abused them economically in much the same way as higher-class men exploited lower-class women sexually. As fathers of families, they had lost the power to protect their daughters' chastity. Despite its sexual imagery, the metaphorical class rape translated potential anger at sexual exploitation to the level of class conflict. Thus, the metaphor effectively prevented working women from publicly voicing antagonism towards men of their own class. The anger given vent in this metaphor was felt by the fathers, brothers and lovers of the women victimised by the actual occurrence.

As Lambertz has found, working-class male concern with

preserving their exclusive sexual rights persisted at least until the turn of the century. According to her, incidents of sexual abuse in factories 'in fact posed a challenge to patriarchal and brotherly prerogatives of female protection (in the literal familial sense)'. As the Chartists had used allegations of sexual misconduct in their attempt to get rid of female undercutting of men's wages, so trade unions or unionised men around the turn of the twentieth century were prone to 'raising the spectre of sexual pressures to facilitate their battles for job control and male retention of skilled, higher-status "men's" jobs'.[31]

Women's withdrawal from waged labour outside the home was conditional upon their acquiring a husband willing and able to provide for them. Advocacy of the man as breadwinner was Stephens's concern in his addresses to working people and was also implied in Watkins's description of the 'cottage of content'.

Chartists fervently advocated marriage, and not only in order to secure women their livelihood. The preservation of marriage was a class issue at a time when it had to bear the combined onslaught of working-class poverty and government measures. *The Friend of the People*, for instance, quoted Louis Blanc as maintaining that only the abolition of want would prevent domestic ties among the proletariat from disintegrating.[32] Doing away with privation was central to Chartism's project, and Chartists thus cast themselves as the preservers of marriage and the family. Moreover, this stand had clearly class-conscious overtones, directed as it was against the implementation of the New Poor Law, which had been framed according to Malthusian principles. Against this doctrine and its embodiment in the workhouse system, Chartists eulogised marriage as the highest state of humanity and declared attention to its duties and the enjoyment of its blessings to be the most holy and sacred of all things.[33]

In response to the attempts at discouraging marriage among the working classes, Chartist novelists reclaimed working people's right to marital happiness by presenting it as being conditional upon the absence of ulterior motives generated by the greed for money. According to Wheeler, it was only among the poor that marriage occurs in unadulterated form.[34] In the same vein, Frost justifies the combination of 'Love and Poverty' in one of the chapter headings of his *The Secret*:

The two words which we have put together at the head of this chapter have been regarded as irreconcilable, but it may be fairly questioned whether there is the minutest fraction of truth in the assumption . . . that poverty is an enemy to passion. . . . So far from love being incompatible with a state of poverty, it may safely be asserted, that there is more of real love among the poor than among the rich, including under the latter denomination both the upper and middle classes. The circumstances under which marriage is generally contracted in the higher circles of society render that holy institution little better than a legalised priest-sanctioned prostitution.[35]

Marriage based on true love is here contrasted with marriage as a bargain, which, by definition, cannot occur among the poor, but is confined to the wealthy ranks of society. The language in which Jones couches the reflections of Laura's father and suitor concerning the tradesman's daughter's marriage denounces their intentions as mere business calculations:

His [the suitor's] capital had been doubled, and he began to entertain a design, of which he would not as much as dreamt of a few years before. This project he subjected to an arithmetical examination, and found that the total was favorable to his interests. Accordingly, he at once set about realising the 'transaction'.

Laura's father

had understood its meaning, and at once had recourse to an arithmetical calculation of loss and profit by the proposed transaction. Having balanced accounts, ascertained Ellman's share in the concern, and considered that by the projected marriage his daughter's dowry would not go out of the firm, he came to the conclusion that the business would be profitable, and that he was justified in giving into it.[36]

In this passage, both father and suitor are mere incarnations of business interests, for no consideration of the human issues involved in a marriage enter into their calculations. The woman concerned is a pawn in the men's scheme. For the father, she becomes a merchandise proffered to the highest bidder, while for the husband she becomes the show-piece of his wealth and splendour.

Both Jones and Wheeler[37] compare marriages that merely support the woman in style, but are devoid of any mutual sympathy, to prostitution. Both rehabilitate the latter at the expense of the former. Jones lets one of his characters reflect:

> what difference there was between the woman who sold herself body and soul to a husband for a social position, and the prostitute who sells herself to the libertine for the bread that shall save her life, unless it is, that the first makes the better bargain, and that a parson plays the broker.[38]

Marriage, unless hallowed by mutual love, is seen as a desecration of human affections, and it is the women who suffer within this perversion most.

And yet marriage was held to be an institution for the particular benefit of women. In Chartist opinion, it was a major achievement of civilisation, enhancing women's protection. Descriptions of foreign customs carried by the Chartist press served to expose polygamy – the antithesis of monogamous marriage – as permitting men irrationally to indulge in passion and pride. These would convert 'the family circle into a caldron of passion most repugnant to concord and happiness'.[39]

Marriage was believed to be essential for regulating male and female passion alike. According to Barbara Taylor,[40] the superiority of reason over passion in forming sexual relationships as a prerequisite for enhancing women's status was a leitmotif running through feminist writing from Mary Wollstonecraft to at least the Owenites. By adopting such a 'rational' view of marriage, Chartists took up a relevant female issue.

Women were presented as being in need of regulations under whose protection they could indulge their passion without harming themselves. In *Woman's Wrongs*, Jones described in the following way a woman giving way to her passion for a man who will never marry her:

> She was his – she felt it – yes, she felt instinctively the full force of that union; hesitation and fear had flown – and she gave herself up, after a passing coyness – the last faint stand of retiring innocence before the foe – to the full torrent of her

generous, ardent, enthusiastic love. She tried to drown reflection in continued ecstasy.[41]

Woman's love, described by three positive epithets in this passage, is presented as a force breaking down the confines of morality and hence its counterpart in female nature, namely coyness and innocence. Women, too weak to stem this 'torrent' on their own, therefore require social regulations to dam their love's force and channel it into marriage.

Yet in the Chartist period, conditions were not conducive to marital happiness among working people. The disruptive impact on marriage and the family was at the forefront of Chartist denunciations of women's labour outside the home. J. R. Stephens, for one, never tired of condemning the factory system for what he considered the upsetting of the natural order of things. Pervaded as he was by the deep belief in God having ordained man and woman to marry and multiply, he was horrified at the factory system's contravening of God's will. In Stephens's opinion, it had made women abhor the very idea of marriage and having children, because they lacked the means of feeding them and were reluctant to expose them to work in factories. By the same token, it rendered men unable to maintain a family, which was why they either did not get married at all, or, if they did, then found that marriage turned from a blessing into a burden.[42]

Male inability to support a family was highlighted by those cases in which men, unable to find employment, were completely dependent on their wives' and children's earnings. It is extremely difficult to gauge their actual frequency, but the cases that did occur provoked extreme concern about the undermining of male familial authority that they entailed. According to Stephens, under such circumstances,

> The holy headship of his own household has passed away from the man. He is no longer king and keeper, good shepherd and feared father over those, who by the ties of blood and kinship ought to have belonged to him. They are his and not his. They hover around him, and yet another covets them and fetches them away from him. They are wanted and they go. He would fain have them to himself but is not strong enough to hold them. He cannot win bread for them to eat; unless they have bread they must die. . . . The man stands here all the day idle,

whilst the woman toils yonder that she may carry back a crust and share it with her shamed and dishonoured husband. . . . Think of the homes that must have been broken, the loves that must have been blighted, the hopes that must have been crushed, the ties of law and troth, of domestic unity and social concord that must have been rudely snapt in two, before a state of things like this could have been established. . . . The understanding is that man is the woman's head, and that their offspring do what they bid them do. The right to bear sway is lodged where it ought to be, and obedience is exacted on the ground and guarantee of efficient superintendence and protection. But this chain of reasons and relations has been broken. Women are their own keepers, and their husbands' keepers also. Children work for their own bread and their fathers' likewise.[43]

Stephens hammered home to his audience the notion of man being the God-ordained provider and, by implication, master of his wife and children. If men only heeded this notion and resolved not to let their wives and children continue working any longer, the political economists' claim that there existed a surplus population would be disproved. If women and children ceased working, all men would find employment, and wages would rise accordingly.[44] Men who failed to act on Stephens's advice came in for scathing criticism: 'The man that can good [sic] himself on the gets [sic] of his wife and little ones, in a factory, is worse than the master whose grasping greed has egged him on.'[45]

True, Stephens favoured an extremely strong and unveiled version of male dominance in gender relations, one that many men, as the Chartist press itself bears out, tried to assert over insubordinate wives by resorting to violence.[46] Yet Chartists in general admonished women to submit to their husbands. Scattered throughout the movement's press are articles to this effect, as well as snippets designed to fill in space. Good temper, accompanied by meekness and gentleness, were considered indispensable in woman to render her marriage successful. These qualities were held to endear her to her husband and to let him even overlook any lack of what was seen as her main asset: beauty. If, however, she indulged in 'keen retort' and 'waspish argument' – the expressions of wifely insubordination most resented by husbands – man would no longer feel tied to her by affection, but by 'stern and frigid duty'.[47] The same sentiment was put more bluntly thus: 'Ladies are like violets; the more modest and retiring they appear, the better you love them.'[48] Conversely, men were reminded that 'Women have a terrible power of torturing their husbands when those act unreasonably or unkindly towards them . . . if men would not be unutterably and intolerably miserable, they must govern their wives by *love*, so far as they govern them at all.'[49] Mellowed by love though men's government of wives was to be, the hierarchical character of marriage was not questioned. In the same vein, women were admonished to keep their marriage vow and to love, honour and obey their husbands.[50]

Awareness of economic superiority as the mainstay of male familial authority pervades the first part of Jones's *Woman's Wrongs*.[51] He aptly describes how the interaction of crumbling male self-esteem and increasing female insubordination escalate into violence. The working-class marriage at the centre of this development is literally one of convenience:

> Indeed, Haspen never loved his wife. She was a servant at his employer's, and he married her because he wanted a wife, and she had saved a little money. He looked on his house merely as a resting-place – at his wife as a servant without wages, whom he found convenient to prepare his meals, and make and share his bed.

Although love is absent from their relationship, their indifference has not turned into hatred yet: 'they bore the character of a happy couple in their court, because Haspen *did not beat her*'.

It is not until the coming of poverty, caused by a reduction in wages, that Haspen begins to vent his feelings of impotence on his wife.

> From his home, where the picture of their misery harrowed him, he rushed to the beer-shop to forget it. The very sight of his mute, but plaintive family, threw him into the rage of helpless despair – rendered still more blind by drunkenness. About this time, cries of pain and anger began to be heard by the neighbours, and the report ran in the court that the bricklayer was in the habit of beating his wife.

Haspen despairs of his inability to fulfil the male role of

provider for his family. His wife responds to her husband's failure to meet her expectation of support for herself and her children by taunting him:

> I thought I married one who had the arms of a workman, and the heart of a man. Why did you not tell me then that you could not work well enough to keep two little children? You want us to leave London! And, pray, what for? Do you suppose I'll go with two girls around my neck, begging from door to door for you? You want to make a trade of the misery of your wife and children, do you? You're out in your reckoning, sweetheart! Follow you I will – but it shall be to cry to the passers-by: 'Do you see this man? He is strong – he is well – but he will not work to give us food'.

She can no longer expect to be provided for by her husband, whom she welcomes with taunts instead of affectionate care. The mutual failure to meet each other's expectations signals the collapse of convenience, on which this marriage was founded. Consequently, the man comes to regard his family as more and more of an encumbrance.

In *Sunshine and Shadow*, Wheeler similarly describes the impact of male unemployment on a Chartist marriage.[52] Unlike the Haspens, Arthur and Mary Morton start out as a blissfully happy couple, completely absorbed in their love for each other. Yet the Mortons' bliss is not to last. Arthur loses his employment, and poverty encroaches on them. Arthur is badly affected by his family's suffering, and Mary has to realise 'that he was no longer the perfect being her young heart had worshipped'. His total inability to alleviate his family's plight endangers his sanity. They now all depend on the scanty wages Mary is able to earn as a sempstress and a washerwoman until she collapses from over-strain. Arthur's personal integrity is shown to be intimately bound up with his position of authority in the family, which rests on his ability to provide for his dependants' needs and thereby to protect them from the evils of want and misery.

The Mortons' fate, though reminiscent of that of the Haspens in Jones's novel, is significantly different. While the Mortons fall victim to the vicissitudes of the economy, Haspen is presented as wilfully bringing poverty on his family by losing his employment for his refusal to work for reduced wages. Unable to procure the means of subsistence for himself and his family, he turns into a criminal and, when arrested, blames his misfortune on his wife and children, whom he has grown to hate. Arthur, too, is driven to a criminal act by utter despair. Yet his fundamentally good character is untainted by this single act, as his relationship to his wife remains totally unaffected by poverty:

> though all the poetry of life had vanished, yet their affection to each other was as pure and undimmed as in the hour of its creation – the depths of misery have but served to render still more strong the ties which bound them to each other. Looking in vain for support from the world, they flung themselves more devotedly into the arms of each other, and when the storm beat loudest, they drew close together, until their hearts became one.

In this passage, Wheeler raises the claim that true love remains unaffected by dire circumstances. This claim, however, stands in stark contrast to the previous description of the effects of poverty on the Mortons' family life. It is precisely in a period of external crisis, whose repercussions extend into the home, that the Mortons' marriage ceases to function as a haven from the storms of life. Wheeler's intention to write realistically here clashes with the ideal he wants to propagate, and it is this clash that reveals his ideal as illusory. Arthur's inability to live up to the masculine ideal of provider and protector could have been met with sympathy by a woman used to fend for herself. Mary, however, is the epitome of the domestic woman, not expecting and actually proving unfit to carry out waged labour. Although the aspirations both Arthur and Mary entertained at the time of getting married have been dashed, neither lasting disappointment nor discord ensues. Instead, all causes of friction are glossed over by a sentimentalised love that is completely removed from the exigencies of everyday life.

While the male protagonist of Wheeler's novel represents the male Chartist ideal, real-life experience showed that adherence to radical political beliefs was no safeguard against recourse to violence in asserting authority in personal relationships. In his autobiography, the Chartist John James Bezer related that his master

> was a great radical – one who'd beat his wife and shout for

reform with all the enthusiasm of a glorious freeman; like many radicals in the present day, who can prate against tyranny wholesale and for exportation, and yet *retail* it out with all their hearts and souls, whenever they have an opportunity.[53]

Unless they were married, working-class women, in Chartist opinion, stood in danger of having to prostitute themselves in order to survive. Inability to procure a husband, Chartists believed, because many working men were incapable to maintain a wife and family, forced women to take this course.[54] Support by a husband was essential in view of the difficulties women encountered trying to obtain suitable or any employment at all.[55] Only if prostitution was the sole available alternative would Chartists relent in their condemnation of waged labour, at least for single women. Prostitution, chiefly attributed to poverty,[56] was interpreted as a by-product of the political oppression suffered by the working class. Consequently, democracy was declared to be the sole cure for this evil.[57]

This was regarded as a class issue in yet another sense, for some Chartists viewed the encounter between prostitute and client – identified as non-working class – as a further instance of exploitation, including sexual, of working people by their social superiors. This was the closest Chartists ever came to analysing sexual exploitation, and it is certainly no accident that this stand was taken in *The National*, edited by William James Linton. He was not only a member of the LWMA, but had also developed views inclined towards Owenism as a result of the influence exerted on him by the women in the circle around W. J. Fox, who were disciples of Mary Wollstonecraft. According to the 'hardwareman' regularly contributing to Linton's paper, the blame society laid on the prostitute was rather more due to her client, who hid his depravity behind a façade of good manners.[58] A similar view was put forward by Frost. For him, prostitution was one of the worst effects of domestic service, which laid servant-girls open to seduction by their masters. Once abandoned, they had nothing but the street to resort to.[59]

Wheeler, while concurring with the view of prostitution as a socially created evil and maintaining that prostitutes were 'driven by want to degradation' also drew attention to them as the victims of male recklessness: 'despoiled of virtue by those who should have supported and not betrayed them, yet have they fallen not so much by their own vices, as by trusting too much in the goodness of others'.[60]

Wheeler depicts prostitutes mainly as the victims of their own goodness and naïvety. These qualities have made them trust those men they have been taught to look to for support. For him, prostitution is not a class but a gender issue, for he does not dwell on the class difference between seducer and seduced, but on men's abuse of their function as the protectors of women.

Jones, on the other hand, presented prostitution as the result of the interplay of a morally deficient character and the prejudice of society, which extends the exclusion from its ranks from criminals to their entire families. Catherine, the daughter of the working man turned criminal, is described as having inherited

> much of the firm, haughty nature of her father – much of that disposition to brave public opinion, which makes either a hero or a criminal, according to the force of circumstances. . . . This callous and depraved reasoning was but strengthened by the intercourse of dissolute young men and abandoned women, the *only society the prejudice of the virtuous allowed her.*[61]

Prostitution appears as something similar to a contagious disease, for 'Her heart was prostituted by the impure contact – long before she had committed any actual sin.'[62] It is essential for all women inclined this way to be debarred from contact with 'this gangrene of foul lusts'.[63] This metaphor reinforces the image of prostitution as a malignant disease, ready to contaminate whoever comes into contact with it. It is like an evil fate hovering over poor women's lives and has to be fended off continually. Jones's *Young Milliner* is full of insinuations as to how the milliner could have supported herself when out of work. Yet being of a morally sound character, a true epitome of virtue, she would rather endure privations than prostitute herself. Thus the author can declare compassionately: 'the orphan had been cast upon the world, in youth, inexperience, and beauty. And bravely had she battled – well had she done – that young girl! More bravely than the proudest hero on the field of war! – against far stronger foes!'[64]

The differences in the way these Chartist novelists viewed prostitution seem to be related to their background. Frost and Wheeler, both of working-class origin, were familiar with the circumstances under which women were driven into prostitution and therefore sympathised with these victims of class society. True, for Jones, the upper-class man turned Chartist, prostitution was one aspect of the rottenness of contemporary society. Yet his revulsion against women who had divested themselves of what, in accordance with Victorian beliefs, he considered their innate chastity and virtue, led him to condemn those who, rather than passively submitting to death by starvation, actively struggled for survival by prostituting themselves.

Having to raise their children without male financial support was recognised by Chartists as a serious problem facing unmarried mothers. This was why they demanded assistance for the women concerned and condemned the punishment that the New Poor Law's Bastardy Clause involved. Against this attempt to hold women alone responsible for their actions, Chartists argued that illegitimate children's fathers were equally, if not more, to be blamed and ought to be punished, while women deserved protection.[65]

Some Chartists at least, such as Peter Bussey, even saw the Bastardy Clause as an instance of ruling-class attempts to conceal the effects of their depravity. He seems to have conceived of illegitimate children as the result of exclusively aristocratic sexual abuse of working-class women. Addressing a meeting at Bradford on the Whit Tuesday of 1838, he said:

> The bastardy clauses of the Poor Law . . . were introduced . . . in order to 'shelter, protect, and screen the despicable aristocrat in all his wicked intrigues and even murder the offspring of those who are the objects of their seducing snares. The result has certainly been the increase of infanticide to a great extent, and as a dernier resort the mother murders her own child.'[66]

To Chartists, infanticide represented the complete reversal of the natural order. Being a mother was described by all Chartist novelists as an important element of being female. Margaret Haspen, Jones's working-man's wife, has silently endured hunger and privation as a result of her husband's loss of employment. One day, however, she is spurred into rebellion by the suffering of her children. In the course of an argument with her husband, she declares: 'I've held my tongue too long – but mark you! I suffered too much hunger in the hunger of these poor little innocents.' The quarrel continues and grows fiercer and fiercer. Haspen is ready to strike his wife, but 'The man paused suddenly before that fury of the tigress defending its young – he felt fear.'[67]

Women, then, were depicted as totally devoted to their children and as doing everything in their power to protect them. Infanticide was therefore an apt expression of a social order so perverted as to drive human beings to act against their best instincts. Chartist papers' reports of infanticide were intended to shock their readers and to heighten their awareness of the deficiencies of contemporary society, particularly the latter's detrimental effects on women, most of all on mothers.[68]

For all these reasons, Chartists objected to free unions as advocated by the Owenites. According to Robert Owen, the obvious and powerful feelings of human nature ought to be given free rein, for they directed 'man' in the right course to physical and moral well-being. Owenites therefore wished for all unions between men and women to be based exclusively on mutual affection and to be dissolvable on principle when their emotional basis had faded away.[69] Opposition to Owenite free unions, however, did not preclude some Chartists from coming out in favour of reforming the existing marriage laws with a view to improving the legal status of married women, particularly with regard to their property.[70] Yet for the vast majority of working-class women this was not a matter of primary importance.

In view of female degradation, which showed in women's waged labour as well as prostitution and their treatment by the Poor Law, working-class women were commonly dubbed 'slaves'.[71] This term not only drew attention to working-class women's total lack of rights; it also highlighted ruling-class hypocrisy. While the plight of the black slaves had provoked the English middle classes into getting up a movement for the abolition of slavery, the same people proved insensitive to the degradation suffered by white, British-born women – conditions that their laws and factories even helped perpetuate.

Chartists eagerly pinpointed other instances of ruling-class hypocrisy, too. While demanding that women be treated with modesty and tenderness, the ruling classes allowed prostitution and the extremely hard work of female labourers to continue. Forcing women to do a slave's work was shown up as going against the lofty opinion held of the worth of woman in her social capacity. While public opinion was outraged by the brutal treatment of women abroad, poverty at home was allowed to drive them into prostitution.[72]

Chartists used descriptions of the luxury enjoyed by rich women to bring out more sharply the misery suffered by the working-class majority of the female sex.[73] By insisting that ruling-class ideology concerning women should lead to the establishment of decent living conditions for all women regardless of class, Chartists demanded for their own womenfolk the right to indulge themselves in the same comforts as enjoyed by the ruling-class members of their sex. Such comforts would make up the decent lifestyle that was central to the Chartist notion of women's rights. It implied the absence of the necessity for women to leave their homes to carry out waged labour and of the threat of having to rely on prostitution as a last resort in the struggle for survival and to evade removal to the workhouse. Instead, women should be enabled to stay at home, supported by a husband earning sufficient wages, and to devote themselves entirely to the care of their families. By drawing such a prospect of what society would be like after the implementation of the Six Points, Chartists addressed themselves to the chief detrimental forces working-class women had to battle with in the England of the 1830s and 1840s.

The main thrust of the Chartist notion of women's rights was not towards opening up new opportunities, but rather towards protecting women from the adverse effects of industrialisation. As a consequence, the suffrage was not an integral part of these rights, although some Chartists did come out in favour of it.

According to prevalent political opinion, women of any class were denied the suffrage on account of their being 'femmes couvertes'. In 1797, during a debate on parliamentary reform, C. J. Fox had explained that women were excluded from the franchise because, by the laws of nations and of nature, they were dependent and their voices were therefore governed by male relations. In his famous *Article on Government* of 1820, James Mill had reiterated this position by stating that women could rightfully be denied political representation, since their interests were included in those of their menfolk. Similar views were also propagated among the working class.[74] In the 1832 Reform Bill, women were for the first time explicitly excluded from the right to vote.

The voices raised against women's exclusion from the franchise were few and far between. Shortly after the passage of the 1832

Reform Bill, Henry Hunt presented a petition to parliament requesting the franchise for all unmarried women with the necessary financial qualification. This petition had been drafted by one Mary Smith, an enormously wealthy Yorkshire woman. Her claim to the suffrage rested on property, not on sex. With the advance of industrial prosperity, there was an increase in the numbers of wealthy unmarried women and widows, to whose interests Mary Smith lent her voice. The right of all women to vote as their only recourse against the injustice they suffered was proclaimed, for the first time, in 1843 by a woman called Marion Reid,[75] about whom nothing else is known.

It is against this backdrop of dominant political beliefs that the Chartist demand for universal male suffrage only has to be viewed. When circulating a draft version of the People's Charter around Britain with a view to inviting suggestions for amendments, the LWMA received one proposal for the inclusion of women in the franchise. Although acknowledging the legitimacy of the demand for female suffrage, the drafters of the Charter objected to it on tactical grounds. Its exclusion was a concession to prevalent prejudices about women:

> Against this reasonable proposition we have no just argument to adduce, but only to express our fears of entertaining it, lest the false estimate man entertains for this half of the human family may cause his ignorance and prejudice to be enlisted to retard the progress of his own freedom. And, therefore, we deem it far better to lay down just principles, and look forward to the rational improvement of society, than to entertain propositions which may retard the measure we wish to promote.[76]

Similarly, Bronterre O'Brien, though considering women to be entitled to the franchise, believed the exercise of this right to be attended with more inconvenience than profit.[77]

In 1842, arguing in favour of female suffrage, John LaMont, a Scottish Chartist, appealed to his comrades not to let themselves be deterred by objections. He listed these and tried to devalue them by attributing them exclusively to Chartism's political opponents. He favoured the inclusion of women in the franchise, 'notwithstanding the amount of blackguardism, and folly, and coercion which will be arrayed against this extension by the aristocratic and royal *debauchee*'.[78]

Although the suffrage demanded in the People's Charter was, once and for all, to be universal for men only, the issue of the female franchise was occasionally raised among male Chartists. The advocates of the enfranchisement of women deemed it most unjust to demand an extension of the suffrage to the most stupid of men, while leaving women unconsidered despite instances of extraordinary intelligence among them in the present as well as the past. The objectors, who counted O'Connor among them, were wary of the interference of female suffrage with domestic happiness, presumably expecting discord to arise from husband and wife voting for different candidates. O'Connor believed it to be sufficient for wives to bring their influence to bear on their husbands over the issue of which candidate should receive his vote. Moreover, he argued, female suffrage would enfranchise women of bad character as well as the female staff at the command of masters, who would consequently support tyranny, prostitution and oppression,[79] thus impeding the improvement that Chartists fought for. It remains unclear, however, why these arguments should not equally apply to certain sections among working-class men.

Chartists refusing women the right to vote on account of their assumed political gullibility came under attack from O'Brien's *National Reformer* for the low opinion they held of the companions of their lives. This paper was also quite exceptional in propagating the belief that female emancipation entirely depended on women's exertions on their own behalf.[80] The representatives of a middle position, finally, were not opposed to female suffrage on principle, but thought it inexpedient to go into this question before the Charter was won.[81]

Yet some men, such as Watkins, realised the injustice involved in restricting the franchise to men and thus leaving the large number of single women without any means of making their influence felt. As women were affected by legislation, they were entitled to the vote. No risk would be incurred by granting women the franchise, for, Watkins maintained, 'I do not know that they would make better laws than men make: they could scarcely make worse.' Yet the vote was not for wives, 'for they and their husbands are one'.[82]

Those Chartists unreservedly in favour of the vote for all women had strong Owenite leanings. William Galpin, for instance, wrote in to *The Northern Star* from Ham Common Concordium, one of the Owenite communities. While acknowledging Chartism to be a most powerful contemporary movement, he totally disagreed with its basis, that is the restriction of universal suffrage to men.[83] William Garrard, the founder and secretary of the Ipswich WMA also supported female franchise.[84] Yet his membership of Goodwyn Barmby's Communist Propaganda Society shows him to have professed Owenite principles at least at some stage of his life.

Goodwyn Barmby himself was involved in both Owenism and Chartism. The part of Suffolk in which he lived was one of the few agricultural areas boasting organised Chartists. In 1841, he and his wife Catherine issued a *Declaration of Electoral Reform*, in which they demanded the inclusion of female suffrage into the 'People's Charter', stating that they were as much opposed to sex legislation as to class legislation and therefore wanted Chartism to be unsexual. Two years later, Catherine Barmby published a tract raising *The Demand for the Emancipation of Woman, Politically and Socially*, in which she reiterated women's right to the franchise.[85]

Chartists particularly resented any criticism of their restricting the vote to men when it came from members of the ruling class. By the later stage of the movement, the Charter had come to be so much a symbol of working-class hopes and aspirations that it was not to be tampered with.[86] *The People* was therefore quite exceptional in proposing the franchise for both sexes on one occasion.[87]

Unreserved endorsements of female suffrage were to be heard only from one of the side-organisations of the movement. The National Association of the United Kingdom for Promoting the Political and Social Improvement of the People, which was established in April 1841 by William Lovett and his political friends in order to promote what was becoming known as Knowledge Chartism, advocated 'the equal educational, social, and political rights of woman as well as of man'. This was also expressed by the motto the Association's paper, *The National Association Gazette*, bore beneath its title: 'The Rights of Man and the Rights of Woman', thus creating an atmosphere in which a heavy attack on Chartists for withholding from women the right to vote could be launched. In a letter to the editor, the drafters of the Charter were compared to those middle-class men who objected to female suffrage for fear of endangering their preoccupations, namely the abolition of the Corn Laws and household suffrage. They were further accused of contradicting the Chartist profession of universal justice. It was ignoble of them to refuse their assistance to those women who, having freed themselves from legally and socially proscribed helplessness, proclaimed their sex's title to equal rights and equal laws. In the writer's opinion, the working class's stand on this issue did damage to its own cause, because they laid themselves open to doubts as to the purity of their motives. Despite its profession of female rights, the National Association took a dim view of women's readiness to improve their condition. Its members believed that women had to be taught to desire freedom as a precondition for attaining it.[88]

Occasional dissension over women's right to vote, however, did not jeopardise the movement's unity, since female suffrage was not considered central to Chartism's project. Chartist political objectives, too, were intimately tied up with the affirmation of male hegemony. The political beliefs of the entire family were to be those of its male head, who was endowed with special powers.

Chartists viewed the suffrage as a natural right belonging to men by virtue of their human capacity. By denying women the vote, Chartists turned them not only into second-class citizens, they even reduced them to the status of second-class human beings. Their interests were to be taken care of by their husbands/fathers as part of the latter's duty to protect their families. This encompassed their obligation to ensure such legislation as would restore women to their proper place in the home.

If men felt the moral dignity of their nature, as *The English Chartist Circular* quoted T. B. Smith, a Leeds Chartist, as saying, they would not suffer women working outside the home or becoming prostitutes. Instead, they would demand participation in legislation to ensure the payment of wages sufficient to maintain a family without the latter's female members having to earn their living.[89] And Chartists were convinced that having to witness the 'slavery' of their wives and daughters would incite Englishmen to rebel.[90] It was precisely these infringements of male supremacy that were expected to prompt men to take political action.

Conversely, the suffrage was an indispensable element of that respectability which, while demonstrating equality of citizenship in public, claimed woman's due regard at home. In return, she would enjoy the protection of a man empowered effectively to

safeguard her status as wife and mother. It is on the interdependence of these two aspects of the suffrage that the following
passage by Watkins turns:

> What woman can respect a man who has so little respect for
> himself as to live a willing slave? . . . Depend upon it, the man
> who is a willing slave can never respect a woman as he ought
> to do; and, if he be an unwilling one, he can never make her so
> happy as he would wish to do.[91]

Chartist aspirations for women involved a marked shift away
from and a redefinition of many of the issues that had loomed
large in previous thinking on women's condition. Mary Wollstonecraft's *Vindication of the Rights of Woman*, which appeared in
1792, is generally regarded as the founding text of modern
feminism.[92] Against the prevalent view of her time that women
had been created inferior beings, she insisted on their deficiency
being the result of environmental impact mediated by education.
Deprived of the exercise of their reason – which she regarded as
the quintessential feature of humanity – women had become
sexual beings, their character and behaviour moulded according to
male notions of female propriety. Having been made to conform
to principles exclusive to their sex, women had effectively become
relegated to a position outside the realm of human beings.
Therefore it was necessary to reinstate them in the ranks of
humanity.

Consequently, Mary pleaded that women should be given the
same opportunities as men to develop their faculties. She pointed
out various occupations that women could hold and thereby
become useful members of society. Their ensuing financial
independence would save them from prostitution and from
marriages contracted merely in order to ensure their support. She
even tentatively suggested that women ought to have the suffrage.
But she was aware that this wish was futile as long as working
people remained unenfranchised.

Mary was unable to conceive of women as the agents of their
own liberation. Despite her consistent denunciation of male oppression, she appealed to reasonable men to bring about women's
emancipation. This she considered not only a precondition of the
progress of all humankind. It would also gratify men's self-
interest, for their relationships with women would become more

satisfying once the latter had been elevated to the rank of human beings.

Mary's conception of female emancipation did not encompass the severing of familial or marital ties, nor did it question the division of labour between the sexes. Recognition of the relevance of this issue owed a great deal to the shift of women's work to factories, a development imminent at the time the *Vindication* was written. It is within the framework of their familial relationships that women were to discharge their duties, foremost among which were those of a mother.

The *Vindication* was available to and known among Chartists.[93] Interest in Mary's writing can be traced to those ramifications of the Chartist movement in which concern with education prevailed. Quotations from the *Vindication* appeared, for instance, in *The English Chartist Circular*, the mouthpiece of the LWMA from 1841 to 1843. The LWMA held the education of the working classes to be the key to the abolition of political tyranny.[94] *The National Association Gazette*, pledged to women's rights as it was, also carried Wollstonecraft quotes, as did *The National Vindicator* and *The Midland Counties Illuminator*. The former served as Vincent's mouthpiece at a time when he was beginning to lean more and more towards educationalism, temperance and an alliance with the middle class. The latter was brought out by Thomas Cooper, the most impressively accomplished autodidact among the Chartists.

In keeping with this bias, it was Mary's arguments for an improved female education that were selected for quotation. All these passages demand the improvement of women's instruction as a means of achieving something else. This object could consist in the general progress of knowledge and virtue, in ensuring that the rising generation was educated in truly patriotic spirit, or in women's conscientious fulfilment of their domestic duties. Finally, improved education was expected to enable women to be men's truly understanding companions and thereby to increase mutual affection. Elementary medical training (a more limited demand) would, by making women efficient nurses of their families,[95] add to their competence.

Like Mary, the authors writing for these periodicals were convinced that an improvement of women's condition was pivotal for the progress of society.[96] Furthermore, they considered women's education crucial for the inculcation of Chartist principles in the rising generation.[97]

The affinity of Mary's analysis to Chartist considerations concerning women was not restricted to the relevant role ascribed to education. There was also agreement on the importance of women's fulfilment of their domestic duties[98] and the emphasis on maternal responsibilities, with which the entire Chartist press abounded.

Yet the marked similarity with regard to some aspects enabled Chartists the more conveniently to ignore or bypass the analysis of male oppression of women contained in the *Vindication*. While Mary did lay great emphasis on improved female instruction, her ultimate goal was not restricted to broadening women's minds. For her, education was the means by which women would attain truly human status and thus equality with men. Chartists diluted the message of passages in which she blamed male tyranny for degrading women into subhuman modes of existence. They did this by making male despotism out to be confined to restricting women's access to education.[99]

Although Chartists, just as Mary, regarded the self-responsible individual as the sole legitimate source of power and hence condemned political tyranny, they did not follow her in drawing the parallel to male despotism in the family. They consistently treated her as an educational reformer rather than as an analyst of sexual oppression.

The next step in the development of a consistent analysis of women's condition was taken in 1825 by William Thompson and Anna Wheeler in their *Appeal of One-Half the Human Race, Women, against the Pretensions of the Other Half, Men, to Retain Them in Political, and Thence, in Civil and Domestic Slavery*.[100] Thompson and Wheeler argued that women were deprived of their human capacity by male oppression, which denied them the right of self-government. For the authors, female inequality was rooted in the competitive organisation of society, which had deformed men and women alike. On their superior strength, men had erected a whole system of 'sexual exclusions' for the sake of indulging their greed for power. According to the *Appeal*, male subjugation of women climaxed in marriage, which required women willingly to acquiesce in their submission.

Thompson and Wheeler deemed women's full equality with men – desirable due to the former's human capacity – to hinge upon competition being superseded by universal co-operation. Under the competitive system, women's emancipation was bound to arouse male hostility. Furthermore, the authors believed female equality to be conditional upon women's exertions on their own behalf. Thompson and Wheeler were convinced that women were both morally obliged and powerful enough to benefit all humankind by pushing the demand for equality.

The *Appeal* amounts to the first manifesto of socialist feminism in that it closely linked women's subjection to social organisation. It refuted all hope for the attainment of full equality of the sexes under a capitalist, 'competitive', system. It is superior, though greatly indebted, to the *Vindication* in pointing to the degrading effect men's subjection of women has on themselves by allowing them to be governed by erroneous notions as to their superiority instead of by that great human asset, rationality. Furthermore, it analysed marriage as that social institution within which women's subjection crystallises and to which all forms of social domination can be traced back. Women, regarded as the pivotal agents in effecting female emancipation, come across as morally superior to men and hence as potential benefactors of humankind by ensuring that all human relations be based on rationality.

Unlike the *Vindication*, from which several Chartist periodicals quoted fairly extensively, the only mention of the *Appeal* consists in an advertisement in the Chartist paper *The People* of 1850.[101] This is not surprising, for the *Appeal* belongs to the communitarian tradition, which has always been both a minority movement and line of thinking. The *Vindication*, on the other hand, was received by Chartists as part of the mainstream, Enlightenment legacy, within which it had evolved.

Another member of the communitarian minority, John Francis Bray,[102] an Owenite and Chartist, did not fare any better at the hands of his Chartist comrades. Although not primarily concerned with women's condition, his *Labour's Wrongs and Labour's Remedy* of 1839 envisaged an improvement of their social position subsequent to social change. Bray held woman's material dependence on man to be a particularly evil concomitant of the contemporary mode of social organisation, which he considered to be based on unequal exchange. Once this had been replaced by co-operation, women's condition would improve. They would be rendered independent of men with regard to occupation and maintenance and thus ascend to that position due to them by virtue of their human capacity, in which they shared equally with men. Bray was convinced that women, once released from male tyranny, would be able fully to develop the potential inherent in their being. Under co-operation, their development would be further assisted by social institutions particularly designed for this purpose, and gender relations would also improve. Against Malthus's political economy, Bray maintained that all impediments to marriage that arose from the unequal distribution of wealth would be removed so that everybody wishing to marry would be able to do so.

Labour's Wrongs and Labour's Remedy was duly taken note of by the Chartist movement in a review for *The Northern Star*.[103] Predictably enough, the reviewer heartily agreed with Bray's view of labour's wrongs, but was totally opposed to a change in the mode of production being proposed as the only possible remedy. After all, by pointing to the insufficiency of governmental as compared to economic change, Bray had levelled a severe criticism against the principal object of Chartist policy. While Bray regarded political structure as a reflection of the economic system, Chartists (as noted above) adhered to the opposite belief. Despite this fundamental difference, Bray's book was lectured upon by McDouall in 1841.[104] Otherwise, Bray's statements concerning women's condition went unnoticed by the Chartist movement.[105]

In various respects, Bray's social analysis is reminiscent of Thompson and Wheeler's. Bray repeated their fusion of Owenism and Utilitarianism in his contention that the class division of society must be abolished before humankind can set about its proper business. Like his predecessors, he shared the utopians' belief in the inevitability of human progress, which was inconceivable without women's participation.

With particular regard to women, Bray, like Thompson and Wheeler, held any genuine improvement of their status to be conditional upon a different organisation of society. All three of them used the term 'slavery' to describe women's contemporary social position and consequently insisted on the necessity for women's independence of men. Quite unlike Bray, however, Thompson and Wheeler argued for the abolition of marriage, which they recognised as the social institution whose only object was to keep women in subserviency to men. Bray, on the other hand, considered marriage desirable and aimed at removing all obstacles to its achievement.

A further difference concerns strategy. In Bray's mind, female emancipation was the inevitable by-product of co-operation, which sustained women's then fully developed human capacity by establishing social institutions designed to this end. Thompson and Wheeler, on the other hand, having analysed male dominance over women in great detail, were aware of the necessity of women's intervention to achieve equality. This was to be the result of their own exertions and would therefore not require the support of any protective institutions.

The women addressed by the *Appeal*, therefore, emerge as stronger, more active, and more self-reliant than those referred to in *Labour's Wrongs*. This may have been partly the result of the impact of industrialisation on women, of which they had to bear the brunt. Borne down as they were by their efforts to cope with the impact of industrialisation on themselves and their families, it was difficult to see how they could have found the strength required for realising the project advocated by Thompson and Wheeler. Bray did perceive degradation, but though still locating it within gender relations, he conceived of it as a result of class relations. In the same vein, the Chartist use of the term 'slavery' to denote women's condition focused on the absence of rights effected by class legislation alone. It is the impact of industrialisation that lies behind the transition from Thompson and Wheeler's ideal woman, self-sufficient, independent, who meets man as his truly human equal, to Bray's woman, who is sustained by protective institutions. Bray wanted to see woman as a 'help-mate meet for man', thereby making man's requirements the yardstick of woman's development. This goal signalled the loss of awareness of the degrading effect of male dominance on men themselves. It is Thompson and Wheeler who had recognised that fully developed humanity, in both women and men, was conditional on the absence of sexual oppression.

Only a year after *Labour's Wrongs and Labour's Remedy* had come out as a book, there appeared a Chartist pamphlet devoted to *The Rights of Woman*. It had been written in Lancaster gaol by Reginald John Richardson, while he was serving a prison sentence for his commitment to Chartism. He had sat as the Manchester delegate in the Convention of 1839, where he belonged to the more militant wing. Through his advocacy of the right to bear arms, he had incurred a prison sentence for sedition and conspiracy. He will feature again (in Chapter 5) in a case study demonstrating the range of gender relations possible in Chartist marriages.

In his pamphlet, Richardson addressed himself head on to one of the most striking paradoxes of the Chartist movement by asking, 'Ought women to interfere in the political affairs of the country?'[106] If viewed against the backdrop of the Chartist campaign – which was aimed at universal manhood suffrage, yet involved large numbers of women – this question contains in a nutshell the ambiguity inherent in the Chartist notion of women's proper social status. This will become clear by unravelling Richardson's argument.

Richardson felt his initial question to be of such importance as to require him to base his answer on the Bible as 'the most authentic record, as well as the most ancient chronicle of human events'. He accordingly turned to the account of woman's creation in Genesis. There he found it clearly stated that God, having made the world, realised man's solitude and therefore created '*woman* as HELPMEET for *man*'. God's intention to relieve man of his solitude by creating a being that shares man's essential human characteristics renders the sexes equal. This equality is unquestionable, resting as it does on divine authority.

Having outlined his notion of woman's paradisaical status (as it were) he proceeded to discuss the effects of woman having been the instrument of the Fall, thereby confronting the main biblical justification for her subordination. As a result of the Fall, woman incurred God's displeasure and was therefore made subject to her husband.

Richardson was now left with the difficult task of having to reconcile two contradictory manifestations of divine will. Having laid so much emphasis on woman's having been created man's equal, he was free to use what he conceived of as God's original intention to temper woman's subjection in marriage. According to Richardson, woman is not intended to be man's perpetual slave 'but only where she enters into a contract with Man to become *his* particular helpmate'. Thus Richardson was driven to the precious and practically irrelevant distinction between women, who are men's equals, and wives, who are subordinate to their husbands.

Conversely, all actions contravening the essential equality in difference of man and woman not only counteract divine will, but are also bound to have the most pernicious effects on man himself as well as on woman, on humanity and on society at large.

Moreover, the husband's power over his wife derives from her consent, modelled as it is upon the political realm, where the force and authority of the head of state depend upon the votes cast by the members of the commonwealth. This definition of the husband's power leaves woman the right to exercise her free will with regard to the marriage contract as well as to all other civil, religious and political affairs.

Indubitable though women's physical inferiority is, it must not be made an excuse for reducing or depreciating her. Her physical organisation enables her to render humanity services that, though different, are equivalent to man's.

> It is true, she is less fitted by nature to endure toil and danger than man; but contrast his bold and rugged form with her soft and graceful person, his high commanding voice with her mild and soothing tones, his inflexible will with her yielding disposition, his boisterous passions with her insinuating and fascinating powers of love; combine them all, and what an agreeable compound do they form! their essence is the spring of life, the fountain of social order, the reservoir from whence all the happiness of mankind flows, the stream that irrigates with all the kind offices of nature the community through which it takes its course.

Richardson, then, believed woman and man to have been created equal, but different, precisely so as to complement one another, and it is the compound formed of the male and female element that bears the most beneficial effects on society. His description of the characteristics by which the sexes differ, however, implies an inherent hierarchy between them. While the male is depicted as a monolith of force and power which pervade every fibre of his being, the female essence consists in flexibility and adaptability.

Richardson admitted that women have in all ages yielded to their subjugation by men, so much so that, had he based his argument on custom rather than on the Bible and natural law, he would have found woman's submission sanctioned by tradition. Despite this overwhelming influence of custom, he was optimistic that a change in women's political status could be effected through concessions on the part of men. Women's own role is confined to urging their menfolk to fight for political rights, defined as the right for men and women to vote. He appealed to women to cease to let themselves be degraded, and to bring up their children in the same spirit. It is up to the women to bring about 'human redemption' thus conferring 'a perpetual obligation on posterity'. Richardson, then, attempted to effect a radical change in women's condition by an appeal to their feeling of moral obligation towards humanity and is scathing in his condemnation of those men who try to prevent this change for the better.

Richardson then reverted to the starting point of his argument by affirming women's natural, civil and political right to interfere in the political affairs of the country. This he regarded, moreover, as her imperative duty the neglect of which would be derogatory to the divine will. He considers woman to be entitled to enjoy to the full all rights that pertain to her in her capacity as human being. He thus extended to women the Chartist natural right argument adduced in support of the demand for universal manhood suffrage.

Woman's civil right is implied in her natural right. In addition, Richardson found no legal ruling excluding her from the exercise of political rights on grounds of her sex, and those instances he had come across he dismissed as dissonant with the law of nature and nations. It was from his belief that a community of persons and of rights would be most conducive to civil liberty that he derived woman's right to an equal share in the law-making of such a community. In his opinion, woman's political right stems from her being a member of the state. Furthermore, by ancient laws of the English constitution, she is admissable to every executive office in the kingdom.

The existing law, though more restrictive, did grant women some legal status. The right of ordinary women to vote was proved by the presence of a female monarch and grounded in the fact that they contributed directly and indirectly to the wealth of the nation.

This is a typical example of the Chartist line of argument employed to prove the people's rights, be it to vote or to arm. There is the reference back to ancient laws, which had sunk into oblivion but would be resurrected by the enactment of the Charter. 'No taxation without representation' was a slogan adopted by the Chartists to express their belief that anyone who is made to pay for the running of a government ought to have a say in its formation. While the aristocracy and the middle class are entitled to vote on account of their possessions, the same right accrues to the working class by virtue of their being the producers of the nation's wealth.[107] Richardson was unique, however, in extending these arguments to prove woman's right to the vote. He moved on extremely unsafe ground, however, where he referred to contemporary legal regulations concerning women, for the vast majority were *femmes couvertes*, that is they did not legally exist as persons.

Richardson went to great lengths to demonstrate women's share in producing the nation's wealth by considering agriculture, mining and factories. His description of the enormous contributions women make in all three spheres of production is pervaded by the feeling of horror he experiences when thinking of women forced to carry out labour that contravenes their nature. Through the overtaxing of her strength, woman 'becomes masculine; and the force of all those tender passions implanted by God in the breast of woman to temper the ruggedness of man, become weakened, her real virtues forgotten, and her proper usefulness destroyed'. Richardson's abhorrence of women performing arduous labour was derived from his conception of the sexes as different and complementing each other. When women are assimilated to men, society is deprived of the beneficial effects exerted by the compound of male and female elements.

The author called upon men to concede women the right to interfere in politics, which the latter are to use to put an end to their suffering. His description of women colliers with its juxtaposition of their emerging from 'these hell holes of coal mines' like 'demons from the lower deeps' with the sentimentalised description of women as angelic creatures chimes in with the views expressed in the public debate on female mine work. Richardson differed from the predominant opinion where he voices his surprise at women's own lack of concern for the degradation of their countrywomen, and at their lack of disgust for the institutions making this possible. In other words he wondered why being witness to such outrage did not turn all working-class men and the women of all ranks into ardent Chartists.

Richardson then referred to the numerous acts of protective legislation, which had proved to be ineffective, since those concerned were excluded from participating in their making. If this were not so, he was convinced, factory women, conscious of being removed from their proper sphere, would have brought about legislation prohibiting female factory work. Instead he called on them to rely on their husbands' financial support while attending to their domestic duties.

As 'God has ordained woman "to temper man"', Richardson maintained, the benefits derived from household decisions made jointly by husband and wife should be brought to bear on the making of laws by adopting the same procedure.

The author concluded by demanding the vote for all men over twenty-one. Curiously, his qualifying age for women was twenty, and he never cleared up this inconsistency. The right to vote, however, should be confined to single women. His demand, then, fell back behind that of his socialist predecessors Thompson, Wheeler and Bray, who had come out in favour of full female suffrage. On the other hand, it transcended the limits of the Chartist demand for universal manhood suffrage only. Unlike James Mill, who had maintained that the interests of all women were included in those of their menfolk, Richardson at least acknowledged that single women lacked anybody with whom their interests could be included.

Although his pamphlet was favourably reviewed in the Chartist press,[108] it did not spark off any discussion. It is interesting to note that the reviewer in *The Midland Counties Illuminator*, while praising the author for the accuracy of his description of the present condition of women in England, found him wanting when measured against Mary Wollstonecraft.

While his predecessors (in the context of this text) had been concerned with analysing the forces oppressing women as a sex, Richardson dealt with the contemporary condition of working-class women only. This shift in focus led to a redefinition of concepts. Tyranny and despotism, terms used in both the *Vindication* and the *Appeal* to denote gender relations characterised by male dominance, are restricted to signify men's denying women the right to political commitment in *The Rights of Woman*. Female rights are accordingly limited to the franchise for single women and to all women's emancipation from waged labour through support by a husband. While his predecessors had demanded comprehensive equality of the sexes, derived from equal opportunities for the full development of human capacity, Richardson argued for equality in difference. Whereas previously, humanness had been claimed as a universal feature appertaining to all human beings regardless of their sex, and the arbitrariness of basing inequality on sex had been attacked, Richardson showed himself to be fully convinced of the inherent difference of man and woman. Yet he did not make this an excuse for a value judgement. He considered man and woman equal by virtue of their human capacity, despite the different forms it assumes in the sexes. Neither masculinity nor femininity alone represents complete humanity. Femininity and masculinity are mutually dependent, and full humanity involves the complementing of one by the other.

What he conceived of as femininity had been denounced by Mary as being the result of an upbringing that warped woman's human capacity so as to render her a willing victim of male subjugation. Masculinity, as understood by Richardson, on the other hand, had been shown by Thompson and Wheeler to be the product of men's indulging irrational passions by dominating women, a conduct detrimental to their own human capacity.

His predecessors had demanded the lifting of all restrictions imposed on women, or, in Bray's case, had at least demanded women's independence from men. Richardson, conversely, argued for barring women from waged labour and for assigning them the home as primary sphere of action, which is particularly conducive to the bringing out of their sex-specific faculties.

While women attend to their domestic duties, men go out and earn the family's livelihood. Each sex brings to the process of decision-making their specific qualities, and the ensuing fusion of the male and female element transcends the segregation of spheres. In the realm of politics, both elements fuse in the ballot, cast by the male head of the household after consulting with his wife. Single women, on the other hand, lacking their individual male complement, are entitled to vote themselves, presumably as a way of balancing the votes cast by single men. Richardson's restriction of the franchise to single women was due to his belief in men's unquestionable authority within the family. He legitimised the power and force of man, as head of the family, through his wife's consent to marry him: his analogy was to the consent of the governed being the sole legitimate source of the head of state's right to rule over them. Where Mary had used this idea, by extending it to the private realm, in order to claim women's right of self-determination, Richardson employed the same idea to underpin male dominance in marriage.

Richardson's notion of the complementariness of the sexes and of its mode of operating in the political sphere can be understood as the conceptualisation of gender relations as these had evolved in the family economy of domestic industry. As these conditions were also highlighted (as Chapter 5 will show) within his own marriage, he can ultimately be seen as generalising from his personal experience. Such conditions were characterised by a high degree of interdependence of husband and wife, whose contributions to the family economy, though different, were valued equally. Despite this rough equality, representation of the family in public was a male preserve, while women were accorded status on the basis of their competent management of the family's internal affairs.

In keeping with the emphasis on sexual difference, Richardson's concept of female degradation differed from that of his predecessors. While they had viewed it as a result of preventing women from attaining full human capacity, Richardson conceived of it as a result of transposing women from their proper sphere, thereby depriving them of the environment conducive to the bringing out of their sex-specific virtues. Degradation, for Richardson, had become synonymous with what was in fact economic exploitation. Viewing the latter as a result of women's transplantation from the home, he was blind to the fact that exploitation was common to male and female workers alike.

What becomes clear from reading *The Rights of Woman* is the shift that had occurred in the radical perception of women's condition. Industrialisation, which relied heavily on female labour power, had pushed women's suffering at the workplace to the centre of radical working-class attention. Concern about the warping of women's character by a gender-conscious education or about marriage as an institution that is particularly oppressive to women, was replaced by anxiety for the well-being of the entire working class, seen as endangered by the removal of women from the centre of the family.

It is Richardson's merit to have rendered a consistent presentation of the Chartist concern for women and to have given a firm biblical grounding to their condemnation of female waged labour outside the home and to their advocacy of marriage as the institution best fitted to secure women's livelihood. His

propagation of the ideal of marriage as the fusion of complementary elements was grounded in the conditions obtaining in
domestic industry. Applied to the factory system, where women
were becoming increasingly less able to contribute to the family
income from within the confines of their homes, this ideal implied
their being deprived of the material base on which rested what
authority they had.

His argument, however, led him, contrary to majority Chartist
opinion, to extend the demand for women's right to interfere in
politics into one for the suffrage for all single women over twenty.
His insistence on women's right to political commitment was
derived from his desire to unite the entire class, men and women
alike, in the endeavour to improve the social system by changing
the political. The motivation as well as the justification of
women's participation in this venture, according to Richardson,
stem from the disturbance of their internal peace or of domestic
happiness. Women's political rights, then, evolve out of and are
circumscribed by gender-specific qualities and by concern with the
home and the family.

In contemporary society, Chartists were convinced, working-
class women were condemned to live under degrading conditions.
In the dedication of his *Democratic Review*, Harney invoked his
readers' aid to destroy 'that vile system', which forced women into
a life of 'degradation and misery'.[109] This, conversely, was, in
Chartist opinion, a most forceful indictment of the society in
which they lived. It destroyed the material base of proper gender
relations by diminishing both male wages and employment
opportunities. The wives and children of the men thus affected
were, according to Watkins, reduced to 'prowl[ing] for food like
unowned dogs'.[110] The image of the stray dogs expresses his belief
that women without a male breadwinner are completely uprooted
and deprived of humanity due to their loss of dignity. Personal
dignity, however, formed one of the chief elements of working-
class respectability – the supreme object of the Chartist struggle.

The women and children roaming about like stray animals mark
the extreme opposite to those enjoying life in the 'cottage of
content'. By thus imaging the worst as well as the best life in
terms of gender relations, Watkins underlined the centrality of
these relations to working-class respectability. They thereby turn
into the touchstone of the quality of a given social system. Proper
gender relations formed an important element in the social setup

envisaged by the Chartists, and the ardent wish to establish men and women in their rightful positions fired much of the Chartist struggle.

From this re-establishment would follow personal dignity, which was, as seen via Watkins, conceived of differently for men and women. Female dignity hinged on women devoting themselves to family care. Preserving that dignity thus involved protecting women from the impact of an industrialising economy that interfered with the proper discharge of female domestic duties. Central to its male complement was the creation of conditions in which female dignity could thrive. This required the fulfilment of the breadwinner's role and, in the last instance, fighting, politically or otherwise, for a social system that enabled men to provide for their families.

The complementariness of male and female dignity followed from the Chartist conception of the sexes as complements, as spelt out by Richardson. Accordingly the effects of Chartist demands for men and women also complemented each other. Each step towards the protection of women from the adverse impact of industrialisation was simultaneously a step towards buttressing male superiority.

The Chartist efforts to reaffirm male hegemony in every sphere of life are indicative of a keen awareness of the erosion of male sexual power brought about by the Industrial Revolution. Chartists responded to the upheaval in gender relations by attempting to revert to pre-industrial patterns of sexual power, at the workplace, in the family as well as in politics.

In the last instance, Chartist efforts to improve the lot of women implied a confirmation of their subordination to men. In a situation characterised by economic exploitation and sexual oppression alike, the Chartist struggle to abolish the former still left women with the latter. In fact, Chartist opposition to women's exploitation was embedded in a conception of a woman's proper social position that put her more firmly in her place by cementing her dependence on man.

3
The Social Profile of Chartism's Female Following

Despite the ambiguities that riddled Chartism's policies for women, the movement did have a sizeable female following. Their exact number, like that of Chartist adherents in general, is impossible to ascertain. As a loosely organised political movement, Chartism was subject to considerable fluctuation in the numbers of its followers. Apart from a hard core of deeply committed supporters, who stayed with the movement more or less for the entire duration of its existence, there were also always large numbers of people floating in and out with the ebb and flow of political excitement. Regardless of the permanence of their commitments, a number of them, including even local adherents, achieved some degree of prominence, usually through the columns of the Chartist press. Yet they only represented a tiny fraction of the people actually involved and of the even larger number who would turn out for public meetings or be prepared to sign a Chartist petition.

The same is even more true of the relatively few female individuals featuring in the movement's press. Women in considerable numbers were part of the crowds congregating to listen to Chartist speakers, while others, possibly an even larger contingent (as Chapter 5 will show), did their utmost to support the movement from within the confines of their homes. By definition, these women were anonymous.

Dorothy Thompson[1] has emphasised the important part played by the local communities in lending Chartism nationally the strength and cohesion for which it has become noted. The shared experience of grievances, rooted in the effects on local industries of economic vicissitudes as well as in central government's onslaughts on a traditional way of life, bound working people together in their attempt to alleviate their plight. This was the promise held out to them by the 'People's Charter'. In rallying around it, people from all over the country fused their local struggles in a national fight for the implementation of the 'Six Points', thus responding also at the national level to the nationwide attacks on their well-being.

Those people turning to Chartism were mostly well-integrated members of their communities, sharing in many of the latter's distinctive features. And this was what made for the particular quality of Chartist association, which Dorothy Thompson has described as being

> not that of an outgroup of sectarians, but . . . based on local community and occupational ties . . . in any area the Chartists were mainly members of the dominant trade of their districts, adhered to the main stream of religious organisations in their area, and took part in the cultural and educational activities in which their neighbours were involved.[2]

It is as members of such communities, in many of whose distinctive features they shared, that women came into Chartism. In fact, the more homogeneous the local employment opportunities, the more they seem to have facilitated women's political activism. Lowe has found that where women were employed in large numbers in major local industries, there was also likely to be a centre of female Chartist activity,[3] usually indicated by the existence there of an FCA. Her observation, however, ignores the extent to which women's political motivation could also derive from the indirect effects of the condition of the local industry on them as housewives.

With the textile trades forming Britain's main productive industries in the first half of the nineteenth century, textile workers, as Dorothy Thompson has noted, formed a large proportion of the Chartist movement – and this was true of factory operatives, outworkers and artisans alike. In the Chartist period, the demarcation between these categories of workers was far from clear-cut. For many men, as she has pointed out, factory employment represented only one stage of their lives, usually when they were at their fittest, and was often followed by retreat into the domestic workshop or some other occupation altogether. This was even more true of women, whose engagement in waged labour inside and outside the home was (as Chapter 1 has underlined) subject to the poverty cycle they and their families went through. Among the textile trades, the weavers of various kinds held the numerically dominant position, which, again according to Dorothy Thompson,[4] accounted for their preponderance within Chartism.

These observations concerning Chartists in general are also borne out with particular regard to women. Lowe has found that references to female supporters in the textile industry outnumber any other in the Chartist press.[5] Moreover, during the 1842 strike for the Charter, which brought the north of England almost to a standstill, female powerloom weavers were active in large numbers, often displaying a higher degree of determination and militancy than their male fellow-strikers.[6]

The pattern generated by particular trades forming Chartist strongholds also bears upon the latter's geographical distribution. Apart from London and Birmingham, Chartism was strongest in two kinds of places: firstly, in the centres of decaying industry, such as the outworking villages of Lancashire and Leicestershire, as well as towns in the south-west, like Trowbridge and Devizes; and secondly, in medium-sized industrial towns, such as Stockport, Bolton, Bradford, that were growing rapidly during the first half of the nineteenth century. Dorothy Thompson, however, rightly regarding close-knit communities as particularly fertile ground for the flowering of the movement, comes up with a more extended list of Chartist bastions, maintaining that

the districts in which the Chartists were for a time in control, and where traditional authority was most threatened, were in the textile towns of the West Riding – Bradford, Halifax, Dewsbury – of Lancashire and Cheshire – Bolton, Oldham, Ashton, Stockport, Staleybridge – of Nottinghamshire and Leicestershire, the mining and ironworking districts of South Wales and northeastern England, and in places like Barnsley or Dundee in which a community of locality, of one or two major industries, and of shared leisure and recreational activities made for speed of communication, common concerns in work and in political action and the kind of mutual knowledge and trust which was essential for the maintenance of organisations which were always on the very frontiers of legality.[7]

There is no doubt, as Dorothy Thompson has claimed, that the main strength of Chartism always lay in the manufacturing districts, on whose traditions of alternative radical politics and religion the movement was able to feed. Within them, she believes, Barnsley, Bradford and Ashton-under-Lyne were the towns with the highest level of Chartist activity throughout the whole period of the movement's existence.[8]

The same geographical pattern applies to female Chartists. Taking the existence of a formally organised FCA as an indication of women's support for the movement, Lowe has discovered that one-third of these were to be found in Lancashire, Yorkshire and the northern half of Cheshire – the heartlands of Britain's textile industry. Major centres of female Chartism were Bradford, Macclesfield, Manchester, Leeds, Oldham and Rochdale. Other textile centres outside this region that boasted important female Chartist groups included Trowbridge and Bradford-on-Avon in Wiltshire. Apart from the textile areas, female Chartism appears to have been particularly strong where the same employment pattern prevailed as in the textile region, that is where local women worked in large numbers in a particular industry.[9] This was the case in Sheffield, where women were employed as burnishers, polishers, dusters and packers in the silver plate and white metal trade. It also applied to the Black Country, where women were engaged in rail, chain, nut, bolt, screw and file manufacture. And Bath and Bristol, the two major centres of female Chartism in the south-west, had local pin industries that employed women. With regard to female Chartists in Nottingham, another stronghold of the movement, Epstein has assumed that the majority of them were seamers, stitchers, lace-runners, menders and knitters[10] – in other words, that they worked in lace-making and hosiery, the major local industries.

This fairly rigid pattern became more flexible following the founding of the Chartist Land Company. This aimed at settling as many working people as possible on the land, thereby draining the labour market of its surplus and thus effecting a general rise of wages. To a large extent, support for the Land Company mirrored that for Chartism in general. As Dorothy Thompson has noted,[11] it centred on the north of England. And E. P. Thompson has claimed[12] that the Land Company held the greatest attraction for the weavers, who seized on it as their last chance of preserving their independence. Yet, as MacAskill's breakdown of Land

Company branches has revealed,[13] apart from the factory operatives, for whom it had primarily been designed, it also received support from craftsmen of the older and smaller towns, a pattern that is also confirmed by looking at the allottees. Moreover, the Land Company was Chartism's first venture to succeed in making inroads into the rural population. Although, in the first half of the nineteenth century, more people were employed full-time in agriculture than in any other occupation, agricultural labourers had been conspicuously absent from the movement. Yet membership of the Land Company was one of the few ways in which farm-workers could associate with Chartism without fear of victimisation. Their participation in the Land Company, as Dorothy Thompson has pointed out,[14] for this very reason by far exceeded that in branches of the NCA, the Chartists' more formally structured national organisation, founded following the failure of the first petition.

In the proceedings connected with the closure of the Land Company in the late 1840s, two membership books have survived in the Board of Trade Papers,[15] giving subscribers' names, occupations and addresses. But their use as indications of Chartist membership does, as Dorothy Thompson has made clear,[16] involve several problems. First of all, the lists are incomplete. Secondly, because they are full of repetitions and overlaps, counting them can produce only a notional idea of the number of people who enrolled in the two years represented – 1847 and 1848. Thirdly, the degree of overlap between members of the Land Company and Chartists proper is unclear. However, Dorothy Thompson has found that in the districts of which she has some detailed knowledge, many of the best-known Chartist names do turn up in the membership lists.

Despite their shortcomings, these documents contain the most detailed and comprehensive information about, at least part of, Chartism's following that is still available. They list 1835 identifiable female subscribers, who represent roughly 4 per cent of the members who joined during those years.[17] This, of course, is only a very incomplete indication of the total number of women involved, for when a couple decided to join, they would usually take out only one share, and that would be in the man's name.

Lowe's breakdown of the occupations of the female members listed in 1848 has yielded the following results:[18] out of a total of 1124, 390 women (34.7 per cent), by far the largest group, were listed as having 'no occupation'. It is not clear, however, whether this indicates that they actually were housewives in the modern sense of the term, or whether they merely viewed household chores and child-care as their primary responsibility, but in fact also engaged in some kind of waged labour, even if only on a casual basis. Among the wage-labouring women, those employed in textile trades – working as spinsters, frame-work knitters, powerloom weavers and so on – formed the largest group (240 women or 21.4 per cent of the complete sample or 32.7 per cent of women in employment). Second came servants (191 women or 17 per cent and 26 per cent respectively), while the third largest group (75 women or 6.7 per cent and 10.2 per cent respectively) were employed producing clothing and comprised dressmakers, seamstresses, milliners and so on. Thirty-two women (2.9 per cent and 4.4 per cent respectively) had some kind of retail occupation, such as innkeeper, shopkeeper, grocer. The remaining 196 women (17.4 per cent of the sample) were scattered in two's and three's over a large number of various occupations.

If one compares this sample with Dorothy Thompson's more localised one of 189 female Land Company members in Lancashire and the West Riding[19] and breaks it down into the same categories as used by Lowe, a rather different picture emerges. If all women who gave their occupation as 'housewife', 'domestic duties', 'no trade', 'housekeeper' or 'widow' are added up, then 97 women, or over half the sample (51.3 per cent), were more or less non-wage-earning. Of the remaining 92 women, 40 (21.2 per cent of the complete sample and 47.6 per cent of wage-earning women) worked in some textile trade, 14 (7.4 and 16.7 per cent respectively) were in domestic service, while 13 (6.9 and 15.5 per cent respectively) were engaged in producing clothing. Eleven women worked in some retail occupation (5.8 and 13.1 per cent respectively), while six women (3.2 and 7.1 per cent respectively) were scattered over various occupations.

While the order of rank among the occupational groupings is the same in both samples, the individual proportions vary considerably. It is surprising that, in regions given over to textile production, the overwhelming majority of female Land Company members should ostensibly be housewives. (This paradox is investigated below.) Conversely, the same factor accounts both for women employed in textiles forming the majority of the wage-labouring contingent and for domestic servants being underrepresented as compared to the national sample.

This, on the other hand, demonstrates the predominance, even at the national level, of women employed in textile trades as well as the relatively high proportion of domestic servants. While the actual status of the women listed as servants in Dorothy Thompson's sample may be somewhat dubious, as she herself has noted[20] – they may in fact have also been co-residing relatives or lodgers performing some kind of service in return, fully or partly, for board and lodging – the status of, for instance, Mary Havard and Harriet Hardwick, both servants at 12 Royal Crescent, Cheltenham,[21] appears to be unambiguous. For women at the beck and call of an exacting mistress, the prospect of leading a more self-determined life on a patch of land of their own must have had considerable attraction.

Moreover, women joined the Land Company in Cornwall and Kent, thus lending support to a Chartist venture in counties in which the movement had traditionally been weak.[22] Some of these places did show some Chartist activity in 1848,[23] which may well have been triggered by individual Land Company members or local Land Company branches.

The Chartist Land Company, then, attracted members from a wider variety of social and geographical backgrounds than Chartism had ever tapped before. It not only managed to organise a fair number of agricultural labourers, but for the same reasons also enlarged its following among domestic servants.

The present author's sample is based on the total number of 1835 identifiable female subscribers who joined the Land Company during both 1847 and 1848. Out of these, 389 (21.2 per cent) lived in typical Lancashire mill towns, such as Ashton-under-Lyne (26 women), Blackburn (35), Bolton (21), Bury (39), Dukenfield (15), Hyde (27), Manchester (118), Oldham (7), Preston (9), Rochdale (11), Salford (22), Stalybridge (18), and Stockport (41). Fifty-eight (or approximately 15 per cent) of these women could be traced in the 1851 census.[24] Of course, this is a statistically small sample, as can be expected given the inevitable limitations of historical data. However, the results obtained from even such a small sample are validated by what is known about working-class women's living conditions in the Chartist period (as detailed in Chapter 1).

Eighteen women (31 per cent of the sample) were allegedly

housewives, their occupation being noted either as 'housekeeper' (seven times), 'no occupation' (eight times), 'domestic', 'at home' or 'coachman's wife'.[25] Of women in employment, the largest group, twenty-three (39.7 per cent) worked in the cotton industry, mainly as weavers (thirteen women or 56.5 per cent of those employed in cotton). The high proportion of housewives in Dorothy Thompson's sample must therefore be attributable to the West Riding. There, domestic manufacture of wool prevailed in contrast to the increasingly industrialised cotton processing of Lancashire. Many ostensible West Riding housewives may in fact have also participated in their families' domestic trade.

In the Lancashire sample, twenty-six women (44.8 per cent) were heads of household, that is they were widowed or, if married, had no co-residing husband, or the husband was absent on census night. With only two exceptions, these women had families. They lived in households comprising, on average, six people and ranging in size from four to twelve people, who included children, children-in-law, other relatives and lodgers. These households, however, were only marginally larger than the average size of 5.5 people, if one takes the entire sample into account. Twelve women (46.2 per cent of female heads of household) were marked as housewives. Given the size of the households, it is reasonable to assume that these women were busy enough doing household chores. Moreover, some of them made money by taking in lodgers, and, with a large number of children around, the family income may have been sufficient to support one family member not engaged in waged labour.

Only seven women (12.1 per cent of the sample) were wives with a co-residing husband. Most of them (five) were registered as housewives. It is interesting to note that all of them, despite their having a co-residing husband, took out a Land Company share in their own name. It is possible that husband and wife may each have subscribed, but at different times, and therefore their names do not appear in the membership list in succession. It seems more likely, however, that the Land Company's specific appeal to women was such as to induce them to take out a share in their own name, with or without their husbands' consent. In the latter case, these women would have had to divert a certain proportion of their housekeeping money towards payment of their shares.

Another sizeable proportion of the sample, seventeen women (29.3 per cent), is comprised of daughters, the majority of whom (twelve) were co-residing with either one or both parent(s). The remaining five were living with siblings. Only two of those co-residing with parent(s) were married, but neither had a co-residing husband. The average age of co-residing daughters was just over twenty-six years, ranging from fourteen to forty-two, while that of non-co-residing ones was, at nearly 19.5, and ranging from twelve to twenty-four, considerably lower. The relatively high age of co-residing daughters would suggest that they were the chief earners of their families at the time and therefore the best able to afford a share, which would give them, as well as their parents, a stake in the Company. The non-co-residing ones, one would presume, hoped merely to better their own prospects, and, without any dependants to support, were able to pay towards a share.

Only six women (10.3 per cent) were single without either dependants or any familial support. Two of them were domestic servants, while the other four were lodgers. The fact that they were without a home of their own, may help explain both their motivation for joining as well as their ability to pay instalments on a share.

Such evidence as there is suggests that the category of person subscribing to the Land Company indicates not so much the age bracket or occupational group displaying the highest degree of interest in this venture, but rather those members of an extended working-class household actually able to afford a share. They were therefore not acting on their own behalf alone, but on behalf of the entire household they were part of. This is borne out by what actually happened when allotments were taken up.

One lot is known to have been occupied by the female allottee, her two daughters, another woman (conceivably a co-residing relative) and a granddaughter.[26] A further indication is the size of the allotments held or won by women. A total number of fifty female subscribers could be identified as either actual allottees on one of the Chartist settlements or as winners of an allotment.[27] The sample is nearly evenly divided between single women (twenty-three or 46 per cent) and women who were either married or had got their allotment on a family ticket with a man who was, one may presume, their common-law husband (twenty-seven women or 54 per cent). In twenty-three cases, the size of women's allotments could be ascertained. The average size of married women's allotments (3.4 acres) was only slightly larger than the average size of those of single ones (2.9 acres). An amazing five (35.7 per cent) of the single women held 4-acre allotments. This validates the assumption that single women subscribing to the Land Company acted on behalf of a whole household. As one case shows, a single woman taking up an allotment even as small as 2 acres could in fact entail a total of six people at least temporarily living off that piece of land.[28]

Moreover, only six families (10.3 per cent of the Lancashire sample) took out more than one share, usually two. One family is exceptional in that they subscribed to four. Significantly, all four subscribers were earning an income. While taking out multiple shares obviously enhanced the chance of winning an allotment, only very few families were able to afford to do so.

The fact that two veterans, aged seventy-seven and eighty-eight respectively, took out shares suggests that people did believe their settling on the land to be imminent. Alternatively, as both lived in large households, a share gave them something of value to bequeath to their children.

The remaining two female subscribers in the sample were a fourteen-year-old girl co-residing with two siblings, and a seven-year-old girl, related to the male head of the household with whom and whose daughter she shared a cellar.

In Dorothy Thompson's sample, eight female subscribers (4.2 per cent) were listed as minors.[29] This tallies with the number of seventy-two (4 per cent) minors among all women joining in 1847 and 1848. This figure does not comprise those minors whose names appear next to that of one or more apparent adults bearing the same surname and sharing the place of residence. Such groupings have been read as parent(s) and child(ren) listed in succession. The label 'minor' indicates children too young to earn, other than casually, and anyway too young to be entitled to keep their earnings. Their shares must have been paid for by their parents, who thereby hoped to ensure their children, and thereby themselves, a life away from the mill.

A case in point is that of Emma Adams of Banbury, who won 2 acres for the Chartist settlement at Snig's End near Gloucester. At the time she took up her allotment, she was nine or ten years old. Her father was a weaver, and probably her parents paid for her share on her behalf. In 1851, Emma, her parents and her three sisters were all living off the produce of their allotment, while in

1861, the family were still tilling their patch of land, though Emma had by then left home.[30]

The majority of female Chartists, one can conclude, lived in the manufacturing districts of central and northern England and were, in one way or another, connected with the local industries. Large numbers of women were associated with weaving. The business cycle of the local economy surely had an impact on them, no matter whether they experienced it directly, as waged labourers themselves, or mediated via family members in paid work. In addition, women in those regions were part of the community, whose values they shared and which they would have wanted, through their commitment to Chartism, to protect from outside pressures.

At a more immediately personal level, membership in the Land Company seems to have been particularly sought by women whose struggle to fend off the impact of industrialisation on themselves and their families required (and may often have been sustained by) large households made up of kin and non-kin, but from which husbands were often conspicuously absent. These women had to make do without male help, were forced to let their children endure the privations of mill work and worked hard to turn their insanitary, overcrowded dwellings into something with the semblance of home. To these women, who had to bear the brunt of industrialisation, the seeming possibility of extricating themselves and their families from the factory system and of reconstituting family life in a rural setting held considerable attraction. Outside the manufacturing districts, female servants formed a sizeable proportion of the Land Company's membership. Apart from marriage, this represented another alternative to life-long service. Chartism's female following, then, on the whole comprised those women (apart from servants, obviously) likely to be suffering most from the socio-economic changes in the wake of the Industrial Revolution.

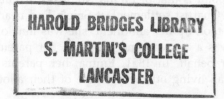

4
The Political Pose of
Women Chartists

The many facets of the suffering that working women experienced as a result of industrialisation formed the core around which revolved female Chartists' public statements, and their addresses in particular. These public utterances were couched in highly stylised language verging on the stereotypical. The uniformity of female Chartists' political articulation and the pose in which it was made are important indications of the constraints under which women operated once they made an explicit stand in public.

The first political address ever to be issued by women Chartists came in December 1838 from the Nottingham Female Political Union. In it, the women pointed out to their 'Sisters And Fellow Countrywomen' that 'At a time like the present', their energies were required 'in aid of those measures in which [their] husbands, fathers, brothers, and children [were] now so actively and zealously engaged.'[1] As the Cheltenham women Chartists explained to their countrywomen in the following year that they had 'Come forward . . . in their relative situation as wives, mothers, and daughters', so nearly all female Chartists reiterated throughout the movement's existence that they had come into Chartism as the female kinfolk of men who were already busy fighting for the Charter.[2]

This pose severely hampered women's political self-expression. It effectively prevented them from establishing themselves as political agents in their own right with needs and aspirations specific to them as women. Easing their entry into the public domain by emphasising their relationships with male Chartists, they extended into the political realm their familial status of men's adjuncts.

Regarding their political status, this pose implied that the women were happy to support a struggle, the primary object of which – universal male suffrage – ostensibly did not affect themselves. As the Cheltenham female Chartists stated about their motivation in fighting for the Charter: 'Too long have our fathers, sons, and brothers been deluded with the semblance of representation without its reality – too long have they been satisfied with the shadow instead of the substance.'[3] The Birmingham female Chartist who had adopted the pen-name of 'Sophia' for her contributions to the movement's press used the ridicule with which parliament had received a speech deploring the lowness of female wages to point out that, unlike the upper and middle-class Members of Parliament, working-class husbands and brothers, in spite of their poverty, were able truly to appreciate women's character. The only guarantee working-class women possessed of having their interests taken care of was to ensure that men of their own class were elected to parliament. That was why, according to 'Sophia', women supported the Charter.[4] Women were reduced to expecting their own condition to improve via the sending to parliament of male representatives of their own class. Common social origin, regardless of gender, was to ensure that working-class women's grievances would be considered sympathetically. Far from addressing any forms of sexual antagonism, such gender-blind political representation helped remove them from the agenda of class politics.

Some women, at least, felt encouraged by the place they had been assigned in the movement, circumscribed though it was, to claim for themselves the same political status as their menfolk aspired to. Thus they affirmed women's right to vote, yet never pressed for the actual recognition of this right by the movement at large. In June 1838, a woman weaver from Glasgow, dubbing herself 'a real democrat', addressed the women of Scotland through the columns of *The Northern Star*, calling on them to join the Chartist struggle. She maintained that it was 'the right of every woman to have a vote in the legislation of her country'.[5] In England, the female Chartists of Ashton, considering intelligence, irrespective of sex, the only precondition for the right to vote, expected female suffrage to follow automatically from the enactment of the Charter.[6] More self-confidently, Helen Macfarlane – the educated, widely travelled Christian socialist and translator into English of the *Communist Manifesto* – maintained, in one of her contributions to the Chartist press, that granting women the franchise was the touchstone of any true democracy.[7]

In their addresses, female Chartists portrayed their commitment to the movement as primarily flowing from their concern for the well-being of their families. As Susanna Inge from the City of London FCA explained, woman had awakened to 'a sense of the social miseries by which she [was] surrounded' at home. Working-class homes had become 'desolate' (an allusion to the prevailing want) and from erstwhile foci of happy families congregating in front of fires blazing in the grate – the physical comfort they spread but a tangible expression of the emotional warmth pervading the atmosphere – they had turned into places with 'deserted and fireless hearth[s]', having become the abodes of 'starving children'.[8]

The inability of mothers to provide for their children's most basic needs, that is to feed and to clothe them, was evoked by the 'tattered garments'[9] worn by 'children in rags'.[10] 'What can be more piercing and heart-rending to a woman', asked the Manchester women Chartists, 'than to hear her offspring crying for food to satisfy the cravings of hunger, and she none to give them.'[11] The theme of the poor mother unable to satisfy the needs of her children climaxed in the image of the baby dying from hunger at its famished mother's withered breast.[12] These were potent denunciations of a social system that frustrated the fulfilment of what was regarded as women's natural maternal responsibility[13] to the extent of drying up 'Nature's sustenance'[14] for infants. Consequently, Newcastle FCA presented Chartism primarily as a movement fighting to 'establish happy homes',[15] and the Cheltenham women stated their intention to turn the 'wretched homes of honest industry' into 'the dwelling places of peace, plenty, and happiness'.[16]

One of the chief obstacles standing in the way of domestic happiness was identified as the factory system. Women Chartists, especially those in the north of England who had the most immediately personal experience of factory labour, forcefully denounced the evils of this system by describing their horribly destructive impact on the family in great detail. The Sheffield female Chartists cast factories as monsters demanding that children be sacrificed to them. 'Go to the factories', they appealed to their countrywomen, 'there you will see men and women emaciated and wretched, their children an offering to mammon, by too early and unnatural labour, crippled and wasted, or brought to an untimely death.'[17]

As the husband failed to earn wages sufficient to support his family, complained the Newcastle female Chartists, 'the wife has been compelled to leave her home neglected, and with her infant children work at a soul and body degrading toil'.[18] Conditions that forced women and children to labour outside the home, turning them into the breadwinners for unemployed husbands and fathers, were denounced as unnatural by the female Chartists of Upper Honley and Smallthorn. 'You who have seen the order of nature inverted', they asked their countrywomen,

> the female driven to the factory to labour for her offspring, and her husband unwillingly idle at home, dependant [*sic*] alike on female and infantile labour for his own existence; will you, can you longer be in love with a base cruel system that makes you and your infants slaves . . . will you refuse your aid, when the object sought is your's [*sic*] and your children's happiness.[19]

Women presented themselves first and foremost as wives and mothers preordained to tend their families at home. On this station rested their female dignity. This was also why women powerloom weavers in Stockport, out on strike because of a reduction in wages, resolved no more to return to work, but rather to attend to their domestic responsibilities. Their action was inspired by the recognition that they were 'wives – not slaves'.[20]

Families were further threatened by government oppression, epitomised by the New Poor Law. The splitting up of families on admission to the workhouse roused female Chartists, here those of Newcastle, to a particularly high pitch of anger.

> We have seen . . . a law enacted to treat poverty as a crime, to deny misery consolation, to take from the unfortunate their freedom, to drive the poor from their homes and their father land [*sic*], to separate those whom God has joined together, and tear the children from their parents' care. . . . We tell the wealthy . . . that our homes shall no longer be destitute of comfort, that in sickness, want, and old age, we will not be separated from them, that our children are near and dear to us and shall not be torn from us.[21]

There were around this time gloomy rumours flying about in radical circles that the children of the poor were to be put to death as a means of combating poverty. Such rumours had, not least, been engendered by the pamphlets written by one 'Marcus',[22] which, driving Malthus's argument to its logical conclusion as they did, were read as forcefully discrediting the latter's work by some, but taken at face value by others. The Ashton female Chartists belonged to this latter category. They expected their countrywomen to 'do all that in you lies, to prevent the wholesale murder of your new born babes, by the Malthusian method of painless extinction'.[23]

The Cheltenham women Chartists, somewhat removed from the scene of the northern struggle against the Poor Law, focused on political oppression. 'Persecution stalks abroad', they wrote in 1839, 'tyranny lays its iron hand on the best and bravest. The bludgeon and the cutlass are the instruments in use – the bullet and the bayonet may yet be resorted to, to attempt the quieting of an oppressed and impoverished people.'[24] 'It was hard to bear the pangs of hunger', proclaimed the female Chartists of Bethnal Green nine years later, 'but it is harder still to know that the only remedies to be afforded are the sabre's gash and truncheon's blow.'[25]

The manner in which female Chartists depicted the current condition of the working class bears witness to the degree to which they had absorbed the movement's political creed. Many Chartist women's political awareness focused on the stark interdependence of the luxury enjoyed by the rich and the misery suffered by the poor. The women Chartists of Bradford calculated, down to shillings and pence, the comfortable living standard a large number of working-class families would be able to sustain on the amounts regularly squandered by royalty:

We see gaunt misery and famine stalking forth in all its horrors and see the useless extravagance bestowed on pampered royalty, when we see a Dowager Queen, who does nothing for the state, yet receiving the enormous amount of £100,000 per annum, when we calculate that she receives £11. 8s. 3½d. per hour, whilst thousands of our fellow creatures are in a state of actual starvation; and again, sisters, we have been insulted by another system of extravagance wrung from the toiling millions in the shape of a royal christening, over which £100,000 has been lavishly expended, which would have maintained twenty thousand families, each family consisting of seven individuals, for one month, at £1 per week each.[26]

Royalty undoubtedly counted among the 'drones of society', as did 'great land-owners' and 'money-mongers',[27] who did nothing but devour the proceeds from working people's labour.

Women Chartists recognised that the working classes were the real producers of all wealth. The female Chartists of Manchester asked

why is it that, in the midst of plenty, we are in such a condition? Why is it that those who are willing to work, that those who have produced everything valuable in society, without whom the factories would not have been built, the machinery made, the railroads constructed, the canals cut, who build and man the ships, who fight the battles, make their hats, shoes, and coats, and till the land – cannot get enough to quell the ravings of hunger?[28]

To this question, the women Chartists of Upper Honley and Smallthorne had the following answer ready: 'all evils of a national nature centre in class-legislation. . . . We tell you that unless class-legislation is destroyed, you can have no hope of being any better, or of obtaining any real benefit.'[29]

Class legislation was imaged as 'the iron grasp of Aristocratic misrule',[30] literally hampering all aspects of the national economy, as the Cheltenham female Chartists spelt out: 'Hence, we see them enacting laws which unduly *press upon* the commerce and industry of the nation; and by their *restrictive* operation limit the supply of food, *fetter* industry, and *cramp* the energies of the people' (emphases added).[31]

The women Chartists of Newcastle, having reflected upon the people's misery,

found that the cause of these evils is the Government of the country being in the hands of a few of the upper and middle classes, while the working men who form the millions, the strength and wealth of the country, are left without the pale of the Constitution, their wishes never consulted, and their interests sacrificed by the ruling factions.[32]

This complete lack of political rights was conceptualised by female Chartists as 'political slavery' with its concomitants, both physical – for example involving 'many hours of slavish toil'[33] – and mental – that is ignorance through being barred from access to education. The working class was thus seen as being in a state of 'political, physical and mental bondage', altogether 'worse than Egyptian'.[34] 'Sisters in bondage' was a common way in which female Chartists addressed each other,[35] and those of Honley and Smallthorn pointed to the particular slavery of mothers and children, denouncing the system that galled women's maternal joy by the awareness that they provided but a constant supply of slaves.[36] As their male comrades had (as argued in Chapter 2) shown up middle-class hypocrisy in fighting slavery abroad while letting similar conditions prevail at home, so female Chartists realised that 'slavery was not confined to colour and clime'.[37] The Bristol female Chartists even suspected that 'Cunning and designing men ha[d] enlisted [their] sympathies in favour of the abolition of negro slavery in [the] colonies',[38] implying that abolitionism was a deliberate diversion of working-class attention from conditions at home. As 'the brand of slavery [was] on their kindred', their supreme object was 'to emancipate the white slaves of England'.[39]

Female Chartists keenly felt that their misery was exacerbated by the degradation it entailed. 'Were we created', asked the Ashton female Chartist, 'to be tortured, starved, and degraded?'[40] What made the prospect of being admitted to the workhouse even worse in the view of the Keighley women Chartists was the fact that its prison-like regulations treated the poor like 'so many felons'.[41]

The emotions provoked by the keenly felt oppression were vented in imagery from the animal realm. Oppression was vividly evoked as a wild beast of prey, whose 'accursed fangs'[42] held a firm grip on working people. The Newcastle women conveyed their contempt of those who had imprisoned Chartists by referring to them as 'those vultures of the human race'.[43] The arrest of Henry Vincent was conceived of by his female followers as a monstrosity perpetrated by the literally 'hideous monster of despotism and tyranny', which had 'stretched forth its homicidal talons' and caught Vincent.[44]

The Nottingham female Chartists had preserved a vivid memory of the reform agitation of the early 1830s and of the

betrayal of the working classes by their former middle-class allies
that the 1832 Reform Act had involved. This had rendered at least
the women Chartists of Nottingham wary of middle-class
waywardness. They were convinced that the latter 'must ever be
considered in the light of false friends, and of no moment
whatever to the people, only to be closely watched to prevent
them doing mischief by their treachery to the common cause'. In a
very clear-sighted manner, the Nottingham women attributed the
unreliability of shopkeepers in particular to dependency on
upper-class customers, stating that the former 'might be tempted
to betray, for the sake of the shop – to gain the smiles of and
custom of the Aristocracy, the great enemies of the liberties of the
people'. In the view of these women, these utterly contemptible
creatures compared quite unfavourably with the men of their own
class. Middle-class men

> in the scale of number and intellect are very inferior indeed to
> the rough and hardy diamonds of the industrious classes, your
> husbands, sons, &c., who if once called out to the field of
> honour and patriotism . . . the affair will soon be terminated;
> we shall then see in whom and where the physical and
> intellectual powers are to be found, whether in the thousands or
> in the millions bent on justice, &c., the former priding
> themselves on their importance behind their counters, with as
> little claim to your respect as possible.[45]

Dwelling on the contrast between rich and poor, attributing it to
class legislation, distrusting middle-class political reliability and
deploring the exacerbation of misery by degradation – all of these
themes echoed the political analysis put forward by Chartist men.

Despite their long list of grievances, however, these women felt
that the latter in themselves were not sufficient to justify female
political commitment. Aware of the extraordinary character of
female public involvement in a political mass movement, it was
with some reluctance, as the Stockport women Chartists declared,
that they departed 'from the limits usually prescribed for female
duties'.[46]

Conversely, the extraordinary aspect of women's participation in
the Chartist struggle, precisely because it involved stepping
outside domestic bounds, was to signal to the government the
extent of working-class oppression as well as the end of the

latter's silent endurance. In this vein, the LFDA argued that observance of the code of female propriety made for 'that apathy and timidity which too generally prevails among our sex', denouncing it as the result of 'the prejudices of a false education'. Instead, they urged their countrywomen to 'join [them] in [their] holy cause, to show the oppressors, that even woman, domesticated woman, leaving her homestead battling for the rights of those that are dear to her'.[47]

The Newcastle female Chartists identified the assignment to women of the domestic sphere as a middle-class doctrine, the observance of which, however, was frustrated by the very same people's way of legislating. 'We have been told that the province of woman is her home', they wrote, 'and that the field of politics should be left to men; this we deny; the nature of things renders it impossible, and the conduct of those who give the advice is at variance with the principles they assert.'[48]

The Bristol women refuted the same doctrine by pointing to the material necessity that had already driven women from their homes to work in factories.[49] And the Keighley female Chartists even maintained that this doctrine was only a device employed by 'the government and moneymongers of this country' to keep the women 'ignorant and divided'. 'It is, therefore, brethren in toil', they continued, 'alike the interest as well as the duty of every working man and woman to declare their political sentiments publicly, in order that both the country and the Government may be acquainted with the wants and grievances of the millions of our oppressed country women.'[50] Only those 'who wish for things to remain as they are', claimed the Manchester female Chartists, questioned the right of women to concern themselves with politics.[51]

The rejection of women's confinement to the home as a ruling-class ideological device to help ensure working-class quiescence helped female Chartists to carve out some space for themselves within the movement by appealing to their brothers' antagonistic feelings towards their social betters. Chartist women's refutation of ruling-class doctrines, however, stopped short of questioning the belief in women's essential home-centredness. That language would have been unpalatable to working-class men. Instead, women used the impact of class legislation on themselves in their familial roles as wives and mothers to justify their political activity. The women Chartists of Bethnal Green did so in great detail:

> Woman can no longer remain in her domestic sphere, for her home has been made cheerless, her hearth comfortless, and her position degrading. . . . Woman's circle has been invaded by hired bands of police ruffians – her husband dragged from her side to the gloom of a dungeon – and her children trampled under foot – and this, for no other crime than that Labour cried for its rights, and Justice for its due.[52]

Women's privations had become intolerable endurance. 'With a fortitude, almost beyond human endurance', the Bethnal Green women proclaimed, 'she has borne poverty, want, disease, privation, and suffering, in their most sensitive intensity, buoyed up with the faint hope that a brighter ray might once more gleam. She feels her tears, her prayers, her supplications have all been in vain.' Now that female supplication had been proved futile and the just demands of the working class had been ignored, it devolved on woman, as the Bethnal Green women maintained, to turn political:

> She will not only be social, but political – no longer stifle her miseries at home, but spread them abroad, till society shall echo forth her note of woe, and Tyranny yield to the omnipotence of her power. Hitherto, she has obeyed the imperious dictates of man, and thought she had no right to political existence; but now, when she beholds nothing but silent despair on the one hand, and cold-blooded cruelty on the other, she feels it to be her duty to step into the arena of political strife, and agitate for the claims of liberty and humanity.[53]

Detailed descriptions of the current miserable conditions, as a result of which women 'as mothers, wives and daughters . . . [found] it impossible to discharge those domestic duties in [their] relative capacities'[54] ran as a persistent theme through the political utterances of female Chartists.[55] Apart from grievances specific to women, it was, as the Newcastle female Chartists pointed out, in their relative capacities – that is mediated through their relationships with working-class men – that women shared in the oppression and impoverishment of their class.[56]

Thus female Chartists can be seen as publicly identifying their social position primarily as one defined by that of their male kinfolk, without, however, denying gender-specific effects of class status. This was the concomitant of their professed adherence to an ideal of a sexual division of labour which, regardless of the actual allotment of tasks, assigned waged work to men and care for home and family to women. This self-portrayal and the highly stylised language in which it was couched indicate Chartist women's awareness that their appearance in public was an intrusion in a male-dominated realm. Both are traces of the women's adjustment to the fact that they were performing in a male theatre to a male audience. Hence also the justification of their political commitment by the elaborate description of the effects of economic privation and political oppression on the family.

This family discourse, though, by enabling the women to speak about the private and the public simultaneously, helped them carve out some space in the male realm of politics. In order to occupy the space they claimed within the movement's ranks, female Chartists tried to forge a group identity as women by giving the general Chartist political analysis a specifically female angle. The detailed depiction of the deeply felt plight of mothers makes for the peculiarly female ring to the presentation of the grievances and political arguments, which were otherwise identical to those put forward by Chartist men. This female tone bears out the fact that the women who signed the addresses were the actual authors, occasionally relying on male assistance though they may have been.

Patriotism is another important theme that shows how women drew on established radical discourse to claim the right to speak publicly. The Nottingham women portrayed Chartism as being headed by 'the first men and patriots of the day' and concluded their address with 'Trusting, sisters . . . that you will respond to us in your kindest and most patriotic sympathies and services in the cause of our common country.'[57] The Cheltenham female Chartists wanted all women to join them 'in working out the redemption of our beloved country'. They were sure that 'The voice of female patriotism ha[d] been heard, and [would] ere long make tyrants tremble for their safety.'[58] The female Chartists of Manchester, finally, explained that their political motivation derived from 'love for . . . [their] country'.[59]

Furthermore, Chartist women were concerned with proving that their struggle was in accordance with God's will. This was why those of Nottingham dubbed Chartism 'the great and holy cause',[60] which, according to the Wotton-under-Edge women, aimed at the 'salvation of [their] country'.[61] While the Keighley women strove to make 'the altar the footstool of God instead of the couch of Mammon',[62] those of Bradford wished all women to unite in order to 'sweep the citadel of corruption from the face of the earth and on its ruins build the temple of Chartism',[63] which, the Blackwood women were convinced, would be dedicated to 'the goddess of freedom'.[64] 'We ask for nothing', explained the Manchester women Chartists, 'but what is consistent with the laws which God has laid down in the unerring standard of divine truth – the Scriptures.'[65] This truth entailed, maintained the Sheffield women, the 'natural right to live upon the terms prescribed by heaven, i.e. to have food and the necessaries of life for our families'. It was not women's political involvement, they claimed, but rather the current deprivation of the working classes that was a contravention of God's will, for 'God is good.'[66]

On a more openly class-conscious note, Chartist women derived their right to political involvement from the existence of a female monarch. The Bristol female Chartists wrote: 'If, as our enemies say, woman has no right to interfere with politics, why should her majesty receive more than £1000 per day from our hard earnings, as the political head of this great empire? Here is the right acknowledged: interest and duty call upon us to exert that right.'[67]

Female Chartists would often cite historical examples of outstanding women who had accomplished marvellous feats. This served both to legitimise Chartist women's own involvement in politics and to provide those women they agitated with examples of female abilities. 'Remember, dear sisters', wrote the female Chartists of Ashton, 'what glorious auxiliaries the friends of the human race have had amongst our sex; ought we not to be proud, that we can point to Joan of Arc, Madame la Fayette, Margaret of Strafford, Charlotte Cordy [sic], Flora M'Donald, and a host of others too numerous to name?'[68] Glorious though these women had been, not even their achievements warranted their rising above the status of 'auxiliaries'. The Bethnal Green women Chartists listed Mary Wollstonecraft as well as the maid of Saragossa, adding Harriet Martineau and Frances Wright as contemporary examples of outstanding womanhood.[69] All these women, as the Newcastle female Chartists noted, had struggled against tyranny and urged their countrymen to be free or die.[70]

Feeling themselves to be interlopers in a male domain, Chartist women displayed their firm grounding in radical ideology as a badge of entry into the movement's ranks, as it were. They not only regarded class legislation as the chief cause of their current misery, but they also shared the men's keen awareness of the oppression of the working people, whom they conceived of as a social class apart, which had to rely on its own resources in bettering its prospects now that the middle classes had lost all political credibility by their conduct in 1832.

Those expressions of gender solidarity that do exist remain closely confined to women of the same class. Thus the Keighley female Chartists addressed themselves primarily to their 'fellow country women' and deferred mentioning the need for cross-sexual class solidarity until the last sentence. Their chief object was to achieve unity among their 'enslaved country women' as a precondition for establishing their freedom from want, a fight they deemed women to be perfectly capable of, as the following passage conveys: 'Stand up with a bold front, like women determined to shake off the bonds, of despotism, and join with us in demanding our just rights; to obtain which we must be united with the rest of our enslaved country women.'

When these women did draw a parallel between themselves and women from other social classes – here, the Queen Mother – it was to highlight the fact that feelings, such as motherly love, were a natural given and therefore unaffected by the social position of the woman harbouring them. '[W]hen our children are starving for want of the necessaries of life', they maintained, 'we can feel for them with an affection as sincere as that possessed by the mother of the Queen upon the throne.'[71] The class-conscious rather than gender-conscious overtones of this assertion stand out even more clearly against the backdrop of prevalent ruling-class beliefs, which considered working-class women unfit to be mothers.[72]

Quite exceptional was the address issued by Susanna Inge of the City of London FCA. Unlike the majority of female Chartists, she wanted women to make use of Chartism to further their own, gender-specific, ends. She believed this to be feasible within the framework of the movement, taking Chartists' insistence on women's right to political involvement as proof of their intention to establish full equality between the sexes. This implied that her concept of equality did not encompass the suffrage nor an overturning of the traditional sexual division of labour.

Susanna shared the belief commonly held in the nineteenth century that woman's condition improved in proportion to the progress of civilisation. While the Evangelicals (as will be shown below) considered this process to have attained its final object, as indicated by Englishwomen's excellency, Susanna regarded this development as being far from over. While affirming the centrality of the sexual division of labour for the well-being of society she asked nevertheless:

> But are we, because we are women, to be excluded from the more rational enjoyments of life? If so, why then was woman gifted with a mind to which in point of delicacy of taste, depth of feeling, and devoted affection, even proud man himself must bow. Why then, if we are thus gifted, are we to be thus treated? . . . Rouse yourselves to a sense of your merits. Assist those men who will, nay, who do, place woman in on [sic] equality with themselves in gaining their rights, and yours will be gained also.

Susanna's views deviated from those of most of her Chartist sisters. She believed women to be men's intellectual equals, if not superiors. It was on this recognition that she based women's claim to their rights, the attainment of which was to be secured in close co-operation with men by women who, out of an awareness of their abilities, took the initiative in bettering their condition rather than relying on male efforts on their behalf. She herself was a prime example of this type of woman (as Chapter 6 will show). She then proceeded to reiterate the reasons commonly adduced by Chartists as to why it was in women's own interest to get involved in the movement.[73]

The evidence available precludes gauging the extent to which Susanna may have acted as the mouthpiece of at least a minority among Chartist women. Her comparatively swift disappearance from the columns of *The Northern Star*, if not from the movement itself, may indicate her lack of support.

Female Chartists spoke primarily as female members of the working class, and not as working-class members of the female sex. Thus they stood in the tradition of plebeian women who had joined radical movements as, often quite militant, wives and mothers. The widespread participation of plebeian women in political and social agitations had begun with Female Reform Societies and continued through Owenism and the Anti-Poor Law movement right into Chartism. Referring to the textile districts in particular, E. P. Thompson has attributed this development to the change in women's economic status in the course of industrialisation, a process that was accelerated during the war years by the increasing demand for labour both in spinning-mills and at the hand-loom.[74] Thus evolved a tradition that viewed women not as passive dependants, but as active participants in all matters affecting themselves, their families and their communities. Yet, as Barbara Taylor has emphasised: 'Female activism of this sort . . . had generally been viewed not as a challenge to women's traditional family role, but as a necessary extension of it, at a time when the rights and needs of all family members were under attack.'[75]

As has been stressed (in Chapter 3), the local community played a vital role within the Chartist movement, giving it a high degree of cohesion. The close-knit community, made up of families still more or less functioning as the units of production, pushed women, as mothers of families as well as productive members of the househould, into political activism. This activism was geared towards preserving the well-being of the entire community, by ensuring women's proper discharge of their family duties.

The female participants in the Reform agitation of the late 1810s were a case in point. Female reformers, like their Chartist successors, felt compelled to justify their interference in the struggle for parliamentary reform. The arguments put forward were identical in both cases: their commitment to the cause arose from their familial function as wives, mothers and home-makers, in which capacity they were made to witness the sufferings their families were subjected to, due to economic conditions brought about by deficient legislation.

If their involvement in the reform movement, these women argued,[76] was the natural extension into the public arena of their specifically female tasks and duties, then nobody could rightfully object to it. What was at stake in 1819 as well as in the Chartist era was not women's subjugation, but the improvement of conditions that prevented them from properly discharging their duties as wives and mothers.

This theme came to the fore again in the movement against the implementation of the New Poor Law. 'Sophia', the Birmingham Chartist, exposed the preconceptions about woman's character and social position that underlay the Poor Law's Bastardy Clause. In her view, this assumed woman to be a reasoning being able to reflect on the consequences of her loss of 'virtue' and prepared to take the penalty for it. Yet in the entire setup of society, this was the only instance in which woman was made independent of man. The law was obviously designed to punish woman for her guilt and imprudence, though for ages she had been taught faith and reliance on man. 'Sophia' did not deny that unmarried mothers had erred tremendously or ought to work for the upkeep of themselves and their children. Yet she strongly objected to the application of the Poor Law until a better arrangement of female society had been achieved. Currently, however, she supposed 'lower-class' women to be constantly exposed to immorality. Lack of education, she maintained, made them the easy prey of upper-class seducers. Girls ought to be properly educated and to be given time for innocent recreation instead of being sent to work in factories. Moreover, the seducers ought to be punished as well as the seduced. One way of achieving this, according to 'Sophia', would be to teach women more of their own rights and less of the doctrine of self-sacrifice. Then, instead of hiding in shame, they would make their seducers known.[77]

'Sophia's' critique of the Bastardy Clause is highly reminiscent of Mary Wollstonecraft's view of female immorality. Both were equally concerned about the injustice involved in treating women in moral matters as responsible beings, while at the same time neglecting their moral education, which alone would enable them to take responsibility for their own conduct.

The critique that 'Sophia' – a middle-class woman though a Chartist[78] – levelled against the Poor Law was not what concerned her working-class sisters most. They simply could not afford to be interested in the niceties of moral concepts involved in legal regulations that, as far as they were concerned, deprived unmarried mothers of the financial support that (as shown in Chapter 1) they considered due to them from the fathers of their children: this argument, however, was not openly put forward in the campaign. Women were determined to resist the Poor Law unto death, as one Susanna Fearnley of Elland, proclaimed. The Elland female activists furthermore explained that their hatred of the Poor Law owed much to the way in which it specifically affected women, who were particularly susceptible to the pain caused by the separation from their children and husbands. Not only had they been accustomed to look to their husbands for support, it was also their duty to be the latter's helpmates and to soothe their sorrows, all of which the Poor Law prevented them from doing. The forcible separation of the family on admission to the workhouse was – as noted above – that feature of the law women hated most bitterly,[79] depriving their families as it did of their maternal and wifely attention, the bestowing of which the women considered their primary responsibility. The hatred inspired by the Poor Law provided much of the impetus for women's commitment to Chartism, which the Anti-Poor Law Campaign merged into.

The pose of radical wife- and motherhood that female Chartists adopted, though limiting their political options, proved strong enough to sustain women's political involvement, and that particularly at a time when the propriety of female appearance in public was severely questioned, particularly among the middle class.

Towards the close of the eighteenth century, when industrialisation was beginning to make an impact on English society as a whole, and ideas associated with the French Revolution threatened to leap across the Channel, the need for consolidating English society was urgently felt. A large section of the upper and middle classes found reassurance from their anxiety in religious enthusiasm. Between 1780 and 1820, the Evangelicals, as they were known, struggled to rebuild the nation through a thorough reform of morals and manners. The emphasis was on a new lifestyle, which, grounded in a new ethic, was equally marked off from the dissipation of the upper orders and the unruliness of the lower. It provided part of the ideological framework for the emergence of the Victorian bourgeoisie.

Central to the new middle-class morality was the conception of gender relations and family life, both of which were regarded as essential for maintaining social order. Due to the emphasis on things domestic, the new lifestyle was to have serious implications and repercussions for women's lives.

The condition of woman was believed to improve in proportion to the standard of Christianity attained by any one nation. Christianity was perceived as a protective shield guarding women against untoward influences that might impair their virtue. This was necessary, because physical weakness formed the chief element of the rigid concept of 'female character' that was allegedly ordained on women by nature. God, by creating women weak, had particularly fitted them for the discharge of domestic duties.[80] The concept of 'female character' thus turned into divine providence what was in fact the result of enforced adaptation.

Physical weakness, or delicacy, was made up for by emotional endowments that prepared woman for eminent moral attainments, such as fortitude, submission, patience, resignation. The commendation of these qualities along with equanimity and forbearance, consideration and absence of selfishness showed the female character to hinge on woman's capacity for self-abnegation, for she was considered essentially a relative creature.[81]

From the considerable emphasis put on the distinctions by which divine creation had marked out the sexes, there derived the notion of two separate spheres, each of which was particularly adapted to what were seen as the natural propensities of each sex. The typical line of argument began with the observation of a difference in physical strength between men and women and, moving through the description of the distinct male and female sexual characters evolving therefrom, ultimately arrived at a division of duties to be fulfilled in separate spheres. While the public sphere, the world of business and politics, formed the male field of action, women were confined to the domestic sphere. Here it devolved on them to run their households and look after their families. This separation of spheres was coupled with and simultaneously maintained women's subordination.

The separation of spheres along gender lines and the concomitant exclusion of women from any position of influence, all traced back to divine law, is thus revealed as a potent social mechanism to ensure male dominance. The natural affinity presumed to exist between femininity and domestic privacy was the ideology that helped restrict women's range of action. Outside the home, there loomed evil forces threatening female purity.[82]

In the domestic sphere, women were entirely to devote themselves to the desires of their husbands. As Basch has pointed out,[83] it was only through deliberate self-effacement that woman could fulfil her *raison d'être*, namely total devotion. The aim of such devotion was to render the home as different as possible from the world outside and thereby to counteract the evil influences man was subject to in the public sphere.[84]

As Houghton has observed, it was the wish, the need even, for a contrast to the principles increasingly governing the world of business and of politics that lay at the heart of the middle-class idealisation of the home.[85] With the growth of the 'mercantile system', as capitalism was often dubbed, the need for a force counteracting the latter's debasing spirit was felt increasingly.[86] This force was seen to be the influence that, by bestowing moral education on her children and setting an example by her conduct, woman was said to exert on society at large.[87]

The object of Evangelical endeavour was not confined to the upper and middle classes alone. With missionary zeal, it was being carried into the homes of the working classes to quell any stirrings of insubordination. It was with this aim in mind that Charlotte Elizabeth Phelan (afterwards Tonna), that prolific author of Evangelical tracts, published *The Wrongs of Woman*. In it she described the wrongs and sufferings inflicted on women of the poor. Her book was aimed at preserving social order by a modicum of social change: the alleviation of female waged labour, for the need for poor women to engage in paid employment was taken for granted. Once freed from the excesses of waged work, working-class women would be able to devote greater efforts to rendering their homes comfortable. Domestic comfort, Evangelicals like Charlotte were convinced, would produce contented men who would thus be dissuaded from rebellion.[88]

Occasionally, female Chartists found themselves being monitored by people who regarded the gaining of an ideological hold on the movement's female members as the key to frustrating the Chartist struggle. The advertisement in *The North Staffordshire Mercury* of a public meeting of local women to discuss the formation of a female political union at Hanley in November 1838 drew forth a condemnatory response from a woman who dubbed herself 'a wife and mother'. She turned out to be a, presumably middle-class, woman steeped in Evangelical beliefs concerning the proper station of her sex. She wanted to see these beliefs adopted among all sections of society, not least among those women thinking of engaging in Chartism. For four weeks, letters from her and her female Chartist opponents alternated in the newspaper, until the debate was brought to a close by some slight pressure exerted by the editor, with whose wishes 'a wife and mother' complied.

Her letters paraded the whole repertoire of Evangelical beliefs counter to women's political involvement. First of all, it was with some reluctance that she herself opened a public debate. 'I feel almost ashamed of troubling you with this letter', she began, 'and I fear that you will think it unbecoming in a woman to appear before the public; but I do assure you, my motives are good. I mean well.' She had decided to write this letter, because, addressed to her townswomen as it was, the newspaper appeared to her to be the proper medium of communication, for 'those amongst my townswomen who attend political meetings will be sure to read the newspaper also'. 'I have been very uneasy, Sir', continued the letter, 'ever since I heard that there was to be a female political meeting, though I did hope there was not a woman in Hanley who would so far forget her proper station as to be seen at it.' For her, such scandalously unfeminine conduct could only be the result of male instigation. Such men must 'either be silly or weak, or else be wicked enough to make us miserable by turning our minds from the important duties which belong to our sex, and leading us to meddle with matters for which we have neither time nor ability'.

The letter-writer worried about what would become of these women's husbands and children while the mothers wasted their time with matters that were of little importance compared with 'their own proper, becoming business'. According to her,

Women have duties devolving upon them, which are much more honourable and useful to society than the repeal of taxes or the carrying political measures. It is a woman's duty, by her kind and affectionate conduct – by her cheerfulness, good temper and industry – to make her father, brother, or husband, love his home, and prefer his fire-side and his family circle, to the public house and the company of strangers. It is her duty to watch over her children; to train them up in right principles and habits, and to make them good and virtuous members of society. Here is plenty of employment for a woman; and surely this is the most honourable employment she can have.

By attending to their specifically female duties, the letter-writer was convinced, women rendered themselves, their families and the country at large happy even more effectively than by any Chartist strategies:

> Let women consider, too, that when they attend most to these duties, they are promoting their own happiness most. Is not a woman happy, who has the affection of her husband, and his company at home, and his assistance and sympathy in the training of her little ones? Is not a woman happy, whose children love and respect her, and by their dutiful conduct towards her plainly show that she has performed a mother's duty to them? And not only would women be happier themselves if they attended more to these duties, but, Sir, I cannot help thinking that if all women were disposed so to conduct themselves, the whole nation would be happier too – yes, happier than if all the taxes were repealed and all the men were allowed to vote as often as they liked. Women love their country, Mr Editor, as well as men, and they can do more for it, too, in a quiet, becoming way. – By staying with their families and teaching them their duty to God and their neighbour, they will be training up men who will know to vote properly; and women, who will in their turn teach their children to become virtuous characters and good citizens.

For her own part, she 'would not exchange [her] husband's affection, and the hope of being useful to [her] children, for any thing on earth '. She concluded by appealing to her townswomen to bring their virtuous female influence to bear on their husbands to ensure the latter's proper conduct, too:

> I do hope my townswomen will consider well, and by their prudence, modesty and firmness in the path of duty, save themselves, and try to save their husbands and sons, their fathers and brothers, from misery, for when once a man gets fond of rambling to public houses there's no saying where it may end. He may become a drunkard, and finish by abusing and ill-treating those whom he should support and love and honour. Women, if you love yourselves, your husbands, your children, and your country, act as women still; stay at home, and do not by your example give the men an excuse for spending their time and money away from their families.[89]

In the next issue of the paper, the female Chartists replied, fully aware that they were dealing with a woman from a different social class. While female Chartists used to address each other and other working-class women as 'sisters' or 'fellow-countrywomen', this letter-writer was called 'madam' and referred to as a lady. Due to the wide social gulf separating her from them, she was held to be unable to appreciate the difficulties working-class women had to struggle with. 'We have read your letter with great attention', the female Chartists assured their opponent. Yet they were sorry to see, 'how little Ladies know of the real condition of poor women, and in consequence how little they feel for them'.

The women Chartists approved of being addressed from the Bible and agreed with much the letter-writer had said concerning their duties as wives and mothers, and they 'earnestly pray[ed] that God [might] mercifully help [them] in the discharge of those duties'. Yet precisely because they felt that they owed their male kinfolk and their children 'the kindest sympathies of [their] hearts', they could not stand by unmoved at the fact that despite unremitting toil, the men could not procure for their families the necessities of life.

In addition, the women Chartists reminded 'a wife and mother' that 'while enjoying their luxuries, these high-born dames perhaps never dream that in a very great degree they are dependant [*sic*] upon the labour of the poor for the possession of these luxuries'. There followed a lesson in political economy explaining to her that taxation diminished wages and rendered food dear, thereby reducing the working people to 'wretchedness and destitution'.

If their opponent, the female Chartists were convinced, were to share their own experience of poverty and to learn that this was due to unjust laws, which would not be amended until the poor were represented in parliament, they could 'not help thinking that [she] would act as [they had] done, and exert [her] influence to obtain for them their natural birthright – a share in the elective franchise'.

They then proceeded to use their opponent's chief argument – that women's primary responsibility ought to consist in the care of their families – to justify their political commitment. '[T]ill you can prove', they challenged her, 'that we have no share in the *miseries* entailed upon our *husbands* and *brothers*, by the scandalous misrule of the present time, you can never induce us to be silent spectators of the scene.'

Furthermore, the women felt their political commitment to be a religious duty, in proof of which they referred to biblical precedents: 'Till you can prove to us from the Scripture, that we are forbidden to sympathise with, and to endeavour to relieve the sufferings of those dear relatives, we will cherish the determined feelings of some of the Mothers in Israel, who got to themselves great renown by assisting to pull down the tyrants of their day.'

There followed the self-assertive claim to the same rights as enjoyed by the Queen:

We think, Madam, that your observations respecting female interference with politics are very ill-timed, considering that the nation is governed by a female: and that your observations respecting our meeting at public houses, having a tendency to encourage our husbands and brothers in dissipation, comes but with an ill-grace, when our gracious Queen deems it needful to be seen at play-houses, opera houses, and banquets, in company with generals, admirals, and bishops all the year round. In short, Madam, the poor women of this district feel as much concerned to enjoy the society and promote the virtue and happiness of their husbands and brothers, as the noblest lady of the land.

By way of concluding, the female Chartists reiterated their determination to support the Charter:

You seem to think us very ignorant, but we know enough to feel the pressure of unjust laws, and we have fortitude enough to stand by those we love, even though it should expose us to suffering and to death. Under these circumstances, we are determined to persevere in the plan we have adopted, and think it a duty that we owe to those we love.

Consequently they signed their letter as the 'WIVES AND SISTERS OF THE OPPRESSED WORKING MEN'.[90]

The following week, the 'wife and mother' was at it again, castigating Chartist women for their erroneous conception of their duties. She was 'truly glad' that the Bible had been accepted by both parties as the common reference point. This was only right, for 'we should be very ungrateful, if, as women, we did not one and all love and reverence that Holy Religion, to which we are indebted for our present happy and honoured condition'. Only Christianity had elevated women to the proper position that was their due. Therefore, women were obliged to regulate their conduct according to Christian principles. She then quoted numerous passages in the New Testament laying down what was proper female conduct. From these she deduced that women had no right to political interference.

For her own part, the 'wife and mother' refuted the ignorance of the people's privations imputed to her by her Chartist opponents. But in view of one's suffering family, she maintained that 'it only made matters worse, to acquire a taste for rambling and gossiping'. These pejorative terms convey clearly that, for her, the quality of female actions was circumscribed by the domestic realm. Once the home had been decreed to be the focus of women's lives, then any movement beyond its boundaries turned by definition into aimless wandering. By the same token, female speech, which in the home served morally to elevate the family, converted, regardless of its contents, into gossip once it had left the confines of the home. Instead, she asked, 'Would it not be our wisest and kindest plan, to endeavour, by increased economy and industry, to make our homes as comfortable as our circumstances will permit?' While, as she agreed, it was women's duty to sympathise with their male kinfolk and 'by [their] devotion and fortitude, [their] affection and frugality, endeavour to relieve [them]', women should leave to their husbands the more manly occupation of 'assisting to pull down tyrants, and to correct abuses'.

In addition, the letter-writer severely questioned the propriety of ordinary women modelling their conduct on that of the Queen. 'For any thing I know', she wrote, 'it may be expedient for ONE female, under some circumstances, to occupy a position which is contrary to the general habits and pursuits of her sex; but this surely can be no reason why all the women in Her Majesty's dominion should quit their natural places to meddle with state affairs.' This would have a most detrimental effect on men.

She concluded by warning her opponents of the dire consequences their political activities were certain to entail for themselves:

Rely upon it, the men who would tempt us to interfere in politics, are not our real friends. Possibly they may mean well, and they may please us by their flatteries, but the effect will be to degrade us, by inducing us to give our thoughts and attention to subjects which will only serve to unsettle our minds, divert our attention from domestic affairs, irritate our tempers, shake our principles, and, it is to be feared, at last alienate from us the affections of our dearest relatives.[91]

This second letter was promptly answered the week after. 'We ourselves scarcely know what Education means', wrote the female Chartists, 'but we are quite surprised it has not done more for a *lady*.' They were particularly incensed by the allegation of having acted without male approval and felt insulted by the 'wife and mother's' apprehension that they might not agree to being addressed from Scripture. Her interpretation of the biblical passages she had quoted against the Chartist women, however, came under severe attack. The female Chartists accused her of 'publicly charging us female members of a union', though they were under the special sanction and approbation of their husbands and friends, 'with usurping authority over them; with neglecting our homes and children; with wandering about from house to house as idlers, tattlers, and busy-bodies, speaking things we ought not, and meddling with things we ought not. And all this, without the shadow of proof. Our husbands, brothers, children, friends, all defy her to the proof.' They then specifically referred to the biblical passage that forbids women to dispute and wrangle in church or religious assemblies. 'Now, really', exclaimed the women Chartists in indignation, 'to quote against us this, is something like applying Scripture to the buttering of pancakes! What, upon earth, can it have to do with our Female Union, formed with our husbands' and friends' entire approbation; and when the very last thing we should think of, would be to wrangle with them!'

Seizing upon the 'wife and mother's' self-confessed political ignorance the Chartist women maintained that they had

yet to learn how that very ignorance of political subjects, [could] possibly contribute to the best training of her children, and the best services of her country; and she [might] be assured, that [they would] follow the directly opposite course. [They would] get [them]selves, and [they would] urge upon [their] children to get, to the utmost, all the very best political knowledge in [their]

power, that by subordinating all to the directions of Holy
Scripture, which [taught them] in the fear of God to love [their]
neighbours as [them]selves, [they might] be the better able to
contribute to [their] country's good.[92]

This correspondence marks the ground on which conflicting
ideas concerning the best way of fulfilling women's responsibilities were fought out. While both parties were agreed that
women had been ordained to devote themselves to the well-being
of their families, the beliefs concerning the forms in which this
duty was best carried out were diametrically opposed. Clash
though they did, both parties felt obliged as well as able to quote
from the Bible in support of each view. While a 'wife and mother'
was convinced that women were essentially unfit to concern
themselves with political matters and were to restrict themselves
to discharging their duties within the confines of their homes, the
female Chartists, on the other hand, claimed that, precisely
because their conduct was primarily motivated by familial
concern, it forced them to leave the confines of their homes and to
attempt to improve their families' lot by joining a political struggle
in the public arena.

Compared to the non-working-class woman who very self-
consciously overstepped her self-imposed boundaries by taking
on the female Chartists in public, the latter fought back in a
very spirited manner, painstakingly refuting their opponent's
arguments one by one, and showing themselves in the process to
be imbued with the belief that their commitment to Chartism was
both a natural and a necessary extension of their domestic care for
their families. The women could be certain that their conduct
would meet with male approval, not least because this meant that
political activities would not take precedence over domestic
chores.

Such steadfastness as displayed by the women of Hanley would
have been equally required by the female Chartists of Cheltenham,
who, in August 1839, staged a visit to the parish church. The
incumbent, the Reverend Francis Close, vented his indignation by
preaching a sermon addressed to

women professing and calling themselves Christians, yet so far
forgetting the delicacy of their sex, and the peculiar virtues
which ought to adorn them, that they step out of their natural

course, and from their fire-side duties, to launch on the sea of
politics; and taking part with their husbands, their brothers, and
their sons, instead of endeavouring to allay the fermentation of
the country, augment it!

What this passage amounted to was the statement that the female
Chartists, by virtue of their political activity, had 'unsexed'
themselves. Close emphasised the unwomanliness of these
women's conduct by stressing their alliance with their male
kinfolk. Precisely the same line of argument was persistently used
by female Chartists to explain the motives underlying their
involvement in the Chartist struggle. The awareness of having
strayed from 'the fire-side duties' was the same on both sides, but,
from the Chartist point of view, familial commitment did extend
into the public sphere.

Significantly, both Close and the Chartists agreed in their
assessment of female support for the movement, on which its
success, or the threat it posed, was deemed to hinge. In order to avert
the threat, Close preached to the women a lesson on how to exert
their influence for the benefit instead of the detriment of the nation.
He went to great lengths to deduce woman's position from the Bible.
Eve forfeited her equality with Adam by being instrumental in the
Fall. Consequently, God made her subject to man, yet mitigated her
curse by making her the vessel of salvation epitomised by Mary.
Close tried to rouse his Chartist listeners to a sense of their obligation
to promote virtue, peace and integrity in gratitude for the privileges
bestowed on them. He particularly exhorted them to exert this
influence in the upbringing of their children:

> In the humbler class of life such a mother of a family . . .
> neglects her children, leaving them in the lanes and streets of
> the city, while she seeks her pleasure elsewhere; perhaps in
> meetings for political discussion, or perhaps in scenes of
> abandonment and vice! what a curse are such women to the
> country! Their children must grow up revolutionists, for they
> have been taught revolution at home.

It was precisely by instilling Chartist principles in their children
that women wanted to promote Chartism; yet never would they
have condoned neglecting children in favour of political
involvement.

By pursuing their present course of action, Close warned his female audience, they were sure to incur damnation. It is interesting to note how, in the following passage, the social upheaval in Britain is ascribed to foreign influence, undoubtedly of French origin. Note also the gradation in the degree to which these women distanced themselves from female decorum. Female Chartism is the worst of all:

Now if these be the duties and the responsibilities of women, how great is their guilt, who in the present day, not only neglect to cultivate these christian duties, but practise the opposite vices! It were bad enough indeed, if they used their influence over their husbands, their brothers, and their fathers, to foment discord, to create a spirit of sedition, and to excite, instead of allaying, the bad passions of those amongst whom they live: but now, alas! in these evil days – these *foreign* days on *British* soil, not content with this, women now become politicians, they leave the distaff and the spindle to listen to the teachers of sedition; they forsake their fireside and home duties for political meetings, they neglect honest industry to read the factious newspapers! and so destitute are they of all sense of female decorum, of female modesty and diffidence, that they become themselves political agitators – female dictators – female mobs – female Chartists! Following the examples of their deluded husbands and brothers, they invade even the sanctuary of God itself, and unite in breaking the repose of the Christian Sabbath! If such proceedings are unbecoming in men, they are actually disgraceful in women! I trust that good sense and female modesty will prevail in future, and that we shall hear no more of *female agitators!*[93]

This impassioned onslaught on female Chartism occasioned a lecture to the local FCA shortly after. The lecturer, one W. Gaskell, employed all the biblical references used by Close to prove the opposite of what his clergyman opponent had maintained. His refutation of Close's arguments culminated in the claim that women's involvement in Chartism was a Christian exigency:

The very question was whether it was not among [woman's] Christian privileges to take part in the political movement of the times. The question was whether, if she did not endeavour to see which was the true view of political affairs, she was not in danger of lending the weight of her natural influence to the wrong side, and thereby of extinguishing the proper influences of Christianity, and losing her Christian privileges.[94]

As this lecture and many more instances prove, male Chartists deemed female support to be essential for Chartism's success. They conceived of women as possessing tremendous influence, because, according to Vincent, 'upon them depends [sic] the morals, religion, and intellect of a nation'.[95]

Evangelicals, too, regarded women as endowed with influence. Their sex-specific virtues were supposed to predestine them to reign in the moral world, whence their influence derived. It was on women, in the last instance, that the moral well-being of society depended, which was why Sarah Lewis could make the following exalted claim: 'We claim for [women] no less an office than that of instruments (under God) for the regeneration of the world, – restorers of God's image of the human soul.'[96]

Believing women to be able to act the part of saviours of humanity, male Chartists recognised the need to show them in which direction this redemption was to be sought. 'If you desire to free yourselves from bondage', wrote Mander May, the president of Tower Hamlets FCA, to the female Chartists of this locality, 'and benefit the whole human race, you must make every sacrifice to build up the sacred temple of liberty and fatherland'.[97] Such sacrifices, the women were assured, would bear their proper fruit, for the Chartist 'cause was good in the sight of God'.[98]

Bronterre O'Brien showed awareness of the weight of female influence, commenting approvingly on a report of a women's meeting at Newcastle: 'This is the right way to go to work! – Only let the oppressed women of England make common cause with their oppressed fathers, husbands, brothers, etc., and no power on earth can prevent their emancipation.'[99] Vincent, addressing 'the Men and Women of the West of England and South Wales', wanted to show them that 'success was certain if the women of England took up the matter in earnest'. He deemed women's support to be essential, because, he wrote:

I have the highest opinion of the judgement of women; – I have the highest opinion of their perseverance, when they are thoroughly convinced, that the cause in which they are engaged

is a good one. We see this strikingly exemplified in the many
benevolent institutions of the country, the principal supporters
of which are women. In matters, even when physical strength is
to be developed, we have often seen the power of women. . . .
In having the women of England, Scotland, and Ireland for
auxiliaries, success is certain.[100]

Indispensable though women's support was considered, their
'auxiliary' role within the movement was not in doubt, not even
for a Vincent, who believed that the efficiency with which women
supported Chartism accounted for much of the hostility the
movement met with among its political opponents. 'Those antique
knaves', he wrote in *The Western Vindicator*, 'who prattle against
women interfering with politics are silenced and confounded by
the shrewdness and enthusiasm of the ladies. Hence their anger –
hence their denunciation of all who have endeavoured to raise
women in the social scale.'[101]

In addition, Chartist leaders derived their recognition of the
indispensability of female support from historical examples of
campaigns in which women had played a crucial role. While
Thomas Clutton Salt of Birmingham thought of women's
participation in moral crusades, such as missionary activities and
abolitionism,[102] Watkins was convinced that 'Women have
frequently proved themselves the better men.'[103] To this effect he
cited several examples, biblical and historical, both violent and
non-violent. And Bronterre O'Brien was fond of alluding to the
'prodigal prowess' women had shown during the French
Revolution.[104] At least for him, women's contribution to any
political campaign was not confined to exerting influence. He
believed in their ability to devise highly efficient political tactics of
their own.

Despite the great store Chartist men set by female support, they
too felt obliged to justify their inciting women to join their
movement. This was necessitated not least (as just seen via
Vincent) by the hostile response women's Chartist activities
provoked. A case in point was a report in *The Times* on a meeting
of female Chartists near the Old Bailey, at which they
had discussed the possibility of electing female Members of
Parliament. The report talked about 'a singular natural phenomenon', namely a meeting of 'hen Chartists'. 'The principal
benefit actually elicited at the meeting', the article went on, 'was a

strong expression of dissatisfaction, on the part of the females, at
not being allowed to make fools of themselves in Parliament;
which they flatter themselves they could accomplish, if people
would let them try.'[105]

Such venomous scorn stung *The English Chartist Circular* into
action and provoked a refutation, containing some of the standard
arguments adduced by Chartists in their unequivocal statements
of women's right to political involvement.[106]

Like the females, male Chartists believed that the existence of a
queen entitled any woman to making her political feelings
known.[107] To see supreme power resting in female hands was
strongly resented by some Chartists for the blatancy with which it
highlighted the differential opportunities accorded to women
along class lines. 'I dislike Kings', William Carrier, the Trowbridge
Chartist, was reported as saying, 'but I dislike Queens much more.
A woman cannot be a parish Clerk, a woman cannot be a Church
Parson, a woman cannot be Prime Minister. Then why should she
be a Queen?'[108] In the same vein, Bronterre O'Brien accused those
who attacked women for their commitment to Chartism of
hypocrisy for not levelling the same critique against the large
number of 'blue stockings' among the aristocracy and against the
Queen herself.[109]

Although itself not in favour of female suffrage, *The English
Chartist Circular* did assert every woman's right to choose for
herself the means, time and place for her political activity,

> whether it be in private or public, through the press or on the
> platform, by works of charity or of zeal, that she seeks to
> vindicate her claim to aid in the moral, social, or political
> advancement of mankind, she is entitled, not merely to the most
> respectful and considerate treatment, but to the encouragement
> of sincere and active sympathy.[110]

This passage marks the contentious issue in the conceptions of
woman's social position. To non-Chartists, women's appearance in
public was anathema. Not only would political activity involve
the overstepping of domestic boundaries and therefore be
improper, but neither were women held to be amenable to the sort
of education that was considered a prerequisite for political
activity.[111] True feminity and politics were regarded as irreconcilable opposites.[112]

In middle-class politics, therefore, if women featured at all, they were assigned an essentially subordinate role, with fund-raising the very limit of their public appearance. The Anti-Corn Law League, a prime example of this type of campaign, embodied its middle-class constituency's beliefs concerning economics as well as women's place in society. The female contribution, vital though it was by helping to lay the foundation for the League's success, did not occur in public and therefore remained invisible. Cultural societies formally excluded women from full participation by detailing the partial forms of membership open to them. Some even thought the question not worth discussing.

The English Chartist Circular, on the other hand, regarded women's political activity as the exercise of female faculties bestowed on them by God for the benefit of their fellow-creatures,[113] thus bringing female political involvement within the realm of women's responsibilities. These responsibilities, Chartists firmly believed, consisted in caring for home and family.

Again and again the men emphasised that the prevailing misery's effects on women and their families not only justified but actually necessitated their political involvement. In his *Address to the Women of England*, Watkins, while unequivocally stating that woman's sphere was the home, maintained that

> when home is affected by any of the causes before mentioned – when it becomes no longer a home – when it is changed into a hell, shall not women come forth and enquire the causes of this? seek the remedy? If they do not, they must part with home and with all that is domestic in their character. The evils that threaten home, threaten all that makes home valuable . . . ought not the woman who values her home – that human nest – to be sensitive of everything which threatens its welfare.[114]

In a more detailed manner, Vincent explained:

> Women, you have often been asked what have you to do with politics! Point to the accursed factory system! Point to the Welsh hills, where women toil like horses! Point to the destitution of your homes and the wretchedness of your families, and then ask if your God intended you to be thus miserable! Point to the high price of your food and clothing! Point to the lowness of your husband's wages! Point to the heavy taxation of the

country, and then ask the fool who taunts you for interfering with politics, how can you possibly be happy under such '*an atrocious cannibal system*'?[115]

The specific effect on women of working-class distress was employed as an agitational device in various ways. In the advertisement for a meeting of the women of Spitalfields and Bethnal Green, they were appealed to thus: 'If you value the happiness of YOUR HOMES! YOUR CHILDREN! YOUR COUNTRY! you will attend this Meeting.'[116] And a placard calling for the Chartist demonstration at Kersal Moor in September 1838 concluded by requesting the women to 'show, by [their] attachment to the cause of freedom, that [they] were determined not to be idle in the holy work of rectifying the wrongs of [their] country'.[117] The last sentence portrays involvement in Chartism as a patriotic duty, a sentiment also endorsed by Salt in his address to the women of Birmingham.[118]

Chartist women stood in the tradition of their radical forebears who had become politically active as militant wives and mothers when they found themselves prevented from the proper management of their homes, which they regarded as their primary responsibility. It was in their familial function as wives and mothers that women presented themselves as experiencing the effects of what Chartists termed 'class legislation'. In their view, this was the cause underlying mass unemployment, starvation-level wages, high taxation and large-scale female and infant labour, all of which combined to render more difficult women's fulfilment of their domestic responsibilities. On the one hand, this pose of militant wife- and motherhood permitted women publicly to participate in political activities, while on the other hand limiting this activism to family issues.

Yet in a period in which the working-class family came under pressure from industrial capitalism and the state alike, the preservation of the small area that afforded what little emotional and material sustenance was to be had must have been a major issue in the on-going class struggle.

The ambiguity discernible in the political attitude of female Chartists accurately reflected the ambivalence of male Chartist agitation of women. Their assertion of women's right to political involvement was double-edged in that its affirmation was confined to issues arising out of domestic concerns. By pointing to the effects of 'class legislation' on domestic arrangements, Chartist men helped ensure that female commitment would solely be geared to an improvement of the conditions under which they fulfilled their tasks as wives and mothers. The nearly total congruence of male and female Chartists' arguments in favour of women's involvement in politics underlines the fact that, in their public statements, Chartist women used that language which they rightly believed to be the most acceptable to the men of their class.

Yet the practical insistence on women's right to become politically active went against the grain of dominant ideology and practice. Chartist women moved beyond the pale of what their social superiors considered true femininity by leaving the domestic sphere in order to create social upheaval. Thus they refused to take on themselves the duty to be missionaries in the task of stabilising a society that brought privation and misery to their homes. Convinced themselves that a woman's proper place was in the home, female Chartists, together with their menfolk, acted out their concern for domestic well-being in the public arena (the only sphere in which, as they well knew, pressure could be brought to bear on political decisions) by resorting to political struggle. In the context of general working-class insubordination, Chartist women's refusal to let themselves be excluded from the public sphere heightened the threatening aspect of Chartism to the ruling classes.

Chartists were aware of this effect and incorporated it into their political strategy. Women's activism was subservient to class objectives. On the organisational level, Chartism thus opposed the predominant content of the concept of 'woman's mission'; on the ideological level, though, the movement adopted certain of its elements, but adapted them to its own political purposes. The belief in the home as women's primary responsibility was infused with a sense of class-consciousness. If this belief was correct, Chartists would argue, then the social setup must not prevent women from properly filling their pre-ordained station. Thus Chartists employed a ruling-class ideological device for their own purposes. Accepting the end – female domesticity – they yet disagreed in practice about the right means to its achievement by furthering women's participation in working-class politics. Yet the failure to question the validity of domesticity on principle laid working-class women open in the long run to increasing pressure to conform to middle-class standards.

5
Chartist Women in the Family

The ambiguity inherent in the pose of radical wife- and motherhood adopted by female Chartists was reflected in and reinforced by the various forms assumed by women's involvement in the movement.

When Chartism appeared on the political stage in England, it was not the first time that large numbers of plebeian women had participated in activities geared towards the improvement of the condition of working people. Female Chartism looked back on and evolved out of a tradition of women's involvement in popular protest. Although, numerically, women's presence in Chartism surpassed that in previous movements, the latter provided a whole range of means to exert political influence and models of organisation for female Chartists to draw upon.

Suggestions as to how women could support Chartism outside the home were geared to using to the movement's full advantage both the extraordinary aspect of female political activism and what were considered specifically female qualities. Female involvement in Chartism was to signal to the government that the misery of the people had become so unendurable as to stir even women into action.[1]

Chartists not only believed women to have specifically female qualities to bring into the movement, but they were also convinced that this was to be done in a specifically female manner. While easing women's entry into Chartism, such beliefs and consequent practice assigned to female adherents to the cause a special status within the ranks of the movement.

The wide variety of forms female commitment to Chartism assumed can be grouped along a scale of increasing visibility, ranging from invisible (in the sense of publicly unacknowledged) activities to those attracting a great deal of public attention.

1 THE HOUSEWORK OF POLITICS

Totally invisible and hardly ever publicly acknowledged were those female Chartist activities that occurred within domestic confines.

Educating Children

Educating children formed the one exception to this pattern, because Chartists consistently called upon women to support the cause by, apart from agitating their husbands in favour of the Charter, forming their children's minds. It was as the primary educators of their children that Chartists believed women to be pivotal for ensuring the movement's success. Vincent, in particular, returned to this theme time and again. According to him, women's interest in politics was the precondition for rooting out deference among the rising generation. Conversely, the necessity of bringing up the young in the Chartist spirit justified women's political commitment, which, in this case, involved the overlaying of child-care with a political purpose.

Addressing himself for instance to the women of the west of England and South Wales, he wrote:

> So long as our rulers could persuade women they had nothing to do with politics, the present unjust system was sure to continue. The tyrants knew that all the children would grow up slaves; but now that women think for themselves, the tyrants feel their end approaching! Talk of putting down the Chartists, forsooth, why every kitchen is now a *political meeting house*; the little children are members of the unions, and the good mother is the political teacher; streets may be filled with troops – dungeons with honest men – lanes with rural police – and a gallows erected to ornament each highway – *still the system will fall*; children will suck in Radicalism with their mother's-milk, and when the present generation sink into the tomb, a race of hardy democrats will wield the destinies of Britain . . . whatever you do, *teach your children*! Make them well-acquainted with their religious, moral and political duties – teach them to value labour and to despise rank and pomp – teach them to LOVE GOD AND HONOUR THEMSELVES, and

root out of their minds any prejudice which a previous false education may have implanted therein.[2]

'Sophia', the Birmingham Chartist (introduced in Chapter 4), emphasised the need for constant self-education on the mothers' part and appealed:

> so let us, as Chartist women and mothers, instruct and encourage each other that our children shall be better informed of their rights as citizens, that their morals be of a higher order; and that, when the time arrives, when they shall receive those rights they shall be better prepared by the training received from their mothers to enjoy them.[3]

Both 'Sophia's' and Vincent's conception of early education – or socialisation in modern parlance – implied at least an idea of the way in which character formation and social structures were interconnected. Within this relationship, character formation was the agent, while social structures were merely acted upon. This left both Chartists with the paradox – never so much as tackled by them – of how mothers brought up in an oppressive society came to adopt democratic principles, to the extent of being able to implant them in their children.

Instilling Chartist principles into their children was rightly regarded by many women as a major contribution they were able to make to the Chartist cause simply by fulfilling one of their familial roles.[4] Naming children after prominent Chartists, a custom with some tradition,[5] was a way of publicly pledging them to the cause. This practice moreover showed the movement to operate like an extended family with figures such as O'Connor nominally acting as godfather to a good many children.[6]

The overlaying of female domestic duties (here, children's education) with a political purpose accorded well with women's own understanding of politics. As the female Chartists of Carlisle asserted in an address to O'Connor, their concept of politics comprised morality, education and religion as well as government.[7] This broad notion enabled them, too, to define traditionally female domains as essentially political.

Chartists knew from personal experience of the relevance of mothers as primary educators and transmitters of political beliefs in shaping their children's outlook on life. John Bedford Leno,[8] the

Uxbridge Chartist, attended his mother's dame school and later attributed his love of learning to her ability to interest her pupils in what she taught. Thus he made considerable progress.

James Watson,[9] the London Chartist and member of the LWMA, owed to his mother not only his taste for reading and for what education he received, but also his radical leanings, for she was a regular reader of Cobbett's *Register*, of which she thoroughly approved.

Female relations had a strong influence on Benjamin Wilson of Halifax, too. His mother had been involved in the reform agitation of the 1810s, and his aunt, whom in his biography he referred to as a 'famous politician', was a Chartist and great admirer of O'Connor. While working for his uncle, Benjamin thus became acquainted with the Chartist movement.[10]

William Adams of Cheltenham was brought up by his washerwomen grandmother and aunts, who took a great deal of interest in Chartism. They possessed a portrait of O'Connor, and on Sunday they regularly read *The Northern Star* attentively. The only reason why they did not keep the 'sacred month' – a general strike proposed for the summer of 1839 – was that they believed the suspension of labour by a few washerwomen to have no effect on the country. For a time, however, they abstained from excisable articles.[11]

Apart from children's education in the spirit of Chartism, male political activism depended on at least the tacit support of their wives. Recognition of this fact as well as the difficulties faced by the women concerned were highlighted at a meeting of female Chartists at Hanley. When they were urged by one of the male speakers not to remonstrate with their husbands for staying out late at political meetings, one of the women present voiced her disapproval of such meetings altogether, while another suggested that they should start earlier. A third found it very hard to wait for so many hours, and a fourth pointed to the expense of burning fire and candles while waiting for the husband's return.[12]

2 GENDER RELATIONS OF CHARTIST COUPLES

More than merely tacit support was required of the wives of Chartist leaders. Many wives of earlier radical plebeian activists had become involved or had found themselves getting involved –

directly or indirectly – in their husbands' politics. During the periods of imprisonment suffered by Richard Carlile, the champion of the struggle for a free press, his London shop, the centre for distributing unstamped papers, was kept open by a string of women, drawn first from his own family and subsequently from strangers devoted to the cause. The first to take over was his wife Jane. Her total lack of sympathy for Richard's freethinking underlines the fact that keeping open the shop, from which the family income derived, was seen by her as part of her familial duties. Despite her opposition to her husband's views, Jane resented the treatment he received at the hands of the government and the sufferings of the whole family as a result of his imprisonment. When she was sent to gaol herself, this did more for her politicisation than years of marriage to a radical husband. This is how she accounted for the change of her views:

> I was neither a politician nor a theologian before being imprisoned, but a sentence of two years has aroused feelings in me I might never have otherwise possessed. I have been made to feel the necessity of reforming the abuses of the Government, as I am sure that under a representative system of government no woman would have been sent to prison for two years for publishing an assertion that tyrants ought to be treated as dangerous beasts of prey. I have been made to think as well as publish it.[13]

Earlier on, Susan Thistlewood, the wife of Arthur, leader of the Cato Street Conspiracy, had presented an example of a woman who was a spirited Jacobin in her own right. She had displayed remarkable composure and courage when her lodgings were searched after the failure of the plot. Nor did she slacken in her visits to her imprisoned husband, although each time she had to submit to a most thorough body search.[14]

Jemima Bamford, although unequivocally in favour of reform, was constantly worried that her husband Samuel's political involvement would lead him into mischief. That was why she was determined to take part in the St Peter's Field rally at Manchester even without Samuel's consent: due to her foreboding that something evil would happen, she wanted to be near her husband. In the ensuing turmoil she lost sight of him, and, having

dreaded the worst, was extremely relieved to find him safe and
sound.[15]

This pattern of wifely support for husbands more or less
prominently involved in politics was also to be found within
the Chartist movement. The way in which Chartist couples co-
operated underlined the indispensability of wifely exertions on
behalf of husbands as well as highlighting the gender relations
existing between them.

Marriage was undoubtedly the family status Chartists aspired
to. Apart from the specific conditions of working-class life in the
first half of the nineteenth century (as set out in Chapter 1), which
made a stable partnership almost a precondition of survival for
women and, to a lesser extent, for men, the Chartist predilection
for marriage pervaded the answers obtained from' Chartist
prisoners during a survey carried out in the winter of 1840–1.[16]

Of the seventy-three men interviewed, fifty-three were married,
one was widowed and only seventeen were single. This latter fact
may well have been related to age. The only notable exception to
this pattern was Feargus O'Connor, who never actually married.
He formed attachments to various women and left several
children behind.[17] Contemporaries observed that his speaking
tours tended to follow the route of the famous actress Louisa
Nisbett. She went and nursed him in his last days,[18] so there must
have been some real attachment.

It is difficult to ascertain what form of marital union Chartists
preferred, whether or not they shared the predominant preference
for church marriage, and how frequent common-law unions were
amongst them. Only two civil marriages among prominent
Chartists have been recorded – that of Henry Vincent, who was a
Nonconformist, and that of George Jacob Holyoake, who turned
secularist.

Marriage was usually followed by children, who were
welcomed by Chartists as a blessing – and not only because they
were expected to support their parents in old age. In addition,
they were regarded as the perfect expression of marital love and
as rendering death less fearful, because, in his children, a man
'leaves copies of himself to succeed him'. The meaning of children
was expressed by Watkins thus:

the sacred names of husband and wife are doubly hallowed
when nature itself pronounces, by the mouth of a child, the

God-honoured titles of father and mother. What more holy and happy creatures than children, those images and heritages of the Lord; those links of being that bind again the bound, that rivet wedlock. Intermediate objects are they of the mutual regard of parents which descends to them, meets in them, and ascends from them to each other.[19]

Of the sixty married prisoners interviewed, nine had no children, fifteen had one child, nine had two children, eleven had three, two had four, one had five, two had six, three had seven, and eight had eight children. Obviously, the longer a couple had been together, the more children they were likely to have. Among prominent Chartists, only the Watsons and the Coopers had no children. That this seems to have been a sore point can be inferred from the following passage of a letter from Thomas Cooper to his wife: 'What trouble Cool and Ann have with *their* children! – what difficulty Harry and his wife must feel to bring up *their* children – and Rose seems to be lost and bewildered as to what *he* is to do with *his* children! What a blessing, darling, it is that we have *none*.'[20] Thomas evidently felt compelled to point to the trouble involved in the bringing up of children. This indicates that not having reproduced caused Susanna a feeling of grief and maybe even of failure.

Children assumed special significance during periods of forced separation of husband and wife, which occurred when, for instance, the husband was transported or imprisoned for his involvement in Chartism. 'Pledges of our mutual love and affection' and 'those little pledges of our undying natural youthful affection'[21] were how two transportees referred to their children. By virtue of their quality as the symbols of their parents' attachment to each other, children were the ties binding together husband and wife despite the obstacles that stood in the way of an actual reunion. As the embodiments of their parents, children substituted for the absent husband, who had thereby left part of himself behind. This is why John Frost appealed to his wife to derive comfort from the hope that 'you may yet see your husband in that son whom he so dearly prized'.[22] The use of the term 'pledge' with reference to children furthermore denotes that they were to ensure faithfulness. Being unfaithful to a husband who was absent through no fault of his own was not condoned. One of the Chartist prisoners interviewed expressed reluctance, on that account, to live with his wife on his release.

In accordance with the pattern prevalent in the working class, a good many Chartists married young. William Sherratt Ellis, who was later to be transported for alleged arson, was twenty at his wedding, as was Joseph Crabtree. Robert Lowery was two years younger, and John Leno stated in his autobiography that he too got married young.[23]

The couple's youth on getting married, combined with adverse economic conditions, predictably resulted in their poverty. The strain this placed on the relationship can be discerned by reading between the lines of Lowery's assessment of that period of his life:

> With love in a garret at twenty years of age hope was high, and we were the world to each other. I am aware that too often, when the difficulties of such early unions come, if there is not sufficient stamina, the parties lose hope and become careless. The husband often turns reckless, and selfishly seeks in the pot-house or elsewhere to escape these difficulties. But if there is manhood in us, a struggle for the sake of those we love will develope [sic] it; and of all the stimulants to exertion, affection for wife and offspring must prove the strongest to a well-constituted mind. We murmured not, but looked forward with hope, and kept our difficulties to ourselves.[24]

Writing from hindsight as a prominent temperance lecturer, Lowery turned the experience of the difficulties of his early married life into an appeal to his contemporary readership to become teetotal. Leno was more honest in stating that 'to say that we never quarrelled would be an untruth; but I can fairly say that our disagreements were on trivial matters, and openly confess that I, in most instances, was to blame for their occurrence'.[25]

For a couple to continue together in the face of the daily struggle for survival required a great deal of mutual affection. When William Sherratt Ellis, for instance, wished to get married, he was strongly opposed by his prospective parents-in-law due to his political convictions and his lack of money. The young pair's attachment, however, remained strong and undeviating, and 'In the midst of successive changes of feeling [William] never lost sight of the affection due to the partner of his bosom for whom he entertained a constant regard.'[26] That love carried many through periods of poverty comes across in the following description of the Lowerys' early married life:

> In passing, I would remark that however in a prudential sense we both afterwards perceived that it would have been more prudent for us to have waited until we had been older, and I had time to fix myself in something, whereby a better provision could have been made for our wants, yet, as Emmerson [sic] has said, in our struggles we had compensation. We were knit into one; and however we improved in circumstances afterwards, we looked back to these days of poverty and love as the happiest of our lives.[27]

And Leno concurred by writing: 'I got mated young, too young many would say, but, for my part, I do not regret it.'[28]

The material base that underlay and, in the long run, sustained the affection on which these relationships were based is revealed in the frequent references to the women's vital contribution to the family economy. The young Lowery, for instance, worked as a slop tailor. If it had not been for his wife's assistance, he would not have been able to make a living, meagre though it was. Ellen Watson ran the couple's bookshop entirely on her own when James was busy printing or engaged in politics. Two months after their wedding, James suffered his last imprisonment for participating in the struggle for a free press. Ellen, still unfamiliar with the business, had to take over, acting on the written instructions she received from her imprisoned husband. If it had not been for her, the shop would probably have been lost. In his autobiography, Leno, also a printer, felt full of praise for his wife's assistance: 'How she laboured at the press and assisted me in the work of my printing office, with a child in her arms, I have no space to tell.'[29]

Chartist marriages were not based on love and affection alone. There was also probably quite a high degree of political intermarrying among them. James Watson, member of the LWMA, married Eleanor (Ellen) Byerley, the daughter of a Leeds radical who was himself a friend of his. Richard Moore, also an LWMA member, in his turn married one of Watson's nieces.[30] Lucy, the daughter of John Cleave, another hero of the unstamped and who also belonged to the LWMA, became the wife of Henry Vincent,[31] himself a member of the same London body. John Livesey, one of the Chartist prisoners interviewed in 1840–1, was married to the daughter of a Manchester political activist.[32] And George Julian Harney married Mary Cameron, who was the daughter of a radical Ayrshire weaver.[33]

One can safely assume that, for many Chartists, their circle of political associates and their friendships overlapped. Therefore the women they were most likely to meet were the relatives of their political friends. A similar example is provided by Thomas Cooper, who, when still an ardent Methodist, married the sister of a fellow-Methodist, with whom he had stayed on a visit to Lincoln.[34]

With some couples, their acquaintance dated back to their early childhood, as was the case with the Ellises. Lowery married his cousin, who had been living with his mother since the death of her own.

Of course, there is more to intermarrying than ease of acquaintance. It furthermore indicates that Chartists – men as well as women – looked for similarity of political outlook in their partners. Or, to put it differently, love and affection sprang from the fertile ground of shared beliefs. This meshing of feelings and politics is instanced by the great number of Chartist marriages in which both husband and wife were active in the movement. Such couples left their mark on virtually every Chartist locality. In Bath, there were the Bolwells. While he was active in the city's male branch of Chartism, Mrs Bolwell was not only a member of the local Female Radical Association, in which capacity she collected for the Vincent Defence Fund,[35] but also acquired fame by chairing a female meeting to receive Vincent.[36] In Exeter, the Clarks were active supporters of Chartism and the Land Company,[37] as were the Flowers[38] and the Lingards in Barnsley, and the Flynns in Bradford.[39] In the same town, the Holdsworths were both involved in planning a rising.[40] So were Mary and Samuel Holberry in Sheffield.[41] Also in Sheffield, Mrs Foden was the secretary of the local FCA,[42] while her husband was involved in the male branch of the movement. In the early 1840s, George Julian and Mary Harney were both active in this town.[43] Mary Grassby, member of the Elland Female Radical Association,[44] remained loyal to Chartism into the 1850s.[45] She was married to a leading local Chartist. The husband of another member of the Elland association, Elizabeth Hanson,[46] was also a local Chartist leader. In London, Mary Ireland sat on the committee of the

Female Democratic Association,[47] while her husband was also actively involved in Chartism. Mrs Simmons, secretary of the Tower Hamlets FCA, was also married to an active Chartist.[48] Mrs Langston, who was often dubbed the 'Mary Wollstonecraft' of Bilston, was married to a leading local Chartist. In Birmingham, the Lapworths were both active in the movement.[49] Nottingham boasted three Chartist couples, the Lilleys,[50] the Longmires and the Sweets. Martha Sweet, member of the local Female Political Union,[51] kept a bookshop together with her husband, who was a local Chartist leader.[52] Anna Pepper, the secretary of Leeds Female Radical Association,[53] was also married to a leading Chartist. In Leicester, Mrs Simpson, member of the local FCA[54] and wife of a leading Chartist, lost her job because of her politics. These couples demonstrate that, for many, Chartism was as much a family affair as production and consumption.

The meshing of feelings and politics was not necessarily peculiar to Chartism alone. When Catherine Watkins, the socialist and feminist, married John Goodwyn Barmby in 1841, he was a leader of Suffolk Chartism and had begun to be interested in Owenism. During the twelve years of their married life, Catherine followed her husband in and out of his different political ventures. Hers was certainly not a case of quiet submission to whatever new turn John's career took, for she actively supported him by contributing to his various papers.[55]

The same was true for Elizabeth Neesom, whose political career closely followed the course taken by that of her husband Charles Hodgson. Both had been involved in the struggle for a free press. In the Chartist period, he was among the founders of the London Democratic Association, while she served as the secretary of both its sister organisation, the LFDA, and its successor, the ELFPA. After spending some months in prison for his involvement in Chartism, Charles turned more towards temperance than political reform. It is highly likely that, around this time, Elizabeth was involved in the East London Female Total Abstinence Chartist Association, which met in Brick lane, Spitalfields. This was also where the Neesoms kept their moderately sized radical bookshop and where Elizabeth ran her little school. Later in life, both became involved in freethought and vegetarian movements.[56]

Sharing the husband's politics did not necessarily result in public political involvement. Many women's active support of Chartism occurred within the confines of the family. Being a good hostess to her husband's political friends, for instance, was important for his political standing, and it was in this capacity that the wives of leading Chartists received praise.

Lucy Vincent joined in Henry's decision to abstain from all excisable articles. In fact, the consent of the wife, on whom devolved the shopping, was essential for such a decision to become effective. Furthermore, Lucy was in charge of the family's finances, not an easy task in view of the precarious situation in which many Chartists were placed. Apart from attempts at finding the money required to cover their personal expenses, her responsibility extended to the financial side of Henry's political ventures. While he was busy touring the country electioneering, Lucy tried to procure the necessary money.[57]

The case of Ellen Watson demonstrates how the wife's contribution to the family income blended with political activity. Her share in the running of the Watsons' bookshop did not only increase their earnings, it also ensured that a shop selling radical literature continued to exist. If necessary, Ellen would also join James in his printing. Without pay, both of them folded and stitched volumes of *The National* for William Linton in order to save him expenses.

Susanna Cooper was another case in point. While Thomas was serving a prison sentence, she began to edit *The Chartist Pilot*. There is a faint feminist ring to the first issue, after the publication of which her state of health deteriorated so badly that Jonathan Bairstow, at that time staying with the Coopers, took over. Thomas did not deem Susanna's remarkable achievement worth a mention in his autobiography. What mattered to him was the fact that he received his wife's support, regardless of the form in which it was rendered. In his mind, editing a paper was not a feat involving stepping out into the public sphere. It did not materially differ from anything else Susanna did for him and formed part of her domestic responsibility, which, in this case, required standing in for the absent husband by furthering the common political cause. This is why the short spell as editor by no means resulted in a break in Susanna's course of life or substantially altered her relationship to Thomas, which continued to be one of unswerving devotion.

Marrying an active Chartist required the woman's readiness to put up with long and frequent spells of her husband's absence. Commitment to Chartism involved lecturing or electioneering tours throughout the country as well as regular attendance at political meetings. It could also result in the husband's loss of employment. He would then have to set off in search of a job elsewhere.

Some wives, such as Lucy Vincent, Sophia O'Brien and Jane Jones, counteracted the separating influence of Chartism by accompanying their husbands.[58] This became more difficult once little children had to be attended to. In this event, personal communication was ensured by regular correspondence. Vincent 'wrote to his home every day when absent, and was ever thoughtful of the comfort and interest of his family',[59] is how Lucy summed up his qualities as a family man in her preface to his biography. When Susanna Cooper became too ill to join Thomas on his tours, long after the demise of Chartism, he wrote to her daily. When away on a tour in 1879, he even enclosed self-addressed envelopes to ensure that her replies would reach him safely.[60]

The frequency and regularity with which Chartist men wrote to their wives testify to the deep attachment they had formed to them and to their wish to sustain the intensity of the relationship in spite of being separated. It was also a way of staying informed about their families. Chartist men, then, took their responsibilities as heads of the household seriously and are rightly described as 'good family men'. The contents of their letters, however, stretched well beyond family matters and encompassed their political activities, on which they dwelt at great length in order to satisfy their wives' curiosity on this point.

The severest trial to which a Chartist marriage could be subjected was the husband's imprisonment or transportation. This was by no means an uncommon fate, given the mass arrests in 1839–40, 1842 and 1848. The wife's support for her husband then became crucial. Chartist prisoners were often subjected to an extremely harsh regime, and their wives' efforts to effect an alleviation of prison conditions were indispensable in ensuring the men's survival. If possible, Chartist wives would carry piles of warm clothes and plenty of nourishing food to the prison cells. Furthermore, they made public their husbands' sufferings. Jane Peddie wrote both to *The Northern Star* and *The Midland Counties Illuminator* informing Chartists of the terrible treatment at the treadmill inflicted on her imprisoned husband.[61] Mary Roberts petitioned parliament for an alleviation of the imprisonment of her husband, a solicitor, who had acted as the counsel for Vincent's defence.[62] Mary Frost, along with her mother-in-law and children, memorialised the Queen on behalf of her husband, asking for the sentence to be revised and pleading for regard of his family, who had not been involved in any offence.[63]

Equally important, at least, was the emotional sustenance that Chartist prisoners gained from being embedded in a relationship characterised by mutual love and affection. Chartist prison correspondence makes this abundantly clear. Separation from the beloved wife increased the horrors of imprisonment. 'Do not suppose that my imprisonment gives me pain; it is not that; it is the separation from you',[64] wrote James Watson to his wife. And this is how William Sherratt Ellis, sentenced to transportation, described the prospect of being separated from his wife: 'I can only say what I have said a thousand times, and proved by every moment of my life; that if I am at last compelled to leave you, the ties that bind me to the world will be snapped; and I would soon release myself from a world, I should hate without you.'[65] Personal experience informed the moving scene of the parting of the prisoner from his wife described by Thomas Cooper at the beginning of Book Nine of his *Purgatory of Suicides*, written while he was serving a two-year sentence in Stafford Gaol.[66]

Conversely, the prospect of being reunited with their wives on their release provided the men with an object to strive for and thus helped them to pull through. James Watson was convinced that his wife's 'love and attachment [would] more than repay all [he had] endured'. And the letter closed with the avowal: 'Take care of yourself! You are to me everything.'[67] And William Ellis wrote: 'though the prospect before me is a frightful one, I will, for your sake, try to bear up under it, still encouraging the cheering hope, that we are destined to meet again under more cheering circumstances'.[68] Reliving in his mind the happy moments of the past was the means Ellis employed to fortify himself during transportation.

Men who were deprived of their mainstay during imprisonment gave themselves up to despair. This was the case with James Burton, one of the Chartist prisoners interviewed in 1840–1. His wife was in very bad health, and he was reported as saying that if she died his home would be broken up and he might as well remain in prison. Loss of the wife was tantamount to the loss of the place of refuge into which she turned the home, the secure haven to which the fighters for Chartism, weary with their struggle, retired to recover their strength.

Intermingled with their suffering was the anxiety the men felt for the well-being of their families they had left behind. 'Oh! I am not permitted to suffer alone', wrote William Ellis to his wife, continuing '[I] wish I could so suffer; the thought of your state of mind is the most galling portion of my punishment.'[69]

It was not only the feeling of loneliness and the worry for their well-being that Chartist prisoners would have liked to have spared their wives. They were painfully aware, too, of the precarious financial situation in which their families were placed by the absence of the breadwinner. When William Cuffay, for instance, was transported to Tasmania in 1848, his wife became destitute and had to move into the workhouse.[70] All the men could do was to find someone to stand in for them in their capacity as the protectors of and the providers for their families. And so they committed their unprotected dependants to God's mercy. In the words of John Frost to his wife: 'May the Comforter of the afflicted, and the Father of the fatherless, be your and my dear children's support and guide in all things!'[71]

Nothing, however, could ease the psychological strain under which the Chartist 'widows' laboured. Many had reason to fear for their husbands' lives. Their anxiety was often exacerbated by the restrictions imposed on the prisoners' right to communicate with their families. Most of them were allowed visitors at long intervals only, and their mail was frequently intercepted and delayed. No wonder, then, that the women's health collapsed under the strain. Eleanor Holyoake fell seriously ill, while George Jacob (having turned meanwhile to secularism) was serving a prison sentence for blasphemy,[72] and Jane Jones's death was attributed in the last instance to the perpetual anxiety caused by Ernest's imprisonment under extremely severe conditions.

On being separated from their husbands, the women spontaneously responded with the wish to reconstitute the family unit, which government interference had torn asunder. Mary Frost, for instance, expressed her desire to join her husband in his exile in Tasmania. While the authorities proved to be unwilling to grant her this favour, John dissuaded her from leaving Britain, where he supposed, she would be more likely to meet with sympathy and support than abroad.[73] William Cuffay's wife, on the other hand, received Chartist financial assistance for her plan to follow William to Tasmania in 1853.

The difficulties of coping with the exigencies caused by their husbands' political involvement were exacerbated in the case of wives from a middle-class background. A working-class woman was accustomed to a life in poverty, and had learned early on to rely for survival on the support networks for which working-class communities were renowned (as described in Chapter 1). A woman from the middle class, on the other hand, entertained well-founded hopes that the reasonably comfortable lifestyle that her father had provided for would continue now that she was living by the side of a husband who was pursuing a respectable career. These hopes were dashed as soon as the husband committed himself to Chartism. It was in such terms that Jane Jones considered her fate. In 1851, she wrote:

> Better much to be the wife of an itinerant pedlar – for then I might probably be fitted by birth and habits to tramp after him, with our children at our backs, and our sentiments being in unison could still enjoy the pleasure of his society – but to be the wife of an itinerant Chartist lecturer! Who could endure it?[74]

A political career might render the man immensely popular, but involvement in working-class politics never paid. Due to their leading position within the movement, Chartists from the middle class were particularly prone to be pounced upon by the authorities in times of crisis. Then their wives were left to their own resources, unable to rely on support from their own families, who were likely to have been estranged by the politics of their sons-in-law.

Sharing in a Chartist leader's career inevitably brought hardship. Sophia O'Brien, for instance, was described by Bronterre's biographer as standing 'by her man loyally through all his vicissitudes, bravely sharing his poverty and the humiliation of being evicted, with her children, from house and home when creditors '"put the brokers' men in"', as they did on more than one occasion'.[75] 'Bravely sharing his poverty' and 'the humiliation of being evicted' are phrases that reveal the writer's belief that women of Sophia's background would be entitled to fare better in life than to share what was the common fate of working-class women. There is no way of telling her own feelings about the turn her life had taken. She seems to have borne up against the consequences of Bronterre's political involvement rather than submitting to them. This can be inferred from the following summary characterisation: 'She seems to have been a woman of character; self-respecting, and possessing a certain independence of spirit.'[76] During Bronterre's imprisonment, she ably acted on his behalf, repeatedly writing to both *The Northern Liberator* and *The Northern Star* to declare the severance of all connections between Bronterre and *The Southern Star*[77] as a result of a quarrel between him and his co-editors. At this time, Sophia was supported to the tune of £1 a week from *The Northern Star*.

Even worse was the downfall that marked Jane Jones's life after Ernest's conversion to Chartism. When Jane Atherley, the daughter of a Cumberland squire, married Ernest, he was rightly considered a suitable match.[78] Coming from an upper-class background, he had the means of keeping his family in style without having to resort to his training for the Bar. Yet he lost his money in an imprudent transaction, and the ensuing bankruptcy was said to have played a not inconsiderable part in effecting his conversion to Chartism. For the entire duration of his involvement in the movement, he never once accepted any payment for his services, and all his earnings went to the cause. This was only made possible by the most rigidly economical running of his own household. Jane's financial situation became even more precarious during Ernest's imprisonment. This resulted in a style of life to which she was completely unaccustomed. During this period, Jane found his demands for economies in the running of the household impossible to meet. Furthermore, her readiness to economise was clearly circumscribed by her wish to keep up a genteel appearance. So she was neither willing nor able to do her laundry herself, she worried about the look of the house in which she had taken lodgings,[79] and she excused her reluctance to economise with the wish not to deprive her children of what she considered was due to a gentleman's offspring.[80]

What was worse, Jane was subjected to two years of constant worrying about Ernest's condition during his imprisonment. The solitary confinement in which he was held and the extremely harsh prison discipline impaired his health greatly. It was not until he had fallen seriously ill that he was removed to the prison hospital. At a later stage of his imprisonment, he was informed that he could petition for a remittance of the remainder of his sentence on condition that he abjured Chartism. This, of course, he found unacceptable. While Ernest was in prison, Jane was supported by Chartist subscriptions, after the payment of half of Ernest's salary had ceased.[81]

During the entire period of Ernest's imprisonment, Jane also received financial assistance from her parents, something that both she and Ernest regarded as a liability.[82] Jane's parents stood firmly by their daughter, obviously unwilling to let her suffer for Ernest's political conduct. Their leniency may have been due to their being more likely to indulge in a certain generosity in political matters than the manufacturing middle class. Yet the strain produced by her precarious financial situation increased to such a degree that, at one point, Jane accused Ernest of want of love for her. Otherwise he would not be so inconsiderate as to make her suffer so much.[83] These sentiments, uttered in a time of crisis, underline that for Jane, Chartism was an affliction and not a cause worthy of support. Yet although she was anything but happy about Ernest's involvement in the movement, she did nothing actively to impede it.

In view of the family hardship in which commitment to Chartism often resulted, the couple's sharing of political principles was a precondition for the success of a Chartist marriage. This is expressed most bluntly by James Watson's biographer Linton. Consequent upon marriage,

> surely he will give up a single man's enthusiasm, and provide first hereafter for the interests of his family and home. He is of more heroic mould. Duty to him is (not independent of, but) higher than wife or home. And his wife is one with him: would not seduce him to play the craven. She has married him to be his helper, not his hinderer.[84]

Sharing her husband's political principles implied a readiness on the wife's part to support his activities regardless of the consequences for him, for herself or for any other member of the family. Lowery's wife, for instance, shared her husband's desire for reading, which characterised working people's quest for self-improvement in the nineteenth century. She therefore consented to going occasionally without dinner on Sunday so that they would be able to afford their weekly subscription for the library.

At times, more than the discomfort of an empty stomach was at stake. In a letter to Susanna, which he wrote when touring Staffordshire, Thomas Cooper stated how he expected his wife to cope with the consequences of his political involvement: 'If they take me prisoner tonight bear up, like a woman.' Endurance, then, was a quality considered to be typically female, which Chartist men looked for in their wives. Thomas went on to explain that he felt morally obliged to expound what he regarded as the true principles of Chartism, and quoted, in support, men who had suffered hardship for the cause they had espoused. He expected Susanna to share his principled stand to the full: 'if they take me up I cannot help it. I must speak the truth. . . . Run away I cannot. Latimer would not – Christ would not. My sweet Love will not expect me to act cowardly.'[85]

He procured his wife's consent to his way of acting by seemingly subjecting himself to her judgement. Susanna's letter, to which Thomas's was the reply, is not extant. But from his attempts at putting her at ease it can be inferred that she cautioned him against provoking the authorities. By terming caution cowardice he employed stigmatisation to force her into acceding to his conduct.

A similar conflict may have underlain Joseph Barker's reply to a correspondent who had enquired about Mrs Barker after Joseph's arrest in the summer of 1848. Barker assured the letter-writer that his wife was both in good health and spirits and only a little excited with regard to the coming trial. According to him, she was convinced that her husband had done his duty, she firmly believed in the ultimate triumph of truth and righteousness as well as in the eventual overthrow of oppression and wrong. She trusted in the Providence of God and in the happiness of the couple's future lot. At least in this reply, Barker claimed to be acting on principles shared by his wife to the full. 'My wife is a good deal like myself', he explained, 'when she believes a thing *ought* to be done, she likes to see it done, whatever the consequence may be. She hates cowardice and treachery as most unmanly vices.'[86]

The quest for respect was one of the driving forces for men's commitment to Chartism. This is how William Sherratt Ellis described what would sustain him during transportation: 'I can brave the heaviest chains, – the darkest dungeon, and the deepest grave that treachery, perjury, and persecution can inflict – consoled with the reflection, that my country, which I have served, and she whom I love respect my memory.'[87]

Ellis was right in assuming that some Chartist wives at least respected the courage their husbands displayed in their commitment to Chartism. In her introduction to Henry's biography, Lucy Vincent wrote:

> In tracing the course of my husband's eventful life, I feel more proud of his utterances in early days, which alarmed timid people and sent him into unjust punishment than I am of the expressions of his matured intellectual power. I reverence and cherish the memory of the indomitable courage which made him dare to resist oppression when resistance was dangerous and Nonconformity unfashionable both in religion and politics. The strong language was a necessity of the time, and few things have pained me more than the apologetic way in which even friends have spoken of it.[88]

Lucy Vincent, however, had been spared the anxiety for a husband suffering for his political activities, for she had not become engaged to Henry until after his release.[89]

Ellis was wrong, however, in assuming that he and his wife had the same priorities. While he put the struggle for the rights of the people before everything else, his wife's political commitment was limited by her familial responsibilities. Having primarily defined themselves as wives and mothers and being reinforced in this view of themselves by Chartism as well as by society at large, Chartist women did not permit their politics to prevent them from performing their duty to their families. When their husbands had been sent to gaol, the wives' sense of duty required them to extend their care to the very prison cell. This is why Samuel Holberry wrote to his wife Mary regarding her tireless efforts to bring about an alleviation of his prison conditions: 'Keep up your spirits, remember you have the satisfaction of knowing you have done your duty.'[90]

'To do one's duty' was what Chartism demanded from both male and female adherents. In the report of his arrest, Ernest Jones was said to have been 'ruthlessly torn' from the arms of his wife, who was portrayed as having remained calm and dignified despite such a severe privation. Such wording implied the denunciation of the government for depriving women of their husbands. Despite the sympathy evinced for Jane's plight, the report emphasised that Ernest Jones had but done his duty for his country. The movement, however, immediately stood in for the arrested husband, and the local Chartists formed a deputation to escort Jane to the railway station in a show of moral support.[91]

Duty had a different meaning for each sex, being solely geared towards the movement in the case of men, but primarily geared towards the family in the case of women. While reinforcing women's acceptance of their domestic responsibilities at the same time as calling on them to do their political duty as Chartists, the movement superimposed its requirements on family pressures; and the women were already trying to meet these anyway. Both sets of requirements were potentially in conflict. If a woman decided to carry on with both, she had to bear the brunt of the conflict in her attempts at combining the uncombinable. Thus, with regard to the political sphere, Chartism reproduced the double burden which, in the work sphere, those women who combined wage labour and housework had to carry.

Mary Holberry's fate instanced what happened to a woman who put politics first. Both she and her husband Samuel were suspected of having planned a Chartist rising in Sheffield. Mary, who was pregnant at the time, was arrested at her home ten minutes after Samuel and conveyed to the Town Hall, where she was held under most degrading conditions. Having been kept without food for eighteen hours, she was brought before the magistrates in order to be questioned. She was repeatedly advised to give evidence against persons in custody and, if she concurred, was promised a substantial reward and her husband's liberty. Otherwise, she was warned, she would have to stand trial for high treason, while Samuel would be transported for life. All attempts at threatening and bribing her, however, failed in the face of Mary's heroic determination. She was eventually discharged due to insufficient evidence,[92] while Samuel did not survive his imprisonment in the Northallerton 'hell-hole'. No wonder, then, that not many women were ready to pursue the same course.

A woman's impending death highlighted her indispensability in her husband's mind. When Eleanor Holyoake's health began to fail, George Jacob took her to Brighton, where he is said to have cared for her tenderly.[93] James Watson's health failed as a result of the anxiety and exertion he had experienced during Ellen's severe sickness.

The relationship of Thomas and Susanna Cooper is particularly moving and illuminating well beyond the years of his actual involvement in Chartism. Susanna was continually ill during the forty-six years of her married life. In the autumn of 1879, her illness took another turn for the worse. Yet Thomas was compelled to leave her for a lecturing tour to make money. The most loving epithets with which the couple's daily letters abound leave no doubt as to their affection. Their effusions of love stand in stark contrast to the rather cool and restrained tone prevalent in the correspondence of other Chartist couples.[94]

Thomas's uneasiness regarding Susanna's state of health increased from day to day. 'The pain that you have passed through I cannot *know* – but I seemed to have a feeling about me all yesterday and in the last night, that you were undergoing a great trial. The hours of today, since I received your letter this morning, I cannot describe. I seem to be all ear – lest a telegram should be brought – tell me you are dead',[95] he wrote to her having actually sensed that Susanna had had a crisis. In view of her impending death, he cherished the hope of being reunited with her one day: 'I will fasten [your letter] in my book of Psalms, that I may have it before me every day as long as I live, to remind me that I am to rejoin you in Heaven.'

By then Susanna's death was imminent, and they often referred to it in their correspondence. Thomas summoned God to help him sustain the heavy loss the death of his wife meant to him. In her very last letter, Susanna thanked God for having endowed her with a kind and good husband:

> Dearest & Best – Accept my most loving thanks [word unclear] for all your loving words and deeds. You're ever before me I bless God for his marvelous [*sic*] goodness in thus providing for my comfort and happiness. The Lord bless you prays Your ever loving wife, Susanna.

Thomas tried to imagine what life would be like for him without Susanna. His feeling of bereavement is clearly conveyed in the following passage: 'I shall have no one left to whom I can speak heart to heart – to whom I shall have to write my daily letter, and tell how I fare, and how I feel and think – to whom my life will be as precious as her own. What a lonely feeling it will be.'

In their correspondence, Thomas and Susanna come across as

two people knit into one. In the case of a couple like this, dissension is not very likely. It may have been with the ideal of a relationship like that of the Coopers in mind that the Chartist demand for universal manhood suffrage was formulated. In this view, the political opinions of both husband and wife merge and find their expression in the one vote cast by the man.

Chartist men showed themselves to be appreciative of their wives' exertions on their behalf regardless of whether these were restricted to the confines of the family or whether their wives had joined them in public political commitment. Charles Neesom's deathbed utterance to his wife, 'Bessy, you have been a good wife to me',[96] implied a compliment of the highest order, for to be a 'good wife' was what Chartist men expected of their wives, who endeavoured to live up to this ideal, which they also shared.

Cooper, summing up Susanna's qualities immediately upon her death, was more explicit about the ingredients making up a 'good wife' by stating: 'She had been my gentle, loving and intelligent life-companion.'[97] The first two epithets describe an attitude that, from the man's point of view, expressed itself as support based on affection. Both qualities are closely related to care and forgiveness, which were indispensable to a woman having to maintain a marriage through all the adversities brought on by political involvement. From the woman's point of view, therefore, love and gentleness implied submission to the person of the husband, and, mediated through him, to principles the couple had in common. The two qualities often bordered on self-abnegation.

Cooper, for instance, was at one stage of life expelled from the Methodist Society. He felt unjustly treated and turned against religion altogether for a while. This caused Susanna, who was the daughter of a Methodist revivalist, considerable grief. In his autobiography, written long after returning to the fold, Thomas was able to admit to having caused Susanna pain and even to quote his wife in support of his self-criticism.[98] But, at the time the break occurred, it was his course that had to be followed.

Love and gentleness, indispensable though they were to a 'good wife', would have been useless unless coupled with intelligence. Intelligence may well be translated here as understanding and acceptance of the husband's politics. Thus the exemplary wife, apart from her unwillingness to impede her husband's political activities, was able to act as his personal counsellor on political issues. The epithet 'intelligent', then, expressed the husband's gratitude and affection for a wife who bestowed on him all the advantages a kindred mind has to offer.

Cooper's sentiments were echoed in John Leno's character-isation of his wife: 'A good mother, an affectionate partner, a wise counsellor, a model of industry. Those words might have been written over her tomb in all truthfulness.'[99] Leno gave precedence to his wife's excellence in her familial function as a wife and mother, put her ability to give advice second, and only then added her contribution to the family income. This may imply a hierarchic ordering of the qualities he saw as part of the definition of the good wife.

In his obituary for Mary, Harney testified to her courage and self-sacrifice in standing unswervingly with him when he was debating with himself whether or not to give up *The Northern Star*. Unswerving loyalty in times of suffering was how Chartist wives were expected to – and indeed usually did – express their gentleness and love. These qualities had to give rise to acts of loyalty in order to be of use to, and perhaps even to be discerned by, Chartist husbands.

It would be wrong, however, to regard Chartist women as mere victims of their husbands' conduct and requirements. In the light of the fact that many of them had been brought up in radical families, it can be assumed that they were eager to show their commitment to the Charter by assisting their husbands as best they could. Thus they were able to endow their domestic function as the homemaker with political significance, thereby transcending the confines of their families. A not inconsiderable number of women went further and became publicly active in the Chartist movement. Unfortunately, too little is known about these women's personal circumstances. Thus it is difficult to ascertain the causes underlying the different forms women's commitment to Chartism assumed. Various factors certainly played a part in shaping women's political participation, such as number and age of children, help from relatives living with or near them, and the necessity and extent to which they had to contribute to the family income.

It would be wrong to assume that women's public commitment to Chartism derived from marriages that could be characterised as partnerships in which both husband and wife held equal rights. What mattered was the fact that the woman supported Chartism at all, which was taken to be as good as sharing her husband's convictions. It was the fact of such support that mattered, regardless of its form – always provided that fulfilment of the woman's domestic duties was guaranteed.

Support for the Wives of Chartist Prisoners

There was a high degree of awareness among Chartists of the clashes that could occur between familial and political commitments and which were highlighted by the plight of the families of Chartists imprisoned or transported for their commitment to the Charter. The serious efforts made by the movement to help women reconcile the requirements of both spheres were motivated by the wish to prevent them from impeding their husbands' political commitment out of concern for the well-being of their families.

This is instanced by the appeal on behalf of the widow of Samuel Holberry, the Sheffield Chartist who died in prison. Mary Holberry qualified for support by virtue of her exertions for Samuel. Moreover, assistance rendered to her was expected to encourage future adherents to the cause to act, like Holberry, regardless of the consequences, knowing that their families would be taken care of by the movement.[100]

The Chartist press was full of appeals for money to support the dependants of Chartist 'martyrs'.[101] In order to be able to grant relief on a longer-term basis, the setting up of comprehensive and permanent funds was considered. With this end in mind, the London Chartists debated the establishment of an 'Exiles' Widows' and Children's Fund' to relieve the families of Chartist transportees. In order to cope with the effects of the government clamp-down on Chartism in the summer of 1848, the 'National Victim Fund' was set up.[102] The increasing frequency and urgency of the appeals in favour of this fund testify to a slackening of support, which was indicative of Chartism's demise as a national movement.

Permanence of relief was best achieved by rendering victimised Chartists' families financially independent. The wife of William Sherratt Ellis, the Leicester Chartist transportee, moved to London in 1844 to take up a house and shop bought for her by Chartists. Previously, she had been supported by subscriptions.[103] It was common for the wives of Chartist prisoners to be set up in newspaper shops, where they would act as agents for *The Northern*

Star and other publications of the movement. Although this
provided them with a living, precarious though it may have been,
it laid them open to harassment from the authorities, who
occasionally seized radical papers for their attacks on the
government.[104] Some women actually managed to provide for
themselves in the breadwinners' absence. This seems to have been
feasible only when the entire family was engaged in some branch
of domestic industry.[105]

In order to facilitate donations for prisoners' families, a wide
range of fund-raising activities were organised.[106] Specific efforts
were made to incite women in particular to contribute to these
funds. The appeal would then allude to female abhorrence of the
Poor Law, depicted as the last resort of women and children
whose breadwinners were in prison. Moreover, such appeals
assumed women's natural sympathy with their sisters thus
afflicted. Addressing itself to the inhabitants of the Potteries and
Newcastle under Lyme, the local WMA asked the women:

> How is it that you should have sunk into apathy – you who
> ought to feel for women and children more than man can feel?
> How is it that you, too, have forgot your oft-repeated pledge?
> Must the all but widows and orphans of our incarcerated
> brothers starve or beg, or, what is worse, be consigned to the
> tender mercies of Poor Law Guardians, Relieving Officers, and
> Bastile [*sic*] Governors? Surely you say no . . . determine that
> nothing on your part shall be wanting to alleviate the sufferings
> of helpless females and suffering children, whilst their
> husbands, and their fathers are suffering the horrors of a prison
> for the cause of liberty.[107]

FCAs similarly used the suffering of imprisoned Chartists'
families as an agitational ploy. The Manchester FCA, for instance,
appealed to non-Chartist women thus:

> Then, Sisters, we call upon you in behalf of upwards of four
> hundred females, who had their husbands torn from them at the
> instigation of class-made law in 1839, and placed in dungeons
> for merely wishing to redress the grievances which press upon
> both you and us; – left without their guardians and protectors at
> the mercy of the public, with a forlorn, sorrowful, and agitated
> mind by day, weeping and mourning and sighing over their

husbands' sufferings; and dreary, restless, and sleepless hours by night, their children bereft of kind and affectionate fathers, and the long affection and concord which existed betwixt them cut asunder by the tyrants.[108]

None of these appeals remained unheeded, and many of the Chartist prisoners' wives were maintained for years, albeit scantily, by the subscription of pennies from other Chartists.

In order to qualify for support, a woman need not necessarily be married to a Chartist. Some women received help on their own merits, as did Mary Willis, whose political involvement dated back to the struggle for an unstamped press. Funds were raised to spare her the degradation of a workhouse funeral.[109]

Another appeal was made on behalf of a long-standing female member of the City Chartist locality, who had fallen ill and had to rely on her widowed mother for support. The Chartists were reminded that the applicant had never refused to give in similar cases,[110] indicating that Chartism, in some respects, operated like an insurance for the mutual benefit of its members.

It is in its efforts in support of the wives of victimised Chartists that the movement comes across most clearly as the champion of the family. The fate of these women was used to highlight government oppression. This was why they were commonly referred to as 'government-made', 'law-made' or 'Whig-made widows'.[111] These terms implicitly denounced the cruelty involved in wilfully depriving a family of their breadwinner and protector.

In their appeals on behalf of the families of imprisoned members of the movement, Chartists proved themselves to be aware of the crucial role played by the man as the chief earner of the family. Following Henry Vincent's arrest, a committee was formed to raise a permanent fund both to enable his mother to maintain herself and family and to buy articles to alleviate Vincent's own condition. While he had to endure winter in gaol, it was pointed out, his mother and family would 'have to struggle through the same season of increased wants and increased expenses, deprived of the counsel and assistance of her inestimable son, on whose exertions, while at liberty, the prosperity of the household had mainly depended'.[112]

The wish to help preserve the family by standing in for the absent breadwinner is also instanced by the following address from the National Union Fund Committee to the People of England, Scotland, Ireland and Wales:

> At the present many are the families of our countrymen sinking into their graves for want of that support which your united mights [sic] would place out of the reach of want, misery, and death. Oh! how heart-breaking it must be to the man that loves his wife and children to think that after risking his life, and now suffering imprisonment, that those which brought him out and cheered him onward and bid him good cheer in the hour of trial and trouble, should not now so much as look upon his family, but allow the finger of scorn to be pointed at them, and his children to be trampled upon as the offscourings of society.[113]

Standing in for the absent husband extended well beyond mere financial support, encompassing overall protection of the family involved. One W. Longson, having, justly or not, slighted the imprisoned Stockport Chartist James Mitchell, was reprimanded for his inconsiderate conduct by William Griffin, presumably the secretary of the local WMA, in the following terms:

> You should have thought about that yourself before you wounded the feelings of Mrs Mitchell. It is not sufficient that she should have her husband dragged from her at the dead hour of night, and placed in a dark damp cell, there to remain five or six days and nights, thence to be sent to Chester and receive sentence for eighteen months – it is not cruel enough that she should be left to maintain herself and child for that length of time – (the child deprived of a father) – but Mr Longson must endeavour to make the public believe that his old scholar is an idle vagabond that would rather get a living by selling beer and pikes, than working at the wheel! How do you think Mrs Mitchell could stand to hear your letter read? If you could have heard her throbs and sighs, and seen the tears running down her cheeks, you would have felt sorry, unless you had a heart like a stone. Perhaps it is better for your health you were not there, for she declared she would measure your head with the square end of the poker, although she is not a passionate woman.[114]

Two Chartist Couples: the Richardsons and the Lovetts

The various strands of wifely support for Chartist men are exemplified by the cases of Elizabeth Richardson and Mary Lovett. Their involvement in Chartism, mediated through their husbands as it was, evolved out of their marital commitment and was sometimes paid for very dearly in personal terms. Unlike their husbands Reginald and William, neither woman ever figured prominently in reports about Chartist activities. Yet, as this section will show, without their assistance, invisible though it largely remained through being mainly rendered within the confines of their homes, their husbands would have found it difficult to attain their positions of prominence within the Chartist movement.

The choice of these two couples for comparison is based on several grounds. There is enough material extant to render them amenable to an analysis of 'hidden' forms of wifely support and of the latter's interdependence with the couple's personal relationship. Moreover, both men were concerned with improving woman's condition. Richardson has already featured (in Chapter 2) as the author of the most comprehensive Chartist publication devoted to this issue, while Lovett's view of women passed into a lengthy poem entitled *Woman's Mission*. Finally, both men were, at least in theory, in favour of female suffrage, though Richardson wished it to be restricted to single women only. It will be interesting to see how both men's thinking about women relates to their marital practice and to what extent their ideas may have been influenced by their wives' personalities.

Reginald John Richardson was originally a master carpenter at Salford. Incapacitated by an accident from working in his trade, he joined his wife in her newspaper shop. As with many other Chartists, his involvement in politics preceded the inception of the Chartist movement. He had received his first schooling in radical activity from the Birmingham Political Union and was a prominent trade union leader in Manchester. He also figured as one of the chief agitators of the Anti-Poor Law campaign in Lancashire. It is not surprising, therefore, that he attended the mass public meeting in Birmingham in August 1838 at which the People's Charter was adopted and which can be seen as marking the official beginning of the Chartist movement. Back in Manchester, Richardson became one of the leaders of the Political Union there, which was responsible for organising the mass meeting on Kersall Moor in September 1838, one of the highlights of early Chartism. In the same month, he spoke at the Palace Yard meeting in London and, for the first time, alluded to the people's right to bear arms. Subsequently he seems to have toured the country on behalf of Chartism, for, at the end of 1838, he was reported as having addressed a meeting of the Female Political Union at Hanley.

The highlight of his Chartist career was his participation in the National Convention as delegate for Manchester. In this capacity he attracted the government's attention. The proceedings of the Convention spurred on government intelligence activities, including the opening of letters. The first such warrant was dated 8 February 1838, four days after the first meeting of the Convention, and concerned four delegates, one of whom was Richardson. Copies of the intercepted letters were sent to the Home Secretary, and this is how some of Elizabeth Richardson's letters to her husband came to be preserved.[115]

Richardson was one of the more militantly inclined delegates to the Convention. He put forward a motion proclaiming the people's right to arm, which he supported by precedents taken from English history. On behalf of the Convention he then toured parts of Scotland. As a result, he reported back that the launching of a general strike would be ill-advised and premature at present. He eventually resigned from the Convention, presumably because he had never received any payment. However, because of his advocacy of the right to arm, a bill for sedition and conspiracy was found against him and he was sentenced to nine months imprisonment in Lancaster Castle. During this period, he wrote the pamphlet *The Rights of Woman* and proposed a complicated new constitution modelled on that of the United States. After his release, he edited *The Dundee Chronicle* for a short while, and in April 1842, he attended the Complete Suffrage Conference convened by Sturge in Birmingham. Thus he severed his connection with mainstream Chartism.

Richardson was a self-confessed educator, constantly encouraging the passion for knowledge and discussion. He owned a Popular Library and wrote and edited cheap political almanacs and the famous Red, Blue and Black Books, which provided the vital statistics on which Chartists based their lectures. His publications encompassed ideas on trade, currency, taxation, banking and the national debt.

Reginald John Richardson, then, was a staunch working-class politician of long standing, who must have been well known in and around Manchester, and certainly acquired national fame as a Convention delegate. He combined militant leanings with a zest for education and was, as far as is known, the only Chartist to theorise on women's suffrage. His Chartist career was confined to the first phase of the movement and terminated, like that of so many of his comrades, in prison.

About Elizabeth Richardson's achievements much less is known. Like any other working-class wife, she found it necessary to contribute to the family income. Not untypically for the wife of a working-class radical, she did so by opening up a newsagent's business selling radical journals and predictably became an agent for *The Northern Star*. Apart from running the shop, she saw to her family. At the time of the Convention she had three sons. Jerry, the eldest, was of school-age, then there was Tom, and finally Alfred, the toddler, only just beginning to talk. In view of her numerous commitments, Elizabeth certainly found her mother-in-law's presence in the household a great boon. But there were other relatives on whose help she could rely. During Reginald's absence in London, his cousin Charles Hulme helped her in the shop. In return, he availed himself of having a relative based in London to further his own professional career as a printer.

Elizabeth's letters to Reginald testify to her efficiency as a businesswoman: she had no difficulty in coping with the responsibility with which her husband's absence had left her. She kept Reginald well informed about the state of the business. In early 1839, *The Northern Star* was causing problems. As it gave away engravings of J. R. Stephens, a large number of customers switched from their regular paper to *The Northern Star* so that Elizabeth was left with stocks of *The Northern Liberator* and Manchester papers unsold. Therefore Reginald was repeatedly requested to write to *The Northern Liberator* for a reduction in the numbers of copies sent. This indicates that while Elizabeth carried out the day-to-day running of the shop, business orders were in his name. As Reginald failed to do so, the request became increasingly urgent. If Elizabeth had been able to stop deliveries herself, she surely would have.

Business increased to such an extent (due to the growing popularity of *The Northern Star*) that Elizabeth, much to her chagrin, had to work Sundays. Moreover, she found herself unable to meet the demand for *The Northern Star* both in terms of numbers and promptness of supply. Therefore Reginald approached Feargus O'Connor, familiarly referred to as 'Feargus', about having *The Northern Star* delivered directly from Leeds in sufficient numbers. This was not the only business advantage to which Reginald turned his stay in London. He also used it for stocking up his shop with recent publications from the capital.

Elizabeth fulfilled an important function in keeping up Reginald's political connections in Manchester. She visited his correspondents and ensured that they remained in communication with him, and she sent him Manchester papers to keep him informed about local politics.

Among the Home Office papers, there are copies of seven letters to Richardson from his family in Manchester. Four of them were written by Charles Hulme, and, except for one, were sent on behalf of Elizabeth, apparently when she was too busy to write herself. One letter dates from the time of her visit to London and was intended to keep the two of them informed about the family. While Charles's letters are grammatically immaculate, Elizabeth's show a certain weakness of spelling, though they are perfectly comprehensible. This may account for her not dealing with business correspondence herself. Saturday seems to have been the favourite day for writing, though it was also the day on which the shop was at its busiest. It was on this day that Reginald's letters from London usually arrived, and the promptness in replying to them indicates the anxiety to keep in close communication.

The letters contain a mixture of news ranging from family issues to business and political matters. Their sequence varies according to their respective importance. The first letter, written by Charles, begins by informing Reginald that Alfred, his youngest son, has recovered from some respiratory disease. The next letter, which is from Elizabeth herself, restates this news showing both the parents' anxiety for the well-being of their children. In fact, Reginald must have been extremely worried, because Elizabeth 'shed a tear on the last letter you sent expressing the feelings of poor little Alfred'. Pandering to his paternal feelings she informed him that Alfred had begun calling for 'Dada', an incident felt worth mentioning by Charles, too, in his next letter to Reginald. Every letter, regardless of its other contents, reassured him that all the family was well, and in little Alfred's case, instances of his recovered health continued to be given to dispel what anxiety might have remained.

This anxiety was mutual, for Reginald was repeatedly requested to write as often as possible, particularly with a view to informing his family about the Convention's proceedings. They naturally preferred a first-hand report to any newspaper coverage, regardless of the latter's comprehensiveness. Elizabeth particularly cautioned Reginald as to what he said at meetings after the resignation of two moderate Manchester delegates, one of whom she had often dealt with on her husband's behalf. In order to support her case, Elizabeth cited other people's opinion on Reginald's negligence as a correspondent. An acquaintance 'would right [sic] out a discharge if he was me for neglect in not righting [sic] oftener has [sic] you could send them free of expense'.

On the other hand, Richardson's family was well aware of the honour reflected on them by having one of them sit on the Convention. From 9 March onwards, Charles addressed his letters to R. J. Richardson MP, showing how seriously the Convention was taken in working-class circles. He got it wrong, however, for the delegates chose to call themselves MC, precisely in order to denote that theirs was the truly representative parliament of the people. Elizabeth asked Reginald to direct one of his letters to her father and to enclose a few lines to him as he would feel extremely honoured to receive a letter from a person of such high standing.

One day, Elizabeth received a handsome shawl and an invitation to join Reginald in London. Although she was greatly tempted by the prospect of seeing her husband and the capital, she was not sure whether they were able to afford the travelling expenses. She herself had very little money left, having just paid bills.

Financial considerations constituted a constant theme of the Richardson correspondence. Like most other delegates to the Convention, Richardson lived on subscriptions made by Chartists to the National Rent. This was presumably the origin of the £10 draft mentioned in one of the letters. There are indications of the Richardsons' need to economise, for instance by avoiding the costs of money orders, which they would try to send free of charge or deliver personally. Elizabeth's financial worries increased after finding out about Reginald's expenses in London. She quoted an acquaintance who was against Reginald's calling meetings on his account, as it was unclear how the expenses he would incur would be defrayed. In order to cut down on personal spending, Reginald considered moving to a cheaper boarding-house.

Despite these financial constraints, Reginald decided to spare the money for Elizabeth's journey to London and told her so in a letter to which Charles replied, as Elizabeth was busy with travel preparations. Unlike Reginald's other letters, which were shown to the entire family and presumably discussed at great length, Elizabeth kept this one to herself. Charles therefore concluded that it was of a very private nature and referred to it as a 'love letter' and 'amor morator' at which she was extremely pleased. Elizabeth's visit to London, however, was not only intended to gratify the couple's personal feelings, but also served to deliver some money to Reginald and to inform him personally about the latest political goings-on in Manchester.

The next letter is from Charles, and was intended to inform both Elizabeth and Reginald about home. An acquaintance had called in every day to enquire about how the journey had affected Elizabeth, who was not an experienced traveller and had therefore dreaded going to London. The older boys were well, she was assured, although showing signs of missing her. Elizabeth had apparently taken little Alfred with her to London, for her mother-in-law expressly sent him a kiss. Elizabeth might have done so because she felt she could not safely leave him in anybody else's care and in order to demonstrate to Reginald the progress of his youngest son's development.

Charles, meanwhile, had rendered himself knowledgeable about London's attractions and suggested to Reginald where to take Elizabeth. The shop proved to be no problem as he had found himself an assistant. Charles wanted to be informed about Elizabeth's time of arrival, presumably in order to meet her, and, much concerned about her safety, advised against her travelling at night. He concluded by wishing Reginald much happiness, alluding to how much it meant to the couple to be reunited.

The last letter in the series is from Elizabeth, written after her return from London. While she usually addressed her letters to 'dear husband', this one was directed to 'dear and most kind husband', and informed him of her safe return home. This occurred a day later than expected by Charles, and so she must have made the most of her stay. Having seen the splendour of London houses, her own home appeared to her rather small, dirty and shabby. An acquaintance, one Mr Willes, made clear that Reginald was very much wanted at home, and that a month's leave could not be granted him. It is not clear whether this acquaintance acted as Elizabeth's mouthpiece, or whether he was in some position of authority over Reginald and therefore able to determine the length of his stay in London.

In this correspondence, the Richardsons come across as a couple who were extremely fond of each other. Elizabeth ably dealt with all matters concerning her family and made a competent substitute for Reginald. Family and political matters mingled in most of her activities. Reginald, although deeply involved in the proceedings of the Convention, found time to express his concern about his family and arranged for Elizabeth to join him in London for a week, because they missed each other, and also because she was his vital link with local politics. He was a loving husband and caring father, and he and his wife seem to have been very much on an equal footing. Although not active in Chartism herself, Elizabeth's support for her husband, rendered more valuable by her political understanding, enabled him to attain an outstanding position in the movement.

William Lovett's involvement in radical politics both pre-dated and survived Chartism. As a leading member of the LWMA he drafted the Charter. In 1839, he served as the secretary of the Convention and had to spend twelve months in prison for his involvement in the movement. He emerged from Warwick Gaol convinced even more firmly that education alone could bring about an improvement in the condition of the people, and it was with this end in mind that he was instrumental in founding a number of political associations. Although a life-long supporter of universal suffrage, he severed his connection with Chartism at the founding of the NCA, which he considered illegal.

The references in his autobiography regarding the women in his family are full of fondness and respect. He felt indebted to them for laying the foundation of his quest for knowledge. His great-grandmother taught him to read[116] and, limited though the learning was that his mother was able to bestow on him, he later thought with gratitude of 'those early lessons of a mother's teaching which have often come across my thoughts in many a long night of study after my day's toil, and which have formed my chief stimulus and most encouraging support'.[117]

During his entire life-time, he thought of women as the primary educators. It is this female function and its repercussions on humanity that Lovett dealt with in his poem *Woman's Mission*, written in 1842. By laying the foundation for the intellectual as well as the moral development of their children, he argued there, women exerted a great deal of influence on them, rendering them virtuous beings and thus ultimately ensuring human progress.[118]

Affection for his mother and grandmother continued to determine the course of Lovett's life. When considering the possibility of moving to London in search of work, he was reluctant to do so without their consent, and decided against going to sea as a rope-maker so as not to cause them any grief.[119] During his imprisonment, he was very concerned about breaking the news to his mother gently and trying to dispel her anxiety.[120] On his mother's death, he summed up her qualities by writing: 'Although dead, poor woman, she yet lives in the memory of her children as the best and kindest of mothers; and, I believe, in that of her neighbours as one who was ever ready with acts of kindness and words of cheering consolation.'[121]

On one important issue, however, William differed from his mother. As a strict Methodist, she insisted on his regular attendance at church and on his reading the Bible. She rendered her creed particularly hateful to William by not allowing him any play on Sundays. Instead she made him attend church three times, and apart from religious books, any reading was prohibited. His mother's rigid enforcement of the observance of religious rites rendered him totally adverse to any form of worship. As late as 1838, he attributed the deplorable fate of an acquaintance to his 'canting Methodism'.[122]

Having moved from his native Cornwall to London and having finally obtained work, Lovett embarked on the improvement of his education until he first set eyes on Mary:

But in the midst of these pursuits after knowledge, my attention was arrested by a new object, by her who for the past forty-nine years has been my kind and affectionate wife. And regarding that meeting as one of the most fortunate events in my life, I think it well to give its brief history.[123]

This passage is important for two reasons. Not only does it rank Mary as another object of enquiry in which William becomes interested, it also justifies his mentioning this event from his private life. Like contemporary working-class autobiographers, Lovett was primarily concerned with the political incidents that shaped his life.[124] Through his autobiography, which abounds with reprints of political pamphlets and manifestos, he aimed at providing the working class with a document of their history by relating those struggles in which he had been involved himself. Moreover, the book was intended as an aid in the exertions of the working class for reform at the time he was writing. It was also designed to give them strategic advice, and represented an attempt at counterbalancing the distorted view of working-class history given by hostile writers. Personal relationships, particularly that with his wife, who was not directly involved in politics herself, did not feature in this context, and their mention indeed required justification.

'All things now seemed bright and prosperous with me', Lovett wrote about his feelings after having been accepted as the future husband. However, an obstacle soon appeared that seriously jeopardised their intended marriage. Mary, who had been brought up a devout Anglican, asked William to take the sacrament with her. Due to his revulsion against all forms of religious rites, he refused to comply, whereupon Mary felt it impossible to marry him. Her refusal threw William into utter despair: 'This avowal I felt with the keenest anguish; and our parting that evening was to me like the parting of mental and bodily powers.'

This passage underlines the depth of his feelings for Mary. It required a great deal of energy on his part to overcome his grief about their parting: 'I tried to summon some little philosophy to my aid, but philosophy I believe has little control over this powerful and strong passion; and months elapsed before I recovered sufficently from the shock to resume quietly my usual avocations.'[125]

This is the nearest William ever came to a public avowal of his love for Mary. The firm believer in the power of knowledge summoned philosophy to his aid, only to find it impotent against unfulfilled love. To search for consolation in a relationship with another woman was totally out of the question, and he resolved to remain a bachelor. In a bid to divert his thoughts from Mary, he plunged into politics and joined a vast number of associations.

He would probably have remained single had it not been for Mary. She sent him a Christmas card, which opened up a controversial correspondence about religious issues and resulted in a reconciliation of their differences so that they could eventually get married.

Unfortunately, William does not record what effected the change of mind in Mary, for it is evident that he did not change his position by one iota. Nor does he state whether the issue was settled once and for all or whether the argument cropped up again. The possibility of his winning her over appears rather slim in view of the fact that his first show of religious dissent had immediately resulted in her refusing him, which seems to indicate that her belief was too strong for her to give it up easily. On the other hand, she must have regretted their parting, for otherwise she would not have taken the first step towards reconciliation. William seems to have convinced her of the principled nature of his stance on religion, while she may have realised that she could never marry him unless she was prepared to tolerate what appeared to her his disbelief. In fact this first recorded argument of their relationship may have set the pattern for their married life. William upheld his principles regardless of the costs to himself and others, while Mary was far more pliable, her flexibility being fuelled by her affection for William.

Many a time his firm adherence to his political principles caused hardship to himself and his family. When William refused to join the militia, a good deal of their furniture was seized by the authorities in payment of the fine imposed on him. Mary let this happen and refused the money she was offered by an acquaintance to exempt her husband.

William's twelve-month imprisonment at Warwick proved to be the hardest trial for Mary. He repeatedly made it clear to her that he strongly objected to any attempts on her part or that of his political friends to effect his release in a way that would compromise his principles. He explicitly forbade her to continue her exertions on his behalf:

And now, Mary, it is my wish that you make no further solicitations on my behalf, either to government or any of its members. I entreat you, therefore, to observe this my request – for if the same justice be denied me, which has been accorded to others under similar circumstances, I shall scorn to sue for it by supplication or importuning myself; and I am equally adverse to my friends doing it on my account.[126]

The hardest blow was still to come. After ten months of the prison term had elapsed, the Home Secretary offered to recommend Lovett for a remission of the remainder of the sentence if he entered into recognisances in £50 for good behaviour for one year. Mary was greatly disappointed by this offer. Although ardently wishing for William's release and unable to detect any compromise of his principles inherent in the offer, she felt that 'it would be exceedingly galling to him . . . I feel sure he will not come out unless quite unconditionally'.[127]

In fact the outcome proved her right. William declined the offer, since it implied the admission of previous guilt. Although aware that his decision would grieve her, he added in his letter to her:

I feel I should have deserved your reprobation and their [his friends'] censure had I accepted my liberty on terms so degrading. No, no, the 25th of July will soon be here and whatever may be my future fate no servility or cringing on my part shall be instrumental in stifling my voice or binding my tongue on that occasion. My powers of usefulness may be diminished by a long and rigorous confinement, or even the thread of my existence may be cut short before that time arrives, but come life or death shall find me true to the just principles I have ever held, and with an honest and self approving conscience.[128]

There is an interesting discrepancy between Mary's and William's response to the offer. While Mary in her anxiety put William's survival before anything else, he was sure of her concurrence with his refusal. This leads one to believe that throughout their married life, Mary outwardly supported William's tenacity regardless of its consequences for herself, presumably knowing well that it was the driving force of his life, of which he must not be deprived. She may also have realised that any contravention of his wishes in these matters would have lost her his esteem.

According to his convictions of what constituted a man's duty, William provided for his impending marriage by making his own furniture so as to provide Mary with a comfortable home. Later in his book *Social and Political Morality*, published in 1853, he stated the proper age for a man to get married. It was attained once biological maturity had been reached, an apprenticeship had been completed and an income sufficient to support a family had been procured.[129]

On his marriage, William gave up his involvement in political associations in order to save money and to preserve the happiness of his home, for

> Perceiving also that much of the bickerings and dissensions often found in the domestic circle had their origin in the wife's not understanding and appreciating her husband's political or literary pursuits; too often coupled with his carelessness and indifference in enlightening and instructing her regarding them; I resolved, if possible, to avoid this evil by pursuing an opposite course of conduct.[130]

This and the following passages contain the core of Lovett's attitude towards women. Unable to develop any ideas of their own, let alone theories, women lack the understanding for men's intellectual and moral mission. It is with men that ideas originate, which it is then their duty to impart to their wives. This image of men as original thinkers and of women as receptacles of male-generated knowledge implies their intellectual inferiority. This view was also put forward in the *Address and Objects of the London Working Men's Association*, in the formulation of which Lovett had participated. It called upon the LWMA members to act as the disseminators of knowledge, instructing their wives and children as to their rights and duties. While ignorant women and children were believed to be 'the most formidable obstacles to a man's patriotic exertions, so when imbued with [knowledge] will they prove his greatest auxiliaries'.[131] Later on, Lovett reiterated in *Social and Political Morality* that, due to the imperfect state of female education, women had to be taught by their husbands so as to be qualified to instruct 'his' (*sic*) children.[132] This view of women accounts for his patronising attitude towards Mary, whom he persistently addressed as 'my dear girl'.[133]

Aware that without Mary's tacit support he would be unable to pursue his avid reading and journalistic writing, he pointed out her duty not to hinder him:

> In all these matters I sought to interest my wife, by reading and explaining to her the various subjects that came before us, as well as the political topics of the day. I sought also to convince

her that, beyond the pleasure knowledge conferred on ourselves, we had a duty to perform in endeavouring to use it wisely for others. I endeavoured to make her understand how much of our social improvement and political progress had depended on past sacrifices and sufferings on the part of our forefathers, and how much the happiness of the future will depend on each and all of us doing our duty in the present as our brave old forefathers had done.[134]

It is for this conviction, which led to his involvement in Chartism, that he had to go to prison. In his first letter from Warwick Gaol to Mary, William signed himself 'yours in the pursuit of knowledge under difficulties'.[135]

William must be credited with keeping Mary informed about his activities and the reason for his commitment. In a process of one-way communication, William expounded his beliefs and Mary absorbed them. He did not aim at involving her in his pursuits, but at preventing her interference in them. One wonders whether Mary knew on her marriage that by procuring herself a husband she had also engaged the life-long services of a lecturer.

William succeeded in gaining Mary's support, of which he was very appreciative:

And in looking back upon this period how often have I found cause for satisfaction that I pursued this course as my wife's appreciation of my humble exertions has ever been the chief hope to cheer, and best aid to sustain me, under the many difficulties and trials I have encountered in my political career. She has ever been to me 'A guardian angel o'er my life presiding – doubling my pleasure and my cares dividing'.[136]

Such were the domestic rewards 'intellectual' men were able to expect for their conduct towards their wives. As he had explained in 1840 by way of arguing the case of improved education:

Intellectual men, too, would regard their *homes* and their *families* with far different sensations than are felt by those superficial and thoughtless members of society who seek for gratification and pleasure anywhere rather than at home; by which conduct habits of dissipation are generated on the one hand, carelessness and bickerings on the other; and domestic happiness, being thus undermined, tends to the destruction of their peace and the ruin of their families. Rightly constituted minds, on the contrary, would feel that, of all other pleasures, *those that spring from domestic happiness are the most enduring and substantial.* Intellectual men esteeming their wives as *their equal companions,* and not the mere slaves of their passions, would labour to cultivate their mental powers, to the end that they should participate in their views and feelings, and be the better prepared to train up their children in knowledge, virtue, and the love of freedom.[137]

Once his principles had been established as the frame of reference in which decisions had to take place, William was prepared to listen to his wife's advice, be it with regard to the care of their daughter or with regard to the livelihood of the family. Therefore, by the time he concluded his autobiography, Mary had advanced from being the receptacle of his knowledge to being his 'best adviser' and 'truest friend'. He felt greatly indebted to the sustenance she had never tired of bestowing upon him:

> To me my dear wife has ever been a second self; always my best adviser and truest friend; ever interesting herself, and sympathising with me in all my pursuits, toils, and troubles; and ever diffusing sunshine of kindness and good temper in our humble home. I know not indeed what kind of man I should have been, if I had not met with such a noble help-mate; and this I often think of with grateful feelings.[138]

Mary was a carpenter's daughter from Kent and joined her brother, who was in business at Boulogne, as his housekeeper. On his subsequent marriage, she became lady's maid in an English family, and it was on one of their visits to London that she met William. After their marriage, Mary, like any other working-class wife, supplemented the family income. She first ran a little pastry shop, which soon failed. Her next appointment was with the London co-operative store for which William had worked previously as a storekeeper. Dedicated to the cause, he had been prepared to accept lower wages than he could have earned at his own trade. Subsequently, however, due to slackness of business, his salary was reduced to a point he found unacceptable and Mary took over at half his pay. Characteristically, William perceived Mary's money-making activities as part of her domestic function and her income as merely supplementary to that of the male breadwinner. Therefore it was not inconsistent for him to condemn married women's labour outside the home.[139]

It is interesting to note that Lovett ascribed the ultimate failure of the early co-operative stores to, among other causes, the unwillingness of women to confine their dealing to one shop. This might have been due to their love of shopping, he conjectured, or to their unwillingness to let their husbands know the exact amount of their dealings. He was unable to understand why women did not support a good cause regardless of the inconvenience it might entail, and of which he was not aware. Instead he depicted women as headstrong and foolish creatures.

After his release from prison, William opened a bookshop, which was managed by Mary. His bad state of health and his political convictions prevented him from working at his own trade as cabinet-maker.[140] The Lovetts had two daughters, Mary and Kezia, named after William's grandmother. Kezia died in her infancy, and Mary was a weakly child, causing her parents much anxiety. She suffered from frequent inflammation of her eyes and because of this was sent to her grandfather's in the country for about two years. Due to an injury received in her youth, Mary senior, who was described as tall, handsome and fresh-coloured at the time of her marriage, became one head shorter than William, her spine having given way as a result of her pregnancies. Her state of health was a constant cause of concern to him.

The worst period in Mary's life was surely the time of William's imprisonment. Being deprived of his company was a severe loss, but his weak state of health, exacerbated by the unsuitable prison diet, greatly added to her distress. Neither of them was certain that he would survive his term in prison.

Mary's anxiety was enhanced by the prison authorities' interference, which rendered the couple's communication highly erratic. Although restrictions on William's right to correspond were lifted shortly after his conviction, his letters were liable to be held back. Whenever this happened, Mary would grow extremely distressed. Furthermore, William was only allowed one visit every three months, and that had to take place in the presence of a turnkey and with a spiked door separating him from the visitor. Mary therefore tried her utmost to effect an improvement in his diet and to obtain his right to free interviews. She memorialised the Home Secretary to that effect, and the ensuing correspondence testifies to her persistence in her exertions on William's account.[141] She also enquired about the treatment other political prisoners received in a search for precedents of improvement.[142] All her efforts were in vain, however, and during the twelve months she was only allowed to see William twice, nor was any substantial change made to his diet. In her concern for his health she even considered moving to Warwick in the hope of being allowed to minister to his needs. Finding it inadvisable to transplant Mary from amongst her friends to a strange place, and altogether doubtful that she would be granted regular admission to the prison, William strongly objected to her plan.

The perpetual veering between hope and despair affected Mary's health, a fact of which William was painfully aware. Hence his calls on her to keep her spirits up. Unlike Mary, he did not place any hope on a favourable outcome of attempts at exerting influence on the authorities, and he appealed to her to resign herself to the inevitable. He reminded her that 'these are the times when such severity is to be expected, and when it comes it must be borne with resignation', and that a change for the better was inevitable, for 'bright sunshine will again appear when this momentary cloud shall have passed away'.[143] The prison correspondence between the Lovetts demonstrates the great extent to which William was sustained by his affection for his family and by the anticipation of reunion with them. He clung to the fact that 'the conclusion of every month will bring us nearer each other',[144] and assured Mary that 'while all goes well with you and Mary [their daughter]I shall not repine'.[145]

Fortunately Mary was able to count on the assistance of William's political friends. In London, there were the members of the LWMA as well as the Bloomsbury Charter Association, with which the Lovetts had been connected[146] and which opened a subscription for the benefit of Mary in October 1839.[147] There was also Francis Place, to whose keen interest in Lovett's fate the preservation of the prison correspondence was due. He helped Mary by drafting letters to be sent to government officials. The Lovetts' greatest asset, however, was James Whittle, a co-delegate to the Convention, who lived at Warwick. He administrated William's money, out of which he bought what extra food William was allowed. He also offered his hospitality to Mary on her visits to Warwick, and, most important of all, as a local inhabitant, he was able promptly to inform her about William's condition whenever she wrote to him, apprehensive from not having heard from her husband.

In spite of all the obstacles, Mary tried her best to alleviate William's life in prison. She sent him warm clothes and books he had asked for. She also had to keep him informed about their business so that he would be able to attend to it from prison. Mary maintained William's links with the outside world. She kept his family informed about him when his letters were held back and, through her, he coordinated his own efforts for an improvement in his condition with those of his London friends. At his request, she collected documents concerning his imprisonment and the political events of that year.

William's instructions, however, show how little she had participated in his activities prior to his imprisonment. Not only did he have to tell her where to procure the political journals he used to take in, he also had to inform her of the state of his business accounts at the time of his arrest so that she could continue them at all. Her function was very much one of running errands for her imprisoned husband. Due to her ignorance of his affairs, she let his address- and account-books be seized by the authorities, which earned her William's censure. In vain, he entreated her not to give up the minute books of the Convention. His instructions also encompassed her domestic concerns. Thus he directed her in her care for their daughter: 'pay every attention to the child and more especially to the improvement of her mind'.[148] When little Mary suffered from a spell of bad eyes he ordered: 'As for "books and work" they must be set aside altogether for a time, for any attempt to apply herself to them will only serve to protract the cure.'[149]

Mary herself was painfully aware of her lack of influence on William's political decisions. After being informed of his intention to go to Birmingham on his release instead of immediately joining her in London, she turned to Francis Place, expressing her anxiety thus: 'I think those persons who wish him to go there are headstrong and madbrained fools and I am afraid they will make a fool of him – or do him great mischief – besides there are so many spies and dangerous persons who would be glad to get him into trouble and disrepute.'[150] She then requested Place to write to William to this effect and advise him about the course to take. This had the desired effect.

In another matter of concern, however, Mary proved unsuccessful. William's political friends in London had resolved on a
particular day for the public dinner to celebrate his release. Their
choice of day would have required the Lovetts to postpone their
visit to Cornwall, where William was to see his mother and
recover his health. Mary, who had been hostess to the LWMA for
quite a while, attempted to have the dinner postponed, but her
considerations for William's health were overriden.

According to his view of a husband's duty, William tried his
best to provide for his family. In *Social and Political Morality* (as
already mentioned), he advocated deferment of marriage until a
man was able to support a wife and children.[151] His own
biography, however, proved his quest for this key feature of male
responsibility to have been frustrated. Economic conditions
coupled with his political convictions prevented him from
providing for his family by entirely relying on his own resources.
Any business failure ran him into debt, and his family's financial
situation became particularly precarious during his imprisonment
when they were supported by subscription.[152] Still, although the
prison correspondence contains numerous allusions to the need to
economise, their situation was not desperate. A friend of theirs, for
instance, took out a lease on the Lovetts' house to enable Mary to
stay. After William's release, the Lovetts continued to be supported
for years by a 'benevolent friend', and an insurance in favour of
Mary was paid for by a collection among friends.

Mary is probably unique among the wives of leading Chartists
in that she actually had the satisfaction of having her merits
publicly recognised. On 23 February 1848, a soirée was held by
eminent radicals in order to present William Lovett with
a testimonial consisting of a tricolor purse containing 140
sovereigns. In the course of the ceremony, the chairman addressed
himself to Mary thus:

> We have thought it not unfit to remember, and have been happy
> in the memory, that Mrs William Lovett still lives, to share, not
> I trust hereafter the trials of her husband, but his triumphs. Let
> us, therefore, while wishing him happiness, remember her who
> has hitherto promoted that happiness in so eminent a manner.
> We desire that the other portion of the testimonial – this silver
> tea service – should especially be presented to Mrs William
> Lovett. We give it to her, because we know that never, even

when the whole of their little property was sacrificed, did she breathe a single murmur or complaint. . . . And in the hour of severer trial – on that occasion to which I have alluded – when prison walls divided her from his love and attention – an hour of trial peculiarly severe to a woman deeply attached to the man with whom she was united, feeling that her domestic happiness might be blighted and destroyed by her husband's bold assertion of political principle, and the inevitable consequence of severe punishment, yet, even then, she shrank not, but patiently rejoiced, far happier in being the partner of the courageous William Lovett, than if surrounded by luxury, and united to a man who had swerved from his duty. . . . Therefore it is to her we present this portion of the testimonial. We present it to Mrs Lovett as an offering of respectful affection and regard.[153]

These sentiments were echoed by William at the conclusion of his autobiography. Mary was praised for her exemplary fulfilment of her role as her husband's helpmate, whose sustenance enabled him to persist in his political efforts. Her achievements were confined to the domestic sphere, and only through her husband's mediation were they translated into the public arena. These eulogies show that the sacrifice of domestic happiness to the husband's political commitment was one of the requirements of a 'good' wife. She was expected as a matter of course to bear the hard burden her husband's political activities inflicted on the family and to do everything in her power to ease its effects.

Both in his *Woman's Mission* and *Social and Political Morality*, Lovett put forward his view of the sexually segregated spheres of life. While it was the husband's duty to provide for his family, it devolved upon the wife to perform or supervise the duties of the household, to rear the children, and to spread cheerfulness, comfort and consolation in the home. She was, in short, to act the part of 'household goddess'.[154] It was this rigid separation of spheres that he enforced in his own family. This is borne out by his behaviour towards Mary and by the terms in which he described his family life. Writing to her from prison, he declared himself anxious 'to enjoy once more the delights of our little world of affection',[155] which stood in contrast to the suffering he had to endure for his public commitment to political struggle. He conceived of the sexes as complementing one another, as 'Twin halves apart – drawn by nature's magic laws, To meet and form a whole of gentle love.'[156] On hearing about a friend's marriage he congratulated him 'on his having filled up that great blank of his existence with a wife'.[157]

Lovett considered the sexes' differential contribution to social life to be of equal value. Women's equality in terms of social usefulness, he maintained, was established by their rendering men fit and willing to labour and thus to produce the nation's wealth:

> And in the performance of these duties, let it be remembered, woman stands on a footing of social equality with man; as her labours and co-operation, in her sphere, are as essential to the production of the wealth of society as is his more hardy, and it may be, laborious portion of the work. For without her solace and domestic aid he would have less inclination to labour, and less of his time to devote to it.[158]

As women's realm was the domestic sphere, they ought not to work outside it, for neglected homes, in Lovett's view, were the cause of all vice and misery. The only explanation he was able to find for female factory labour was their husbands' idle, drunken and inconsiderate conduct, which called forth his most severe condemnation: 'Such a man must indeed have lost all self-respect or sense of duty, thus to allow himself and offspring to be dependent on a woman's labour.' He took up the issue again in his autobiography, in which he commended it to the attention of his fellow working men:

> Another most important subject, that should engage the serious attention of working men, is the employment of *married women* in our factories; which I think reflects anything but credit on our manufacturing population, masters and men. For every reflecting person must perceive that children cannot be properly brought up without the careful nurture and superintendence of the mother; nor can a man's home – in which his chief happiness should be centred – be much other than a mere resting place or nightly refuge when the wife is taken from it to labour, too often to supply the man with mere sensual enjoyment. It is a folly therefore for such men to talk pompously of right and justice for themselves, while their wives and mothers of their children are thus treated; nor indeed, until

they are placed upon a footing of equality, socially and politically, with themselves, and to occupy the station for which they are best fitted. Women, however, unmarried, or without husbands to support them, should be at liberty, equally with men, to earn their living in any business they choose.[159]

Lovett acknowledged the necessity for single women to work for their own upkeep. Furthermore, he considered men's right to demand an improvement of their position to be conditional upon their recognition of women's equality, which was to operate within the restrictions imposed by a rigid sexual division of labour. Lovett claimed to have included the demand for female suffrage, which was later abandoned, in his original draft of the Charter, and the National Association for Promoting the Political and Social Improvement of the People, of which he was a founding member, advocated women's political rights.[160]

William Lovett, who was undoubtedly very fond of his wife, displayed an extremely paternalist attitude towards her. Indeed he was the epitome of a patriarch attempting to act as both provider and protector. In his efforts to do so, he was sustained by Mary's pliability towards a husband for whom she had great affection and respect. Her untiring exertions on William's account were most effective when confined to the domestic sphere from which she never had the opportunity to escape having served the needs of male kinfolk throughout her entire lifetime.

While inequality characterised William's relationship with Mary, equality was what he advocated in *Woman's Mission* as women's principal object. Their current subjugation by men, he argued there, prevented them from fulfilling their mission as the improvers of society. Women's elevation to this position was consequently what all should gear their exertions towards. Woman was to appeal to man to accord her equal status, and the latter

> must at once his gothic laws annul,
> Fling back her dower, strive only for her love
> And proudly raise her up all rights to share.[161]

Women, according to Lovett, would attain equality with men by being raised to this status through male agency. Their equality, by thus being conferred upon them, ultimately only reinforced their inequality.

The preservation of male self-interest formed the backcloth against which all of Lovett's efforts, purportedly made for the sake of women, reveal their true meaning. As he made clear in *Woman's Mission*, it was in order to evade the damage that his subjugation of women was doing to himself that man was obliged to grant woman her request for equality:

> For ruling man no perfect freedom lives,
> Whilst by his laws woman remains in bonds:
> In sober truth, he's but in heart a slave,
> Whose power controls, whose home a slave contains.[162]

To overcome the degrading effect of man's subjection of woman on himself had also been one of the concerns of Thompson and Wheeler (as noted in Chapter 2). For them, this hinged on transcending the limits inherent in both the male and female sexual character towards a true humanity, centring on rationality. Lovett, on the other hand, confined the changes envisaged to women, thus making men – as currently constituted – the yardstick against which female development was measured.

It is through the preservation of male interest that Lovett's extremely patriarchal relationship with his wife and his lofty demands for female equality are reconciled. Women's equal status, by remaing conditional upon male agency, merely perpetuates male hegemony in a different guise.

If the Richardsons and Lovetts are anything to go by, the degree and scale of support – both material and immaterial – that Chartist men received from their wives was inestimable, although obscured by being blended with the women's other familial functions. This blend of the personal and the political characterised both Elizabeth's and Mary's involvement in the Chartist movement. Removed from the political forefront as they were, they had to content themselves with the personal gratitude liberally bestowed on them by their husbands and to forego all public appraisal of their exertions. Yet this was of no account to them, the happiness of their families unquestionably being their primary object.

Although home-centredness characterised both women's lives, Elizabeth Richardson and Mary Lovett instance the range of possibilities inherent in a life centred on the home. The Richardsons' marriage came very close to a partnership on equal terms, with each spouse responsibly fulfilling his or her tasks assigned along gender lines. In view of the abilities Elizabeth displayed in doing so, Reginald would have been most foolish not to consult her about important decisions to be taken. Having experienced the beneficial results of a sensible woman's counsel, it comes as no surprise that he wanted to see the practice of household decisions taken jointly by husband and wife extended to the political sphere. This he argued in *Rights of Woman* (as shown in Chapter 2).

In the Lovetts' marriage, tasks were also divided along gender lines. Yet William, by shutting Mary out of all public matters, used gender segregation to assume a position of power. He was the medium through which Mary was connected to the outside world, both in terms of physical contact and intellectual conception, which was imposed upon her by William's teaching. Educate his wife he did, but not with a view to rendering her intellectually independent. On the contrary, Mary's education was to make her more serviceable for his purposes. As he was inspired by the wish to be instrumental in effecting the improvement of humanity, he felt justified in making everything and everybody subservient to this object. The rigidity he displayed in pursuing this course was complemented and sustained, on Mary's part, by a pliability and devotion to her husband that bordered on self-abnegation. Mary thus foreshadowed the type of woman that would have resulted from Lovett's ideas had they ever been fully realised.

6
Chartist Women in Public Politics

1 THE EXTENSION OF DOMESTIC RESPONSIBILITIES INTO THE PUBLIC ARENA

The first step out into the open for many Chartist women consisted in an extension of their domestic responsibilities into the public arena. There were various ways in which Chartism sought to mobilise specifically female skills to further its aims.

Although favouring female political involvement, Chartists did not expect women to support the movement in the same way as men. Thus the Hull WMA appealed to the men and women of Hull:

> Men and women of Hull – We ask you to join with us in our effort to obtain freedom and happiness for the masses – we call upon the men to join in holy brotherhood with us as members of the Working Men's Association – we call upon the women to cheer us on with the smiles of their approbation, and to encourage us with their support.[1]

The women's special task was seen to consist in lending male Chartists the moral support deemed indispensable to the victory of the movement. Again and again they were called upon along the following lines: 'Lend us then your powerful assistance, animate us in the glorious struggle, cheer us by your approbation, enliven us by your presence, and we cannot, we will not fail of success.'[2] Women were exhorted to lend men moral support by 'smiling them on to victory', as the standard phrase went,[3] thus doing for the movement at large what every woman was supposedly accustomed to do at home, namely to cater for her family's psychological needs.

The large number of fairly well endowed Chartist funds – most of which were set up for the relief of Chartist prisoners' families (as noted in Chapter 5) – owed their existence to women's ability to economise, even though the actual donation might have been made in the husband's name or in that of a male association. Frequently, however, women themselves featured as contributors,[4] especially to funds set up for the relief of Chartist prisoners' families.[5]

The difficulty working-class women had in eking donations out of a scanty income is demonstrated by the actual amounts given. The high average percentage (13 per cent) of female contributions in aid of the 'Welsh widows' amounted to a meagre total of £4. 14s. 9½d.[6]

Women's lack of financial power was taken into account by the movement. As Caroline Maria Williams, a Bristol Chartist, had done in 1842,[7] so the executive of the Defence Fund – set up in 1848 to cover the cost of procuring legal defence for imprisoned Chartists – suggested that women should sell handmade articles of needlework for the benefit of this fund. Significantly, the male executive took the occasion to assign a political meaning to the employment of specifically female skills in a typically female setting by arguing:

> Indeed this work of benevolence seems peculiarly adapted to, and should call forth the energies of the female mind; for what more noble and pleasurable enjoyment can a woman find, after the performance of her domestic duties, than in exercising her talents in the formation of some useful or fancy article, consoled by the reflection that her industry will counteract the venomenous [*sic*] sting of tyranny, dry the widows' and orphans' tears, and shed the sunshine of the heart upon the house of the desolate.[8]

Chartist women were not the first to engage in activities geared towards the relief of the families of political activists. In July 1832, a number of politically active London women had formed themselves into a group called 'The Friends of the Oppressed'. They had aimed at giving moral and financial support to the families of political prisoners, especially those involved in the struggle for a free press. This kind of activity arose out of women's awareness of the plight of a family deprived of the male breadwinner's earnings. By alleviating the sufferings of the families thus afflicted, these women helped sustain political movements by easing male activists' anxiety for the survival of their families in the event of imprisonment.

In their capacity as the chief purchasers for their families, women employed the tactic of exclusive dealing to put pressure on the newly enfranchised shopkeepers either to vote for Chartist candidates at elections or to donate to the movement's funds. Robert Lowery devoted an entire pamphlet to this issue.[9] Predictably enough, he began by reminding his readers of the treachery he found the middle-class shopkeepers guilty of through their conduct in 1832. In that year the Reform Act had been passed, the result of a campaign uniting the unenfranchised working and middle classes, from which the latter alone had benefited. Lowery proceeded to argue that shopkeepers' prosperity, and thereby ultimately their franchise, depended on the spending power of their working-class clientele, a power currently curtailed by heavy taxation. Thus he argued an identity of interests between shopkeepers and Chartists, which, once perceived, would, he hoped, convert the former to the Charter.

Lowery then focused on the moral power underlying exclusive dealing. He was convinced that this practice would unite the working class by a double tie, principle and self-interest. Moreover, it would get them used to habits of regularity in their plans, and this, along with their determination in carrying these out, was sure to topple tyranny. Rigorously applied, he maintained, exclusive dealing would, by ultimately pulling the financial base out from under the middle class's feet, turn them into working people and thus enhance the power of the working class.

Lowery realised that the carrying out of this plan would not be feasible without women's co-operation, and he therefore appealed to them:

> Women of Britain! On your co-operation much depends; without your aid we cannot be successful! You have the laying out of our wages. . . . Remember that no woman is worthy of the name of a working-man's wife, who will lay out his hard-earned wages in the shops of those who insult him and deny him his political rights.

This passage is remarkable for the underlying awareness of the highly political significance of everyday tasks such as shopping. Such awareness, which (as shown above) was not confined to Lowery, eased women's entry into the movement by imbuing their housewifely duties with political meaning and placed them in a key position with regard to at least this Chartist tactic.

Although Lowery's claims as to the ultimate effects of exclusive dealing were somewhat exaggerated, the practice proved effective in the short run, for shopkeepers in working-class districts were in fact unable to afford losing their clientele. The amount of pressure exerted on them aroused a great deal of concern among the authorities.[10]

The practise of exclusive dealing was confined to the early period of Chartism. This may be attributable to the shift of female support, which will be discussed later (in Chapter 8). Nevertheless, the tactic's previous success motivated attempts to revert to it at later stages. The political analysis underlying this tactic also survived. As late as in the summer of 1848, the female Chartists of Bethnal Green reiterated Lowery's argument of the identity of interests between shopkeepers and the working class in an appeal to the former to join the Chartist ranks.[11]

Vincent, while also advocating exclusive dealing in an address to the women of the west of England, advised them to abstain additionally from all excisable articles and 'to do all in their power to deprive the government of money'.[12] He himself in fact acted on this principle (as noted in Chapter 5).

Without the efforts of its female membership, the Chartist movement would never have become renowned for its well-developed social life, which was made up of countless tea and dinner parties, picnics, soirées and similar events.[13] On these occasions, a committee was usually formed to see to the necessary catering arrangements.[14]

Apart from providing food, the catering involved decorating the room in which the gathering was to take place. To this end, women not only used flowers abundantly, but also hung up portraits of their Chartist champions or caps of liberty to point to the political context in which the social occurred.[15] The women's efforts were duly acknowledged, usually by proposing a toast along the lines of: 'The Tea Committee, thanks to them for their labours'.[16]

By getting up these socials, women not merely brought to bear on Chartism the domestic skills they had acquired in their homes, but also imbued them with their own sense and understanding of female political involvement. Conversely, by attributing political significance to women's domestic skills, Chartism enabled women to participate in the movement without, however, opening up forms of activity that transgressed the boundaries of female domestic responsibilities. The movement's insistence on the manifold ways in which women might utilise the fulfilment of domestic tasks to further the Chartist cause certainly enabled Chartism to tap a larger pool of potential female support. Simultaneously, though, it confined women to a secondary role within the movement.

2 FEMALE CHARTISTS' APPEARANCE IN PUBLIC

Boosting Chartist Ranks

Women's presence within Chartism became visible, even to outsiders, and was acknowledged, both inside and outside the movement, whenever it involved engaging in one of the wide variety of public activities connected with the Charter.

A very important task was the collection of money for Chartist funds. Women's exertions in procuring money for these were recognised as pivotal.[17] Chartist women went about collecting money quite professionally. Those of Barnsley, for instance, formed a relieving committee and subdivided their town into districts.[18]

Women also went round their neighbourhood making house-to-house calls in order to obtain signatures to petitions.[19] In addition, women put their own signatures to each of the three National Petitions. By allowing women to sign, the movement afforded them the opportunity of voicing their grievances before that political institution all Chartists looked to for redress.

Petitioning, of course, was the oldest form available to non-electors of bringing pressure to bear on parliament. Women, too, had employed this means of seeking redress for their grievances. Very early precedents had been set in the 1640s and 1650s, when women petitioned parliament for peace, against the detrimental effects of the decline of trade, against bishops and the Laudian innovations, and for the release of their husbands from prison. The women petitioning, entirely independently of men, for measures to counteract the depression of trade were mainly tradesmen's wives and widows. They were not driven, they stated, by any desire to claim equality with men either with regard to authority or wisdom, but were motivated by the fear of their inability to support themselves and their families. Like that of female Chartists, these women's political activity was rooted in their responsibility for the well-being of their families, which encompassed the need to earn a living. This is obvious in the case of tradesmen's widows, but the running of the family business may also have increasingly devolved on the wives of those tradesmen who were preparing to take up arms in a country on the brink of civil war.

As Chartist women traced the misery of the people back to class legislation, so the early female petitioners attributed their sufferings to what they saw as Catholicism and to the abuse of power by its supporters. It was their particular vulnerability as females that incited the women of the seventeenth as well as those of the nineteenth century to seek the help of parliament. Both groups felt compelled to justify their interference in politics by pointing to their equal share with men in the suffering of the people. Moreover, both adopted mainstream oppositional ideology in order to do so. The grounding of their action in the belief in spiritual equality irrespective of sex – one of the tenets of seventeenth-century Protestant sects – enabled these women to realise self-confidently that they were not merely justified, but had an actual right to interfere in politics.[20] Nineteenth-century radical ideology, on the other hand, clearly assigned women to the role of caring for home and family, but justified their interference in politics whenever the proper discharge of domestic duties was in jeopardy.

During the Anti-Poor Law campaign, several petitions signed exclusively by women were submitted.[21] In view of the determination with which women insisted on making known their abhorrence of the Poor Law, male campaigners had to give in and brush aside all constitutional misgivings about letting women sign petitions.[22]

In the Chartist era itself, women petitioned parliament to make known their stand on the Ten Hours Act passed in 1847. Regardless of whether women approved of the shortening of hours for enabling them to devote a larger portion of their time to domestic chores, or disapproved for fear of losing their jobs and thus being deprived of any means of supporting their families,[23] the attitude of female operatives towards the Act hinged on what effects it had on the well-being of their families.

Female Chartist petitioners thus stood in a tradition in which women had appealed to parliament for help whenever they had believed the integrity of their families to be under extreme pressure. Significantly, women made up a relatively larger proportion of signatories in areas where the Anti-Poor Law campaign had taken hold and where there existed precedents for female petitioning.[24]

Women also drew up their own memorials to the Queen, praying for a pardon of the leaders of the Newport Rising.[25] By memorialising the Queen, female Chartists hoped to arouse the assumed natural sympathy of the woman on the throne with the plight of other members of her sex – here, the wives of transported Chartists. Such ventures met with the movement's approval, as long as they did not divert support from Chartism's fight for universal suffrage.[26]

Women featured in large numbers at all kinds of Chartist meetings, be they of an exclusively political character, or a social activity blended with a political object. Examples of the latter kind were the extremely popular socials (featured above in section 1). Special efforts were made at rendering these social gatherings particularly attractive to women. Sometimes, for instance, the admission entitled male visitors to bring a female along free, and women generally had to pay less than men. The getting up of entirely teetotal entertainment was intended as another incentive to female attendance. Thus, it was hoped, the women would naturally join their Chartist kinsmen in their entertainment.[27]

It was with precisely this object in mind that Bronterre O'Brien addressed himself to his 'unrepresented brethren in England and Scotland' from Lancaster Castle. In the early days of the movement, a public dinner would be held on significant occasions. This, however, began to change, not least because of the reason adduced by O'Brien. 'I prefer soirées to public dinners', he wrote, 'because they are less expensive, interfere less with working hours, and above all, because working men may more conveniently take their wives and sisters to soirées than to public dinners.'[28]

From then on, as Eileen Yeo has noted,[29] tea parties, soirées and balls came increasingly to replace public dinners. They were very much multipurpose occasions, cheaper than dinners, but providing more food – mainly sandwiches and cakes – as well as dancing and music or theatrical entertainment. While dinners had been all-male affairs, these occasions enabled the whole family to socialise together, because they cost less and possibly also because of their teetotal nature. Chartism thus reconstituted, at least temporarily, the happy family life for the preservation of which women had become involved in the movement in the first place.

Apart from enjoying the entertainment laid on, women themselves contributed by singing songs, some of which they had composed themselves.[30] Social events of this kind were an effective means of tiding Chartism over periods of lull by providing its members with a focus. However, the number and frequency of recorded Chartist socials declined after about 1842.[31]

Women formed a regular component of the crowds turning up at Chartist rallies, some of which, such as the meetings on Kersall Moor and Peep Green in the late 1830s, were highlights in the whole history of the movement. Famous Chartists were also commonly greeted by large demonstrations on their release from prison.

For the banners carried on these occasions, women frequently chose quotations from the Bible to denounce the current political system as a contravention of God's will. Significantly, the system's godless character was attributed to lack of regard for those God had particularly assigned to the protection of the powerful. The corruption and ruthlessness of those in power was condemned thus: 'Thy princes are rebellious and companions of thieves, every one loveth gifts, and followeth after rewards; they judge not the fatherless, neither doth the cause of the widow come unto them.' Other banners directed God's wrath onto the heartless by the slogan: 'Whoso stoppeth his ears at the cry of the poor he also shall cry himself, but shall not be heard. Prov. XXI, 13.' Women also showed themselves to be familiar with the founding fathers of radical ideology, taking up the Paineite slogan: 'Every man has the right to one vote in the choice of his representatives; and it belongs to him in the right of his existence, and his person is his title deed.'[32]

Women boosted the audiences of Chartist sermons,[33] as well as attending the more formal political lectures, listening to speeches dealing with a wide range of subjects.[34] Foes of Chartism commonly pointed to the attendance of women at Chartist events as a means of disparaging the movement. To such people, the interest taken by women in Chartist proceedings devalued the movement and ridiculed its political aspirations. It must have been in order to counter this particular view that a brief notice in *The Northern Star* of a lecture at Shipley asserted that it had been delivered 'to a very attentive audience composed not of women and children, but of intelligent adults'.[35]

Rioting

At least verbally, female Chartists occasionally declared themselves to be prepared to resort to violence in order to attain the Charter, or to condone what came to be called 'physical force'. The female Chartists of Ashton, while stating their abhorrence of bloodshed, quoted the Bible in justification of violent opposition to severe oppression. Three months previously, the Nottingham female Chartists had proclaimed that they would 'glory in seeing every working-man of England selling his coat to buy a sword or a rifle for the event'. They were convinced, that is, that the current system of government would only yield to force, asserting that 'a great and deadly struggle must take place ere our tyrant oppressors yield to reason and justice'.[36]

However, Chartist recourse to armed militancy in a given situation caused controversy among male and female Chartists alike. To many female Chartists, the acceptability of violence varied with its object. While believing an oppressed people to be entitled to effect its emancipation by violence, they condemned this very same strategy when it served as the tool of oppression in the hands of tyrannical rulers. Growing working-class reluctance to let themselves be used for the purpose of internal oppression was hailed by the Sheffield female Chartists as the inauguration of a new era, which would be characterised by an absence of oppression and thus by internal peace.[37]

To oppose oppressive rulers – and this may be the meaning underlying all this violent female rhetoric – women were determined to hold out even if their lives were at stake. This was why at a public meeting of the Fraternal Democrats in London prior to the rally on Kennington Common in April 1848, West, the delegate for Stockport, was able to claim that the women of the north were adamant to have the Charter and 'ready to take the place of the men who [were] cut down should it come to that'.[38]

The English Chartist Circular and, to a lesser extent, *The Friend of the People* reinforced such female determination to resist oppression unto death. Both papers portrayed women of remarkable military achievements who had acted from commitment to a cause which Chartists approved of politically, such as national liberation.[39] The best-known example of this type of woman was Joan of Arc. Her life was serialised in *The English Chartist Circular*.[40] The 'Maid of Orleans', in particular, was used to demonstrate that, underneath male attire, her 'truly feminine essence' was not lost. And this belief may account for the portrayal of these women in a paper like *The English Chartist Circular*, which was very much the mouthpiece of the LWMA's moral-force-cum-education views. These encompassed the belief that women's 'truly feminine essence' was crucial for generating the moral feeling of a nation, and consequently strong opposition to all attempts at blurring the essential difference between the sexes.[41]

Acceptance of violence on the part of female Chartists did not always remain mere rhetoric. Whenever Chartists rioted, women were also involved.[42] Apart from the fact that female violence always received more publicity than the male variety anyway, on account of its allegedly extraordinary character, women's presence in Chartist riots was often conspicuous. In the disturbances in Sheffield following the arrest of two Chartists, the women were reported as being more violent than the men, reminding *The Northern Liberator* correspondent of the female inhabitants of Paris who had participated in the French Revolution,[43] incidentally another example of female militancy approved of by Chartists.

Following the abortive Bradford rising in the summer of 1848, local women resorted to a practice reminiscent of 'riding the stang' – a type of charivari – usually inflicted on individuals who had infringed community customs. In this case, the punishment was administered to the principal witness against local Chartists, who was attacked by a large crowd of boys and women on his way home from a pub, where he had bragged about his activities. He was beaten, robbed and flung into a stream[44] by women who felt incensed at such boasting about what they must have perceived as a flagrant breach of community solidarity.

Such outbreaks of angry female militancy, whether spontaneous or not, had already occurred prior to Chartism. They had been sparked off by marked and sudden economic deterioration, and had been aimed at immediate redress. Riots over the prices and supply of food had customarily seen women as instigators and leaders in their capacity of chief purchasers for their families. In the first half of the nineteenth century, women likewise featured prominently in the struggle of many Welsh people against the enclosure of common land and in many Scottish people's fight against Highland clearances. A very early precedent for female militancy had occurred in 1643, when a group of women, having failed to have their petition (mentioned in the preceding sub-section) accepted, attempted a 'rush' on the House of Commons to force parliament to listen to their grievances.

All these women had acted from a strongly felt concern for the integrity of their families, whose material base they perceived to be threatened severely. Under such circumstances, women had shown themselves to be determined to have customary conditions restored, even if this required recourse to violence, which, fired by female desperation, could turn out exceedingly difficult to suppress. During the Welsh anti-enclosure riots, the authorities were known to complain about the greater trouble they had with women than with men. Instead of bringing a restraining influence to bear upon the crowds – as apparently expected – women were at the forefront of the struggles, driving the men on with their taunts and provocations.[45]

When women acted in a militant manner, they differed from men not with regard to the scale of violence used, but with regard to the slight amount of planning and organising that female forms of violent behaviour required. Food riots, for instance, evolved out of women's daily routine, such as buying in the market-place. Moreover, they were firmly grounded in the customs and beliefs of the local community, which these women helped to enforce.

Rioting, then, appears as a form of protest particularly suited to women's lifestyle. Not only did it arise over issues that concerned women's familial responsibilities, such as shopping for the family and generally safeguarding the home against encroaching powers, but whenever it occurred spontaneously, it also proved least disruptive of the fulfilment of these duties that the issues at stake had interfered with in the first place.

Equally, concern for the well-being of their families motivated women's participation in the general strike of 1842 – often also referred to as the 'Plug Plot' – in which factory operatives struck work to obtain the Charter as a precondition for better wages. Often, it was women who stopped the mills and brought the working people out. Although the reduction in wages rendered the condition of factory operatives acutely desperate, many of the women involved in the strike aimed at a more thorough-going change than a mere pay rise would have represented. One Eliza Walker, a married woman, was reported as observing at an exclusively female meeting at Macclesfield to the loud cheers of her audience:

A married woman's occupation ought to be the management of her own house. The man ought to be the bread-provider, and the woman the bread-distributor. But the scales had been sadly turned. Women had to toil in factories from their earliest infancy, and it was no wonder that so many of the women of Macclesfield were stunted in their growth, and no bigger than herself.[46]

It was for the restoration of the traditional division of labour between the sexes that large numbers of female operatives held meetings, sent their delegates, drew up their terms, proposed resolutions and made speeches,[47] thus bringing political expertise – possibly gained within the framework of Chartism – to bear upon the strike.

Great numbers of female strikers were placed in the middle of a procession of Lancashire turn-outs marching to Halifax. When they were halted by the military, women seized soldiers' bayonets, turning them aside with the words, 'We want not bayonets, but bread!' Others went up to the cavalry exclaiming, 'You would not hurt a woman, would you?'[48] Women's belief in their relative immunity from retaliation by the authorities was justified to a certain degree. In the food riots, for instance, although the law came down as harshly on women as on men once they were brought up for trial, the former seem to have had some initial advantage over soldiers and magistrates because of their sex. Yet when Chartist crowds did clash with the military, women were at the receiving end of a good deal of armed violence.[49]

With regard to legal punishment, however, women on the whole fared better than men. No female Chartist was ever transported, and the severity of the prison sentences passed on female rioters depended on how seriously the incidents in which they had been involved were taken by the authorities.[50] After the failure of the first Chartist petition in 1839, both male and female Chartists began arming and drilling, mainly in the north. In a period when tension between classes was at a high pitch, the arming of women increased the alarm felt by the authorities anyway. At Cockermouth, for instance, the following public notice was put up appealing to what the authorities conceived of as women's femininity and Englishness in order to dissuade them from arming:

> To the Chartists generally, we earnestly address ourselves. We implore you to restore peace and quietness to the town, and confidence to trade, by withdrawing from this wicked Association; it is said, but we hope without truth, that some of your women have been seen armed with Daggers, surely, anything so un-feminine and un-English was never heard of before – English women have always been considered adverse [*sic*], even to look on deeds of violence, but never inclined to partake in them. Think what a sad example you are setting to your children; how can you ever expect to receive respect and obedience from them, when they see you preparing violence and mischief for others. . . . We therefore entreat both men and women to return to a course of right conduct.[51]

Conversely, in a more relaxed atmosphere, the presence of large contingents of women among Chartist crowds was taken by some authorities as an indication of the movement's weakness.[52]

Joining the National Land Company

The rejection of the second National Petition in 1842 was final proof for many Chartists that the Charter was not to become the law of the land for a long time to come. Following this failure, the Chartist movement entered into a period of lull, both in terms of members and enthusiasm. In this situation, the Land Scheme proposed by O'Connor was seized upon by Chartist leaders as giving them something to offer to the people that was closely related to the latter's aspirations and desires. The Land Plan aimed at improving the condition of the working class by settling as many people as possible on the land, thereby draining the labour market of its surplus and thus effecting a pay rise for those remaining dependent on a wage income. Many working people were attracted by the seeming possibility of extricating themselves from the factory system and living the rural life of their forebears. Seen retrospectively, a life regulated, not by the sharp ring of the factory bell and the incessant noise and clatter of machinery, but by the cycle of the seasons, acquired a golden hue. This goal was presented as a realistic, short-term feasibility and was in fact realised, at least temporarily, for a tiny proportion of the Land Company's membership. All it seemed to require was thriftiness so as to be able to pay up one's share, on which depended one's eligibility to settle on one of the five Chartist estates. In view of the scanty income of working-class families, this was not feasible without the fullest co-operation on the part of the women.

The Chartist leadership realised this, and, following the establishment of the Chartist Land Co-operative Society in 1845, began to appeal specifically to women to join. Great care was taken to point out to them what particular advantages the scheme entailed for women, not the least of which was safeguarding them against the Poor Law.[53]

In *The Labourer*, which was set up by O'Connor and Jones for the specific purpose of propagating the aims of the Chartist Land Company, there appeared a fictitious story entitled 'The Charter and the Land', in which women's objections to their husbands' involvement in Chartism and the reasons for their favourable response to the Land Plan were dealt with. The story is set among a family of weavers at Stockport. The wife is totally opposed to her husband's attending a great number of Chartist meetings in the vicinity, because this not only deprives her of his company, but it also results in frequent imprisonment. Having been blacklisted after his release from prison, the husband is unable to obtain work and takes to drinking, which makes it even more difficult for the wife to make ends meet. At the establishment of the Chartist Land Company, however, the husband undergoes a dramatic change. He abandons the public house under the condition of receiving a weekly allowance of one shilling from his wife, to which she gladly consents, not knowing that he uses the money to pay up for a share in a Chartist settlement. After the birth of their third child, the husband obtains a share in the O'Connorville estate. His wife is overjoyed at this news, since it means no more work for a master and more time to look after her children. While she has always conceived of the Charter as getting one into trouble, she is in favour of the Land Plan, as it puts one in bread. Her joy turns into apprehension, however, when her neighbours consistently point to her husband's unfitness for agricultural labour. Her fears are dissipated by him, as he reminds her of his rural descent and explains to her how they will be able to provide the rent money by harvest work in the summer and other work in the winter, apart from saving expenses for food. Having obtained a share in a Chartist estate, he feels, has made all his sacrifices for the Charter worthwhile. At O'Connorville, which is dubbed 'Holy Land' in the story, the family are pleased with their living conditions. The story ends with the husband attending a vestry meeting, where he is met with the respect due to the holder of a vote.[54]

This piece of Chartist propaganda is fairly unique in pointing to the hardship brought on their families by the men's commitment to the Charter, and of which the women had to bear the brunt. Thence their understandable opposition to the movement. This was presented as standing in stark contrast to the real gains they would derive from settling on the land, which would do away with the submission to the laws of factory work. Furthermore, it would give back to the settlers the feeling of personal dignity, of which their status as factory workers had deprived them. For them, settling on a Chartist estate was supposed to imply a prospect of paradise on earth.

In his speech at the opening of O'Connorville (or Heronsgate), O'Connor described in detail the particular benefits women would derive from living on this first Chartist settlement. The prospect centred on the restoration of the sexual division of labour prior to industrialisation. While women and children would be spared the hardship of working in factories, men would be reinstated into their proper position of breadwinners instead of living in enforced idleness and dependency on the labour of their wives and children. Moreover, the outdoor life afforded by the rural setting would benefit the children's health. Finally, O'Connor promised that drunkenness would not be tolerated on any Chartist settlement.[55]

True to his promise, O'Connor actively encouraged sobriety at O'Connorville. At the end of the first summer, he designated a premium of £15 to those settlers who cultivated their land best. Even more consideration, however, was given to the men's conduct, sobriety and treatment of their wives and children. In his judgement, O'Connor was not content to take the men's word for it, but actually went and asked the wives' opinion.[56]

It was the prospect of being reinstated into their proper position of mothers of families that women responded to with great enthusiasm. When the first colonists moved into O'Connorville, the women showed themselves to be even more delighted than the men. *The Northern Star* chimed in with the prevalent feeling by stating that 'the free mothers, rescued from the cold gripe of Mammon, with their own babes in their arms, added great dignity to the spectacle'.[57]

The string of social events hitherto distinguishing the Chartist localities throughout the country soon extended to the settlements. A new feature in the annual round of Chartist events were the so-called 'harvest home festivals', which were celebrated at least at O'Connorville.[58] There the allottees also had a party to mark the fourth anniversary of the settlement's opening.

The Land Company had branches in many parts of the country, and women seem to have taken an active part in their proceedings as a way of furthering the Land Company's goal as well as expressing their commitment to Chartism in general.[59] In some localities, ordinary Chartist branches seem to have existed side by side with Land Company ones, while in other parts of the country, the Land Scheme was effective in recruiting new members to the movement.[60]

Many of the new recruits to Chartism may have been women (as maintained in Chapter 3), who would have been more ready to commit themselves to the Land Plan than to other Chartist ventures which inevitably put the family into jeopardy. O'Connor himself was convinced that the Land Company's success was due to female exertions.[61] Visits to the settlements and interviews with female allottees confirmed this picture of overwhelming female contentedness with rural life in a Chartist setting.[62]

The quality of the cottages in particular was so good as to turn into a bone of contention. O'Connor insisted on high building standards and took great care over the design and furnishing of the cottages with what he considered indispensable conveniences. Their layout and equipment greatly facilitated housework. While accounting for women's delight with their cottages, the quality of these dwellings caused resentment among many Land Company members elsewhere. Having had to resign themselves to the atrocious housing conditions prevailing in the factory districts (described in Chapter 1), they would have preferred the money to be spent on acquiring more land so as to enable a greater number of people to leave the factory towns for good.

As time wore on, the allottees began to find living off the land more and more difficult. Apprehensions as to the ability of factory operatives to work the land proved well justified.[63] Yet when the Land Company began to show signs of being financially unsound and O'Connor came under attack for not taking proper care of the financial side of his scheme, letters of support from both company members and allottees started pouring in.[64] Despite a massive show of support, the Land Company was dissolved in 1851, a defeat which exacerbated O'Connor's mental instability, signs of which had previously begun to show.

Learning and Teaching

The Chartist concern with education was embedded in the radical tradition that went back to Paine's *Age of Reason* and Godwin's *Enquiry*. Their emphasis on the formative power of education had derived from the Enlightenment idea that mental characteristics were formed as a result of the impact of external circumstances. On this belief in turn was based the theory of human perfectibility. Chartist adherence to such ideas can be traced through the relevance they ascribed to mothers as the primary educators of their children in ensuring the movement's success (as noted in Chapter 5).

In relation to this Chartist belief, professed by Vincent in particular, Lovett's brand of Knowledge Chartism represented the application of this notion to society in general. He considered women to be pivotal for ensuring the progress of humanity. In his *Chartism; A New Organisation of the People*, written in conjunction with Collins, he described the tremendous influence he saw mothers as having on their children. From this, in turn, followed the demand that women themselves be well educated so as to be able to educate children to the best possible advantage. Lovett asserted that

> women are *the chief instructors of our children*, whose *virtues* or *vices* will depend more on the education given them by their mothers than on that of any other teacher we can employ to instruct them. If a mother is deficient in knowledge and

depraved in morals, the effects will be seen in all her domestic arrangements; and her prejudices, habits, and conduct will make the most lasting impression on her children, and often render nugatory all the efforts of the schoolmaster. If, on the contrary, she is so well informed as to appreciate and second his exertions, and strives to fix in the minds of her children habits of cleanliness, order, refinement of conduct, and purity of morals, the results will be evident in her wise and well-regulated household. But if, in addition to these qualities, she be richly stored with intellectual and moral treasures, and make it her chief delight to impart them to her offspring, they will, by their lives and conduct, reflect her intelligence and virtues throughout society; for there has seldom been a great and noble character who had not a wise or virtuous mother.[65]

The same view was also put forward by Samuel Smiles – still, at this time, in his Chartist phase – in *The Labourer*. He attributed the contemporary weakness and oppression of the working class to a lack of education, which alone could turn them into rational beings. Women held a central position in his concept of education, too. 'Woman, especially', he maintained, 'stands in need of education; inasmuch as she is one of the great instruments by which the people themselves are to be educated. She is, indeed, the great Teacher. The moral condition of a people is almost entirely her work.'[66] Smiles looked to the improvement of female education 'as one of the most efficient means of reconciling and allaying the now discordant and jarring elements of society'. Such reconciliation between the elements – or classes – of society was not far removed from the type of conviction-through-enlightenment Chartism favoured by Lovett.

As a concomitant of the centrality ascribed to the education of women, female intellectual faculties were highly regarded by Chartist educationalists. Views ranged from belief in the inherent intellectual equality of the sexes[67] to the conviction that man and woman had different propensities.[68] 'Sophia', whose Wollstone-craftian leanings have already been noted (in Chapter 4), self-confidently claimed, in tones highly reminiscent of her famous predecessor, that the standard of women's intellectual abilities could not be judged unless given a fair trial. She therefore called upon Chartist women to prove their intellectual equality with men by stating:

We, as Chartist women, have then a far mightier effort to make than the men of the same good name. Not only have we to assist *them* in the regeneration of our beloved country, but to contend against those old prejudices which have so long militated against our improvement and consequently our happiness. We have to *prove* our capacity for enjoying all intellectual pleasures equally with the other sex, by our eagerness to abandon frivolities and seek *knowledge*.[69]

The Chartist view of female intellectual abilities stood in stark contrast to the increasingly dominant Evangelical image of woman. This conceived of the sexes as essentially different, as antipodes, with women embodying emotions, men rationality. Men were characterised by physical and mental strength, an ambitious and enterprising spirit, courage, activity and perseverance, ability for close and comprehensive reasoning,[70] all of which woman lacked. She, on the other hand, was construed as tender, compassionate, gentle, disinterested, conscientious, pious, contented, gay, cheerful, all of which qualities she was said to possess to a greater degree than man. Woman's mind, like her body, was chiefly characterised by weakness, rendering her prone to failings and surely unfitting her for any kind of serious application. The mental powers woman was believed to possess were all geared towards alleviating the sorrows and anxieties besetting the lives of her fellow-beings.[71]

The female character, as conceived of by the Evangelicals, was so artificial as to require careful education for its creation. The emphasis was on moral education as opposed to the development of the intellect. This would bring out the spirit of devotion – that necessary requisite of femininity – ensure woman's acceptance of her proper sphere, and guard against presumption.[72]

Chartist educational efforts have to be viewed against the notoriously deficient facilities available at the time for the education of women, particularly in the working class. Women rarely had equal access to available forms of adult education. It was at least the partial knocking down of such barriers that 'Sophia' had in mind when proposing that women be admitted to Mechanics' Institutes' lectures and reading rooms, 'of course, under severe restrictions, and altogether separate from the youths'. She called for the recognition of women's right to attend lectures on any subject, but particularly those dealing with the human frame, education and the right treatment of children. This was because she considered women to be entitled to knowledge on everything to do with children's minds and persons. Moreover, she advocated lectures be followed by discussion and suggested that lectures concerning women in particular be delivered by female speakers.[73]

Despite the variety of forms of female adult education provided, the course-content was remarkably uniform, encompassing the three R's, sewing, cooking and some limited general knowledge. On the whole, the curriculum was geared towards improving women's domestic and child-rearing skills, thereby reinforcing the sexual division of labour within the working-class family.

This was the professed intention of Chartist educationalists, who maintained that the instruction of women must not estrange them from their domestic duties, which, troublesome as they might be, were considered an integral part of women's lives. Thence the emphasis on the following demand: *'Female education cannot be complete without a thorough knowledge of domestic arrangements.'*[74] 'Sophia', like many other Chartist women, considered it to be their particular duty to prove that their education would not only not interfere with their attendance to domestic matters, but actually improve it.[75]

W. E. Adams, the Cheltenham Chartist, likewise eulogised the beneficial effects of good housewifery. A visit to a Chartist couple, whose 'humble cottage' was kept 'spotless clean', gave rise to the following observations:

> Riches are not necessary to produce the blessings and comforts of home. A bright fireside is not incompatible even with poverty, or at least with the very humblest of means. . . . If all Chartist homes had been as well kept as Larry's, there might have been less discontent in the country, but there would have been more force and vitality in the movement to which the masses of the people gave their sanction.[76]

Such ideas shaped the educational provisions envisaged by Chartists. According to *The Labourer*, the girls on Chartist settlements would receive instruction in mending, shirt-making, stocking-making, baking and straw-plaiting, and Lovett planned for the girls attending the schools set up according to his ideas to be taught sewing, knitting and cutting out their own clothes.[77]

As a concomitant of this gender-specific curriculum, the schools on Chartist settlements were segregated accordingly.[78] A certain degree of sexual segregation was also to be observed in the schools planned by Lovett and Collins in *Chartism; A New Organisation of the People*.[79] *The People*, on the other hand, advocated an education for girls the gender-specificity of which showed not in the curriculum, but in the application of knowledge to practical and benevolent purposes.[80]

Chartists conceived of female education as being tantamount to women's stepping out of their domestic confinement;[81] the transgression of domestic boundaries was restricted to the intellectual realm. Women were expected to piece together their image of the world from reading and other sources of information. Through improved education, Chartists aimed at rendering women not intellectually self-sufficient, but more useful to their families. Although a large number of women benefited from educational facilities laid on by the movement, it is significant that none of the female Chartists who come across as independent-minded individuals owed their education to the movement.

Furthermore, Chartist educationalists repeatedly emphasised that better educated women would increase men's happiness. Female education would enhance domestic harmony by the mutual understanding generated by the intellectual equality of husband and wife. In the words of Lovett:

> *how much of men's happiness depends upon the minds and dispositions of women* – how much of comfort, cheerfulness, and affection their intelligence can spread in the most humble home – how many cares their prudence can prevent, and their sympathy and kindness alleviate?[82]

It was the blending of a comprehensive education with feminine virtues that men were presumed to appreciate most in women.[83]

As it was seen to lie in men's own political interest to further female education, 'Sophia' appealed to them thus: 'we earnestly implore the intelligent and right thinking of the other sex, to stretch out their hands to save us, and the future generation, from the sins of commission and omission, into which our parents were betrayed by ignorance'.[84]

Such appeals did not remain unheeded, and educational ventures were prominent among Chartist endeavours. Several

Chartist leaders were involved in running Sunday schools at some stage of their lives. These were particularly encouraged by the Chartist Church in Birmingham, which ran one in several districts of the town. O'Connor himself demonstrated the relevance Chartists placed on education by occasionally attending the quarterly examinations of the pupils at Chartist Sunday schools.[85]

Conversely, participation in educational efforts for the benefit of the working class seems to have produced some degree of affinity to Chartism, as was at least shown by the handloom weavers who ran their own school in north-east Lancashire.[86]

Yet there were also specific efforts made to improve the education of female Chartists. The Radical Association of Elland, for instance, decided to start classes in their association rooms. Women were to be taught free. A month later, members were reported being 'as anxious in the affairs of politics, as that of writing, accounts etc.'[87] This observation underlines the mutual reinforcement of Chartism and education, both of which aimed at the same goal, namely self-improvement.

Elizabeth Neesom, the secretary of the ELFPA, shared with the members of her association the Wollstonecraftian belief that women were men's intellectual equals had they but the same opportunities of education. In order to provide some such opportunity, she advertised in *The Northern Star* that she would attend the Trades Hall on Mondays at 7 p.m., one hour before the commencement of the ELFPA's business, in order to instruct in writing and other elementary skills any of the female members choosing to attend.[88]

At Nottingham, Mary Ann Abbott attained some prominence as a local Chartist, not least through the Sunday school she ran together with her sister at the Democratic Chapel, the chief venue of local Chartists. Her pupils, who comprised adult women as well as children, achieved high standards on examination. This may not least have been due to the books they received from members of the local FPU, who had a subscription for this purpose.[89]

These schools certainly all served the dual purpose of imparting knowledge and providing the women running them with a living. That this was often quite precarious was instanced by Caroline Maria Williams, the Bristol Chartist. She had opened an infant school with a fair prospect of success. Yet the local clergyman went round the neighbourhood advising parents against sending their children to her school, since she was a Chartist.[90]

All these examples tend to confirm the correlation discovered by Dorothy Thompson between areas where Chartism was strong and those with records of educational provision.[91] There is a sense in which the whole Chartist movement can be seen as one great educational venture. Many of the speeches made at Chartist meetings were intended for the instruction of the audience, and the same was more obviously true for the numerous lectures. Moreover, Chartism was renowned for the vast number of journals and newspapers it produced. The reading and discussions they provoked were also instructive, and this not only in a narrowly political sense. In addition, the regular Chartist meeting places used to be furnished with at least a small library.[92] And Wearmouth has emphasised the educational value of the Chartist class-system, in the framework of which many Chartists learned to read, discuss, speak, debate and instruct.[93]

Through their involvement in the movement, therefore, women benefited from the educational by-products that commitment to Chartism entailed.

Contributing to the Chartist Press

The Chartist press received a large number of contributions from women, either in the form of articles, or, more often, in that of letters to the editor. Their exact scale can only be guessed at, for almost any proportion of the contributions that were only initialled or submitted entirely anonymously may have been of female origin.

The obstacles female contributors had to surmount, in terms of both literacy and conventions, are illustrated by the following opening to a letter sent by a working woman to the editor of *The National Association Gazette*. She self-consciously apologised for all grammatical and orthographical mistakes and implied that, had the paper not previously inserted contributions from other women and were her own long-standing adherence to Chartism not likely to induce the editor to leniency, her courage would have failed her. Her letter began thus: 'Please to excuse all faults, and put this letter in your *Gazette*. Myself and husband are both Chartists, and read your paper every week; and we have seen there, [*sic*] letters from women, therefore I thought you would put in mine.'[94]

While this letter was a one-off venture, other women, who possessed self-confidence and knowledge enough to do without such timid introduction to their writings, contributed theoretical articles to Chartist journals on a regular basis. Outstanding among these was 'Sophia', whose middle-class origin has already been noted (in Chapter 4).

Another example was Helen Macfarlane, also from a non-working-class background, as can be inferred from her education. She had an excellent command of French and German and possessed a wide knowledge of philosophy, literature and art. For several years, she lived on the Continent, where she witnessed the severe repression following the Vienna uprising of March 1848. In 1850, she returned to Britain, where she met Marx and Engels and subsequently translated their *Communist Manifesto* into English. The translation appeared in Harney's *Red Republican*. Up to June 1850, she signed her articles in this paper with her own name, while from July of that year onwards, one 'Howard Morton' appeared. Due to the similarity of both their articles with regard to form, type of argument, style and literary allusions, 'Howard Morton' was presumably a pseudonym used by Helen Macfarlane.[95] After a party of the Fraternal Democrats in December 1850, at which Mary Harney was allegedly rude to her, 'Howard Morton's' articles disappeared from Harney's paper. Engels thereupon castigated Harney for what he called an unfortunate break with 'the most outstanding and capable contributor to *The Friend of the People*'.[96]

Helen Macfarlane's articles encompassed a wide range of topics. Apart from a critique of Thomas Carlyle's pamphlets, in which she advocated the principles of social democracy, she openly favoured a social revolution in various of her articles. Consequently she railed at those who professed education to be a means of improving the condition of the masses and scorned 'charity' as something that granted the masses only that of which they had been robbed previously. Her deeply rooted conviction of the inevitability of a social revolution was due to her conception of the opposition of labour to capital, which she regarded as irreconcilable, as well as to a sharpening of class divisions. Her articles were tinged by Christian Socialism, casting Jesus as a proletarian prototype. In her more topical contributions, she came out against working-class contributions to a monument to Sir Robert Peel, exposed the hypocrisy of the Frankfurt peace congress by demonstrating the necessity of a standing army for maintaining order in exploitative systems, and denounced *The Morning Post*'s sympathy with Haynau,[97] who had become notorious for his cruelty in crushing the Hungarian revolution.

'Sophia's' articles on the education of women and children, on specifically female forms of political interference and on the Poor Law's effect on women have been quoted extensively (both in this chapter and in Chapter 4). These were the topics around which the bulk of her writing for the Chartist press revolved.[98]

It is significant that both women were not only non-working class and therefore had no difficulty in engaging in written forms of communication, but also felt strongly about women's rights. While 'Sophia's' proximity to Mary Wollstonecraft has repeatedly been noted, Helen Macfarlane imagined the 'veritable republic' she strove for as being peopled by 'free men and women'. Despite the assets that a good education and slightly feminist leanings represented, both women seem to have been self-conscious about the unconventionality of some of their views and of voicing them in public, for otherwise it would not have been necessary for them to hide behind pseudonyms (always assuming, that is, that 'Howard Morton' was really Helen Macfarlane).

In accordance with newspapers' topicality, female contributions to them concerned matters of immediate interest. *The Northern Star* in particular published reports about local Chartist proceedings which were sent in by the local associations' secretaries. In the case of FCAs, these were often women, who thus formed a large contingent of female contributors, although usually remaining anonymous in their capacity as reporter.

Another large group of letters contained enquiries or sought legal advice.[99] These letters became fairly frequent in *The Northern Star* after its opening of a legal department to make cheap legal advice available to working-class people. Letters of this kind testify to the women's belief in the editors' expertise in all kinds of issue. Moreover, they demonstrate that Chartist papers took their working-class readers so seriously, and on the whole treated them so respectfully, that even women dared address themselves to them. Women's contributions generally received appreciation and praise.[100]

The disdain working-class people experienced from papers other than their own was mirrored by the fact that Chartist women used the columns of *The Northern Star* to defend themselves and Chartism in general against false accusations published in the non-radical press.[101]

If the contents of a letter could be considered unlawful, the editor would decline insertion for fear of the authorities' response, a fate not uncommonly befalling female contributions, perhaps no less than male.[102] It is impossible to ascertain, however, what exactly constituted their unlawful character, whether they could be considered libellous by the government, or whether the editor found their contents outrageous precisely because they had been written by women.

Joining Female Chartist Associations

Apart from sexually mixed ventures, the Chartist movement provided the framework for women's structured participation with the founding of FCAs, which were exclusively female, at least in terms of membership. A total of just under one hundred and fifty of these have been found to exist at least at some stage of English Chartism between 1838 and 1852. This amounts to about one-ninth of the number of WMAs listed by Dorothy Thompson for the years 1839, 1841, 1842, 1844 and 1848.[103]

The life-cycle of FCAs also showed a different pattern from those of their male counterparts. The latter had their climax in the years 1839 to 1842. Numbers had dropped down markedly by 1844, but had picked up considerably by 1848. Yet in that year, the number of WMAs was only half that in 1839.

The number of FCAs, too, reached a peak in 1839, only to drop down dramatically in subsequent years. The revival in 1842 amounted to only about a third of the number attained in 1844, while in 1848, the FCAs managed only a meagre third of their number in 1842, or under one-eighth of their strength in 1839. This picture is somewhat distorted by the fact that, after the founding of the NCA in 1841, it became possible for individuals of either sex to join local branches. Actual structured female support of Chartism was therefore greater than that measured by numbers of FCAs.

The vast majority of FCAs were formed in the years 1838–9. They were created as much to campaign against the Poor Law as for the Charter. This underlines the importance of opposition to the 1834 Act in bringing women into Chartism. Following the reorganisation of the movement that began in the spring of 1840, numerous FCAs sprang up in new localities, while others re-formed. Of the seventy-six FCAs set up over the year as NCA branches, forty-four had had precursors in 1838–9, while the remainder were completely new local ventures. In 1847, the third life-cycle began with only a handful of FCAs coming into existence. Some of the FCAs recorded were re-formed once or twice. Outstanding among them was Sheffield FCA, which featured in all three stages of Chartism. It has to be borne in mind, however, that the exact date of foundation was not always given, nor can one definitely date the death of an association. They simply ceased to be mentioned in the press. This also makes it difficult to trace the continuity of an association's existence.

The strongholds of FCAs were to be found in the heartlands of Britain's textile industry. The bulk of them clustered in Yorkshire, which was closely followed by Lancashire, including the northern half of Cheshire. FCAs thus mirrored the geographical pattern of female Chartism already outlined (in Chapter 3). In areas where women's support of Chartism was very strong anyway, there was consequently an increased likelihood of their formalising their commitment to the movement by founding one of its female branches.

Membership of FCAs varied over time as well as according to the size of the population in a given locality. Birmingham, a comparatively large town, had, unlike London, only one central FCA boasting at one stage over 1300 members.[104] This was quite exceptional, for the average FCA numbered between thirty and fifty women.

From among the female committee members whose names were reported in the Chartist press, the overwhelming majority (sixty-one) were married, while only nineteen were single. It would appear that being married helped to enhance a woman's status, thus increasing her willingness to stand for, and that of others to elect her into, office. The City of London FCA was unique in being exclusively organised by single women.[105]

Furthermore, FCAs seem to have afforded several generations of women from one family scope for political activity. The Tower Hamlets FCA had a Miss Simmons as treasurer and a Mrs Simmons as secretary. On the committee of the London Female Democratic Association, there sat one Sarah and one Mary Dymmock,[106] who were almost certainly related.

All FCAs were run by a committee that usually comprised a

president or chairwoman – a term actually used by Chartists[107] – a secretary and a treasurer. Membership involved the willingness to pay weekly subscriptions, which ranged from 1*d*. in the case of the ELFPA to 2½*d*. in that of the South Shields FPU.[108] Subscriptions were thus adapted to the different economic conditions in various parts of the country, which determined what amounts women were potentially able to set aside for their own political activities from a family budget that would in many cases have included political expenses incurred by the husband.

Each FCA would resolve upon a particular day for their weekly meeting. The ELFPA, for instance, had theirs on Monday evenings at eight o'clock and finished not later than ten.[109] The fixing of a time-limit is an interesting indication of how female Chartists' political activism operated within restrictions imposed by their family commitments, and perhaps also by considerations of respectability and safety. Some FCAs met at the house of one of their members, while others, mostly those of large and active localities, were able to use Chartist meeting places.[110]

The regular weekly meetings of FCAs followed similar patterns all over the country. New members were enrolled, both national and local events as well as tactics were discussed, and resolutions expressing opinions or setting out a course of action were passed.

Apart from the weekly meeting, there were quarterly and general ones as well. General meetings were open to both members and women wishing to enrol and to have the principles of Chartism explained. Every now and then, the local WMA and FCA might hold a joint meeting, either to give women the opportunity of hearing a lecture on a topic of relevance to them or in order to increase Chartism's impact by rallying the movement's united forces. It also seems to have been common for FCAs to send a delegation to public Chartist meetings in their locality which were of special significance, for instance because of the attendance of O'Connor.

The resolutions adopted at the meetings of FCAs did not essentially differ from those of WMAs. Again and again the women would pledge themselves to support their kinsmen in their struggle for the Charter.[111]

The means of exerting political influence that were employed by FCAs were modelled on those of their male counterparts. FCAs would participate in Chartist demonstrations parading their own banners, which expressed specifically female concerns. Banners

bearing inscriptions such as 'our children cryeth [sic] for Bread' or
'Mothers, claim the Rights of your children' emphasised that it
was in order to safeguard their children's interests that many
women had come into Chartism. Equally, opposition to the Poor
Law inspired many banners. At a procession to meet the Chartist
White on his visit to Newcastle, the local FCA carried a flag with
the inscription: 'We Live and Die Together – Down with the
Bastiles [sic]'. Other banners would indicate the function of the
FCA along the lines of 'The Nottingham Female's [sic] Association;
Established to Assist in obtaining the People's Charter.' This
banner moreover expressed women's conviction that Chartism
was certain of success, since it aimed at putting into practice
divine principles. The corresponding caption read: 'Why grind ye
the faces of the poor saith the Lord, Freedom's cause cannot be
lost, It is sacred before the Lord of Hosts.' Other banners simply
reiterated common Chartist slogans, such as 'Universal Suffrage –
No Corn Laws', which was paraded by Bolton FCA at the Kersall
Moor demonstration in May 1839.[112]

Despite their scanty means, the members of FCAs spent large
amounts of money on embellishing their banners.[113] The females
of Botchergate, Carlisle, chose what must have been one of the
most popular motifs within the iconography of early female
Chartism. Their flag showed a keeper of a workhouse about to
part mother and children. The caption read: 'Tyrants beware! think
you that a mother's love is not stronger than your laws.' On the
reverse side, the same figure was shown about to part husband
and wife, and the motto read: 'Whom God has joined together let
no man put asunder.'[114]

FCAs were very important in boosting contributions to the
Chartist funds[115] and also actively supported Chartist prisoners, be
it by petitioning on their behalf or by collecting useful articles.[116]

Inviting lecturers to speak on some aspect of Chartism was a
regularly recurring feature of FCA business. Many lecturers served
to impart political knowledge, thus supporting FCA members'
own efforts in this field.[117] In the same vein, Vincent conceived of
FCAs as political schools from which their members would set out
to impart their newly acquired knowledge.[118] In order to make
their political beliefs known, FCAs would publish political
addresses (which have been quoted from extensively in Chapter
4). Some of these were issued at the release of political prisoners
from gaol. The earliest example of this was an address from

Elland FCA celebrating the restoration of the Tolpuddle Martyrs to Britain.[119] Frequent recipients of FCAs' addresses were O'Connor[120] and, in the early years, J. R. Stephens, who was praised for his success in enlisting women's support by depicting the atrocities of the Poor Law and the deplorable condition of the children labouring in factories. The women of Brighton, as the authors of such an address, particularly thanked him for his repudiation of the grievous wrongs inflicted on their sisters in the north.[121] It is particularly significant that women of the south, themselves spared the sufferings inflicted by large-scale industry, took J. R. Stephens's exertions on behalf of other members of their sex as an occasion to assure him of their sympathy.

FCA addresses went through three cycles. The first address was adopted by Nottingham FCA on 26 November 1838 and was succeeded by many others up to the autumn of 1839. The next cycle began in early 1841 and terminated in the June of the following year. Addresses of these two cycles thus clustered around the time when National Petitions were presented to Parliament. These periods marked the high points of the movement, and the women used their addresses to add extra momentum to the general Chartist campaign. The third cycle, on the other hand, comprised only four addresses and extended from June 1848 to February 1849. They were a desperate last attempt to stem the tide of growing disintegration.

These addresses often formed part of the business of FCAs and served as a means of communicating with one another. They can also be shown to have influenced each other and thus to have been instrumental in women's forging a group identity.[122] Apart from the various political activities FCAs engaged in, they also had their convivial side, which provided a welcome outlet from the misery and drudgery that characterised the everyday lives of working-class women.[123]

Clearly the members of FCAs formed an inner core of supporters, whom many other women sympathetic to the cause would join for special events or in times of great activity nationally. This accounts for the certain degree of overlap between activities listed as those of FCAs in this section, but also considered (in the subsections above) as activities engaged in by individual women.

Chartist leaders also perceived the vanguard function of FCAs by hoping they would win non-organised women over to

Chartism. Congratulating the female Chartists of Bristol upon their founding of an FCA, Vincent described its purpose thus:

> it will be the means of concentrating the political principles of your fellow women around the great principles of human liberty. . . . In forming a Female Political Society, you have set a noble example to the women of Bristol; an example they will not fail to follow. You will be the means of making them acquainted with our political principles; you will teach them the value and importance of the rights we wish to confer upon their husbands, fathers, brothers and friends; you will teach them to reject the . . . talk about *blues* and *yellows*, and win over their sympathies in favour of right principles which will increase the happiness of all the people.[124]

Vincent regarded women as best able to agitate their sisters.

FCAs were rooted in the tradition of sexually segregated organisation both within trade unions and political campaigns. With the spread of waged labour, followed by the introduction of factories, which heavily relied on a female workforce, conditions of work and pay had begun to affect male and female workers alike and had inspired resistance regardless of sex.

In the early stages of workplace organisation, exclusion on grounds of sex was not always total. Within trades employing a sexually mixed workforce, combinations had reflected this, even where women's status as secondary workers had long been established.

The increased competition for jobs between men and women in conjunction with industrial reorganisation following the Napoleonic Wars, and the debasement of craft skills, heightened sexual antagonism at the workplace, and the segregation of women into separate organisations became common. At the formation of the Grand General Union of Spinners in 1829, it was resolved to exclude all female workers from coming into spinning. However, recognising the futility of excluding women from work they had once virtually monopolised, the men recommended them to form their own unions, in which endeavour the women received male help and advice. This could well be an instance of what Barbara Taylor has described as sexual segregation resulting from a compromise with men wanting to exclude women from their trades and unions altogether.[125] Four years later, the same men backed women's demands for male wages. Male claims for equal pay for women over the next hundred years were based, as Lewenhak has noted,[126] on fears of losing work to women, who undercut male wages. It was also seen as a device to keep women out of the job entirely, for men believed that the implementation of the 'rate for the job' would give them preference in employment.

Male powerloom weavers, on the other hand, realised that any attempt at organising without the women who dominated this branch of the industry would be doomed to failure. Some weaving associations, therefore, made it a rule not to accept any man as a member unless all his womenfolk working in the trade would join as well.

In 1834, with the formation of the Grand National Consolidated Trades Union, a deliberate attempt was made at unionising women in the face of a mounting tide of unskilled labour. The members of the GNCTU's female lodges were mainly women working in the clothing industry. Women organised in separate lodges, even when they were employed in mixed trades, and men's lodges seem to have taken all joint leadership initiatives without meeting with any female protest. Male dominance in the organisations thus persisted despite the high level of sexual solidarity prevalent in Owenite unions. Male bids for dominance met with little resistance, for women viewed themselves as a group apart – as women first and workers second.

This self-perception, however, did not prevent women from taking action when they felt their rights to be infringed upon. When this occurred independently of male support, some middle-class observers became greatly alarmed. They saw it as foreshadowing women's questioning of male hegemony in all spheres of life.[127]

Female Friendly Societies formed a tradition of female organisation that would at times merge in the early trade-union movement. Women set up their own all-female Friendly or Benefit Societies or Box Clubs, whose members were entitled to sickness, unemployment or funeral benefit. Many of these societies enforced a rigorous moral code and refused money to any member falling ill of venereal disease or any other disorder contracted by a 'loose' lifestyle, or to unmarried mothers. The emphasis on thrift, self-help and sobriety indicates the extent to which these societies were influenced by Methodism. Felony, elopement and living in open adultery all led to the exclusion of the member thus guilty.

The 'sisters' were expected to maintain a certain level of respectability and to refrain from swearing, drunkenness, lying and gambling. Female Friendly Societies may be interpreted as the formalisation of women's neighbourhood support networks, which had long not only dispensed material aid to neighbours in need, but had also kept a close watch on people's morals. Any transgression of the community's moral code incited women's disapproval, and the charivari was perhaps the best known means of enforcing adherence to community customs.

Some Friendly Societies admitted men to meetings on payment of a fine, but in general strangers were not welcome. The rules of these societies were businesslike and democratic, and the appointment of officials and admission to membership went by vote. The clubs also had their convivial side, which would provide a release from the hardship and drudgery of everyday life. Around 1800, about 750,000 men and women were organised in such societies. Lancashire, where there were 820 of them, boasted the biggest single concentration. These societies were not restricted to members of one particular trade and were therefore not trade unions proper. At the later stages of their existence, they occasionally used their funds for strike pay. Moreover, in Manchester, for instance, one Female Friendly Society campaigned for a ten-hour day.

Female Friendly Societies were thus the earliest form of indigenous female working-class combination, and as such they provided the model for later associations of women, including Chartist ones.[128] Although carefully abstaining from overtly political involvement, they laid the foundation for women's expertise in running associations, which Chartist women displayed to such a remarkable degree. Furthermore, Lancashire was not only a stronghold of Friendly Societies, it also boasted a large number of Reform Societies as well as a high concentration of FCAs later on. It can therefore be assumed that each generation of female associations provided the training-ground for the leadership of its successor.

In the 1810s, Samuel Bamford, the Reform leader from Middleton, introduced at Reform meetings the issue of women's right to vote. This was a new idea, and, as he reported, 'the women, who attended numerously on that bleak ridge, were mightily pleased with it, – and the men being nothing dissentient,

– when the resolution was put, the women held up their hands, amid much laughter'.[129]

Despite the novelty, however, this became common practice. Once women's right to participate in political matters had thus been acknowledged, female political unions were formed, complete with chairwomen, committees and other officials who, in true Jacobin style, rotated. The first of these societies originated at Blackburn and speedily sent out a circular letter calling upon the wives and daughters of workmen in different branches of manufacture to form sister societies in order to co-operate with men. Involvement in the Reform movement thus often turned into a family concern, with all members joining. These women came forward as the female kinfolk of workmen, the support of whose political exertions was thereby placed within the framework of family responsibilities. Precisely the same attitude was to be adopted by Chartist women twenty years later. The same is true for women's efforts to instil into the minds of their children a hatred of their tyrannical rulers. As Barbara Taylor has observed,[130] this concept of radical action as a necessary extension of women's family duties both encouraged female militancy and limited the forms this militancy assumed. In terms of organisation, the sexual divisions of labour and power, which were rooted in the family, became superimposed on working-class campaigns.

Through their involvement in the Reform movement, women participated for the first time in a long-term campaign for an overtly political goal – electoral reform – that was somewhat removed from their daily cares and responsibilities.

However, separate organisation of women within the Reform movement was riddled with difficulties. At the second meeting of the Stockport Female Society on 19 July 1819, Mrs Hallworth, on being elected president, somewhat apologetically asked the men present to withdraw,

not . . . with a view to transacting anything of a secret nature, for it is commonly said that women can keep no secrets, but merely that if in our debates (for it is something new for women to turn political orators) we should for want of knowledge make any blunders we should be laughed at, to prevent which we should prefer being by ourselves.[131]

This passage – not least its self-deprecation – shows the

cautiousness and timidity of women aware of the novelty of overt female interference in political matters. The novelty, moreover, posed a variety of practical problems, such as the proper way of addressing a female audience. Speakers were reported as struggling with 'Mrs President and ladies' and 'Mrs President and sisters'.[132] This difficulty, however, had been overcome by the time Chartist women began to feature in politics, and 'chairwoman' and 'sisters' were well established forms of reference to leaders and members of FCAs.

The women involved in the Reform movement were keenly aware of the hostility they met with even among male fellow-reformers, and this despite the fact that their determination to achieve reform did not lag behind that of the men. 'We do not wish for irony and flattery', wrote one of them, 'we wish you to address our reason.'[133] These women, then, had to struggle hard in order to establish their place in a political movement, a struggle from which Chartist women benefited, because their right to political involvement was never questioned; on the contrary, their contribution was welcomed as essential in winning the Charter.

When reform became the dominant radical issue again around 1830, women played a less noticeable role in the movement. Female political unions seem to have been clustered in the manufacturing districts, and the major unions admitted women as members. The tone for this decision may have been set by John Cleave, later to become one of the founding members of the LWMA, who argued for the free admission of members' wives to meetings, because the latter would be ornamented by the women's presence, and it would reduce political argument at home. Furthermore, although he was convinced that women were generally Tories, he was confident that, if induced to attend, they would shortly turn into republicans and would raise their children in this belief.[134] This view of women as inherently politically conservative was echoed eight years later by Salt, the Birmingham Chartist, when advocating the formation of FCAs.[135]

Owenism, which both preceded and partly overlapped with Chartism, was unique among working-class organisations of the late eighteenth and early nineteenth century in that it addressed itself to the issue of sexual oppression. The movement's endeavours to implement women's equality within its own ranks were part of an overall attempt to establish a society based on co-operation, which would not only improve the lot of the working class, but would also ensure the equality of the sexes. Despite Owenism's explicitly feminist ideology, it failed to make inroads into male hegemony at the organisational level.

The Owenites welcomed women into all their assemblies, and many branches made active efforts to ensure that female voices would be heard on such occasions. Theoretically, women were expected to play an equal role in the government of the movement, both at the local and national level. But only a few female officials featured, and women seem not to have voted for each other. There were several reasons for the lack of effect of the Owenites' feminist principle on their own power structure. Male prejudice on the one hand was equalled by female diffidence on the other. This marginalisation of women, as Barbara Taylor has argued, has also to be seen as part of a broader development within working-class politics. There occurred a shift away from locally based, direct-action mobilisations towards more formalised structures of national political organisation. With the replacement of trade unions and co-operatives in Owenism by the Rational Society, with its executive councils, delegate meetings, united conferences with agenda and elaborate rules of order, this type of political organisation proved to be too time-absorbing and intimidating to women, who had less free time at their disposal and lacked the public confidence which many of their husbands evidently possessed.

By the time working people began to rally round the Charter, sexual segregation had been firmly established as an organising principle in plebeian movements. It was based on and expressive of male hegemony in political and social agitations. Within trade unions, it owed its inception to the rising tide of sexual antagonism at the workplace, which made many men regard female union branches as the best option short of women's total exclusion. In political campaigns, on the other hand, sexual segregation resulted from men's deliberate attempt at securing female support, while maintaining women in a subordinate position.

The idea of forming separate FCAs originated with Salt, one of the middle-class leaders of the Birmingham Political Union, the body that had suggested the getting up of a national petition praying for the enactment of the Six Points of the Charter. Salt had for a long time believed in involving women in radical politics, and had already urged them to be active in the Reform Bill agitation.

To this end, he convened a public meeting of the women of Birmingham at the Town Hall on 2 April 1838. Three resolutions – presumably written by Salt – were passed. Firstly, the women stated that the prevailing want and misery had driven them to leave their homes, their proper sphere, in search of employment, which was increasingly difficult to obtain and less remunerative. It was in order to consider these difficulties that they had met in public. Secondly, they affirmed the pointlessness of hoping for an improvement of their condition from parliament, which had proved itself impervious to working-class pleading and had persisted in passing acts of class legislation. Therefore they had, thirdly, come to the conclusion that any improvement of their condition hinged on universal male suffrage, backed up by the remaining five points of the Charter, to the full support of which they pledged themselves.[136]

Salt reported that this meeting had been attended by about 12,000 women and, as he seems to have felt obliged to emphasise, had been conducted in a most enthusiastic and orderly manner. He also revealed that his main motive for organising women was to prevent them from impeding men's commitment to Chartism out of ignorance:

> I believe (I might say I know) that hitherto, the women have thought so little upon politics, and being so utterly ignorant of the connection of our system with their poverty and degradation, that they have either not interfered, or persuaded their husbands from meddling with politics as a thing of no profit. We cannot afford their neutrality or hostility; they must be our enthusiastic friends.[137]

That was why he wanted to see women's meetings repeated all over the country. Moreover, he intended the National Petition to be twofold – one signed by men, one by women.

In the middle of July 1838, the women of Birmingham met again. The main speech was by Salt, who went to great lengths justifying his convening of public women-only meetings. According to the report in *The Birmingham Journal*,

He confessed that it had required considerable resolution on his part to take so unusual a step, as to convene a meeting entirely composed of women. The bravest of his friends had shrunk from the risk of so novel an experiment. Some feared the ridicule which low minds might attempt to cast on it, but one master fear so possessed his (Mr Salt's) mind, that he was inaccessible to any other, that fear was the continuance of the misery of the people.

In order to illustrate his belief that 'nothing was done well but what was done by women', he greatly flattered his female audience by choosing household chores as an example:

> Let any of them set their husbands to clean the house and mind the children, and the experiment would be decisive of his qualification. The dirt would be barely swept into the corners, every thing would be out of place; the broom would be left on the floor to break people's shins, and all would be hopeless confusion, but let the woman come home, see the broom in her hands, I'll warrant she'll make a clear deck of it.

No wonder that such respect for female circumspection in domestic matters was greeted with laughter and applause. Salt then extended his observation to the political arena by reminding his audience of the 'bungling job' the men had made of the 1832 Reform Bill. This was why he currently had to call on women, assuring them that on 'that day the women of Birmingham would obtain the immortal honour of setting the example to the women of England'. He went on to assert that women bore the brunt of the current misery, which he described in detail. In view of the exigencies of the present state of the country he felt justified in appealing to women to bring their powerful influence to bear upon the cause.

> He volunteered the acknowledgement that it was not an influence that ought to be appealed to upon ordinary occasions. There was a sacredness about the character of woman in the retirement of her home, that must not be lightly trespassed upon. He was the last that would wish to see her habitually taking part publicly in angry political discussions; but every privilege of their sex had been disregarded when they were

dragged from their homes to the slavery and demoralization of factory labour, and he assembled them to assist in recovering the respect and protection due to the females in a civilised country.[138]

This concluding paragraph of Salt's speech highlights once again the ambiguity inherent in the Chartist agitation of women. Chartist leaders unequivocally welcomed female support – provided female commitment remained geared towards the restoration of a clearly demarcated sexual division of labour.

On 16 August 1838, Salt made a final effort to involve the Birmingham women in the agitation around the National Petition by publishing an open letter to them. This reiterated the arguments commonly to be found in the Chartist agitation of women (as set out in Chapter 4).[139] From then on, Salt was regarded as the founding father of FCAs, whose plan to involve women in Chartism was defended by Bronterre O'Brien against attacks in the conservative press.[140] By likening working-class women's right to political involvement to the right of aristocratic 'blue stockings' – a term actually used by O'Brien – to concern themselves with politics and to the Queen's right to supreme power, he removed women's participation in Chartism from the gender-specific plane on which Salt had located it and brought it within the realm of class politics. This difference of argument highlights Salt's rootedness in middle-class thinking.

Salt's open letter to the women of Birmingham seems to have marked the actual beginning of the local FPU, founded as a sister organisation to its male counterpart, for subsequently meetings began to be reported in the local paper.

True to Salt's intention, the Birmingham FPU did in fact provide a model. It is interesting that Birmingham served as a model for the Newcastle FPU despite the different balance of support in these centres for moral and physical force. Although pledged to the latter, Newcastle took cues as to how to organise women effectively from the Birmingham FPU.[141] After Birmingham and Newcastle, the founding of FCAs snowballed throughout the country.

Like the Birmingham FPU, a great number of FCAs were formed at mixed meetings. Famous Chartist leaders were also instrumental in setting up FCAs by writing to or visiting Chartist localities.[142]

Elsewhere, the WMA nominated delegates from among themselves to assist the women in establishing their association. Accordingly, the meetings at which the local male Chartists resolved to form a female branch seem not to have been attended by women.[143] The fact that many FCAs were set up at male instigation was often reflected by the sex of their officials.[144] A great number of FCAs, however, were formed at meetings of women wanting to lend Chartism their support on a regular and formalised basis, at times with male help or at male instigation, at other times evolving from female initiative.[145] Sometimes the meeting at which an FCA was to be formed was advertised in *The Northern Star* coupled with a call upon the women to attend.[146]

FCAs that were formed at female instigation and boasted all-female committees were most likely to be found in localities with a long tradition of female involvement in radical politics, and where there consequently existed the expertise and personnel required for the running of such a formalised political body. Several FCAs, mainly in the north, had had Anti-Poor Law antecedents.[147]

In places where FCAs were the first instance of women organising themselves politically, this attracted a great deal of attention.[148] The women themselves were very much alive to their embarking on something out of the ordinary and, at least initially, might behave very self-consciously.[149]

The female associations founded called themselves Female Political Unions, Female Democratic Associations or Female Radical Associations to denote their close links with the respective – and often similarly named – male body of their locality. The East London women chose the name of East London Female Patriotic Association[150] in accordance with the belief held by many Chartist women (as noted in Chapter 4) that commitment to the movement was a patriotic duty.

Yet the formation of an FCA was not necessarily conditional upon the existence of an equivalent male association. Several localities boasted FCAs, while lacking a male counterpart. At Birmingham, the FPU showed more longevity than the Birmingham Political Union, surviving the latter by several months.[151] After the founding of the NCA, women were able to join its local mixed-sex branches, as happened at Cradley and Netherton. When a sufficient number of women had gathered, the local NCA branch might decide to start a female association.

Men like Salt and other Chartist leaders intended FCAs to be
mere auxiliaries. Yet the existence of all-female associations within
the framework of Chartism is significant in that it did afford
women scope for turning them to their own purposes, if they so
wished. The lack of any evidence of this happening does not rule
out the possibility that women may quite simply have appreciated
this opportunity to meet among themselves. Moreover, FCAs did
help turn politics from an exclusively male affair into a family
activity, and one that went beyond convivial occasions such as tea
parties and picnics (mentioned in section 1). It is in FCAs founded
at female initiative and run exclusively by women that evidence of
such rudiments of female self-awareness as existed within
Chartism were most likely to be found. This becomes apparent in
their rules and regulations. Unfortunately, only those of the LFDA,
of the ELFPA and of Barnsley FCA were recorded in any detail in
the movement's press.

While other FCAs saw their task chiefly as one of assisting their
male kinfolk to obtain the Charter (as shown in Chapter 4), the
LFDA emphasised its wish to co-operate with the other female
and male Chartists (in this order) throughout the country in their
struggle for the Charter. Secondly, the London women expressed
their determination to fight the New Poor Law, and thirdly, they
wished to co-operate particularly with the women of the north in
crushing the factory system, which was hated for its evil effects on
children. Not affected by the factory system themselves – on
account of the different economic structure of London – the
women of the LFDA made the plight of their sisters the reason for
their own struggle. Fourthly, they pledged themselves to support
those suffering for their commitment to Chartism.[152]

The ELFPA seems to have evolved out of the LFDA in October
1839. This is suggested by the fact that Elizabeth Neesom served
as the secretary of both.[153] In their official objects, the East London
women put unity with their sisters in the country before assisting
the men in their fight for universal suffrage. Secondly, they aimed
to help each other in cases of need and affliction. Thirdly, they
pledged themselves to support those suffering for Chartism, and
fourthly, they were determined to practise exclusive dealing.[154]

Continuity between LFDA and ELFPA is further suggested by a
comparison between their rules, which gave priority to sexual
solidarity within the framework of the working-class fight for the
Charter.

The 'Laws and Qualifications of Members' of the ELFPA ruled that the weekly subscription of 1*d*. per member was to be equally divided between the support of imprisoned Chartists and relief for members afflicted by illness. This may have been tantamount to the forming of a lying-in fund and would show the ELFPA to stand in the tradition of Female Friendly Societies. The fifth clause laid down that membership of the association be restricted to women, and the sixth that no man be admitted without the invitation of the majority of the members present. Furthermore, the same condition, plus a week's notice, applied to people wanting to lecture to the ELFPA on religious subjects or on the marriage laws. Both were highly contentious issues, which the ELFPA thus tried to remove as the causes of possible dissension. While, at least in public, Chartists on the whole chiefly ignored Owenite proposals concerning marriage reform, *The New Moral World* carried an account of one female Chartist attacking the Owenite marriage doctrine at a public meeting.[155]

The regulations of Barnsley FCA were also reminiscent of Friendly Societies in that women pledged themselves to orderly behaviour. The rules furthermore testify to the highly democratic character of at least this FCA. The committee of nine, to be elected to manage the business of the association, was to retain office for three months and then to be either re-elected or succeeded by fresh members.[156] This potentially ensured that a maximum number of women was involved in running the association, and this always under close scrutiny from members.

There were several attempts at uniting FCAs regionally or nationally other than by virtue of their being female NCA branches. In 1842, the Chartist Council of Birmingham resolved to recommend to the women to form a separate body to be called 'The Women's National Charter Association'.[157] Thereafter, 'FCA' was the most common label to be found, although no national all-female organisation seems to have come into existence.

The Birmingham call may have been responded to in London, for in September of that year, Susanna Inge, the secretary of the City of London FCA, published an appeal in *The Northern Star*. She urgently called on all her 'Sister Chartists' in London to attend a general meeting of the 'Females Association' to deliberate on some rules and regulations for improving its organisation. Although no more was heard of this metropolitan women's association, Susanna seems to have tried to expand it nationally. In

May 1843, all secretaries of FCAs throughout the country who had not previously communicated were requested to send their addresses to her.[158] Yet in 1848, another brief attempt seems to have been made to form a National Female Charter Association. This is at least suggested by the address issued by the Bethnal Green FCA, which called itself 'The National Female Chartists Association (Branch No. 2)'.[159]

The regularity with which the efforts to unite Chartist women nationally failed can be taken as an indication of the extent to which class issues predominated over those of gender in the political motivation of female Chartists. Moreover, women who were anyway overburdened would have found it extremely difficult to take on the extra work involved in running an organisation on the national scale.

The indefatigable Susanna was a member of the City of London FCA, which, as has been noted, was exceptional among FCAs for being exclusively managed by single women. These, as the example of Susanna showed, were both willing and able to devote a great deal of time and effort to political organisation. They also possessed a fair amount of self-confidence. While it usually devolved on men to advise FCAs as to how to render their organisation more efficient, Susanna thought nothing of breaking this male privilege. She suggested that every locality hang up the plan of the organisation in a conspicuous place so that all members might thoroughly acquaint themselves with it. The by-laws and rules of the locality should be read before the commencement of business at every meeting. If any officer of the association failed to do his (*sic*) duty, a special meeting of members should be called to investigate the case, which should not be made public unless private remonstrances had proved futile.[160] These suggestions speak volumes about Susanna's political experience. It is not clear whether this was gained in her capacity of secretary to her FCA, in which function she was first mentioned in May 1843,[161] or whether experience acquired previously made her eligible for this office.

When, in July 1842, she published an address to the women of England (quoted from in Chapter 4), she signed herself simply as a member of the City of London FCA. Her address was outstanding for being issued by an individual woman who disdained seeking shelter from political and personal attacks behind an office in a political organisation. Moreover, the address differed from those of other female Chartists with regard to the assertive manner in which it claimed women's equality with men.

Although exceptional among female Chartists in her self-assertion and in the slightly feminist bias of her thinking, Susanna met with a response from at least one other woman. Caroline Maria Williams, the Bristol Chartist, whose various contributions to *The Northern Star* (noted above) betrayed a similar spirit of independence, asked for Susanna's address.[162] Significantly, both of them were single women, and while the Londoner's origin remains obscure, Caroline Maria Williams is known to have been middle class.[163]

Lecturing

In the limelight of the movement, there stood a few female lecturers who possessed sufficient confidence to agitate for the People's Charter before audiences who were often sexually mixed. Female lecturers appeared in 1839, in the years 1842 and 1843, and in 1848–9. Paradoxically, female lecturing thrived after the rejection of the National Petitions. This would suggest that women speakers appeared whenever the movement entered into one of its more reflective stages, considering how to proceed from the petitions' defeat. At such junctures, female help in sustaining the movement oratorically was likely to meet with less resistance, presumably because men were less fastidious about women's appearance in public.[164]

The dominant female figure of the late years of Chartism was Mrs Theobald. In October 1848, she spoke at Sheffield on the following subjects: 'Co-operation: or the accumulation of wealth by the working classes considered', 'Woman's duties or man's rights: or the justice of the People's Charter, and the way to its speedy accomplishment'. She was reported as having avowed principles of physical force to the extent, as the reporter of *The Sheffield Times* stated with a noticeable shudder, of considering the conduct of the woman who shot eight men during the revolution in Paris 'glorious' and 'womanlike'. She thought that if the women of Sheffield were to combine, they would be more than a match for the policemen.[165]

Like her male colleagues, Mrs Theobald would embark on exhausting agitational tours around the country, delivering her lectures in a different locality each day.[166] She was exceptional in the geographical sweep of her lecture tours – most of the other female Chartist lecturers seem to have been tied to their home towns and neighbourhood by other commitments, such as work and family care.

Significantly, none of these women felt particularly concerned about female issues. Even Mary Ann Walker of the City of London FCA, although supporting female suffrage,[167] was not reported as having lectured on any aspects of women's rights. She appears to have confined herself to the mainstream of Chartist themes. An exception was Helen M'Donald, a Scotswoman, who at the age of eighteen delivered two lectures at Perth on the neglect of female education or the rights of woman.[168] Consideration of the influence that the specifically Scottish brand of Chartism might have had on Helen M'Donald's concern with woman's condition is outside the scope of this book. All these women were very able lecturers and possessed sufficient self-confidence to hold their own against members of the audience who considered the appearance of a female speaker as, in itself, a good excuse for heckling.[169]

Female public speaking, cloaked in a religious guise, can be traced back to the religious sects that emerged during the Civil War. These separatists stressed the spiritual equality of the sexes. Once admitted into a sect, women had an equal share in its government and were allowed to preach. The emphasis on the individual in his or her search for godliness helped to undermine any authority other than that authorised by the individual conscience. This affected the authority of the monarch over the nation as well as that of the father over his family, and thus opened up new lifestyles for women. However, even the most radical sects, once institutionalised, became conservative as regards the organisation and discipline of the family and firmly restricted equality to the realm of spirituality.

Female ministry sprang up again as a concomitant of popular revivalism. Among eighteenth-century Methodists, for instance, female preaching was common practice, but became more restricted in the course of the nineteenth century. The founding of Primitive Methodism can, at least partly, be ascribed to the wish to defend female ministry. As with the Civil War sects, institutionalisation militated against women preaching. It was precisely within the framework of popular revivalism that many working women acquired the expertise required for participating in structured plebeian radical politics.[170]

3 CONCLUSION

Women's support for Chartism, displaying a wide variety of forms, was strongest in fields where it did not jeopardise the well-being of the family. This was true for all kinds of activities in which women overlaid their daily reproductive tasks with political meaning. Conversely, these forms of commitment were particularly welcomed, since they could most easily be used by the movement.

The ambiguity discernible in the Chartist agitation of women likewise characterised the forms of their involvement in the movement. Women's chief task was defined as rendering assistance to the men, and this firmly relegated them to a subordinate position of auxiliaries within the Chartist ranks. This relegation, rather than being counteracted, was actually reinforced by the women-only FCAs. Any suspicion that sexually exclusive combination might be an indication of female autonomy[171] is not borne out by the evidence available. Neither the Chartist view of women's primarily domestic duties nor the female Chartists' self-image allowed for the latter to use the space provided by FCAs to further gender-specific goals.

All these conditions combined effectively to preclude the development of the self-assertion and self-sufficiency conducive to a way of thinking and acting that was inclined towards feminism. The few women who did display these characteristics, such as Helen Macfarlane, 'Sophia', Caroline Maria Williams and perhaps Susanna Inge, were middle class and did not owe their qualities to Chartism.

Given women's family and job commitments, it can be assumed that by far the largest, albeit most hidden, number of them worked for the cause within the confines of their homes. Even so, the outstanding feature of Chartism, compared with all other movements during the period, was the relative scale and extent of female support that was visible and therefore publicly acknowledged.

7
Gender Relations within the Chartist Movement

Women's involvement in Chartism was characterised by an ambivalence that has been traced from female Chartists' own pose of radical wife- and motherhood (demonstrated in Chapter 4) through the movement's agitation of women, which reinforced the female self-portrayal (also shown in Chapter 4), up to the various forms female commitment to Chartism assumed (outlined in the preceding chapter). This ambivalence necessarily followed from a concept of female political activism in which the primacy of women's responsibility for the welfare of their families was central. While both actuating and legitimising political commitment in times of crisis, the chiefly familial concern at the samen time circumscribed the scope of women's activities as well as defining their position within the Chartist movement. The entry of women on to the political stage primarily as wives and mothers had repercussions on the relationship between male and female Chartists that will be explored in this chapter.

One important indication of the gender relations within Chartism was women's veneration of the movement's leaders. Believing these men to have particularly exerted themselves for the cause and, by implication, for the women involved in it, female Chartists presented them with marks of their esteem.[1] Consciously or not, Chartist women thus continued a custom that had been started by the female reformers, who used to give handmade caps of liberty to those men whose services to the cause they valued particularly highly.

Within Chartism, O'Connor, as the national leader, received a great deal of female praise. In his reply to an address by Sunderland FCA, he put forward his view of women's entirely secondary role within Chartism. He began by stating his pleasure in perceiving the identity of feelings that prevailed between men and women in their struggle for political rights. Although, he maintained, women were unable to help men in the battlefield, they could give them courage. He confirmed his wish to keep the women's respect and reiterated that he was more pleased by a female address than by a male one.[2]

This speech was another instance of O'Connor's anti-feminist views, which have already been noted (in Chapter 2) with regard to female suffrage. Underlying his explicit high appreciation of female Chartist activities was his belief in women's inherent political backwardness. Hence his greater degree of pleasure about a female address, and hence also his emphasis on unity across sexual lines, which – within this context – implied the submerging of specifically female issues by those of class. Moreover, he flatly denied any female inclination towards militancy, by assigning to women the role of moral supporters.

Nevertheless, female Chartists not only continued to venerate O'Connor as the great leader of Chartism, but even freely submitted to his literally patriarchal pretensions by casting him in the role of the father of the movement. Thereby they echoed O'Connor's practice of addressing the Chartists as his 'dear children' in the columns of *The Northern Star*. In the image of the father merged the respect that female Chartists felt was due to him on account of his non-working-class background and their gratitude to him for having so entirely devoted himself to the working-class struggle for the Charter. Elizabeth Dewhirst, for instance, one of the allottees at Bromsgrove, wrote to O'Connor via *The Northern Star*, praising him for his efforts to place the poor on the land. She appealed to him thus: 'Whatever you find in this paragraph that is not right you must attribute to ignorance and not presumption; and I hope, as this is the first letter I ever addressed to a gentleman of your order, you will receive it as a father.'[1]

Significantly, only Susanna Inge, the independent-minded London Chartist (introduced in Chapter 4), refused to exempt the conduct of Chartist leaders from critical assessment on account of their exertions for the movement. She did not even hesitate to tackle O'Connor himself over his habit of recommending to Chartist members, through *The Northern Star*, those people he thought fit to take over vacant offices instead of letting members decide for themselves. This criticism was refuted by the editor in tones suggestive of his feeling that Susanna had far overstepped the boundaries of women's place within the movement. He sneeringly remarked that she was 'very much in love with her ideas of democracy', which, however, were not shared by anybody else; he proceeded to reject her allegation as completely unfounded. This point of view was by no means uniquely male. In the following issue of *The Northern Star*, Susanna came under what must have been a severe·attack by the female Chartists of Nottingham. Yet insertion of their letter was declined, because, as the editor explained, 'We must not have the women "quarrelling", the men make "mess" enough.' A fortnight later, the editor informed his readers that some non-Chartist paper had taken Susanna's letter to assert a regular split to have taken place between 'He and She Chartists', with the writer of the letter and Mary Ann Walker, her co-member of the City of London FCA (introduced in section 2 of the preceding chapter), leading the opposition to O'Connor. For *The Northern Star* this assumption of a split along gender lines demonstrated the detrimental effect of the original letter[4] and closed a debate that left O'Connor's leadership as unquestioned as before.

On their release from prison, Chartists received tokens of female esteem in appreciation of the sufferings they had endured for the cause.[5] In this manner, the women expressed their acknowledgement of the men's sufferings, as well as pressuring them to continue as 'faithful' as before. And they were right in assuming no Chartist leader to be willing to forfeit women's respect. In reply to an address from Trowbridge FCA, the imprisoned W. P. Roberts, who had been the counsel for Vincent's defence, maintained:

> MY DEAR FRIENDS, – For the very flattering ADDRESS you have so kindly presented to me, I beg to offer my most sincere thanks: as a mark of your esteem and confidence I shall value it to the latest hour of my life; and should all other motives fail, this proof of your regard will stimulate me to renewed exertions in favour of UNIVERSAL LIBERTY.[6]

In their exertions for the movement, Chartist leaders were to be able to count on women's own efforts. Echoing the feelings of many FCAs, that of Blackwood affirmed that they 'consider[ed] it a duty incumbent upon [them] as a society . . . to ease the rugged path of persecution . . . by showing [the imprisoned patriots] that [they were] determined to render all the assistance in their power towards carrying the principles of the Charter into law'.[7]

Despite their willingness to support the cause to the best of their ability, the women considered their own part to be that of mere auxiliaries, while regarding male exertions to be pivotal. This view was even shared by Susanna Inge. She conveyed the feebleness of female political exertions by picturing woman, aroused by the social misery surrounding her, as 'embark[ing] with her light boat upon the ocean of agitation, to assist in steering the shattered bark of liberty to a smooth and sheltered haven'.[8]

The women's high esteem for their efforts sustained Chartist prisoners psychologically, thus helping to alleviate their sufferings. As Roberts wrote in reply to an address from Trowbridge FCA:

> But talk of it and laugh at it as we may, fetters *are* galling, dungeons *are* both cold and gloomy, and solitary confinement, with scanty and unwholesome food, are but a poor prospect for men with active minds and energies ennobled by a cause like ours; and therefore it is that we so desire your sympathies, prayers, and exertions, and prize so dearly every proof of your will and approbation. . . . Again let me thank you for the kind and generous feeling with which you have ever received me. The knowledge of this has been a solace and a joy, at times when sadness and gloom might else have overwhelmed me.[9]

Of all the Chartist leaders, Vincent was undoubtedly the one enjoying the highest degree of popularity among the female membership. The ease with which he related to those in his constituency, in the south-west of England and in Wales, was never achieved by O'Connor, who, as a national figure, was somewhat remote, and as the 'father' of the movement enjoyed the respect rather than the affection of female Chartists. The women consistently addressed Vincent as 'brother' in what Blackwood FCA termed 'the language and feelings of sisterly affection',[10] while he reciprocated by calling them 'sisters'. Only as late as 1846 did Harney make a habit of addressing Chartists as 'brothers and sisters';[11] but, with him, the practice remained one-sided.

The language of kinship was thus being used as a metaphor to refer to fellow-Chartists as members of an extended family. In the communication between Chartist men and women, the use of such language indicates a strong feeling of class solidarity. Yet the same terms also served to express solidarity along gender lines, as the many FCA statements addressing other Chartist women as sisters (presented in Chapter 4) demonstrate.

Vincent was cast in the role of female Chartists' communal brother, who valiantly engaged in the struggle for the Charter.[12] In return for his efforts, Vincent's female supporters were prepared physically to defend and protect him from political enemies.[13]

Vincent endeared himself to women by the high value he placed on their influence both within Chartism and society at large (as noted in Chapter 4). The meetings he attended gave cheers regularly for 'our wives, sweethearts, and ourselves'.[14] Moreover, true to his belief in women's centrality, he took practical steps towards involving them in Chartism. When touring the country he was in the habit of convening exclusively female meetings at nearly every locality he visited.[15] He was the only Chartist leader who is known to have done so.

Women responded warmly to Vincent's high estimation of female exertions.[16] He himself was well aware of his effect on women. Reporting on a meeting he had convened at Stroud he remarked: 'I flatter myself that I have made nearly all the women of Stroud Radicals.'[17] He took a genuine delight in the many FCAs that formed, not least through his own doing. This comes across in the following announcement in *The Western Vindicator*: 'Mr Vincent will hold a Meeting of his excellent friends, the Ladies of Bath, at the earliest opportunity. He is very desirous of meeting them all again, and again.'[18]

Vincent's convening of single-sex meetings might have been attributable to a certain awareness on his part of the intimidating effects on women of dominant male behaviour at sexually mixed events. This is indicated at least by his attempts to make sure that the male Chartists of a given locality would be otherwise engaged at the time of the female meeting. The announcement of a women-only gathering at Hull concluded thus: 'The Meeting being exclusively for the Ladies, the MEMBERS of the WORKING MEN'S ASSOCIATION, are requested to meet on the same evening at the ROYAL OAK, Blackfriargate, at Half-past Seven o'clock, on important business.'[19]

Of course, men were extremely curious to know what went on at such exclusively female gatherings with Vincent. On one occasion, a crowd of around 4000 women assembled in a park outside Bath to receive him, while vast numbers were unable to gain admittance. Except for Vincent himself, no man was allowed to witness the proceedings. Gammage, the only authentic historian of Chartism (introduced in Chapter 2), gave the following account of this meeting:

> It so happened, however, that notwithstanding this prohibition, a member of the rougher sex, with a curiosity that might have been excused in one of the gentle fair, by ensconcing himself in female attire gained admission to the gardens. The trick was, however, speedily discovered, and almost as speedily communicated to the meeting, who in the best possible humour buffeted the intruder from their presence.[20]

This account is significant for the gender-specific stereotypes it purports. While downplaying male disquiet at Vincent's pull on women, Gammage seems to have regarded the intruder's conduct as somewhat unworthy of a member of the male sex, considering curiosity a typically female characteristic.

Gammage, while noting Vincent's appeals for female elevation, could not help attributing his sway over women to his attractive appearance: 'With the fair sex his slight handsome figure, the merry twinkle of his eye, his incomparable mimicry . . . rendered him an universal favourite.' In the West Country in particular, women enrolled in FCAs in large numbers and, according to Gammage, displayed even more enthusiasm than the men in their support of the movement. For him, the reason for this was obvious: 'Doubtless the fascinating personal qualities of Vincent had their share in rousing the patriotism of these fair Democrats',[21] and this although Gammage found him very illogical in his speeches.

True, there was a certain touch of gallantry about Vincent's relationship with female Chartists, added to, no doubt, by the fact that he was single (he married in 1841). At Trowbridge in 1838, a young woman presented him with a silk scarf on behalf of the single women, while William Carrier, a local Chartist and a married man, received one from the married female Chartists of that town.[22]

The message of Gammage's assessment of Vincent's relationship with female Chartists, however, is clear. For him it was inconceivable that women's political commitment should be attributable to their accepting what were presented to them as the best means of improving their condition. Instead, he saw their involvement as hinging on a male personality. He held this man's attractiveness and oratorical skill to have a greater impact on women's political attitude than the ideas put forward. Underlying this interpretation of Vincent's relationship with women was a view of the latter as deficient in mental penetration and as easily swayed by appearance. With regard to anti-feminism, Gammage was thus a good match for O'Connor, whom in other respects he so scorned.

Gammage was right in pointing to the strongly personal element in women's relationship with Chartist leaders, which, however, operated differently from the way insinuated. The kinship relations to male Chartists that brought women into the movement in the first place were transferred to its leaders. The latter assumed the role of the strong male, for instance by acting the part of the collective father, as in O'Connor's case, or brother, as in Vincent's, striving to afford women the protection they sought from the adverse impact of social change on their lives as wives and mothers. They expected Chartism to reinstate them in what they conceived of as their rightful position of mothers of the family, according to the motto on the banner carried by Warwick women at the Birmingham demonstration to celebrate O'Connor's release from gaol: 'The rights of women – instruction, affection, protection'.[23]

Those leaders who most energetically devoted themselves to the Chartist struggle, as did O'Connor – or who most vociferously denounced those aspects of the new social order women suffered from worst – thereby rendered themselves extremely popular with female Chartists. J. R. Stephens, for instance, never tired of condemning the evil effects inflicted on the family by the New Poor Law and the factory system. He therefore was another of the women's champions.

Following Stephens's arrest at Leigh, the female Chartists of that locality expressed their regret at this incident and assured him of their moral, financial and religious support. They particularly praised his exertions on behalf of women, stating:

> We also reflect with exquisite pleasure on the eloquent, the tender and generous manner in which you plead the cause of

the female – the poor, defenceless, and almost unprotected, the overlooked and undervalued female, whose misery in the distress of her country has been almost forgotten. . . . We have long viewed with heartfelt sorrow the infringement oppression has made on our rights and liberties; and our best thanks are due, and the finest feelings of our nature are sensibly alive to all those noble-minded men who are using every effort to unnerve the strong arm of tyranny, and thus release us from its iron grasp.[24]

Apparently, the women felt strongly the need for male denouncers of their suffering who showed an awareness of their plight.

Chartist leaders, by devoting themselves to a struggle aiming at an order of society that would afford women the protection they felt in need of (as noted in Chapter 2), anticipated the restructured gender relations Chartists expected to follow from the attainment of the Charter (as also argued in Chapter 2). In the conditions of unchallenged male hegemony then established, all working-class men would be reinstated in their position of protectors of their families, a position that the Chartists of either sex assumed naturally to appertain to men. In this vein, Nottingham FCA called on Chartist women to urge their male kinfolk 'to consider themselves bound by the sacred ties of nature – to protect and shield their wives and children from that system of cruelty and starvation now stalking through the land'.[25] Other Chartists took it for granted (as already noted in Chapter 2) that the 'slavery' of their wives and daughters which 'Englishmen' had to witness would incite them to rebellion.[26] This view implied that female suffering and degradation, apart from the plight of the women concerned, signalled the diminution of the hegemony of men whose function of protector was being eroded.

The same reasoning underlay the address of the female Chartists of Upper Honley and Smallthorn in which they reminded men of their duty to protect their families – a duty, moreover, incumbent on them as destined by nature to be the 'strong' sex:

Men, (we appeal to you), should this be so? you who pride yourselves on your superior intellect, strength and courage; should you be apathetic; you, with all your boasted advantages, should you be indifferent to the suffering [sic] privations and

destitution of your wives, your children and yourselves? Surely
not. It cannot be, that the father of a family can endure to see
the wife of his bosom, the children of his love, pine and die for
want, when a remedy lies open before his eyes, a remedy easy
to be obtained and only wanting the united energies of labour's
sons to obtain that which would at once and for ever arrest the
downward march of labour's children, and put an end to all
those evils now so severely felt by all.[27]

In its agitation of working-class men, too, the Chartist
movement played on male pretensions to act as the protectors of
their families. An advertisement of a public meeting at Darlington
appealed to them thus: 'Working Classes, attend, your wives, your
children, and your homes are at stake!!!'[28]

These pretensions, moreover, probably helped arouse the
sympathy of the middle classes. In their wish to act as the head of
the family, Chartist men knew themselves to be in unison with all
men regardless of class allegiance. In a public address to the
middle classes, the Council of Durham County Charter Association cited the misery of their families as the motivating force of
their Chartist commitment and as proof of their disdaining
violence and militancy.[29]

Conversely, the very same family commitment was adduced by
Chartists at a Birmingham meeting as instigating them to violent
action. The motto on their banner read: 'For our Children and
Wives / War to the Knife – so help us God.'[30] And at the dinner
following an Anti-Poor Law demonstration at Newcastle, this toast
was proposed: 'Our country women - our mothers, our wives, and
our daughters; they never shall be *slaves*, nor insulted by Poor
Law Despots.'[31]

While believing it to be men's duty to provide for their families,
moral-force Chartists were not prepared to condone resort to
violence in doing so. Lowery recalled attending a meeting at
Newcastle at which the speaker exclaimed: 'If I had a wife I
would fight for her, I would die for her!' One in a group of
working-class women was thereupon overheard by Lowery as
remarking rather sceptically: 'He doesn't say he would work for
her!' According to the author, 'This woman understood the duty
of man.'[32]

It was in fact not least in order to alleviate working-class
women's lot that men committed themselves to Chartism. Take

Richard Pilling, a powerloom weaver from Stockport, who later moved to Ashton, where he became a local Chartist leader. He had to stand trial for the prominent part he had played in the 1842 Plug Plot. His commitment to the movement was motivated not least by his wish to defend the interests of his family, which, in his belief, hinged on defending those of the working class as a whole. In his famous defence speech, with which he achieved his discharge, he exposed the condition and treatment of women factory workers, describing in detail the long hours they had to work, sustained by insufficient nourishment, and how they had to have their babies brought into the factories for breastfeeding.[33]

It is true that in his defence, Pilling was carefully trying to evade the political charges brought against him. But the wider context of the Chartist movement lends credibility to his presenting the wish to alleviate his own wife's and all other working women's plight as the chief motive of his actions.

In the political sphere, male hegemony was preserved (as noted in Chapter 4) by defining women's commitment to Chartism as an extension of female domestic concerns into the public arena, necessitated and legitimised by the working-class experience of crisis. Consequently, women's political involvement never lost its extraordinary aspect.[34] Given the amazement male Chartists felt at the scale and scope of women's commitment to the movement, FCAs could be held up in the Chartist press to set their male counterparts an example of political efficiency. Underlying this device was the belief that men had a natural propensity for political business, while it required great exertion on the part of women to translate their political motivation into efficient action. Women's achievements in this respect were therefore bound to help spur men into action in order to affirm their superiority in the political sphere.

For the able conduct of their business, some FCAs were instanced as examples to the men, along the lines of the following comment on the ELFPA:

The business-like manner in which this association conducts its proceedings, reflects not only great credit upon the president, secretary and committee, but on the members generally; and offers an example worthy of imitation by many men's associations we have visited; fully proving the capability of woman to think and act for herself, a privilege too often denied them by men professing the most ultra-radical principles.[25]

This complimentary comment may have been well deserved by the ELFPA, which (as has been noted in section 2 of the preceding chapter) displayed at least rudimentary female self-awareness. The extent to which other FCAs did present examples of women thinking and acting for themselves will be further discussed below.

Reports about the progress of FCAs commonly noted that the Chartist women were about to outnumber the men in a given locality.[36] Moreover, competition between the male and female sections of the movement were directed towards tasks at hand.[37]

It was precisely because of the extraordinary aspect of female political commitment that Chartists believed women to be in some roles more effective political agents than men. The resolution adopted at a meeting of female operatives at Ashton-under-Lyne to appoint women to go round collecting for the National Rent drew the following comment from *The Northern Star*: 'We confidently anticipate, that no man can refuse the applications of these fair patriots, who are laying aside their natural timidity, in hopes to mend their unhappy condition, by assisting to make the People's Charter the law of the land.'[38]

Chartist women themselves were aware that their commitment could incite men to exert themselves. Caroline Maria Williams, the independent-minded Bristol Chartist (introduced in the preceding chapter) urged her Chartist sisters thus:

> Remember the eyes of the men are fixed on us, and if they can but see we are in real earnest about the matter, there is not a man of them who would not rather die to attain with us our freedom, than turn aside ingloriously. Unity is strength. Our aid added to the men's will soon make our tyrants yield to us our rights, or perish.[39]

In 1848, the female Chartists of London resolved to unite in the fight for the Charter, thereby removing themselves as impediments to their menfolk's political commitment. Considering love of their family to be the chief motive of male actions, the women regarded their own political involvement as decisive for politicising men. They maintained that

The feeling of love, which now engenders fear, would act in the opposite direction, and form a powerful ally with the love of liberty that dwells in the British bosom. Our husbands, brothers, and sons, would follow out [*sic*] example, and fear would give way to courage. The police, degraded as they are, would feel some little regard for our sex; and if they did not, our gallant troops would never shrink from the duty of defending their mothers, sisters, and daughters, who, goaded by injustice, reduced to want, subject to insult, had united for the purpose of convincing their oppressors, that union is strength, and liberty worth struggling for.[40]

The London female Chartists were convinced that their example in supporting Chartism would stir the men into action, who would thus live up to female expectations of male protection.

Ten years earlier, the women attending the founding meeting of Hanley FCA had voiced their belief that women had to take matters into their own hands as men had failed to prevent the worsening of conditions. One participant maintained: 'It's time for us to act', while another asserted that 'The men ha[d] done nothing a great while!' The women were therefore resolved to urge the men forward. As one of them observed: 'By influencing the men, we might do some good. Many husbands, if ruled by wives, would do a deal more good.'[41]

Such 'ruling' of men by women was condoned, provided that it was geared towards promoting the Charter. The women attending a public meeting at Bedlington were reported as egging their men on,[42] and, according to *The Northern Liberator*, the women at a gathering at Colne exceeded the men in enthusiasm, demanding most vociferously that they and their 'lads' should be free.[43]

With regard to the means of exercising women's 'rule', Leicester FCA resolved on its formation that if the men became apathetic they would arouse them by every moral and physical means.[44] And Mrs Lapworth, a member of Birmingham FPU, advised the women attending a Chartist soirée not to fulfil any duties for their husbands, material or immaterial, until the Charter had been passed.[45] If put into practice, such resolutions would have amounted to women refusing to attend to their domestic duties as long as men failed to take on the responsibility involved in the position of the head of the family by actively promoting Chartism. As it was, such threats remained mere rhetoric and must be read as expressing the high degree of women's determination to stir their menfolk into action.

The competition between male and female Chartists, who were officially set to vie with each other for efficiency and devotion to the cause, was the only form in which sexual antagonism was allowed to surface in the Chartist movement. Subservient as it was to the furtherance of a cause that was recognised by all as essential to the entire class, this competition effectively channelled what antagonistic feelings there were into exertions for the movement.

Yet before women were able to engage in this kind of political competition, they had to surmount the obstacles many men placed in the path of their womenfolk's political commitment. Those contemplating joining the movement were warned of men's opposition, which these female sympathisers were told to suffer in the awareness of the moral effects they would produce by thus accelerating the intended reform.[46] Although female Chartists were not necessarily cast as martyrs to the cause, there was an awareness that without her husband's or father's consent, any woman was hardly able to engage in Chartist activities, let alone join an FCA. This was why men were called upon to let their wives attend women's meetings, while at the same time being warned against unduly pressurising them into attending.[47]

Some Chartist women, however, were not willing to be pawns in men's political schemes. While believing men to be endowed with greater political rights than women, the female Chartists of Carlisle held the former's right to freedom to be conditional upon their granting the latter the right to make up their own minds about political issues. As they maintained in their address to O'Connor: 'If men have a right to *freedom* they must prove that right by maintaining for women *their* sacred right of *judgment, reason,* and *opinion.*'[48]

Chartism's persistent casting of women as the female kinfolk of male activists rendered difficult the task of involving those who could not rely on male relatives for introduction into the movement. Calling on the women of London and its vicinity, the Metropolitan Delegate Meeting urged every wife to accompany her husband to Chartist meetings and every other 'female' to go with her brother, sweetheart or other relative. Women lacking Chartist kinfolk were encouraged to go along nevertheless. Doing so was portrayed as one of the duties incumbent upon the female sex.

Furthermore, participation in Chartist activities would place them on a more equal footing with men, rendering them more valuable, more endearing to 'those to whom God ha[d] given [them], as his choicest gift, his greatest blessing'.[49] Quite blatantly, women were encouraged to join Chartism as a means of enhancing their sexual value. On top of being a competent housewife and earning her own upkeep, a good working-class woman was expected to be a committed Chartist. By thus fulfilling male requirements, unaccompanied women engaged in Chartist activities did not, in this sense, transgress the boundaries of working-class femininity, since their actions were solely geared towards meeting male expectations.

This argument could be turned on its head by portraying only men committed to Chartism as worthy of women's love. This is what Watkins did in the following passage:

> The beautiful are the best, and those who possess beauty will not be backward in true bravery. As all the honest among men are Chartists, we shall consider none among the women to be beautiful but those who are Chartists. 'None but the brave deserve the fair!' Women used formerly to set their lovers a task to prove their love. In the age of chivalry, a man could have no pretensions to the hand of a woman, much less to her heart – she would give him neither – she would give him nothing but scorn, unless he could boast of some noble deed of benevolence. Women were wont to arm the men for battle. Let them smile on the Chartists, and encourage them to seek that freedom, without which a man is not worthy [of] a "woman's love!".[50]

Women adopted the same line of argument themselves. The members of Ashton FCA were determined not to have relationships with men other than avowed Chartists:

> we are determined that no man shall ever enjoy our hands, our hearts, or share our beds, that will not stand forward as the advocate of the rights of man, and as the determined enemies of the damnable New Poor Law . . . be sure then to remind your husbands, fathers, brothers, sons, and kinsmen all, that he that is willing to live a slave deserves not the smiles of a lady!!![51]

In the same vein, Chartist leaders, such as Harney, called upon the women to practise exclusive dealing both in trading and in loving as a means of converting men to Chartism.[52] At the founding meeting of Newcastle FPU, Harney emphasised that 'He would not recognise that man as a Democrat who did not love his mother – (loud cheers) – his sweetheart or his wife; and if they would emancipate their fatherland, they would only do it with the assistance of the females.' The last speaker to address the meeting underlined the importance of Chartist women inciting the men to acts of bravery.[53] These remarks highlight the way in which Chartists conceived of the interrelation between class politics and gender relations. Female political commitment was seen as enhancing a woman's sexual value by ensuring her acquiescence in her husband's political activities. With regard to male activists, on the other hand, regard for women's concerns was defined as an indispensable ingredient of a democrat.

Although welcoming women at all kinds of meetings, the legitimising by Chartists of female political involvement can be seen via the manner in which female presence was reported about. Numerous women attended a public meeting at Bridgeton (to take just one example from *The Northern Star*), 'who seemed to pay the deepest attention to the proceedings'.[54] Again and again, the reports emphasised the seriousness and understanding displayed by female Chartists in an attempt at refuting all allegations that the large-scale presence of women diminished the earnestness of the Chartist struggle. In so far as they were intended to combat internal opposition to female involvement, these reports testify to the extent that male Chartists needed converting to this idea. With regard to external opposition, this manner of reporting proves the movement to be a champion of women's right to become politically active (as already noted in Chapter 4).

In his memoirs, Lowery recalled a meeting at Carlisle, at which he exposed the reduction of wages as the chief cause that forced all members of the family to work. His speech was very well received, but what he valued highest was the response of a young woman, whom he described thus: 'she was some twenty years of age, had a Saxon face, with a fair complexion, light hair, expressive blue eyes, and an intellectual forehead, while her coarse vestments could not conceal her graceful form'.[55] She seems to have been overwhelmed by what she had heard, for she grasped me [Lowery] by the hand, not in a forward manner, a soul of feeling was in her eyes. She uttered no words; the utterance was in the grasp and look. We stood as if both were mesmerized for a minute, when the pressure of others seemed to recall her recollections; she unclasped her hand, but still spoke not, and passed away.

It was this kind of soul-stirring response that Chartist speakers sought to arouse among the female section of their audience in particular. This ambition implies a view of women as standing in need of political enlightenment to be brought to them by men. Once having grasped a political idea, however, women were believed to be able to cling to it more devotedly than any man was thought to be capable of.

This was why Chartists professed that once women took up the cause, success was certain. O'Brien, for instance, claimed in *The Northern Star*:

Let the women of the manufacturing districts only make common cause with the men, as they are now doing in Birmingham, and I will venture to say that within twelve months they will have done more for Universal Suffrage than the men have done for the last twenty years. Were the question ever to be decided *vi et armis*, the Radical women of England would be more than a match for all the Whig and Tory Sybarites in the three kingdoms. The very *eyes* of the women would decide the victory without a blow on either side.[56]

The chivalrous terms in which the praise of women's contribution to the movement were couched stemmed from the belief in the distinct otherness of the female character. This was assumed (as noted in Chapter 2) to render women unfit for physical exertion at the workplace and, by implication, in politics, while particularly fitting them to make a moral impact. The more highly elevated they were in this respect, the less power they actually wielded.

Yet Chartist chivalry did not stop at veiling women's lack of authority within the movement. It was moreover common practice among correspondents to remark on the latter's clothes, pointing to their respectability or even elegance. This was to be visible proof to all that women's political involvement did not impair the performance of their domestic duties, even in economically hard times.[57]

The need to emphasise the respectability of female participants in Chartist events reflects the growing restriction of women's public appearance in the middle class. Reporting on a Chartist dinner at Sheffield, the local non-Chartist paper described the women present as 'respectable-looking females, most of them without bonnets'.[58] The lack of headgear was obviously taken here as an indication of women Chartists overstepping the boundaries of female propriety. This is further corroborated by a report to the Home Office noting that a Chartist procession at Manchester was led by 'a large party of young women, very decently dressed'. They and the men following were arranged in regular file, 'and nothing could be apparently more respectful and peaceable than their demeanour'.[59] The 'apparently' indicates that the respectability of appearance and peacefulness of conduct were seen by this observer as an outer shell only just containing a violent potential that might flare up at any moment.

It was precisely to refute such suspicions that the movement drew attention to the respectablility of the women attending Chartist meetings and, according to one reporter in *The Northern Star*, furnishing 'greater inducement to order in the rougher sex'.[60] In the same vein, a meeting of Calton and Mile End FCA was said to have been crowded by a well-dressed, highly respectable assemblage of male and female Chartists, which led *The Northern Star* to conclude: 'We can state with safety that we never witnessed a better behaved or more agreeable audience.'[61]

Occasionally, mention of respectability was coupled with that of intelligence to drive home the message. Of the female Chartists attending a meeting at the National Charter Hall near the Old Bailey it was said that 'for decorum of conduct, [they] could not be surpassed, and for mental intelligence and worth, [they were] an honour to their country'.[62]

Apart from the attire of female Chartist, their beauty was regularly emphasised. At meetings, 'The number and beauty of the ladies was dazzling in the extreme'; or else a 'galaxy of female beauty' was noticed whenever 'members of the fair sex graced [a gathering] with their presence'.[63] In addition, women were frequently referred to as 'the fair sex' or quite simply as 'fair faces',[64] thus being reduced to their outward appearance.

This type of chivalrous language, while reducing women to

ornaments adorning Chartist events, simultaneously betrayed a distinct feeling of pride in the female section of the working class. Male Chartists took an obvious delight in the looks of their wives and daughters, and by applying to them the chivalrous epithets that had by then become the stock in trade of the middle classes, they tried to bring their own womenfolk into the pale of respectable womanhood, thereby claiming for them the supposed privileges already enjoyed by women of those classes. This was not the least reason why women active in the movement were consistently referred to as 'ladies'.

In addition, the emphasis on female Chartists' good looks – and this was also contained in the passage from Lowery's memoirs referred to above – underlined that their engagement in politics by no means rendered them unwomanly. Thus they were in no danger of jeopardising their 'truly feminine essence', which Chartists believed to be central to women's beneficial influence (as noted in section 2 of the preceding chapter).

In *Woman's Wrongs*, Jones, too, put forward the view of working-class women being entitled, by virtue of the qualities belonging to their sex, to the same conditions as enjoyed by the female section of the other classes of society. For him, women's claim to social equality rested on beauty, which he presented as a feature specific to the sex regardless of class. As to beauty, the milliner of Book Two of *Woman's Wrongs* is equal to any woman from the upper class, and her awareness of this equality renders even more galling her inequality with regard to possessions and easiness of life. Watching a society ball from outside, 'she felt she was as beautiful and as good as the bright, fair things that were dancing, and singing, and listening to love within'.[65] As one of the concomitants of the class system, working-class women, due to their exposure to all kinds of privation, were denied the extended enjoyment of beauty as the precondition of happiness and a title to equality. The absence of beauty in women thus served as an indication of the state of society. Society, ideally ordered, would safeguard women's physical integrity and thus preserve their beauty.

Some Chartists did not content themselves with claiming equality of beauty for their womenfolk; they even considered them to surpass their social superiors in this respect. The women who attended a grand soirée at Halifax in honour of Jones received the following compliment from one of the male speakers:

Well may Halifax be proud of its daughters, for we may safely
assert that never in the mawkish assemblies of royal courts have
we seen so great an array of female loveliness and grace, while
the face of maid and matron alike were beaming with a pure
enthusiasm and joy unknown to the worn-out votaries of
heartless fashion.[66]

This passage would suggest – and this was also insinuated in the
paragraph from Watkins's *Address to the Women of England* quoted
above – that the beauty Chartists praised in their womenfolk was
not so much a physical property, but rather a cipher both for the
pleasure men derived from having women fighting by their side
and also for the sympathy they felt with them.

Women's role of adorning Chartist events was not only
conveyed by the reports in the movement's press. When attending
formal gatherings, female Chartists were subject to a strict code of
behaviour, many elements of which were strikingly similar to
those governing middle-class women's appearance in civic life. At
indoor meetings, men and women were usually seated apart from
each other. Often the female participants were confined to the
gallery of the meeting-room, thus being effectively reduced merely
to watching the proceedings. Alternatively, female Chartists were
assigned the pit and/or boxes, or they occupied the platform.[67] Yet
wherever they sat, the seating arrangement signified them to be a
group apart.

Being admitted onto the platform along with the principal male
speakers was a distinction conferred only upon women who had
made special efforts to further the Chartist cause, usually the
leaders of the local FCA.[68]

At outdoor meetings, on the other hand, distinguished women,
such as the wives of Chartist leaders, were sometimes allowed the
use of carriages.[69] This not only ensured that they were in the best
possible position to follow the proceedings, with the vehicles
stationed near the platform or the hustings, it also spared them
the bother of being part of a large crowd.

If the function was a public dinner, which (as has been noted in
section 2 of the preceding chapter) were exclusively male affairs,
and on those occasions when women were allowed to be present
at all, they were accommodated in a separate room. Alternatively,
they were not admitted until after the meal. At the more convivial
tea parties and soirées, moreover, people sometimes had to take

turns sitting down to eat for want of room. These sittings-down could also be sexually segregated.[70]

In public, women were more restrained than men in making their feelings known. While the men present at Chartist meetings would clap their hands or cheer in order to express approval, the women would wave their handkerchiefs.[71]

The code of behaviour imposed on and adhered to by the women active in the movement, coupled with the structural impediments to women's attaining any position of prominence, amounted to an effective control of female participation in Chartism.

After the founding of the NCA, many women joined this national Chartist organisation (as noted in section 2 of the preceding chapter), either individually or as members of an FCA. The NCA rules provided for female membership by describing members as 'persons'. NCA officials, on the other hand, were consistently referred to in the male form.[72]

Accordingly, except for the exclusively female associations, there were no women holding offices in Chartist organisations. At Bradford, however, which boasted a variety of Chartist localities, at least in August 1841, two FCAs elected one of their members to be their delegate at the town's General Committee,[73] and this although such councils were no longer mentioned in the revised NCA rules of February 1841.

There is no indication of the extent to which women were able to exert any influence on these bodies. While – to cite a Scottish example for once – Dundee FCA was refused representation on the local executive by the men, Manchester FCA thanked their council for their strenuous exertions in promoting the interests of the association.[74] In the summer of 1843, Oldham FCA once and Nottingham FPU twice put up a full slate of female candidates for the elections to the General Council,[75] in whose hands lay the national government of the NCA. Obviously none of the women proposed was elected, and it remains obscure why they made the attempt in the first place.

There were, however, female delegates chosen for specific occasions. One Mrs Cooper represented the women of Bromsgrove at a meeting of the Chartist executive with delegates, and Elizabeth Ellis and Elizabeth Semper acted for Bradford FCA at a delegate meeting at York to celebrate O'Connor's release from gaol.[76] Judging by the reports in the Chartist press, these are unique examples of women striving for and actually attaining office in a Chartist body of other than exclusively female composition. Both cases seem to have been connected with Chartist celebrations of O'Connor's release from prison, an occasion certainly seen as warranting female participation at all levels.

Women found it difficult enough to take on responsibility in FCAs,[77] not to mention sexually mixed committees at higher levels within the organisational structure. Such female lack of confidence in their own political competence reinforced the movement's bid to restrict participation in important proceedings to men. All delegates to the Chartist Convention of 1839 were male, with two working-class women looking on, as was also the case at a delegate meeting at Birmingham in 1841.[78]

For a female Chartist to raise her voice at a mixed meeting was quite extraordinary – the only exceptions were the very few female lecturers (considered in section 2 of the preceding chapter). The women who did occasionally address a sexually mixed audience were distinguished activists. It was their specific task to call upon their sisters to come forward and help attain the Charter. These appeals were apparently believed to be particularly effective, coming as they did from women who had already adopted the course they advocated. Alternatively, female speakers dwelt on topics of specific concern to women.[79] Not even when female Chartists presented a prominent leader with a mark of their esteem was the accompanying address necessarily read out by a woman.[80]

The majority of the women speaking before sexually mixed audiences were distinguished from the ordinary female members of the movement. Some of them, such as Catherine Moore of Carlisle, Mrs Whitaker of Bath or Mrs Campbell of Sunderland,[81] held official positions within their local FCA, which gave them a certain standing. Others were related to male Chartists who had attained local prominence, such as Mrs Lapworth of Birmingham,[82] or Mrs Cully of Leicester, whose father, Thomas Raynor Smart, had been one of the earliest radical leaders of the county. She chaired a huge meeting, allegedly attended by around 4000 people, at which Leicester FCA was re-formed.[83] It would therefore appear that close familial ties with famous male Chartists gave the women concerned the confidence required to speak publicly, thus inevitably attracting a great deal of attention.

They seem to have used their family's reputation to legitimise their behaving in such a 'forward' manner, while simultaneously being able to rely on this very reputation for a favourable reception.

Their behaviour stood in stark contrast to that of politically active women, such as Emma Martin and Margaret Chapellsmith, two of the Owenite lecturers, who, without such props, expertly chaired and spoke at meetings, and also proposed and seconded motions.[84]

Of the very few female Chartist lecturers, at least Mary Ann Walker keenly felt the extraordinary character of her appearance in public. There is a detailed report about her first lecture, which took place at the National or Complete Suffrage Association Hall, High Holborn, and dealt with the social evils afflicting the state, and the Charter as the only remedy. The fact that the lecturer was female resulted in a great number of women attending. Mary Ann appeared in the company of many friends, including some women, and was enthusiastically greeted, with only a few hisses. Her friends may have been brought along to sustain her morally. After a detailed description of her dress, her unusual wanness was ascribed to her anxiety to do justice to her subject and to satisfy her audience. It testified to the stress involved for a woman in speaking before a mixed audience. In his introductory remarks, the chairman showed himself to be delighted to have one of 'the softer sex' advocating the principles of the Charter. Being destined to remove the evils from which people suffered, the 'female class' ought to be considered the best of 'propagators' of the cause. He praised Mary Ann and Susanna Inge for coming forward for the cause of humanity, and finished by asking the audience to listen without interruption, since it was Mary Ann Walker's first address to a large assembly. She began by expressing her awareness of the difficulty of her situation. But in view of her country's and her brothers' and sisters' sufferings, she had no apology to make for presenting herself. She came out at her country's call, thence her boldness to step out of her retirement. She went on to describe the misery of the people, particularly of the women, and suggested that those in need ought to be paid with money that would be gained by reducing the support given to the Royal Family. She ably dealt with interruptions from some Tories, and consistently instanced the prevailing misery by its effects on women. She concluded by saying that if her coming out saved at least one individual, she would feel herself repaid despite all consequences. When she had finished, Emma Miles, the president of Mary Ann's City of London FCA, moved and one Mrs Watts seconded the thanks of the meeting in what can be interpreted as a show of solidarity with a sister who had thus exposed herself. As a prelude to lecturing, Mary Ann had participated in the discussion following a lecture by a male Chartist.[85]

Female speakers were highly praised for their efforts. At a meeting of Birmingham FPU that was also attended by men, these were said to have been 'enraptured' by the female president's speech.[86] And this is how *The Northern Star* reported about a speech by Mrs Langston, often dubbed the 'Mary Wollstonecraft of Bilston'. At a tea party there, 'a highly intelligent female', that is Mrs Langston, addressed the meeting in a 'neat and exceedingly clever manner', pointing out the necessity of interrupting the dancing so that those absent at the beginning could hear the invited speakers.[87]

The following account of Susanna Inge's lecturing activities contains the whole range of Chartist motifs of chivalry. It noted the combination of beauty and intelligence discernible in the female lecturer as well as very favourably comparing her faculties with those of male speakers, and proceeded to conclude from this evidence women's entitlement to political rights:

> a young lady of prepossessing appearance, who, with an energy and spirit, worthy the great and glorious cause – 'The People's Charter' – which she has in company with so many others of the high and virtuous-minded women of England, taken up, delivered what may be termed a very splendid lecture – a lecture which, we may without flattery say, would do honour to the highest talents of man, and which proved that woman, 'mentally' considered, is in every way fitted and endowed by nature for the exercise of political rights.[88]

Significantly, the appearance of a female lecturer encouraged other women to take part in the proceedings.

Despite the strongly chivalrous overtones, such approval did imply a measure of encouragement for women to speak up publicly. Some felt thus emboldened to the degree of actually criticising Chartist proceedings. At a public festival in London to commemorate Tom Paine's birthday, one Miss Dyer stated amid loud cheers: 'It is not possible for man to be free whilst woman is a slave.' She reminded the meeting of Richard Carlile, whom she thought worth remembering along with Paine and gave as a highly applauded sentiment: 'Woman – and may she continue to detect errors.'[89]

The predominantly female character of FCA meetings, which were usually chaired by one of the association's members, did not preclude men from speaking. On them devolved the task of explaining the principles of the Charter, often with a focus on the specific benefits women and their families could expect from its attainment. They also urged women to form FCAs by detailing the advantages the latter would entail. Often, they reported on their tours of the country, reviewing the current state of the movement elsewhere, sometimes with a particular view to the progress of FCAs in other localities, even reading out an address from one of these. Their reports would include assessing outstanding Chartist incidents. Again and again, as an agitational ploy, men depicted the suffering inflicted on women by the New Poor Law and by class legislation in general. In order to impress on their audience the necessity of FCAs, women's right to political involvement as well as the value placed on female assistance were repeatedly stressed. To the same end, male speakers praised female exertions for the cause, sometimes proceeding to make suggestions for increasing the efficiency of the FCA addressed, often by recommending exclusive dealing.

Male speakers thus provided members' vital links with those branches of the movement beyond the boundaries of an FCA's locality. While highlighting the manner in which Chartist women, unlike their male companions, were tied to their home community by family commitments, these speeches also testify to the deliberate efforts the movement made to involve its female members in Chartist activities nationally.

In addition, men often played the part of political advisers to FCAs, thereby satisfying a demand from Chartist women, who wanted to take advantage of the political experience accumulated by the movement's leaders. An address to Vincent, currently imprisoned in Monmouth Gaol, from Wotton-under-Edge FCA praised him for his unceasing political activity stating that 'though [he was] immured in a dungeon far from [them, they] still enjoy[ed] [his] valuable counsel and advice, of which [they] at the present time [stood] in need'.[90]

At the founding meeting of Hanley FCA, which originated with women, one Mrs Timmis was voted to the chair. 'The CHAIRESS, as she was termed', read the newspaper report on this event, 'after taking her seat said, that not being able herself to explain the object for which they were assembled, she hoped some gentleman would undertake the task.' R. J. Richardson, the author of *The Rights of Woman* (analysed in Chapter 2) then began to speak. The following meeting was to be attended by another male Chartist, for, as one woman affirmed: 'We are only scholars, learning the ABC of it.'[91]

Chartist leaders were only too happy to comply with the women's request.[92] In September 1838, Mrs Lapworth concluded the proceedings at a meeting of Birmingham FPU by thanking the male speakers thus: 'It was true as yet the women knew little of politics, but they were daily becoming better acquainted with them and ought to be thankful to these gentlemen who took the trouble to instruct them.'[93]

Requests for such instruction, however, were not made indiscriminately. Another meeting of Birmingham FPU did not want to be addressed by Salt – despite the respect they felt they owed him as the founder of their association (as noted in section 2 of the preceding chapter).[94] By this time, the FPU had begun to diverge from Salt's political views, which had a strong middle-class bias. This incident indicates that the hierarchical relationship between FCAs and their male advisers did not necessarily preclude criticism on the women's part.

Yet the overall division of political labour along sexual lines remained unquestioned. A month later, Birmingham FPU's president reaffirmed that 'women were obliged to sue for countenance to men', deploring that during the London sitting of the Chartist Convention, women had had to speak themselves, for lack of Chartist men available for the purpose.[95]

Many FCAs seem to have been adopted, as it were, by one local male leader, who would speak and dispense his advice to the association on a regular basis. The ELFPA was frequently addressed by Charles Neesom.[96] He had already been present at the founding meeting of the LFDA, as the ELFPA had initially been called (as explained in section 2 of the preceding chapter), which he had addressed at the women's request.[97] He was not only a member of the London Democratic Association, the LFDA's male counterpart, but also married to the latter's secretary. The male political advisers were not frowned upon as intruders into a female realm, but rather seen as helpers easing the latter's entry into the male domain of politics.

The degree to which many FCAs relied on male help disproves the claim quoted above, which *The Northern Star* had made with regard to the ELFPA, namely that the female section of the movement afforded woman the scope of 'fully proving [her] capability . . . to think and act for herself'.[98] The fact that even the ELFPA, whose rules and regulations (as noted in section 2 of the preceding chapter) safeguarded against male intrusion, frequently turned to its secretary's husband for guidance, indicates the scale of influence that Chartist men were able to exert on FCAs and which enabled them to check what tendencies towards a degree of female autonomy there might have existed.

While Chartists such as Vincent and Harney, as variously noted, sincerely wished women to take an active part in the movement, other sections of Chartism encouraged female participation to a far lesser degree. The prime example of this attitude was the LWMA, which, at the organisational level, treated women in very much the same way as Lovett, its prime mover, did his wife at home (as analysed in Chapter 5).

The attitude towards women displayed in the Association's address is one of paternalist benevolence aimed at using them for the LWMA's aims. Men are seen as those among whom political ideas generate, which it is then their duty to impart to their wives, thus raising them to their own level. Women are only regarded as participating in the men's knowledge, but unable to develop any ideas of their own, let alone theories. Consequently women are implicitly excluded from membership. Women, who passively absorb knowledge but do not actively seek for it, never come within the range of the address, directed as it is at 'fellow labourers in the pursuit of knowledge'.[99]

Although women's participation in the Chartist movement was warmly welcomed and in many ways encouraged, the code of female Chartist behaviour was strikingly similar, in several respects, to that at work in middle-class campaigns, which were extremely hesitant about admitting women into their ranks. Serious misgivings militated against respectable female speakers addressing 'promiscuous assemblies'. Even when women were allowed to attend public meetings, propriety was preserved by segregating the seating, a strategy with respectable ecclesiastical precedents. One frequently employed method consisted in relegating women to the gallery.

Within Chartism, women were confined to a subordinate position. They were constricted by a code of behaviour geared towards a respectability of distinctly middle-class overtones; their public speech was channelled into utterances of familial and community concerns; structural stumbling-blocks were put in the way of those women striving for positions of prominence. These subtly operating mechanisms extended even into the inner life of FCAs, which, at the organisational level, functioned as mere adjuncts to their male counterparts. On a larger scale, FCAs thus held the position of auxiliaries assigned, on a smaller scale, to the individual woman in the family. Chartism's behavioural requirements, coupled with the restriction of women to inferior positions, were modelled on the sexual division of labour and power characteristic of the plebeian household. This (as has been noted in Chapter 1) was being eroded by industrialisation, a development that the Chartist movement tried to counteract by enforcing unchallenged male hegemony within its own ranks in anticipation of the gender relations it aimed at establishing after the attainment of the Charter. In this attempt, the movement met with little resistance on women's part. Stretched on the rack as they were by the increased difficulty of meeting their families' demands in an expanding capitalist system, most working-class women seem to have gladly given themselves up to social and political protection by men who professed to know, and to lead, the way out of working-class misery.

8
Working-class Women's Post-Chartist Activities

In 1848, with the presentation of the third petition praying for universal suffrage, Chartism reached its third and final climax. This was less intense than the two preceding ones of 1839 and 1842, and foreshadowed the movement's definite decline. As in 1839, the petition's rejection sparked off clandestine preparations for violent outbreaks, this time both in the north and in London, but the Chartist risings at Bradford and elsewhere were soon overpowered by the combined forces of police and military. Wholesale arrests of the movement's leaders – both national and local – began in June 1848. Within a few months, the futility of all attempts to establish the Charter by force had been brought home to even the most militantly inclined.

Those few who remained committed to the cause despite this major – and, as it turned out, lethal – defeat assembled in London at the end of March 1851 and adopted a *Programme of Agitation*, which spelt out what had by then become encapsulated within the slogan 'The Charter and Something More'. This programme differed from the previous petitions in that the emphasis had shifted from the Six Points to the social reforms to be introduced subsequent to the winning of the Charter. Foremost among these was the nationalisation of land and the exclusive levying of tax on land and accumulated property.[1]

Despite the shift of emphasis, which testified both to the attempt at tapping fresh reservoirs of support and to the influence exerted by socialist ideas, the programme essentially failed to transcend the radical frame of reference that had been the hallmark of Chartist ideology (as argued in Chapter 2). Still attributing the ultimate cause of working-class misery to 'class government', the programme put forward the extension of the franchise to working men as the precondition for implementing the social changes outlined. This inability to accommodate the

247

reforms enacted by the state over the past decade or so (as claimed in Chapter 2) lay at the heart of the utter failure to restore to the movement the mass following it had once commanded. Thus Chartism petered out, although the NCA dragged on a crippled existence until 1860 when it was finally dissolved.

The falling away of mass support was of course also reflected in the dwindling number of women involved in Chartism after 1848. There are, however, indications of some degree of female presence where local associations did survive.[2] *The People's Paper* was devoted to chronicling Chartist activities, and judging by it reports in 1858 – the last year of its existence – social events had by then come to preponderate over directly political ones, and it was predominantly in the former that women continued to participate. In the period of Chartism's long-drawn-out death, they were completely marginalised.

In Sheffield, however, women, at least initially, adopted a rather different course. The Sheffield Female Radical Association had evolved in 1839[3] and was one of the longest-lived FCAs in England, continuing until 1851. In that year, it began a new phase in its existence. In January, Mrs Rooke, one of Sheffield FCA's members, received a letter from the Chelmsford Quaker Anne Knight. She had been born in 1792 and was to live until 1862, devoting her life to conducting a single-handed campaign for women's rights. She had been involved in the anti-slavery cause, but the refusal of the Anti-Slavery Conference held in London in June 1840 to accept female delegates deeply affronted her, hardening her determination to advocate women's rights. Apart from lecturing on this issue at peace and temperance gatherings, she brought out two-inch leaflets with quotations from whatever source she could find in support of female suffrage. The first of these seems to have appeared around 1847. In it she based her demand for female franchise on the necessity of bringing to bear on the country at large the combined qualities of men and women, conceived of as complements, in order to ensure the best possible government of the nation.[4] Moreover, she wrote copious letters and followed and tracked down every person or organisation that could remotely be influenced in favour of female enfranchisement. One of her correspondents was Isaac Ironside.

Ironside, a Chartist and Owenite, had by the late 1840s become the undisputed leader of Sheffield Chartism. In 1851, he passed on to Anne the names of seven local Chartist women eager to take action on female suffrage.[5] It may well have been his commitment to Owenism that rendered him sensitive and sympathetic to this issue.

Sheffield FCA had had a tradition of female self-assertion. The association (as noted in section 2 of Chapter 6) had been among those that evolved without male guidance. Furthermore, very early in its existence, the Sheffield women held a soirée at which one of their number spoke on the 'necessity of admitting the female portion of society into political existence'.[6]

The seven women whose names Ironside transmitted to Anne had waited on him, requesting him with great determination to cease abstaining from voting in the Town Council, of which he was a member.[7] This would indicate that they formed the most active and energetic section of Sheffield female Chartism.

Thus, on 20 January 1851, a letter came to be penned at Chelmsford to Mrs Rooke, one of the seven named. Anne called on the Sheffield women to press for a revision of the Charter to encompass female suffrage. So far, she pointed out, women had only organised to form charitable societies, whereas the gaining of female franchise was sure to effect such changes as would render charities superfluous. She urged the female Chartists not to rely on men changing their point of view, but to take action themselves by reviving the Charter thus revised.[8]

Anne was not the first woman to object to the male bias of Chartism. In 1843, a woman using the pseudonym of 'Vita' had written to *The Northern Star* to complain of Chartist delegates giving their sanction to the word 'males' instead of 'persons' in the rules of the NCA. While regarding such explicit opposition to women's rights as tainting Chartists' reputation as advanced people endowed with superior social and political knowledge, she had welcomed such open avowal of the Chartist stand on women's rights as enabling the latter to withdraw from a movement from which an improvement of their status was not to be expected. She had scathingly remarked that

> whatever may be thought by future and more enlightened ages, of the wisdom, policy and humanity of the Chartist decree, by continuing in their new constitution the civil disabilities of women, they will have earned for themselves as a body the reputation of honest men (no small price), by a public avowal of their views – so that woman may no longer remain in ignorance

of the social condition reserved for her by the movement party, who, it appears, is not yet prepared to feel an enlightened abhorrence of slavery![9]

In 1849, Anne herself had for the first time criticised the Charter for calling exclusively male suffrage 'universal'. While Joseph Barker, the editor of *The People*, to which she had addressed her letter, was not averse to granting the suffrage at least to single women,[10] Harney, her other correspondent, strongly objected – not, apparently, on principle, but on tactical grounds. He took Anne's isolation in raising the issue as proof that the time was not yet ripe for putting this demand. 'Political formulas must be the fruit of generally accepted ideas', he maintained, 'otherwise they are premature and non-effective.' This may have been why he never fulfilled his promise to publish a selection of Anne's papers. Undeterred, she took up her pen again, claiming in another letter to Harney's *Friend of the People* that the extension of the suffrage to women was dictated by common sense, for otherwise the term 'universal' would be meaningless. This time, she was not even favoured with an answer.[11]

In Sheffield, however, Anne met with a far more favourable response. On 5 February 1851, more or less immediately on receipt of her letter, a public meeting of women was held at the Democratic Temperance Hall, Queen Street, the local Chartist venue. This meeting adopted the first ever petition – to be submitted to both houses of parliament – that prayed for the enfranchisement of women. Significantly, as the Chartists had based their claim for women's right to political involvement on the existence of a female monarch (as noted in Chapter 4), so now the Sheffield women derived their claim to the suffrage from the fact that a woman enjoyed royal prerogatives.[12]

At their next meeting, the women elected a council and corresponding secretary to hold office for the ensuing three months.[13] As their Chartist predecessors, they thus continued the Jacobin tradition of rotating offices.

On 26 February 1851, an address to the women of England was adopted. Having for several years observed campaigns for the improvement of government, the Sheffield women claimed to have been 'brought to the conclusion that women might, with the strictest propriety, be included in the proclamation of the people's charter; for we are the majority of the nation, and it is our

birthright, equally with our brother, to vote for the man who is to
sway our political destiny' by imposing laws and taxes that
affected women equally with men. This argument extended the
Chartist notion of the vote as a natural right from working men as
a class to women as a sex. This presupposed the recognition of
sexual oppression as an issue apart from and additional to class
oppression. And in fact the address illustrated 'male tyranny' (as
sexual oppression was termed), by tracing it, somewhat summar-
ily, to all spheres of society, including political organisation:

> does woman not toil early and late, in the factory, and in every
> department of life, subject to the despotism of man, and we ask,
> in the name of justice, must we continue ever the silent and
> servile victims of his injustice? – to perform all drudgery of his
> political societies, and never to possess a single political right?

In order to redress this grievance, the Sheffield Women's Political
Association (also sometimes called the Sheffield Women's Rights
Association) had been formed to devote itself to the 'entire
political enfranchisement of [the female] sex'.[14]

The address was published both in *The Northern Star* and *The
Sheffield Free Press*, with *The Northern Star* version being slightly
less feminist in tone. While also containing the demand for the
inclusion of women's suffrage in the Charter, it omitted the
mention of female subjection in political societies – after all an
insight that was the result of the Sheffield women's experience
within Chartism. The address that appeared in *The Northern Star*
seems to have been revised especially for publication in that
paper, because it particularly appealed to O'Connor for support.

In March 1851, Anne herself approached O'Connor in a letter
printed in *The Northern Star*. She desired an interview with him,
obviously believing him to be sympathetic to female suffrage on
account of *The Northern Star* coverage of the Sheffield women's
activities. She intended to entreat him to make women's rights
more especially his cause, and she reiterated her critique of the
Charter for the logical inaccuracy involved in its use of the term
'universal'. Moreover, she deemed this a political injury of the
interests of women – the majority of the nation. She concluded
thus: 'My object was to endeavour to submit to thy heart-interest
this momentous cause, that men of political action may banish
from their politics the vice of sex, as nothing is more unjust than

to suffer their sisters in this state of helotage.'[15] This appeal was predictably wasted on O'Connor, whose strong anti-feminism has variously been noted.

On the other side of the Channel, however, the Sheffield women's venture was warmly welcomed by two like-minded sisters. In June 1851, the association received a letter from Paris, written by Jeanne Deroin and Pauline Roland, whose insistence on their rights had gained them a prison sentence. Jeanne Deroin, a journalist, had stood for the Constituent Assembly. Although her candidacy was declared illegal, she had managed to address a number of groups and to publicise her demand for women's right to stand for election until she was arrested. Pauline Roland had claimed her right to vote in the election both for the mayor of the town in which she had lived and for the Constituent Assembly.

Links between the French revolutionaries and Sheffield had been established in 1848, when Isaac Ironside personally delivered to the French provisional government an address adopted at a mass meeting in his home town and which hailed the recent events in France as 'the greatest revolution ever known'.[16] This may explain how the two Frenchwomen came to know about the Sheffield Women's Political Association.

In their letter, Jeanne Deroin and Pauline Roland assured the Sheffield association of the sympathy of their French sisters, emphasising that the improvement of society could never be complete without the emancipation of women. They proceeded to list the various ways in which women were subject to men, including the Constituent Assembly's neglect of female rights. They advised women, in their search for allies, to look to workers, whose willingness to support female rights supposedly grew out of working-class men's and women's common involvement in the production process. Although the Sheffield association had been formed precisely as a result of the futility of all attempts at having their rights recognised by working-class men, the letter was loudly acclaimed.[17]

The following week, the association received support from a different political quarter. J. A. Roebuck, the Radical MP, confirmed his intention of presenting the Sheffield women's petition to parliament. He explained to them, however, that while concurring with the demand for female suffrage, he would be precluded by parliamentary rules from supporting the petition's contents in the presentation speech.[18] Roebuck's previous critique of the Charter for its use of the term 'universal'[19] showed him to be an early sympathiser and may have accounted for his willingness to advocate women's cause in parliament.

In August 1851, Jeanne Deroin and Pauline Roland, in a show of practical solidarity, attempted to bring their influence to bear on Sheffield's male Chartists by sending them a letter. They again attacked the Charter for omitting the demand for female suffrage, reminding the Chartists that the liberty and equality of a society were conditional upon the latter's extension to men and women alike, for, they maintained, 'Man wishing to constitute liberty for man alone only constitutes the right of might. Man wishing to constitute equality only amongst men constitutes partiality.' They furthermore asserted that prejudices depriving women of political influence were a relic of barbarity when only the right of the strongest had been recognised. Establishing women's equality was a precondition for children developing into good citizens, for this required the abolition of man's preponderance over his wife and children to maintain their dependence. According to the two Frenchwomen, the Charter needed to be turned from a programme for the benefit of the male working class into one for the universal improvement of the condition of everyone suffering from deprivation. They emphasised that 'The work of enfranchisement [could] not be complete and durable but by the radical extinction of all privileges of sex, race, caste, birth and fortune.'[20]

The men on the Sheffield Chartist Council responded with the prevaricating attitude so common among those Chartists not prepared to condemn outright the demand for female suffrage. They unanimously subscribed to the principles set out in the letter and acknowledged the defect in the Charter itself. This, they were convinced, would be obliterated some day in the future. However, the unanimous acceptance of the Frenchwomen's criticism is an important pointer to the political atmosphere in which the self-assertion displayed by the Sheffield women was able to thrive.[21]

On O'Connor's visit to the town in November 1851, the association renewed its attempt at inducing him to throw in his weight behind their campaign.[22] Appreciation of his past exertions on behalf of Chartism seems to have overridden any possible questioning of his stand of strong and explicit anti-feminism.

A less illustrious, but far more sympathetic, visitor arrived about the end of that month, however. Speaking to the association,

Anne reiterated why she held women to be entitled to the vote and instanced the unsuccessful female struggle for the suffrage. By way of concluding, she suggested the adoption of a memorial to the Home Secretary praying for universal male and female suffrage.[23]

In the meantime, the Sheffield women had appointed one George Hows their agent. His job was to establish sister organisations everywhere on the model of the Sheffield association. The women also contemplated sending out two of their number as missionaries.[24] This manner of proceeding was strikingly similar to that of FCAs, which (as noted in section 2 of Chapter 6) had spawned sister associations in other parts of the country. WMAs, moreover, had also sent out missionaries to agitate for the Charter. The necessity of building up their own network may have been due both to the movement's reluctance to let the women use Chartist connections and to the women's refusal to rely on an organisation they were breaking away from.

The Sheffield example was in fact followed in Glasgow, Leeds, Edinburgh and several other places. Encouraged by such success, the women, in May 1852, adopted a plan for national organisation and established a National Woman's Rights Association with Anne as its first president.[25]

Reports in *The Northern Star* on the association's activities continued until 1 May 1852. By then, the initiative for improving women's condition seems to have passed to the middle class. In July 1851, Harriet Taylor had published an article on 'The Enfranchisement of Women' in the *Westminster Review*. In May 1852, as *The Northern Star* was able to inform its readers, the Woman's Elevation League, predominantly middle class in tone and social composition, was formed with Anne as a member of its council.[26] It remains unclear whether she had by then severed her connection with the National Woman's Rights Association or whether she had brought the latter with her into the League. This was rather a short-lived venture, too, and more than a decade was to elapse until middle-class women's sustained campaign for the franchise took off.

The Sheffield association's rootedness in Chartism has already been noted with regard to the arguments it put forward and the political strategy it employed. Nor were its activities confined to campaigning for female suffrage. Like any Chartist body, it concerned itself with a variety of radical issues. In true Chartist style, it even held a bazaar to raise money for the local Refugee Fund.[27]

In addition, there was some overlap between the personnel of the local FCA and the Woman's Rights Association. Furthermore, the Democratic Temperance Hall, the traditional local Chartist venue, at which the association met, belonged to one G. Cavill, who was very likely to have been a sympathiser if not active in the movement himself. One Mrs Cavill, certainly his wife, served as the association's treasurer at some point.[28]

For some of its female members, Chartism had provided a period of political apprenticeship, in the sense that the movement both provided a framework for and enhanced female self-assertion and in that it taught women how to translate the latter into political action. Realising that no improvement of their own political status was to be expected from men firmly relegating women to a subordinate position in the movement and, for the future, in society at large, these women decided to break away. As the Sheffield example indicates, there may have existed some dissatisfaction among the movement's female section with Chartism's overall treatment of women.

But conditions were not everywhere as conducive to female ventures as in Sheffield. There, Chartism seems to have been shot through with a good deal of Owenite thinking, due to a number of people combining commitment to both movements (as Isaac Ironside). This may also have been true of some of those women who ended up as members of the Women's Political Association. If so, this would underline the observation (made in Chapter 2) that the demand for the extension of universal suffrage to women was frequently inspired by Owenite ideals of sexual equality.

Although the Sheffield Women's Political Association temporarily transcended its local base, it never managed to grip women on a scale comparable to the movement from which it had evolved. With its demise, the public and organised life of the working class became marked by the almost total absence of women. Thus lapsed the tradition of sustained plebeian female participation in formally structured movements fighting for long-term political and economic goals. Chartism had been the last instance of this tradition of organised female militancy, of which it had formed the high point in terms of numbers involved.

* * *

Women's reappearance in working-class movements during the 1880s marked a new stage of female participation in class politics. In 1883, female co-operators set up an organisation of their own, the Women's Co-operative Guild, primarily to campaign for improving the condition of working-class wives and mothers, while later on broadening out into wider issues. Workplace conditions, on the other hand, were taken care of, to however slight an extent, by the new trade unions established around 1890 in a bid to organise the considerable potential of unskilled – and largely female – labour. This new departure had been heralded in 1888 by the London female match-workers who came out on strike for higher pay and improved working conditions and subsequently formed a union. Outside textiles, when women re-entered working-class organisations in large numbers, they found themselves confronted with a marked reluctance on the part of their male comrades to acknowledge, let alone support, female demands that went beyond workplace concerns and which were not ultimately geared towards phasing women out of the labour market altogether.

Significantly, it was in the north-west with its continuous tradition of large-scale female employment in the cotton mills that, around 1900, working-class women began to take action on their dual oppression as women and waged labourers. They focused on the vote as a major step towards an improvement of women's overall condition, and brought to bear on the campaign they built around it an experience many of them had acquired in a trade-union context.

Dorothy Thompson has been the first to address herself to the issue of women dropping out of working-class politics. However, she has not seen this as taking place with the decline of the Chartist movement, but as having already occurred in the mid-1840s.[29] This development was accentuated, she has claimed, by the increasing influence of the temperance movement on working-class women, which resulted in their growing reluctance to attend political meetings held at beer-shops. With the number of active members dwindling, on the other hand, fewer localities were able to maintain their own meeting places and therefore had more and more to resort to the local pub.

Certainly, this aspect should not be belittled. Thus it was precisely in this vein that, in the early 1850s, Jones strongly advised against the holding of Chartist meetings in taverns as this was deterring many adherents, and especially women. Reiterating the standard argument of the latter's centrality to Chartism's success on account of their influence on men and children, he emphasised that no respectable man would take his womenfolk to the pub.[30]

His article was warmly welcomed by Abiah Higginbottom on behalf of the Sheffield Women's Political Association. She took the occasion to link the extension of the Charter to the removal of meetings from the 'pot-house' as preconditions for gaining that female support in whose centrality she believed along with Jones.[31]

Temperance undoubtedly appealed to working-class women, who were finding it extremely difficult to make ends meet on a scanty income even without any member of the family squandering meagre and hard-earned wages on drink. The popularity Vincent enjoyed among female Chartists (as noted in the preceding chapter) certainly owed a great deal to his combining Chartism and temperance very early on in his career.[32] Temperance thus not only held out the prospect of an increase in material comfort; many believed moral improvement to follow from sobriety, which was seen, moreover, as pivotal for domestic happiness.[33]

The relevance of sobriety – both for the competent conducting of political campaigns and for the domestic well-being of the working class – was widely recognised within the Chartist movement. Leaders of the NCA were asked to abstain from drink and tobacco. In Scotland, north Lancashire, and the west, this was almost a condition of office. In the early 1840s, having emerged from prison convinced of the superiority of moral over physical force, Vincent was instrumental in establishing teetotal FCAs in Bristol, Bath and the west. Even O'Connor – although totally opposed to any deviation, which he regarded teetotal Chartism as an example of – was determined to enforce abstinence on Chartist settlements (as noted in section 2 of Chapter 6).

In London, Vincent's teetotal ideals were shared by the Neesoms (introduced in Chapter 5). By January 1841, the ELFPA had changed its name to the East London Female Total Abstinence Chartist Association, still with Elizabeth Neesom as its secretary. In an address to their sisters throughout the country, the women argued that contemporary government, notorious for its acts of class legislation, was in fact sustained in power by the tax-money it derived from the large amount of alcoholic drink consumed by the very people suffering from its oppressive legislation. Therefore the London women were convinced that the only remedy lay in relinquishing 'the use of all intoxicating drinks, to become a thinking and strictly moral people, and acquire sound political knowledge'. Here again, sobriety was emphasised as the key to politically improving the condition of an oppressed people. The women advocated abstinence in order to avoid the effects of alcohol on physical and mental health, to set children a good example and to enable people to secure for their offspring an education independent of state and church provision. In continuation of the self-assertive stance adopted by their two predecessor organisations (as noted in section 2 of Chapter 6), the London female Chartists urged their sisters to obtain an education in order fully to develop the mental faculties they believed women to possess. Then husband and wife would be able to try and excel each other in knowledge and morality. They therefore appealed to their sisters to form Total Abstinence Chartist Associations everywhere and concluded by quoting what they considered to be the key sentence from Vincent's address on total abstinence. This read 'That no Government can long withstand the just claims of a people who have had the courage to conquer their own vices',[34] a sentence indicating the strong belief of temperance Chartists in the pressure a concerted show of will-power was able to exert.

Thus the East London female Chartists' quest for moral improvement through abstinence was intermingled with a good dose of female self-assertion. The LWMA, by contrast, advocated a brand of moral respectability in which a pronounced variety of patriarchy (as noted in the previous chapter) was an integral part. Dorothy Thompson has missed this aspect of the combination of temperance and patriarchy on account of her failure to address issues of sexual oppression. The LWMA's rules and regulations stipulated that members should be 'honest, sober, moral, and thinking' men, as against 'the veteran drunkard' and 'the profligate railer'. All members were supposed to share 'aspirations beyond mere sensual enjoyments'. Neither were they 'forgetful of their duties as fathers, husbands and brothers', nor did they 'drown their intellect amid the drunken revelry of the pot-house'. The worthy LWMA member was a man – the rules and regulations were unambiguous about members' sex – dominated by rationality, in full possession of his intellectual capacities, and conscious of his familial duties. Conformity to this standard of respectable manhood was considered a political necessity. The opposite of respectability was profligacy, which was believed to turn people into 'the ready tools and victims of corruption or slaves of unprincipled governors'. Intemperance, 'this politically debasing, soul-subduing vice', was therefore resisted for both political and moral reasons. Accordingly, LWMA meetings were to be convened at members' homes instead of public houses. The Association aimed at blending study with recreation and at sharing in 'rational amusements (unassociated with the means of intoxication)'. 'Rational amusements' were the useful pastimes of those seeking more than 'mere sensual enjoyments'.

The most beneficial effects on society at large were expected as a result of establishing a vast number of associations modelled on the LWMA. These would bring together 'the honest, sober, and reflecting portion of every town and village in the kingdom', who would devote their time to self-instruction. In this manner, they would set an example of 'propriety' to their neighbours and enjoy 'even in poverty a happy home'. Domestic happiness was seen to derive from 'a cheerful and intelligent partner . . . dutiful children, and . . . means of comfort which their knowledge has enabled them to snatch from the ale-house'.[35] The promising prospect of temperate husbands diverting drink money to the support of their families ensured women's acquiescence in male pretensions of dominance, to which moral superiority was central. This, in turn, involved a system of self-instruction that was envisaged as a male preserve (as noted in Chapter 5).

The temperance many female Chartists favoured was shot through with a good deal of radicalism and could therefore be lived out within the movement, which enforced a certain degree of abstinence because it recognised the relevance of sobriety to the well-being of the working class. This inclination for temperance was recognised by the Temperance movement proper, which tried to build upon it. *The English Chartist Circular* published an appeal for female support by the National Anti-Tobacco and Temperance Association. This was addressed to the 'ladies' of England and Wales and stated that, while 'native delicacy and public opinion' prohibited women from appearing in the 'arena of strife and contention', other opportunities were open to them. Underlining the crucial role played by women in forming the human character, the address appealed to them to exert their influence in favour of temperance.[36]

While Chartist women were not inhibited from making use of the scope for activities afforded to them by their movement, they had heard a great deal of – and themselves believed in – the relevance of female influence (as noted in Chapter 4). This argument may have spoken to the women regardless of its class origin. The high value placed on temperance by many Chartists and middle-class proponents alike did help pave the way for something like a *rapprochement* between these classes in the long run.

In working-class neighbourhoods, the pub was not narrowly defined as a place primarily designed for the consumption of alcoholic drink. Rather, as Eileen Yeo has pointed out,[37] it formed an important part of the 'free zone' in which working-class culture, including political meetings, was allowed to thrive. Chartists hired rooms in the local tavern for all kinds of events, including teetotal functions and even religious services. Several FCAs (as noted in section 2 of Chapter 6) held their weekly meetings at their local pub as well as the tea parties and similar social events they organised for the benefit of the movement. Thus many female Chartists used the tavern in very much the same way as some of their predecessors of the Female Friendly Societies, who combined visits to the local ale-house with the strict enforcement of sobriety among themselves (as also noted in section 2 of Chapter 6).

Apart from those working-class women concerned about the effects of alcoholism on their families, many others regularly called in at their local pub for a drink. For the period 1870–1914, Ross[38] has found a veritable female pub culture to have existed in London. Women of all ages frequented public houses, bringing their children with them until the entry of the latter was restricted in 1908. The local was the place for gossiping, but women workers were also known to have organised pub 'Christmas Clubs'. In some east and south London districts, certain pubs were even exclusively visited by women.

It therefore seems doubtful that the penetration of the female section of the working class by a middle-class brand of temperance – which stigmatised the consumption of alcohol and women's presence in public spaces, such as the ostensibly named public house, alike – was as wholesale as has been suggested.

Nor can women's disappearance from working-class movements be conclusively attributed to the latter's increasing formalisation and sophistication. As a result, commitment to them required a great deal of time, something women with large families on their hands and jobs to do simply could not spare. The application of sophisticated rules, moreover, intimidated them.[39]

While most working-class women certainly did not have the time or the freedom of movement to attend meetings other than at their place of residence, there is no reason to assume that involvement in organisations at the local level, which had been feasible in the early Chartist period, should all of a sudden have ceased to be so. Moreover, the existence of Chartist female itinerant lecturers even as late as 1849–50 belies the utter impossibility of women being active other than locally. Women's commitment is far more likely to have been proscribed by the number and age of their children and by the degree of need for taking up a regular job than by the structural changes occurring in a political movement.

FCAs as well as their predecessors were run by their often all-female committees with an efficiency that was commonly acknowledged. Rather than speculate that this expertise, acquired over decades, had vanished quite abruptly, it is necessary to note the structural mechanisms operating within Chartism itself (as analysed in the preceding chapter) and which prevented women from attaining any position of leadership outside their FCA even at local level.

In addition, a considerable number of FCAs evolved under male guidance (as noted in section 2 of Chapter 6). This placed the male founders in a position of authority, which could be used either to help lay the foundation for female self-determination or to nip it in the bud. The predominant adoption of the latter course is suggested by the greater longevity of female as compared to male-dominated FCAs. The latter enjoyed an average lifespan of about one and a half years, with no FCA of this category existing for more than two. Female-dominated FCAs, by contrast, had an average lifetime of four and three-quarter years, with Sheffield FCA's twelve years representing an unparalleled maximum.

Chartism exerted a contradictory pull on its female supporters, encouraging them to involve themselves in politics while at the same time confining them to an auxiliary, secondary role. This combined with the evident defeat of two petitions submitted in relatively rapid succession. Taken together, both aspects must have made for a decline in women's readiness to come forward when Chartism issued to them a third, much weakened call. This reluctance, incidentally, was shared by the movement's male followers, and the campaign of 1847–8 lacked the momentum of the previous two. Rather than turning away from politics altogether, women chose to channel their energy into a project that more convincingly promised short-term redress and which, moreover, was uniquely suited to being promoted from within the confines of the home. Nor did it carry with it the risks to the well-being of the family that public forms of commitment to Chartism entailed. The home (as shown in Chapter 5) had always been the site of the bulk of female support right from Chartism's beginning. In the mid-1840s, therefore, rather than dropping out of politics, women began to join the Chartist Land Company in large numbers. In fact, the adoption of the Land Plan resulted in an upsurge of measurable female membership (as maintained in Chapter 3).

Furthermore, it is important to bear in mind that women's absence from working-class movements was by no means tantamount to a passive acceptance of their general condition. Not even in the heyday of female support of the movement had women been in a position, from within Chartism, to confront male transgressions (for example sexual violence) of the customary power structure in gender relations. Such matters had been – and certainly continued to be – settled by recourse to informal, popular means of protest, which women had also occasionally employed to further the cause of the Charter (as instanced in section 2 of Chapter 6).

With its subordination of female followers, coupled with a move away from community pressure politics towards a more centralised and formalised organisational structure, Chartism formed the link between those earlier campaigns in which women had been central and those later ones in which their supposed interests were taken care of exclusively by men, and frequently even without consultation. The middle of the nineteenth century witnessed a downright split in working-class politics along sexual lines. The increasing masculinisation of working-class organisations, which succeeded in improving the conditions of at least the skilled – and by definition male – labourers, marginalised women, whose multifarious oppression continued to find an outlet in angry outbursts of militancy. By the middle decades of the nineteenth century, however, power structures had become almost totally impervious to this type of spontaneous protest, which thus increasingly came to demonstrate the impotence of those women who engaged in it within both the productive and political spheres.

Discussion of the other cause of women's disappearance from working-class politics – the filtering down of the middle-class ideal of female domesticity[40] – leads right into the key argument of the next chapter.

9
Gender and Class in Chartism

The first half of the nineteenth century witnessed important changes in the economic sphere, and these had serious repercussions on social, including gender relations. In many trades, cheap, unskilled and often female labour was given preference over skilled men demanding higher wages. In textiles – and cotton in particular – an ever larger share of the production moved from home into factories, which relied on a predominantly female and juvenile workforce. This transition of labour from formal to real subordination under capital resulted in significant changes, at least in weaving, among the male personnel wielding authority over the female and juvenile operatives.

The potential – and to a certain degree actual – substitution of women for men as the chief breadwinners, combined with the loss of control exercised by many working-class men over their dependants' labour (as noted in Chapter 1), undermined the material base on which male supremacy in the family rested. The marked and prolonged economic depression that began in 1837 led to large-scale unemployment and a sharp drop in wages, thus giving an edge to the feeling of many working-class men that their dominant position within the family was being challenged.

It was at this juncture that the demand for universal male suffrage was revived. In Chartism, working men fought for the franchise (as argued in Chapter 2) as a token of their civic status, which they felt was due to them as the producers of the nation's wealth. Thus they wanted to buttress at the political level, too, their hegemony that was being eroded at the workplace and in the family.

At the workplace, Chartists demanded women's withdrawal from waged labour outside the home (as noted in Chapter 2). This was to ensure the proper discharge of female domestic duties and thus the well-being of the family. As an alternative to employment

264

outside the home (as also noted in Chapter 2), Chartists advocated marriage, which, by affording women male protection from the drudgery and alleged moral perils of waged labour, had a definite and hierarchic structure. In the political sphere, the vote cast by the male head of the family was to demonstrate his position of authority in public (as argued in Chapter 2). The reassertion of male supremacy in all spheres of life was coupled, at the ideological level, with a shutting out of any notion of sexual oppression (as also argued in Chapter 2).

Working-class women themselves (as analysed in Chapter 4) conceived of the care for the well-being of their families as their primary duty. It was when prevented from properly attending to their domestic responsibilities that they took to political action geared towards establishing conditions in which their performance at home could improve. In its agitation of women, Chartism (as also demonstrated in Chapter 4) reinforced their political pose of radical wife- and motherhood. This in turn circumscribed the various forms that female commitment to the movement assumed (and which have been noted in Chapters 5 and 6). A great deal of support was rendered from within the confines of the home. Within its own ranks, the movement kept its female adherents firmly confined to a secondary, subordinate role (as argued in Chapter 7). Any attempts by women to assert themselves by pressing gender-specific – as opposed to class-specific – demands inevitably resulted in secession from Chartism (as shown in Chapter 8).

The essence of Chartism's concern with women was that their defining characteristic was their devotion to home and family. The different strands of domesticity cohered into a female Chartist ideal-type that Wheeler created in his novel *Sunshine and Shadow* (introduced in Chapter 2). He unequivocally welcomed female participation in the movement. In accordance with the tone of Chartist press reports on women attending political meetings (as noted in Chapter 7), he had his hero notice 'the enthusiasm, good sense, and propriety displayed by the numerous females who attended these gatherings'.[1] The propriety that Wheeler wished to govern women's conduct accorded with attendance at political meetings, but not with public speaking. True, he partially attributed the renewed vigour of the movement in 1842 to the appearance of female speakers on Chartist platforms, believing the extraordinary aspect of their conduct to have aroused people's curiosity. In the long run, however, this may have frustrated rather than enhanced Chartism's prospects: he implies this by remarking sceptically: 'Whether the labours of these female orators were beneficial or not to the cause we leave others to decide.'[2]

The true model Chartist woman is presented in the shape of Mary Graham. She owes all her qualities to her upbringing by an exemplary mother:

> Mary Graham was fortunate in possessing a mother who united in herself all the qualities necessary to form the character of a young maiden in the class to which she belonged; frugal and a good housewife, yet possessing sufficient energy and romance in her disposition, to prevent her ever becoming a domestic drudge – possessed of a strong mind, and owing some slight advantages to education, she seemed by instinct to comprehend any subject which attracted her attention. Amongst these was politics; and in correctness of reasoning and a happy appreciation of, and expression of ideas, few men could compare with her; but it was only in private company, or in the domestic circle, that this faculty was observable; for though a great frequenter of public assemblies, her character was of a retiring nature – more fitted to adorn home than shine in public.[3]

This, then, is the stuff Wheeler's ideal woman is made of! She possesses enough energy to be not only a model of industry in the fulfilment of her domestic duties, but also to be interested in affairs beyond the confines of her home. She works like a drudge without becoming one. For any lack of education she makes up by 'instinctive comprehension' – no mean achievement indeed! Mary's mother's quick grasp of politics does not make her 'forward', but, owing to her 'retiring' nature, she displays it only in the domestic circle. While not denying women the ability to understand political affairs, Wheeler did not approve of their making it an excuse for exhibiting their political commitment in public beyond the attendance of meetings, at which they played the part of passive listeners.

The author dexterously wove elements of female Chartists' real-life experience into his description of Mary Graham's relationship to Arthur, the novel's hero, to make the point that women work the most beneficial effects by leading an essentially domestic life. Mary and Arthur meet at the various Chartist functions that both of them attend regularly. This is the constellation in which love flourishes: 'their feelings, their ideas were similar, both were connected with the same movement, and both impelled to action by the same hopes and aspirations'.[4]

This experience was actually shared by many Chartist couples (as noted in Chapter 5). Common interests, however, do not make Mary and Arthur equal partners in their relationship. In the initial period of their marriage, Arthur is described as educating his wife by reading to her so that 'under Arthur's instructions, Mary rapidly progressed in intellectual attainment'.[5] By making up for the deficiencies of his wife's education, the husband asserts his familial position of authority, based on his superiority with regard to education and experience. There existed a real-life model for Wheeler's characters in Lovett, who also set himself the task of educating his wife (as also noted in Chapter 5). Where Morton was able to build on his wife's Chartist commitment, Lovett tried to awaken his wife's understanding of his politics.

Arthur's is the guiding hand in a relationship to which Mary brings the ardour of hopeful enthusiasm.[6] It is not only good behaviour that renders Arthur, the Chartist, different from other men, but also the fact that he focuses on the woman he loves the profusion of feeling he harbours for all humankind: 'he had loved her with a love which was the only outlet for the hoarded and passionate musings of his romantic life; upon her he had lavished all the tenderness of a heart, overflowing with love towards all mankind'.[7]

Mary's upbringing in the spirit of Chartist womanhood comes to full fruition once she is married. Now she can actively right the 'inversion of nature' – as Wheeler branded female employment outside the home – by busying herself about the house and leaving waged labour to her husband. Wheeler's description of the Grahams' home[8] is highly reminiscent of Watkins's 'cottage of content' (introduced in Chapter 2).

Mary fulfilled the prescript laid down by Watkins in his *Address to the Women of England*, in which he used biblical language to underline the eternal validity of his view:

The proper sphere of woman is home; and a proper woman should be suffered to rule there. Man goeth forth to work and returneth for that rest and refreshment which his labour at once needeth and procureth. Woman, in the mean time, fitteth and prepareth the good things provided by his toil, and she cheereth his worn spirit by words and looks and deeds of love.[9]

It does indeed absorb a woman's entire strength – something open only to one free from the need to labour for wages outside the home – to safeguard her domestic realm against the influence brought to bear on it by the society in which it is embedded. It is interesting to note that Chartism itself counts among 'the cares of business' from which the husband retreats into the home, for 'Politics were almost forgotten in the honeymoon of his bliss.'[10]

When Arthur resumes his Chartist activities in the period leading up to 1848, his renewed commitment is denounced as an attempt at escaping from his home, which still reminds him of how he was once previously unable to provide for his family properly, on account of unemployment. Chartism is portrayed here as a threat to the domestic happiness of the family, by demanding the man's commitment. Thus the aims Chartists were striving for – the alleviation of people's misery so as to render them happy in the family circle – had to be, at least temporarily, abandoned in the Chartist struggle itself. This observation coincides with the painful experience of domestic disruption that many female Chartists suffered following their husbands' imprisonment (as noted in Chapter 5).

As the example of Mary Graham shows, the Chartist advocacy of female domesticity was intimately bound up with the preservation of male dominance. In every sphere of life, the model female Chartist was man's helpmate, not his competitor. Her qualities are summarised in the following epitaph: 'a better wife, a more devoted mother or a truer democrat never existed'.[11] The three domains assigned to woman were – in order of priority – marriage, motherhood and Chartism. Her excellence in all three derived from her exertions being directed solely to the benefit of others. She made a good wife for her husband, devoted herself to the upbringing of her children, and her democratic attitude was devoid of any selfish motive. The devotion displayed in all three domains bordered on self-abnegation, which, on the part of women, was to complement male self-assertion.

The Chartist emphasis on female domesticity had its roots in the conception of the sexes as complements, which, together with the concomitant gender relations, were defined in accordance with the notion of respectability. This had evolved from the older, Puritan virtues of hard and regular work, thrift and sobriety, which had been reworked and adapted to working people's condition.

Respectability hinged on independence as a result of property in skill. The skilled man had earned wages high enough to enable him to support himself and his family at a customary standard without recourse to charity or the Poor Law. In the domestic sphere, respectability comprised a positive evaluation of home and family and a rather sedate sexual life. These standards were shared by artisans, by domestic outworkers experiencing the threat of industrialisation, as well as by degraded skilled workers in the textile industry – irrespective of whether they worked in factories or at home – and united them across any divisions that might otherwise have existed between them.

Respectability was predicated upon a rigid division of labour by sex. With the exclusion of women from skilled trades, property in skill became by definition male and formed the basis for men's position of authority in the family. Both skill and familial position had been established as defining criteria for the economic, legal and political subject (that is, an independent person enabled to act for her -- or here invariably his – self) in radical popular speech during the discussions triggered by the Levellers in the seventeenth century.

Women were thus excluded from attaining status as political subjects. Instead, they were assigned, as their primary responsibility, care of their husbands and children. While expected to earn their own upkeep, this was never to take precedence over their familial duty. Despite their social inferiority, their efforts and achievements in this realm were recognised and valued.

Women's ability to live in a respectable manner depended on the degree of respectability achieved by their husbands. Regular housekeeping, clean, well-fed children, and a stable domestic life – the hallmarks of decent womanhood – were conditional upon a steady male income. Ross[12] has drawn attention to the crucial role played by working-class women in maintaining respectability and demonstrating this to the neighbourhood. Variations in female dress, public conduct, language, housekeeping, child-rearing methods, spending habits and sexual behaviour were subtle markers of the degree of respectability attained by a family.

Drawing on the tradition of respectability and emphasising male supremacy was William Cobbett, who, according to E. P.

Thompson,[13] created the Radical culture of the 1820s and thus had a great deal of influence on Chartism. In his *Advice to Young Men*, Cobbett drew up a list of the desirable qualities of a wife. These were, in order of priority: chastity, sobriety, industry, frugality, cleanliness, knowledge of domestic affairs, good temper and beauty.[14] His ideal was the active, energetic woman, able to render her husband valuable support through good housekeeping. In doing so, she was clearly subordinate to him.

Cobbett could not conceive of marriage as other than a hierarchical relationship in which the husband dominated the wife. Accordingly, the power to make decisions was to be the husband's alone. Cobbett argued for the right of wives to be consulted on matters of minor importance. Decisions in matters of importance, however, such as style of living, disposal of property, children's education, politics – to name but a few – must be left to the husband, or else family harmony would be seriously disrupted. This very argument was echoed by O'Connor in his refutation of women's demand for the suffrage (as noted in Chapter 2).

As a corollary of the concept of man as the head of the household and hence the political subject, Cobbett excluded women from the right to vote, considering the exercise of the franchise to contravene female nature. Natural propensities precluded women not only from voting, but also from enjoying any other kind of liberty. 'For *freedom*', Cobbett argued, 'means an exemption or departure from the *strict rules of female reserve*; and I do not see how this can be *innocent*.'[15]

Rooted within this indigenous working-class tradition though the Chartist notion of femininity was, it displayed many similarities with the middle-class conception that has come to be summarised as the 'angel in the house' view of women (spelt out in Chapter 4). Not only was domesticity central to both, but concordance can also be traced in a number of beliefs that followed from it. Domesticity was predicated upon a concept of female nature defined as inherently different from and complementary to its masculine counterpart. Consequently, the sexual division of labour and women's subordination were regarded as part of natural or divine prescription, assigning each sex that sphere to which it was naturally fitted. Female nature was conceived of as static and devoid of any historical dimension. In this manner, a socialised stereotype ossified into a concept of femininity, unchanged and unchangeable over time.

This concept of femininity is also discernible in Chartist novelists. Jones repeatedly asserted the different character of love in men and women. For the latter, love is a 'religion': 'Truly man loves not so truly, so religiously as woman.' This is why his female characters, when unable to live out their love, die of a broken heart. Woman's essential dependence on the beloved being is brought out most clearly in the way Anna, the young milliner, refers to her lover: 'Charles is my life – my hope – my all! If you take him away from me, you kill me. I have grown so to feel the need of seeing him – of hearing his voice; let me remain near him as his servant – as what you please – but let me be near him.' The woman in love is a being whose personality is wiped out and who receives her vital impulses from the man she loves. Hence separation equals death. The love relationship does not imply equality of the people involved, since physical proximity is all the woman requires for her happiness. Once she has given way to her love she has ceased to exist as a person in her own right.

Anna, the lamb, is the image on which Jones's metaphorical language plays in this passage: 'Lamb-like, she followed; she felt that she was helpless; with confiding or reckless resignation – gentle, impulseless, as though she had no longer a will of her own, she obeyed his every word, followed his every motion.' The lamb metaphor alludes to Anna's predestination as a victim. The lamb has not found in her lover the protecting shepherd to complement her: 'Alas, for her, whose sole refuge and dependence is the constancy of man!'

As in love, so in motherhood, women can give free rein to the flow of their emotions. In diffusing maternal love, even the ugly woman is beautiful and assumes angelic qualities. In Jones's *The Working-Man's Wife*, Margaret, about to be hanged for the murder committed by her husband, reaches out for her children one last time from the gallows:

> she leant forward – all the mother came rushing to her face – an involuntary blessing hovered on her lips – oh! despite years of hardship and hunger – despite grief and age – she looked beautiful – very beautiful – that moment! . . . 'Hush! – Mary! – Don't cry so, Mary!' and the soft cajoling tenderness of the mother turned her choking tones into angelic music.

While her husband has been hardened by the privations he has had to endure, Margaret has been able to preserve her maternal feelings despite her suffering. These women seem to be impervious to the evils of the world.

In Anna, too, motherhood works a dramatic change in the woman's attitude: 'Until then Anna had observed a meek and suppliant attitude, but wounded now in the dearest, holiest, sanctuary of her young heart – her dawning mother's love – the weeping girl suddenly raised her death-pale forehead, and stood erect, proud, noble.'[16] Anna, who has been writhing under the scorn of society as the mere mistress of the man she loves, becomes aware of her dignity through her pregnancy. Dignity is conferred upon women solely through their reproductive capacity. And only in that capacity do women come into their own.

On account of their natural function, women were seen as being closer to nature than men and as requiring to remain so in order to preserve their purity. This is how Wheeler describes one of his female characters:

> Brought up in retirement with her father, she possessed but few of the courtly graces of the fashionable lady, but in all the charms of unsophisticated loveliness she abounded. Pure and simple in her manners, as the sylvan tribes by which she was surrounded, she lived the life of a flower, glowing in the light but closing to the shade, flourishing alike amid sunshine and darkness, drawing the sweet elements of her beauty alike from both, and both seemed to disrobe themselves of their harshness, and mingle their purest influences in her creation. She was truly Nature's child; she had no desires that the quiet retirement of Newland Hall would not gratify – no wishes that strayed beyond their domestic circle.[17]

By imbibing natural sweetness, woman becomes a flower, which symbolises moral purity and physical weakness coupled with beauty.

Woman, the flower, is not made to grapple with the adversities of life. This incapacity generates her dependence on male protection, which, due to her lack of power, can easily be abused. This is acknowledged by an observer of the young milliner, who, abandoned by her lover, falls ill of a broken heart: 'An instinctive feeling of regret overcame him, to behold so sweet a flower so cruelly torn and trampled.'[18] Conversely, undue exposure to society imperils female purity, as Jones's eponymous lady of title instances:

> of no staid and settled disposition, no firm character well-founded by a wise education, with generous impulse, good intention, and ardent feelings, she, like so many more of the children of rank and wealth, were [sic] thwarted and perverted from the cradle, to be bandied to and fro, like waifs, amid the shallows of society.[19]

The following description of another of Wheeler's female characters, reiterating the flower-image of woman, shows beauty to be the physical expression of inner purity.

> Julia North was a beauteous and well-trained flower growing in a wild and uncultivated garden, possessing beauty of a rare order . . . there was still a nameless charm about her that it was impossible to trace to any mere combination of features, a form rather short than tall but most exquisitely proportioned, flaxen hair falling in ringlets on her delicate shoulders, eyes of the purest blue, and a complexion in which the rose and the lily were so completely blended, that art would try in vain to imitate it. Though there was nothing decidedly intellectual in the cast of her countenance, its beauty being of the order that would attract the attention of the sensualist rather than that of the philosopher, yet no one could gaze upon her and not at once pronounce that Nature could not have committed the anomaly of so fair a body without a corresponding soul.[20]

This detailed description contains the core of the character's destiny, which is developed in the course of the novel. In the woman's complexion are blended the rose, symbol of the sensuous female, and the lily, denoting the pure, unworldly, angelic creature. The rose, however, preponderates, for the woman's beauty is more attractive to the sensualist than to the philosopher. Unless she indulges the sensuous side of her nature, the woman is destined to fail – having disregarded her natural propensities. Wheeler obviously did not conceive of women as essentially asexual beings, for in some at least, the rose and the lily blend.

This would imply that the author regarded sexual compatibility as part of desirable marriage.

By denying herself the gratification of her love, the woman divests herself of the earthly, human constituent of her being and assumes angelic quality. This is recognised by the man who loves her, and who, in his farewell letter, makes extensive use of religious language and imagery, thus emphasising the adored woman's transmutation into an angelic being:

> Beloved companion of my youth, – With feelings of pain have I received my dismissal from the temple of my adoration, where I knelt – oh! how humble a worshipper! – content with my lot, dreaming, not of higher aspirations. Alas! even this happiness must no longer be mine. I must still continue to worship, but the shrine will be forever removed, and my dark and chequered lot lose the only star that illumined its erratic course. Hard and unfeeling man, could not aught else have soothed thy pride without making shipwreck of my treasured happiness? Lady Baldwin, accept my hearty thanks for your kind remembrance, and if a love, holy as that of angels, pure as the dreams of infancy, be an acceptable offering, oh! receive the oblation. It will not tarnish the virtue of the altar, but will ascend as the grateful incense of a devotee to the shrine of the Most High.[21]

The man who loves the woman, being denied the sensuous side of her nature, is left to adore the angelic, the lily side of her, who is thereby turned into a saint. A woman's destiny, then, is determined by her natural propensities. If they are given room to flourish, the woman's life will be a success; if not, a failure. Suppressed female nature results in death of a broken heart. Not only is a woman's development circumscribed by inherent traits, she is also denied the power to shape the conditions that bear upon her life. Women are depicted as the victims of fate or society, on the workings of which they have not the slightest influence. The servant-girl of Frost's novel, realising that her lover will never marry her, becomes aware of 'the force of circumstances which were as much beyond her control as the motions of the planets'.[22] And this is how Wheeler commented upon his heroine's attempt at wielding her own destiny:

> Julia North . . . thinks that she could give up wealth and title to

reside in a cottage with the chosen of her heart – that her destiny is in her own hands – that she has to choose between love on the one hand, virtue and matronly pride on the other. Poor moth! fluttering around the light, thy destiny is irrevocably fixed, thy mingled yarn is nearly spun, the sister fates will spare ye not.[23]

As any attempt at breaking the bonds of her status as victim would be in vain, woman reaches excellence in passive endurance of all hardship. When borne down by misery, it is said of the servant-girl in Frost's novel, for instance, that 'there was in her pale countenance more of that uncomplaining patience which her sex usually possesses in so eminent a degree'.[24] This observation is echoed by Wheeler thus: 'O the patient virtues of womankind, how they shine when compared with man's selfish engrossments; never does sympathy with the distress of others forsake the breast of woman; never does their own grief make them callous to the feelings of their fellow-sufferers.'[25] Through the contrast with man's 'selfish engrossments', woman's sympathy with others comes across as self-abnegation in the face of misery. Having presented his heroine as the ideal embodiment of such female virtue, Wheeler leaves 'her humble abode with higher notions of woman's fortitude, and woman's devotion than [he] had hitherto imbibed'.[26] The telling juxtaposition of fortitude and devotion implies that woman is strongest when annihilating herself by serving others. The strength with which she has been endowed is worthily applied only when spent for the benefit of others.

It was this capacity that Chartist men seem to have looked for in their wives[27] and that they couched in the increasingly clichéd image of woman, the vine, clinging around man, the oak, to whom she gives sustenance in times of adversity.[28]

Conversely, it was precisely because woman was of the weaker, softer sex that the Reverend J. R. Stephens committed her to male protection by demanding that 'man, whose is the wisdom, as hers is the love, by man, whose is the strength and the power, as hers is the gentleness and kindness of the milk of nature, so is she, by man . . . to be cherished, protected, and defended'.[29] Cheltenham WMA chimed with this call by solemnly vowing to follow their countrywomen into the struggle for the Charter, because, as they explained, 'we prize the jewel, woman, as [God's] first greatest gift to man; we honour her fortitude; we venerate her truth; we are charmed by her loveliness; we are humanized by her tenderness'.[30]

Men's protection of women implied male dominance. As in Chartism, so in the middle class, male hegemony in society at large was mirrored by gender relations in the family. Obedience and deference were due to the husband on the part of his wife. Self-abnegation, that principal female virtue, was to be practised, first of all, towards him. The literature abounds with rules of conduct to be observed by wives towards their husbands. They ought continually to try and please them, chiefly by preserving a good temper and remaining unobtrusive. Mrs Ellis, the Evangelical writer, summed up the requirements demanded of a wife thus:

It is to sound judgment, then, and right principle, that we must look, with the blessing of the Bestower of these good gifts, for ability to make a husband happy – sound judgment to discern what is the place designed for him and for us, in the arrangements of an all-wise Providence – and right principle to bring down every selfish desire, and every rebellious thought, to a due subserviency in the general estimate we form of individual duty.[31]

Chartist periodicals variously quoted from works propagating the 'angel in the house' view of women.[32] Yet dissenting views were also noted, and that mainly in Chartist periodicals with an educationalist bias. Examples include Marion Reid, who, in her *Plea for Women*, refuted the orthodox view of femininity, even demanding female suffrage, as well as Lady Morgan, the novelist, and Harriet Martineau, the writer on politics and economics, who likewise insisted on women's rights and on an extension of their sphere.[33]

For many Chartists, proper marriage, church or civil, had become a badge of respectable womanhood and led them to disapprove of common-law unions, regardless of their stability. For this reason Eliza Sharples, who had formed a common-law union with Carlile and had actively supported him in his struggle for a free press, came in for censure. A letter to *The Northern Star* drew attention to the fact that she was about to die in distress. The correspondent emphasised her tenacious adherence to her political principles in order both to account for her current isolation and to induce Chartists to come to her assistance in spite of any moral misgivings.[34] That the writer anticipated criticism of Eliza Sharples's lifestyle shows the restrictive thrust of the Chartist notion of female respectability.

The belief in the moral power of female influence, which was kept strictly subservient to the furthering of class interests, indicates the general direction in which this restriction worked. Chartist and middle-class concordance concerning women's moral power did not extend to the manner in which it could best be exerted (as noted in Chapter 4). By involving women in the movement, Chartists clashed head on with the dominant middle-class opinion that female influence depended on women's confinement to the domestic sphere for coming to full fruition. Yet conformity to this belief contained the potential of pointing women the way to release from subjection.

Opposition to male dominance arose out of concern for its deleterious effects on woman's character. Instead of having her intellectual development impeded in order to keep her firmly subject to man, woman should be given full scope for the application of her faculties to the regeneration of society. The early Victorian feminists therefore demanded better education for women, not only in order to enable them to bring up their children properly, but also because they were entitled to it in their own right.[35] Improved education, however, should be part of a broader social and civil equality for men and women.

To grant women influence while denying them power in the manner of the Victorians, argued Marion Reid for instance, meant in fact to nullify the influence from which such beneficial effects were expected. This was why she came out in favour of female suffrage (as noted in Chapter 2).[36] These early feminists did not call the overall assumptions about femininity into question, but wanted to remedy certain particular injustices. They used the image of woman as 'helpmate' – of equality through difference – to widen her sphere and to justify her education.[37] The ideal of womanliness they embraced resembled the Victorian ideal of masculinity in its emphasis on self-reliance, industry, forthrightness, and independence. As Murray has argued, 'In a culture in which women were brought up to pride themselves on their selflessness, the creation of any standard by which they could affirm a strong moral character was one of the most basic ways to resist the limitations of their positions.'[38]

The female Chartists' struggle, too, was often inspired by a deeply felt sense of the power of their influence. Cheltenham FCA asked the local women:

> Will you not come forward and with your casesses [sic] stimulate and strengthen the weak – with your all-powerful influence rush in between the oppressor and the oppressed, and stop the current of persecution . . . come forward, we say, and let posterity halo the period of the nineteenth century, when it may be said that *a female band led their sons to victory, by the moral power of their influence, their energy, perseverance, and matchless patriotism.*[39]

The female Chartists of Bethnal Green were not only convinced of the moral power of their influence, but regarded it as favourably distinguishing them from those men who were notorious for mere physical or military power.[40] Yet the firm entrenchment of male dominance within the Chartist movement prevented these seeds of female self-awareness from germinating into fully fledged self-determination. Instead, belief in women's moral power seems to have been in inverse proportion to their actual influence.

Despite the various similarities between the Chartist and the middle-class concepts of womanhood, there existed a fundamental difference concerning the ultimate end towards which these notions were geared. This can be clearly suggested via the comparison of two works of fiction. Charlotte Elizabeth wrote her *The Wrongs of Woman* (introduced in Chapter 2) to plead an alleviation of female waged labour in order to safeguard social stability. Proper attendance to their domestic duties would enable working-class women to exert that beneficial influence which would quell any feeling of dissatisfaction and thus prevent social upheaval. The striking resemblance as to title and subject matter between this book and Jones's *Woman's Wrongs* (introduced in Chapter 2) suggests that the former may have inspired the latter, at least to a certain extent.

Both authors agree on mothers' centrality for their children's moral education[41] and on the pernicious impact of waged labour on women. For Charlotte, this is a gender issue. She attributes female employment outside the home to the depravity of men who, in order to spare themselves the physical exertions of labouring, send their female dependants to earn wages for them.[42]

For Jones, conversely, the issue at stake is the whole social setup. He describes female suffering in order to denounce 'the vile mechanism of our system'. Where Charlotte wants to rouse female sympathy and compassion, Jones's novel is directed at a general readership. Neither philanthropic effort nor 'amelioration' is his object, but social change. Hence the call on his readers to 'go! try to alter [the world] and BEGIN AT HOME'.[43] Jones describes social evils, instanced by women's plight, to drive home the malleability of society and consequently the possibility of social change.

Social stability and social change denote the ultimate and diametrically opposed goals to which middle-class and Chartist notions of female domesticity were respectively related. For Chartists, achievement of this end was conditional upon asserting their class interests in the political arena. For this show of strength to have the maximum impact, the involvement of the largest possible number of working-class people was required. Agitational efforts were directed towards the family, which Chartists conceived of as the basic social as well as productive unit within the community. It was to reinstate the family in its state prior to industrialisation that Chartists took political action, and this was why women were indispensable to the movement's project. Their coming into Chartism, not as political subjects, but via their familial function accounts for the clear clash that occurred between their political activism and the ideal towards which it was geared, namely female domesticity. By viewing the female adherents of the movement as essentially domestic beings whose public political appearance was legitimised by the current exigencies of working-class life, Chartists were able to condone, if not to acclaim, whatever form women's determination assumed. The striking discrepancy between women, conceived of as flowers, unable to wield their destiny, and the actual female activists, some of whom occasionally did not even shun most violent forms of militancy, is an important indication of the main thrust of Chartist notions of femininity. The emphasis on domesticity involved a shift from an active to a more passive female lifestyle. This meant a general narrowing of the options open to women, and thus helped bring the working-class home closer to the middle-class ideal.

Significantly, the Chartist novels here considered all appeared (as noted in Chapter 2) between 1849 and 1852, that is well after the final high-point of Chartism. During the course of the movement (as shown in Chapter 6), the visibility, if not degree of commitment, of women's involvement had considerably dwindled. This development was both reflected and reinforced by the novelists looking back upon the ebbs and flows of Chartism. They consistently depicted women as lacking the power to shape their destinies. The defeat of a movement that had, at least to some degree, relied on a good deal of women's, often militant, support, served as an indictment of precisely these forms of female involvement. And this makes for the wide gap between women's treatment in fiction and the reality of their lives.

This is further corroborated by Wheeler's female Chartist ideal-type. It stood no chance of becoming incarnated in many actual working-class women, except perhaps temporarily in that small fraction whose husbands managed to earn enough wages to make a completely home-centred life viable. However, as an ideal-type, it lingered on, helping to power many more working-class campaigns in the years to come.

The frictions between the realities of working-class life and the aim of the Chartist struggle in the realm of gender relations also account for the variations in the views Chartist leaders professed with regard to women. Some, such as Vincent, hoped that the victory of Chartism would result from men and women's concerted efforts; this involved recognising an active female contribution to the condition of the entire class. By contrast, others, such as O'Connor, were more concerned with keeping women in a subordinate position by emphasising the auxiliary and secondary character of their support.

What occurred in the Chartist period, then, was not simply a filtering down of Victorian values into the working class. Instead, in dealing with the dominant ideology, Chartism could rely mainly on notions of proper womanhood that had evolved and actually been lived among working people and which formed a more or less independent tradition. Still, whatever their different class origins, the middle- and working-class concepts of femininity shared a number of basic assumptions, and these opened avenues to something like assimilation (the mode of which will be discussed in the following chapter).

Underlying the emphasis on female domesticity was the growing insecurity at all levels of life that arose because society was becoming increasingly dominated by capitalist values. In the realm of gender relations (as argued in the beginning of this chapter), this was experienced as undermining male supremacy, a feeling sharpened by the economic disruption of the 1830s and 1840s. In the middle class, women's time and energy were absorbed by their efforts to create homes designed to be refuges from the troubles of the world outside. The stiffening of competition in the economic sphere affected middle- and working-class men alike, albeit in different forms. Hence the attraction for working men of home as a space for emotional respite. Feeling at the mercy of powers beyond their control in the economic sphere, men of both classes had a psychological need for clearly defined power structures at home which, moreover, by placing them at the head of the household, endowed them with authority over the lives of their dependants.

This was a consensus built along gender rather than class lines, and the Owenites were presumably alone in not joining it. What marked them off from most contemporary radical movements was their challenge of both the social and sexual hierarchy. Possessing a clear conception of sexual oppression, the Owenites made the full equality of the sexes an integral part of their campaign. Thus they created an environment conducive to some Owenite feminists' use of the notion of woman's mission and her specialness for buttressing their claim of female superiority. However, among the working class, Owenite ideas attracted merely a minority. Chartism, by contrast, became a mass movement, not in spite, but on account of its clinging to customary gender relations and its emphasis on the family and the marriage union as the unit of production. This was put into practice on the Chartist settlements, which attracted a much wider group of people than those colonies governed by the Owenite stress on communalism.

As Barbara Taylor has argued,[44] the opportunity the latter afforded of leading a life that was not defined by marital status may have had some appeal for single women carrying on a precarious existence in the borderland between lower middle and upper working class. Working-class women, on the other hand, were facing fundamentally different problems. Stretched on the rack by their efforts to reconcile the requirements of waged labour with those of their families, they very often willingly consigned themselves to male protection in marriage, even though this

ultimately meant acquiescing in male dominance. Marriage to a
husband earning a steady income held out the promise of relief
from at least part of their burden. In addition, the sexual crisis of
the 1830s and 1840s (outlined in Chapter 1) heightened women's
sexual vulnerability and made marriage even more desirable. In a
period when it was becoming virtually impossible for working-
class women to survive on their own – and, when married, to
cope with the burden of family support – the Chartist struggle for
female domesticity must have looked a highly convincing solution
to their problems. The pressures of economic insecurity and
overwork were so daunting as virtually to preclude women from
recognising the potential economic independence of men inherent
in wages earned by labour. In a different setting, these wages
could have laid the base for personal autonomy and given rise to
a feminist line of argument. Only in a few cases (discussed in the
preceding chapter) was women's frustration about their subordination within Chartism inspired by notions of sexual equality.

10
Chartism's Transitional Character

Towards the close of the 1840s, it became evident that industrial capitalism had irreversibly established itself as the dominant mode of production. Within the working class, coming to terms with the new conditions therefore began to take precedence over the wholesale rejection of the factory system and of its concomitants. This rejection had been at the heart of the Chartist project. In this movement, whole communities, men and women alike, had responded to the threat that industrialisation posed, albeit differently, to all their members.

In the struggle to avert these threats, working people came to see themselves as a social group living under conditions and having needs that, while knitting them together as a group, set them apart from other sections of society. In the course of their opposition to the socio-economic changes under way, working people developed their ideas about the kind of life to which they aspired. This they imaged in terms of healthy family relations. Central to them was the fulfilment of the evolving standards of proper man- and womanhood and of the gender relations attendant upon them. The 'good man' was cast as the provider, whose function as the family's sole breadwinner would confirm his headship. His familial authority would be reflected and enhanced by his civic status, enshrined in the right to vote. Endowed with such status and power, he would be able to afford his wife the protection it was felt she needed.

Relieved by the male breadwinner from the need to earn her own upkeep and to expose herself to the dangers, both physical and moral, believed to lurk in the world of work, the 'good woman' would be able to devote herself exclusively to home-making. She was regarded as essentially unable to fend for herself and as best fitted to see to her family's needs at home. The wage-earning wife, once a common feature of the plebeian household, came to be viewed as signalling the man's degradation.

The emphasis placed by Chartists on the family, both actually and metaphorically, can thus be seen as an important device in forging class identity. Coherence was achieved by casting all working people as members of a large family, within which each filled the station allotted to them according to gender and age. Class homogeneity thereby took precedence over gender heterogeneity, and thus helped submerge sexual antagonism. The Chartist idea of gender relations became the movement's legacy to subsequent generations of workers. This legacy was no less fundamental in shaping working-class politics and social relations than the legacy of political defeat, which has, understandably, preoccupied generations of historians.

Indeed, the ideas about gender persisted longer than those about politics. The radicals' view of government as that instrument by which the ruling classes were able to shape society to their exclusive benefit had, by the end of the 1840s, definitely proved incapable of accounting for a number of actual reforms in favour of those excluded from political power. Consequently the belief had to be abandoned. Along with the ideology, the movement that had been its vociferous champion was undermined.

Not so Chartism's sexual ideology. The attainment of female domesticity appeared feasible in the long term despite continued large-scale female waged labour in and outside the home. The gradual improvements won by concerted class action sustained the hope that, even within industrial capitalism, the working class would eventually be able to enforce female domesticity within its own ranks. Unlike Chartism's political ideology, the movement's sexual beliefs persisted due to their adaptability to changed economic conditions. Both this quality and the fundamental way in which these beliefs responded to the needs of working-class men and women ensured the survival of this sexual ideology, independent of the movement that had nursed them. For these needs were shaped by economic and social conditions: this book has consistently pointed to such conditions as the reason why Chartists of both sexes held to and, via their movement, strengthened these beliefs.

The effects of involvement in the Chartist movement therefore differed along gender lines. Commitment to Chartism bolstered men's shared identity as men, by promoting their common identification as family breadwinners who waged a political struggle for conditions in which they would better be able to secure their families' economic survival. Women's self-definition as wives and mothers was reinforced, too, by the working-class version of female domesticity that evolved in the Chartist era. Yet conformity to this standard involved a significant shift away from radical wife- and motherhood. Precisely by giving priority to familial responsibilities, many such women had fulfilled them energetically and actively outside the home as well as inside. It was via this pose of radical wife and mother that Chartist women became subject to greater pressure towards domesticity. In the family, the reaffirmation of the sexual division of labour that domesticity implied left women to grapple with reconciling the requirements of family care and waged labour. In the productive sphere, by underscoring the primarily familial definition of female work, it further facilitated gender-specific exploitation. These developments were exacerbated by women's political dis-empowerment. By enforcing female domesticity, the Chartist movement did much to deprive women of any effective means to exert an influence on the forces shaping their lives. This disempowerment was captured by the description of women in Chartist novels as lacking the power to shape their destinies.

The Chartist notion of proper gender relations proved a perfect fit for the requirements of industrial capitalism. This created, or underpinned, gender segregation of jobs and wage differentials, and consolidated women's work as secondary both in the family and at work. This specific way in which industrial capitalism appropriated patriarchal structures was an important safeguard of the material base of male familial authority. The Chartist reaffirmation of male supremacy, albeit in a shape adapted to the changed conditions of production, eased working-class men's accommodation both to industrial capitalism and to the political ideology that was to evolve with it.

Despite its different social origin, the Chartist notion of manhood displayed a significant degree of overlap with middle-class men's idea of masculinity. Cross-class gender solidarity may, in the long run, have subtly helped undermine class conflict as working men affirmed their masculinity as much over their wives as against their employers. The set of shared assumptions in the realm of gender relations surely contributed to the *rapprochement* between both classes, and indirectly reinforced the growth of working-class Liberalism. Subsequent struggles, though not necessarily fought less fiercely than in the Chartist era, remained essentially confined to a capitalist frame of reference. The reforms sought – whether wage rises or restrictions on the participation of women and young people in the labour market – may admittedly have been aimed at improving the condition of the entire class, but they ultimately hardened the sexual division of power between men and women. A social system allowing for the attainment and enhancement of male privileges was sure to win some kind of political consent from working-class men, especially when, up to 1918, the opportunity for expressing that consent – the vote – was repeatedly granted as a further male preserve.

With the crushing of all hopes of ever reverting to pre-industrial conditions, Chartism's female followers were left to their own devices in reassessing their status under the changed conditions. The dwindling support for women – a process that began during the Chartist struggle itself – seems to have deadened, in most of the movement's female adherents, any desire to join this or subsequent campaigns. Thus the transition was made from pressure politics – taken up by whole communities – to the overpowering masculinity that shaped working-class politics in the second half of the nineteenth century.

On a wider canvas, the picture that emerges from the evidence available is one of middle- and working-class women beginning sharply to diverge over gender issues around 1850. Middle-class women, who had effectively been relegated from the public arena, craved for fields of action other than the home on which to bring to bear their specific knowledge, skills and energy. What started off in philanthropic ventures broadened out into more openly political areas and culminated in their standing up for their own rights. In this achievement, they were sustained, at the ideological level, by their class's belief in the power of female influence, which they cleverly turned to their own advantage. At the practical level, they were able to draw on the experience gained in movements such as the anti-slavery and Anti-Corn Law campaigns. Although confined, in both, to working behind the scenes, the female participants were able to claim at least part of these movements' success as their own.

It was not only in this respect that Chartist women, just emerged from a lost cause, differed. Overburdened as they were in their daily lives, their hope was not so much to broaden as to narrow down their multifarious fields of action, without apparently realising that, in the long run, this would be to their detriment. The intersection of class position and dominant sexual ideology thus produced, at least temporarily, diametrically opposed results in middle- and working-class women.

It could be argued that, after the demise of Chartism, women dropped out of working-class politics not least because of the movement's obvious failure – given its inability to arrest the pace of industrialisation – to reinstate them into what was commonly agreed to be their proper position of wives and mothers. Most women turned away from political and trade-union campaigns, devoting their energies instead to attempts to improve domestic life directly, such as the mid-century co-operative movement. Women's large-scale involvement in the Chartist Land Company could thus be seen as the first move in this direction.

In the long run, the Chartist preoccupation with restoring male authority by enforcing female domesticity thwarted the ability of most working people to create a vision of class and gender equality such as had been proclaimed by the Owenites. The Chartist version of gender relations spoke more reassuringly to the anxieties suffered by men and women who felt themselves threatened in the very core of their beings by the erosion of a traditional way of life. For men, who identified themselves primarily through their work, their personal identity was at stake. This was the fabric intricately woven from pride in skill and family headship. Women, who defined themselves chiefly through their familial responsibilities, felt that their performance as wives and mothers was seriously impaired by the combination of economic crises – which threatened living standards – and the need, for increasing numbers of them, to engage in waged labour away from home. The mutual reinforcement of working people's anxieties, Chartist gender images and the patriarchal structures appropriated by, and operating in, industrial capitalism accounts for the difference in size between the Chartist and Owenite movements.

With its insistence on female domesticity, women's views as workers were subdued in the working-class consciousness taking shape in the Chartist struggle. Thus Chartism paved the way for the exclusionist attitude of its successor movements, which was reciprocated by women's apparent reluctance to join organisations that discriminated against them, be it as waged labourers or be it as women.

When women did reappear in working-class politics during the closing decades of the nineteenth century, they found themselves confronted time and again with the now firmly entrenched working-class belief in female domesticity. Women were forced to set up organisations of their own – such as the Women's Co-operative Guild – in order to take care of gender-specific issues. Others, like the suffrage movement, served as a base from which to rattle at the portals of male privilege, including the privilege rampant in working-class organisations themselves. The life of late-nineteenth-century female activists was therefore in many ways similar to that of their Chartist sisters after about 1842. They still had to shoulder the double burden of housework and the need to contribute to the family income. Additionally, they overcame their predecessors' resignation and began to assert themselves in the face of male hostility – a hostility that, frequently enough, came from men of their own class. These often interlocking pressures on their strength exasperated even the strongest-willed and most energetic among them.

Considerable time was to elapse before women were able to begin again to challenge simultaneously their economic exploitation and sexual oppression. This, as it turns out, was not to happen on a large scale until the growth of socialist feminism from around 1970.

Notes

Place of publication is London unless otherwise stated.

List of Abbreviations Used

BT   *Board of Trade Papers*
HO   *Home Office Papers*
PP   *Parliamentary Papers*

Chartist Newspapers and Periodicals

The years indicated are those studied for this book.
The Charter, 1839–40.
The Chartist Pilot. Leicester, 1843–44.
The Democratic Review of British and Foreign Politics, History and Literature, 1849–1850. Reprinted 1968.
The English Chartist Circular, and Temperance Record for England and Wales, 1841–1843. Reprinted New York, 1968.
The Labourer; A Monthly Magazine of Politics, Literature, Poetry, etc., 1847–8.
The London News, 1858.
McDouall's Chartist Journal and Trades' Advocate. Manchester, 1841. Reprinted New York, 1968.
The Midland Counties Illuminator. Leicester, 1841.
The National. A Library for the People, 1839. Reprinted New York, 1968.
The National Association Gazette, 1841–2.
The National Instructor, 1850.
The National Reformer and Manx Weekly Review of Home and Foreign Affairs. Douglas, Isle of Man, 1846–7. Reprinted New York, 1969.
The Northern Liberator. Newcastle upon Tyne, 1837–40.
The Northern Star and Leeds General Advertiser. Leeds, 1838–44; continued as *The Northern Star and National Trades Journal*, 1844–52; continued as *The Star*, March–May 1852; continued as *The Star of Freedom*, May–November 1852.
Notes to the People, 1851–2. Reprinted 1967.
The Operative, 1838–9.
The Penny Times, 1860.
The People: Their Rights and Liberties, Their Duties and Their Interests. Series I, Wortley, 1848–51, series II, Wortley, 1851–2. Reprinted Westport, Conn., 1970.
The People's Paper, 1857–8.
The Red Republican and The Friend of the People, 1850–1. Reprinted 1966.
Reynolds's Political Instructor, 1849–50. Reprinted Westport, Conn., 1970.
The Weekly Telegraph, 1858.
The Western Vindicator; or, Memoirs and Correspondence of an Editor. Bristol, Bath, 1839; continued as *The National Vindicator and Liberator of the West and Wales*. Bath, 1841–2.

Parliamentary Papers

Annual Reports of the Poor Law Commissioners for England and Wales for the years 1834–47/8.
Annual Reports of the Registrar-General of Births, Deaths and Marriages in England for the years 1839–52.
Copies of Correspondence Relating to the Treatment of William Lovett and John Collins, Prisoners in Warwick Gaol. PP 1840. XXXVIII.
Prisoners for Libel: Returns from each Gaol and House of Correction in the United Kingdom of the Name and Designation of every Person confined for Charges for printing and publishing Seditions or Blasphemous Libels, etc. PP 1840. XXXVIII.
Reports from the Select Committee on the National Land Company; together with the Minutes of Evidence, and Appendix. PP XIX. 1847–8.
Reports of the Central Board of His Majesty's Commissioners for inquiring into the Employment of Children in Factories for the years 1833–7.
Reports of the Inspectors of Factories for the Half-Year Ending 31st October 1848. 1849. XXII (1017) (1084.)

Introduction

1. E. P. Thompson, *The Making of the English Working Class*, 3rd edn (Harmondsworth, 1972) p. 801.
2. R. G. Gammage, *History of the Chartist Movement, 1837–1854*, issued in parts in 1854–5.
3. D. Thompson, 'Women and Nineteenth-century Radical Politics: A Lost Dimension', in J. Mitchell and A. Oakley (eds), *The Rights and Wrongs of Women* (Harmondsworth, 1976).
4. See ch. 6 of M. I. Thomis and J. Grimmett, *Women in Protest, 1800–1850*, 1982; D. Jones, 'Women and Chartism', *History*, LXVIII (1983); ch. 7 of D. Thompson, *The Chartists* (1984). There have also been two MA dissertations written on the subject: C. E. Martin, 'Female Chartism', University of Wales (1973): J. E. B. Lowe, 'Women in the Chartist Movement', Birmingham University (1985).
5. L. Davidoff and C. Hall, *Family Fortunes: Men and Women of the English Middle Class, 1780–1850* (1987).
6. For a detailed analysis of Owenite sexual politics, see B. Taylor, *Eve and the New Jerusalem* (1983).

Chapter 1 Changes in Plebeian Women's Living Conditions

1. L. A. Tilly and J. W. Scott, *Women, Work, and Family* (New York, 1978) p. 12.
2. The latter is maintained by H. Medick, 'The Proto-industrial Family Economy: The Structural Function of Household and Family in the Transition from Peasant Society to Industrial Capitalism', *Social History*, IX (1976) p. 312.
3. M. Hewitt, 'The Effect of Married Women's Employment in the Cotton Textile Districts on the Organization and Structure of the Home in Lancashire, 1840–1880', Ph.D. London University (1953) p. 55.
4. *PP* 1834. XXIX. p. 467.
5. G. N. Gandy, 'Illegitimacy in a Handloom Weaving Community:

Fertility Patterns in Culcheth, Lancs, 1781–1860', D.Phil. Oxford (1978) pp. 196, 232, 245.

6. D. Levine, 'Industrialization and the Proletarian Family in England', *Past and Present*, no. 107 (1985) p. 184.

7. Gandy (1978) pp. 183, 188, 202ff.; cf. also Levine (1985) p. 185, who reports on a close analysis of illegitimacy in four communities, which has shown a very direct connection between rising prices and skyrocketing annual illegitimacy ratios. These findings underpin the dependence of marriage on material circumstances.

8. *PP* 1834. XXIX. p. 467.

9. J. R. Gillis, 'Peasant, Plebeian and Proletarian Marriage in Britain, 1600–1900', in D. Levine (ed.), *Proletarianization and Family History* (Orlando, Fla., 1984) pp. 135, 150.

10. Medick (1976) p. 312.

11. These calculations are based on the list of estimated average weekly earnings of various classes of cotton operatives in Lancashire and Cheshire in G. H. Wood, *The History of Wages in the Cotton Trade During the Past Hundred Years* (1910) p. 131.

12. *PP* 1834. XIX. p. 471.

13. *PP* 1834. XXXVI. p. 69i.

14. *The Morning Chronicle*, 8 November 1849, p. 5.

15. B. R. Mitchell and P. Deane, *Abstract of British Historical Statistics* (Cambridge, 1962) p. 187.

16. P. Joyce, *Work, Society and Politics: The Culture of the Factory in Later Victorian England* (Brighton, 1980) p. 60, for his refutation of Smelser's belief that the spinning family was broken up as a productive unit between the 1820s and 1840s (cf. N. J. Smelser, *Social Change in the Industrial Revolution* (Chicago, 1959) p. 224).

17. Hewitt (1953) p. 18; M. Hewitt, *Wives and Mothers in Victorian Industry* (1958) pp. 14, 102; R. B. Lichfield, 'The Family and the Mill: Cotton Mill Work, Family Work Patterns and Fertility in Mid-Victorian Stockport', in A. S. Wohl (ed.), *The Victorian Family: Structure and Stresses* (1978) pp. 183, 185.

18. O. Banks, *Faces of Feminism* (Oxford, 1981) p. 29.

19. *The Morning Chronicle*, 22 October 1849, p. 2.

20. For example, *A Copy of the Evidence Taken and Report Made, by the Assistant Poor Law Commissioners sent to inquire into the State of the Population of Stockport* (Stockport, 1842) p. 125.

21. *PP* 1849. XXII. pp. 158, 179, 183, 190, 204; *PP* 1833. XX. pp. 26, 111 D.2; *PP* 1834. XIX. p. 516.

22. Cf. movements of infant workhouse inmates in Rochdale charted in J. Cole, *Down Poorhouse Lane: The Diary of a Rochdale Workhouse* (Littleborough, 1984) p. 80.

23. *The Morning Chronicle*, 12 November 1849, p. 5.

24. For example, W. Cooke Taylor, *Notes of a Tour in the Manufacturing Districts of Lancashire*, 2nd edn (1842) p. 199.

25. Lichfield (1978) pp. 186, 191.

26. M. Anderson, *Family Structure in Nineteenth-century Lancashire* (Cambridge, 1971) pp. 71, 72–3.

27. S. Alexander, A. Davin and E. Hostettler, 'Labouring Women: A Reply to Eric Hobsbawm', *History Workshop*, no. 8 (1979) p. 178.
28. For example, R. Heywood, *Private Minutes of the Magistrates' Court* (Bolton Central Library) 22 October 1835.
29. *PP* 1833. XX. p. 9 D.2; *PP* 1849. XXII. p. 158.
30. *PP* 1833. XXI. p. 188.
31. *PP* 1849. XXII. p. 183.
32. *The Morning Chronicle*, 22 October 1849, p. 2.
33. Hewitt (1958) p. 64.
34. *PP* 1849. XXII. pp. 177, 204.
35. *PP* 1833. XX. p. 9 D.2.
36. *PP* 1849. XXII. p. 188.
37. J. Foster, *Class Struggle and the Industrial Revolution: Early Industrial Capitalism in Three English Towns* (1974) p. 92.
38. *PP* 1833. XX. p. 15 D.3.
39. *PP* 1833. XXI. pp. 188, 190.
40. *PP* 1833. XX. p. 111 D.2.
41. *Appendix to the Reports of the Select Committee of the House of Commons on Public Petitions* (House of Lords Record Office) App. 269, 1847, p. 132.
42. *PP* 1849. XXII. p. 204.
43. *The Morning Chronicle*, 19 November 1849, p. 5.
44. Ibid., 25 October 1849, p. 5.
45. R. Roberts, *The Classic Slum: Salford Life in the First Quarter of the Century*, 3rd edn (Harmondsworth, 1977) pp. 53–4.
46. Hewitt (1953) pp. 180ff; (1958) p. 129.
47. Anderson (1971) pp. 74, 142.
48. Cooke Taylor (1842) pp. 182–3.
49. *PP* 1849. XXII. p. 178, 181.
50. Anderson (1971) p. 74.
51. For example, J. R. Coulthart, *A Report on the Sanatory Condition of the Town of Ashton-under-Lyne; With Remarks on the Existing Evils, and Suggestions for Improving the Health, Comfort, and Longevity of the Inhabitants* (Ashton-under-Lyne, 1844) p. 21.
52. Mitchell and Deane (1962) p. 36.
53. Foster (1974) p. 97.
54. Hewitt (1953) pp. 200–1; see also *The Morning Chronicle*, 15 November 1849, p. 5.
55. Hewitt (1953) pp. 187, 192–3.
56. W. Dodd, *The Factory System Illustrated in a Series of Letters to the Right Hon. Lord Ashley* (repr. 1968) p. 64.
57. Hewitt (1953) p. 189.
58. *The Morning Chronicle*, 15 November 1849, p. 5.
59. *PP* 1833. XX. p. 3 D.2.
60. For example, *Poor Law Commissioner's Report on Stockport* (1842) p. 120.
61. For example, *The Morning Chronicle*, 29 October 1849, p. 5.
62. *PP* 1833. XXI. pp. 17–18 D.2.
63. *The Morning Chronicle*, 29 October 1849, p. 5.

64. D. Vincent, *Bread, Knowledge and Freedom: A Study of Nineteenth-century Working Class Autobiography* (1981) pp. 79ff.
65. Anderson (1971) pp. 132, 166–7.
66. Coulthart (1844) p. 30.
67. Foster (1974) p. 97.
68. Lichfield (1978) p. 192. The original quote reads: 'age of parents when older children began to work and when younger children were likely to leave home'. This, however, must be a misprint and the sequence of 'older' and 'younger' be inverted so as not to distort the meaning of the passage.
69. M. W. Dupree, 'Family Structure in the Staffordshire Potteries, 1840–1880', D.Phil. Oxford (1981) p. 416.
70. For example, *Rochdale Poor. A copy or extract of any report made by Mr Tuffnell, or other Assistant Commissioner, to the Poor Law Commissioners, in October 1841, as to the State of the Poor in Rochdale* (1841) pp. 4ff.
71. L. Faucher, *Manchester in 1844: Its Present Condition and Future Prospects* (1844) pp. 27, 63, 65.
72. F. Engels, *Die Lage der arbeitenden Klasse in England. Nach eigner Anschauung und authentischen Quellen,* MEW 2, (Berlin, DDR), p. 331.
73. *The Morning Chronicle,* 11 November 1849, p. 5.
74. *The Annual Report of the Manchester and Salford City Mission, with a List of the Subscribers, and Extracts from the Journals of the Missionaries* (Manchester, 1838) p. 15.
75. J. J. Bezer, 'The Autobiography of One of the Chartist Rebels of 1848', in D. Vincent (ed.), *Testaments of Radicalism: Memoirs of Working-Class Politicians, 1790–1885* (1977) p. 164.
76. E. Ross, 'Survival Networks: Women's Neighbourhood Sharing in London Before World War I', *History Workshop,* no. 15 (1983) p. 7.
77. Quoted in P. Thane, 'Women and the Poor Law in Victorian and Edwardian England', *History Workshop,* no. 6 (1978) p. 35.
78. *PP* 1849. XXII. pp. 158, 165.
79. *Appendix on Public Petitions,* App. 694, 1847–8, p. 369.
80. National Association for the Promotion of Social Science, *Trades Societies and Strikes. Report of the Committee on Trades' Societies* (1860) p. 220.
81. J. Liddington and J. Norris, *One Hand Tied Behind Us* (1978) p. 100.
82. For example, P. Gaskell, *Artisans and Machinery: The Moral and Physical Condition of the Manufacturing Population* (1836) p. 105.
83. Cooke Taylor (1842) p. 45.
84. For example, *Reports of the Manchester City Mission* (1838–50).
85. For example, *The Bolton Free Press,* 9 November 1844, p. 3.
86. For example, Heywood, *Private Minutes,* 11 September 1835.
87. For example, *The Bolton Free Press,* 9 November 1844, p. 3; 23 November 1844, p. 3.
88. *Blackburn Strangers' Friend Society. Report,* 1850 (Blackburn Central Library) pp. 4, 9.
89. These difficulties are mirrored in the marriage pattern of Lancashire, which was predominantly Anglican throughout the 1840s; cf. *Annual Reports of the Registrar-General of Births, Deaths and Marriages in England for the years 1839–1852 in PP.*

90. Cf. Mitchell and Deane (1962) p. 6.
91. For example, *Rochdale Poor* (1841) pp. 5ff.
92. *The Morning Chronicle*, 25 October 1849, p. 5; 12 November 1849, p. 5.
93. For the Lancashire cotton district, this is borne out by, for example, *Reports of the Bolton Society for the Protection of the Poor and District Provident Society* (1840–58).
94. For example, *The Bolton Free Press*, 7 September 1844, p. 3; 23 November 1844, p. 3.
95. For example, *The Bolton Free Press*, 5 October 1844, p. 3; 23 November 1844, p. 3.
96. E. Ross, '"Fierce Questions and Taunts": Married Life in Working-class London, 1870–1914', *Feminist Studies*, VIII (1982) p. 594.
97. A. Clark, 'Rape or Seduction? A Controversy over Sexual Violence in the Nineteenth Century', in The London Feminist History Group, *The Sexual Dynamics of History: Men's Power, Women's Resistance* (1983) p. 19.
98. For example, *The Morning Chronicle*, 8 November 1849, p. 5.
99. For example, *PP* 1833. XX. p. 39 D.1.
100. N. Tomes, '"A Torrent of Abuse": Crimes of Violence between Working-class Men and Women in London, 1840–1875', *Journal of Social History*, XI (1978) p. 334.
101. For example, Heywood, *Private Minutes*, 24 September 1835, 5 November 1835.
102. Tomes (1978) pp. 332, 338–9; cf. also Ross (1982) p. 582; (1983) p. 8.
103. Vincent (1981) p. 55.

Chapter 2 The Chartist Prospect of Society

1. C. E. Martin, 'Female Chartism', University of Wales (1973) ch. 1 and conclusion; M. I. Thomis and J. Grimmett, *Women in Protest, 1800–1850* (1982) pp. 120, 123; D. Thompson, *The Chartists* (1984) pp. 142–3; J. E. B. Lowe, 'Women in the Chartist Movement', Birmingham University (1985) p. 17.
2. G. Stedman Jones, *Languages of Class* (Cambridge, 1983) p. 100.
3. R. G. Gammage, *History of the Chartist Movement, 1837–1854* (repr. 1976) p. 9.
4. Stedman Jones (1983) pp. 161ff.
5. *The English Chartist Circular*, no. 13, p. 49.
6. *The Western Vindicator*, 23 March 1839, p. 2.
7. *The English Chartist Circular*, no. 94, p. 165; *The Democratic Review*, February 1850, p. 347; Samuel Smiles in *The Labourer*, vol. 4, p. 251 (I am grateful to Angela John for bringing this article to my attention); *Notes to the People*, p. 361; *The National*, no. 5, pp. 66–7. The same item also appeared in *The English Chartist Circular*, no. 8, p. 31.
8. *Notes to the People*, pp. 630–1.
9. *McDouall's Chartist Journal*, no. 17, pp. 131–2.
10. *The National Instructor*, pp. 21–2.
11. *The National*, no. 5, pp. 66–7; *The English Chartist Circular*, no. 8, p. 31.
12. *The English Chartist Circular*, no. 94, p. 165; *The Democratic Review*, February 1850, pp. 347–8; *Reynolds's Political Instructor*, no. 4, p. 31.
13. *The Western Vindicator*, 23 March 1839, p. 2.

14. *Notes to the People*, p. 361.
15. Ibid., pp. 149–50, 768. *The Northern Star*, 27 October 1849, p. 3.
16. Smiles in *The Labourer*, vol. 4, p. 241.
17. E. W. Binney quoted in *The English Chartist Circular*, no. 66, p. 54.
18. *The English Chartist Circular*, no. 66, p. 54; *The National Association Gazette*, no. 22, p. 174; *Reynolds's Political Instructor*, no. 18, p. 141.
19. *McDouall's Chartist Journal*, no. 19, pp. 146–7; Smiles in *The Labourer*, vol. 4, p. 249.
20. *The English Chartist Circular*, no. 66, p. 54.
21. *The Western Vindicator*, 23 March 1839, p. 2.
22. *The English Chartist Circular*, no. 66, p. 54; no. 94, p. 165; no. 143, p. 361; *The National Association Gazette*, no. 22, p. 175; Smiles in *The Labourer*, vol. 4, p. 250.
23. J. R. Stephens, *The Political Pulpit: A Selection of Sermons* (1839) p. 12.
24. *The People*, no. 22, p. 173.
25. N. J. Smelser, *Social Change in the Industrial Revolution* (Chicago, 1959) p. 299.
26. *The Northern Star*, 2 May 1840, p. 8; *The Western Vindicator*, 23 March 1839, p. 2; *Notes to the People*, p. 361; *The National Instructor*, p. 22.
27. *McDouall's Chartist Journal*, no. 20, p. 155.
28. W. Cooke Taylor, *Factories and the Factory System* (1844) p. 41.
29. D. Phillips, *Crime and Authority in Victorian England: The Black Country, 1835–1860* (1977) p. 152, quoted in A. Clark, *Women's Silence, Men's Violence: Sexual Assault in England, 1770–1845* (London, New York, 1987) p. 96.
30. For example, *The Northern Star*, 3 March 1838, p. 5.
31. J. Lambertz, 'Sexual Harassment in the Nineteenth Century English Cotton Industry', *History Workshop*, no. 19 (1985) pp. 34, 43.
32. *The Friend of the People*, no. 1, p. 5.
33. *The People*, no. 14, p. 104; no. 37, p. 291.
34. *The Northern Star*, 15 September 1849, p. 3.
35. *The National Instructor*, p. 155.
36. *Notes to the People*, p. 789.
37. *The Northern Star*, 19 May 1849, p. 3.
38. *Notes to the People*, p. 790.
39. Lady Sydney Morgan quoted in *The Northern Liberator*, no. 140, p. 3; *The English Chartist Circular*, no. 113, p. 244.
40. B. Taylor, *Eve and the New Jerusalem* (1983) p. 47.
41. *Notes to the People*, p. 671.
42. Stephens (1839) pp. 21, 60.
43. *The Ashton Chronicle*, 14 April 1849, p. 4.
44. Ibid., 23 June 1849, p. 1.
45. Ibid., 14 July 1849, p. 3.
46. For example, *The National Reformer*, no. 1, p. 4; *The Northern Star*, 3 March 1838, p. 5; *The Star of Freedom*, 28 August 1852, p. 4.
47. *The Northern Liberator*, no. 137, p. 3.
48. *The People*, no. 65, p. 98.
49. Ibid., no. 157, p. 419.
50. *The National Reformer*, no. 13, p. 14.

51. *Notes to the People*, pp. 518, 520, 549, 570.
52. *The Northern Star*, 27 October 1849, p. 3; 5 January 1850, p. 3.
53. J. J. Bezer, 'The Autobiography of One of the Chartist Rebels of 1848', in D. Vincent (ed.), *Testaments of Radicalism: Memoirs of Working-Class Politicians, 1790–1885* (1977) p. 170.
54. *The People*, no. 147–8, p. 350.
55. *Reynolds's Political Instructor*, no. 16, p. 122.
56. M. Wollstonecraft quoted in *The National*, no. 11, p. 145; *The National Association Gazette*, no. 17, p. 131; G. Wakefield quoted in *The Western Vindicator*, 9 March 1839, p. 4.
57. *The People*, no. 147–8, p. 350.
58. *The National*, no. 10, pp. 129–32.
59. *The National Instructor*, p. 22.
60. *The Northern Star*, 19 May 1849, p. 3.
61. *Notes to the People*, p. 571.
62. Ibid.
63. Ibid., p. 592.
64. Ibid., p. 651.
65. *The People*, no. 108, p. 31.
66. *The Bradford Observer*, 7 June 1838, quoted in A. J. Peacock, *Bradford Chartism, 1838–40* (York, 1969) p. 15.
67. *Notes to the People*, pp. 549–50.
68. *McDouall's Chartist Journal*, no. 7, pp. 50–1; no. 26, pp. 206–7.
69. *The National*, no. 11, pp. 145–6; no. 24, p. 327.
70. *The People*, no. 21, p. 161.
71. *The English Chartist Circular*, no. 66, p. 54; no. 94, p. 165; no. 143, p. 361; *The National Association Gazette*, no. 9, p. 72; no. 18, p. 142; *McDouall's Chartist Journal*, no. 7, pp. 50–1; *Reynolds's Political Instructor*, no. 4, p. 30; *The Labourer*, vol.4, pp. 241ff.; *The Democratic Review*, October 1849, p. 183.
72. *Reynolds's Political Instructor*, no. 4, p. 30; no. 9, p. 69; *The National Association Gazette*, no. 22, p. 174.
73. *McDouall's Chartist Journal*, no. 25, p. 195.
74. E. Swaine, *The Political Franchise, a Public Trust, demanding an Intelligent and Virtuous Care for the Public Good. A Lecture to Working Men . . . at the Request of the Congregational Union. With an Appendix on the Exclusion of Women and others from the Franchise* (1849) pp. 33ff.
75. Mrs Hugo Reid, *A Plea for Woman* (Edinburgh, 1843) pp. 51ff.
76. *The People's Charter: Being an Outline of An Act to provide for the Just Representation of the People of Great Britain and Ireland in the Commons' House of Parliament*, 3rd edn (1838) pp. 2–3.
77. *The Operative*, 4 November 1838, p. 1.
78. *The English Chartist Circular*, no. 83, p. 111.
79. *The Northern Star*, 2 October 1841, p. 1; 1 July 1843, p. 1; 24 October 1846, p. 8.
80. *The National Reformer*, no. 26, pp. 5, 6. This had been Bronterre O'Brien's position all along, cf. *The Operative*, 4 November 1838, p. 1.
81. *The Northern Star*, 24 October 1846, p. 8.
82. *The English Chartist Circular*, no. 13, p. 49; see also a clip from *The*

Examiner in W. Lovett, *Proceedings of Working Men's Associations* (Birmingham Public Library) pt. 2, p. 257; answer to Sir Lytton Bulwer in *The Northern Star*, 20 October 1838, p. 3.

83. *The Northern Star*, 23 September 1843, p. 7.

84. D. Thompson (1984) p. 203.

85. C. Barmby, 'The Demand for the Emancipation of Women, Politically and Socially', *New Tracts for the Times*, vol. 1 (1843) no. 3.

86. *The Democratic Review*, June 1849, p. 391.

87. *The People*, no. 145–6, p. 331.

88. *The National Association Gazette*, no. 1, p. 1; no. 6, p. 43; no. 11, p. 84.

89. *The English Chartist Circular*, no. 42, p. 166.

90. Ibid., no. 94, p. 165.

91. Ibid., no. 13, p. 49.

92. Of course, the feminist tradition is far from monolithic. A case in point is Mary Astell, who lived from 1666 to 1731. She not only remained single throughout her life, but actually managed to make a living out of writing. Her works combine staunch High Tory views with urgent demands for better education of women, not least in order to lighten their lot in marriage, of which she took a dim view. With regard to her emphasis on female education, Mary Astell can be viewed as an early precursor of Mary Wollstonecraft, whose *Vindication*, however, was embedded in a politically radical tradition. See two recent studies of Mary Astell by B. Hill (ed.), *The First English Feminist: 'Reflections Upon Marriage' and Other Writings by Mary Astell* (Aldershot, 1986), and R. Perry, *The Celebrated Mary Astell: An Early Feminist* (Chicago, London, 1986).

93. In 1841, John Cleave, the printer and member of the LWMA, brought out a cheap edition of the book; cf. *The English Chartist Circular*, no. 27, p. 108.

94. *Address And Rules of the Working Men's Association, for benefiting Politically, Socially and Morally, The Useful Classes* (n.d.) p. 4.

95. *The English Chartist Circular*, no. 22, p. 88; no. 27, p. 108; *The National Association Gazette*, no. 21, p. 166; no. 24, p. 193; *The National Vindicator*, 4 December 1841, p. 7.

96. *The National*, no. 11, p. 143; *The National Association Gazette*, no. 9, p. 71; no. 17, p. 138; no. 19, p. 150.

97. *The English Chartist Circular*, no. 26, p. 102.

98. For example, *The English Chartist Circular*, no. 16, p. 63.

99. *The Midland Counties Illuminator*, 20 March 1841, p. 24.

100. The *Appeal* was written in refutation of James Mill's *Article on Government*.

101. *The People*, no. 134.

102. Born in the United States in 1809, Bray came to England in 1822. His family settled in Leeds, where he became a working compositor. His active connection with the working-class movement can be traced back to 1835. Two years later, he was elected treasurer of the newly formed Leeds WMA, which had been modelled on the LWMA. In this capacity, he delivered a series of lectures on 'The Working Class – Their True Wrong and Their True Remedy', which were favourably received. At

the end of 1838, he began to publish these lectures in weekly instalments, which did not arouse much interest among workers and received an unfavourable press. In 1842, following the decline of Chartism, Bray returned to the United States, where he continued to propagate his ideas and to be active in the labour movement up to his death in 1895.

103. *The Northern Star*, 7 September 1839, p. 7.
104. Ibid., 9 October 1841, p. 1.
105. Ibid., 2 December 1848, p. 4; *The People*, no. 134.
106. This and all the following quotes are from R. J. Richardson, *The Rights of Woman: Exhibiting Her Natural, Civil, and Political Claims to a Share in the Legislative and Executive Power of the State* (Edinburgh, 1840; repr. Manchester, 1986). *Rights of Woman* is worth quoting in detail, for hitherto only the second half of the pamphlet has been available in D. Thompson, *The Early Chartists* (1971) pp. 115ff. The text in its entirety, however, has a somewhat different slant than appears when the latter half is seen in isolation.
107. Second National Petition in *The English Chartist Circular*, no. 40, p. 159.
108. *The Northern Star*, 30 January 1841, p. 3; *The Midland Counties Illuminator*, 13 February 1841, p. 3.
109. *The Democratic Review*, no. 1, dedication.
110. *The English Chartist Circular*, no. 13, p. 49.

Chapter 3 The Social Profile of Chartism's Female Following

1. D. Thompson, *The Chartists* (1984) p. 6.
2. Ibid., p. 116.
3. J. E. B. Lowe, 'Women in the Chartist Movement', Birmingham University (1985) p. 2.
4. D. Thompson (1984) pp. 112, 209.
5. Lowe (1985) p. 18.
6. For example, M. Jenkins, *The General Strike of 1842* (1980) *passim*.
7. D. Thompson (1984) p. 62; see also D. Jones, *Chartism and and the Chartists* (1975) p. 27, whose list of Chartist strongholds largely overlaps with Thompson's.
8. D. Thompson (1984) pp. 106, 124.
9. Lowe (1985) p. 19.
10. J. Epstein, *The Lion of Freedom: Feargus O'Connor and the Chartist Movement, 1832–1842* (1982) p. 232.
11. D. Thompson (1984) p. 113.
12. E. P. Thompson, *The Making of the English Working Class*, 3rd edn (Harmondsworth, 1972) p. 326.
13. J. MacAskill, 'The Chartist Land Plan', in A. Briggs (ed.), *Chartist Studies* (1959) pp. 322, 331.
14. D. Thompson (1984) p. 174.
15. *BT* 4/474–6 (Public Record Office).
16. D. Thompson (1984) p. 94.
17. The nearest estimate of overall membership in those years is 42,000, given by A. M. Hadfield, *The Chartist Land Company* (Newton Abbott,

1970) p. 45, as the number of people joining between August 1847 and January 1848.
18. Lowe (1985) app. 3, pp. 282ff.
19. D. Thompson (1984) p. 128.
20. Ibid.
21. *BT* 4/474–6.
22. Jones (1975) p. 27; see also the appendix of 'Location and Timing of Chartist Activity' in D. Thompson (1984) pp. 341ff.; see also the two maps showing the wider geographical distribution of Land Company branches in the summer of 1847 as compared to NCA branches in 1841 in Jones (1975) pp. 9–10.
23. Appendix in D. Thompson (1984) pp. 341ff.
24. *Census Enumerators' Books* for the 1851 Census in *HO* 107.
25. In the early censuses, the use of the category 'housewife' was highly problematic. Often it indicated the census-takers' view of women's proper function rather than accurately describing women's multi-faceted employment, waged or not, in the home.
26. P. Searby, 'Great Dodford and the Later History of the Chartist Land Scheme', *Agricultural History Review*, XVI (1968) p. 36.
27. 'List of Allottees or Occupiers on the Estates' in Hadfield (1970) pp. 224ff.; see also Searby (1968); see also *The Northern Star, passim*.
28. P. Horn, 'The Chartist Land Company', *Cake and Cock-Horse*, II (1968) pp. 21, 23.
29. D. Thompson (1984) p. 128.
30. Horn (1968) pp. 21, 23. In the ballot list, Emma Adams incorrectly appeared as Emma Andrews, see Hadfield (1970) p. 232.

Chapter 4 The Political Pose of Women Chartists

The Roman numbers used below refer to the addresses of the following FCAs:

I	Nottingham Female Political Union in *The Northern Star*, 8 December 1838, p. 6.
II	Ashton-under-Lyne FCA in *The Northern Star*, 2 February 1839, p. 3.
III	Newcastle FCA in *The Northern Star*, 9 February 1839, p. 6.
IV	London Female Democratic Association in *The Operative*, 12 May 1839, p. 16.
V	Stockport FCA in *The Northern Star*, 25 May 1839, p. 5.
VI	Wotton-under-Edge FCA in *The Western Vindicator*, 29 June 1839, p. 3.
VII	Bristol Female Patriotic Association in *The Northern Star*, 2 August 1839, p. 6.
VIII	Bath FCA in *The Western Vindicator*, 17 August 1839, p. 4.
IX	Cheltenham FCA in *The Western Vindicator*, 24 August 1839, p. 2.
X	Blackwood FCA in *The Western Vindicator*, 31 August 1839, p. 3.
XI	Keighley FCA in *The Northern Star*, 12 October 1839, p. 3.
XII	Trowbridge FCA in *The Western Vindicator*, 30 November 1839, p. 4.
XIII	Newcastle FCA in *The Northern Star*, 26 December 1840, p. 6.
XIV	Manchester FCA in *The Northern Star*, 31 July 1841, p. 8.

XV   Cheltenham Female Political Union in *The Western Vindicator*, 24 August 1841, p. 8.

XVI   Upper Honley and Smallthorn FCA in *The Northern Star*, 29 January 1842, p. 8.

XVII   FCA of Manchester Road, Bradford in *The Northern Star*, 19 February 1842, p. 7.

XVIII   Sheffield FCA in *The Northern Star*, 4 June 1842, p. 8.

XIX   Susanna Inge, member of the City of London FCA in *The Northern Star*, 2 July 1842, p. 7.

XX   Bradford FCA in *The Northern Star*, 19 December 1842, p. 7.

XXI   London FCA in *The Northern Star*, 24 June 1848, p. 6.

XXII   Bethnal Green FCA in *The Northern Star*, 8 July 1848, p. 1.

1. I.
2. IX; see also II, VII, XV, XIV, XVII, XXI.
3. IX.
4. *The National Association Gazette*, no. 12, p. 9.
5. *The Northern Star*, 23 June 1838, p. 3. The significance of this woman's Scottish origins is beyond the scope of this book.
6. II.
7. *The Democratic Review*, April 1850, p. 423.
8. XIX.
9. I; see also VII.
10. II.
11. XIV.
12. XXII.
13. I, XVIII, XXII.
14. XXII.
15. III.
16. IX.
17. XVIII; see also II.
18. III.
19. XVI.
20. *The Northern Star*, 2 May 1840, p. 8.
21. III; see also IV, VII, XI.
22. 'Marcus', *On the Possibilities of Limiting Populousness* (1838), *The Book of Murder* (1839).
23. II.
24. IX.
25. XXII.
26. XX; on the theme of the contrast between the rich and the poor, see also I.
27. VII.
28. XIV.
29. XVI.
30. For example, address to Wotton-under-Edge FCA in *The Western Vindicator*, 29 June 1839, p. 3; VIII; XII. The fact that this image cropped up in three addresses that appeared in the same regional paper testifies to the extent to which they influenced each other.

31. IX.
32. III; for the attribution of contemporary misery to class legislation, see also I, VII, IX, XX, XVIII.
33. I; see also VII.
34. VII.
35. For example, XIV, XX.
36. XVI.
37. VII.
38. VII.
39. III.
40. II.
41. XI.
42. VIII; see also XIII, which mentioned 'the fangs of your oppressors'.
43. XIII.
44. X.
45. I.
46. V.
47. IV.
48. III.
49. VII.
50. XI.
51. XIV.
52. XXII; see also the address of Newcastle FCA to released prisoners in *The Northern Star*, 26 December 1840, p. 6.
53. XXII.
54. V.
55. III, XI, XVIII.
56. III.
57. I.
58. IX.
59. XIV.
60. I.
61. VI.
62. XI.
63. XVII.
64. X.
65. XIV.
66. XVIII.
67. VII; see also XIV.
68. II.
69. XXII.
70. III.
71. XI.
72. In a period when the chief remedy for poverty and crime was believed to consist in preventing the poor from reproducing, Chartist women made a bid for cross-class female equality by stressing their right to motherhood by virtue of their womanhood. This, to them, was apparently more relevant than differences of child-rearing practices that the middle class emphasised. In the light of this specific context,

Chartist women's claim to maternal feelings does not necessarily indicate their falling for what E. Badinter, *Die Mutterliebe: Die Geschichte eines Gefühls vom 17. Jahrhundert bis heute* (München, Zürich, 1981) would call the myth of the maternal instinct in human beings. The conclusions she has presented are far too general, even in the French, let alone the European context. For the serious methodological flaws of her work such as lack of a chronological and sociological dimension see also S. Wilson, 'The Myth of Motherhood a Myth: The Historical View of European Child-Rearing', *Social History*, IX (1984).

73. XIX.
74. E. P. Thompson, *The Making of the English Working Class*, 3rd edn (Harmondsworth, 1972) p. 454.
75. B. Taylor, *Eve and the New Jerusalem* (1983) p. 80.
76. *The Black Dwarf*, 10 May 1820, quoted in M. I. Thomis and J. Grimmett, *Women in Protest, 1800–1850* (1982) p. 96.
77. *The National Association Gazette*, no. 17, p. 131.
78. Her brothers held high ranks in the army, and she realised that her parents would have been horrified had they lived to see her become a Chartist; see *The English Chartist Circular*, no. 33, p. 129.
79. For example, *The Northern Star*, 3 February 1838, p. 5; 17 February 1838, p. 8; 1 September 1838, p. 8; 29 December 1838, p. 7.
80. For example, T. Gisborne, *Enquiry into the Duties of the Female Sex* (1797) pp. 19–20; Mrs J. Sandford, *Female Improvement* (1836) vol. 1, p. 142; 'A Woman' (Mrs Richard Napier), *Women's Rights and Duties* (1840) p. 4.
81. H. G. Clark, *The English Maiden: Her Moral and Domestic Duties* (1841) pp. 6, 11; Sandford (1836) vol. 1, pp. 52, 67; S. Stickney Ellis, *The Women of England, Their Social Duties and Domestic Habits*, 2nd edn (1839) p. 64.
82. For example, P. Wakefield, *Reflections on the Present Condition of the Female Sex; with Suggestions for its Improvement* (1798) p. 109; Mrs J. Sandford, *Woman, in Her Social and Domestic Character* (1831) p. 63; 'Woman' (1840) vol. 1, p. 210.
83. F. Basch, *Relative Creatures: Victorian Women in Society and the Novel, 1837–67* (1974) p. 5.
84. S. Stickney Ellis, *The Wives of England, Their Relative Duties, Domestic Influence, and Social Obligations* (1843) p. 110.
85. W. E. Houghton, *The Victorian Frame of Mind, 1830–1870* (Yale, 1957) p. 343.
86. A spate of books were written in order to point out to women the best ways of exerting their moral influence; for example, S. Stickney Ellis (1839); *The Mothers of England, Their Influence and Responsibility* (1843); 1843 (*Wives*); *The Daughters of England, Their Position in Society, Character, and Responsibilities* (1845).
87. For example, Gisborne (1797) pp. 12–13.
88. Charlotte Elizabeth (i.e. Charlotte Elizabeth Phelan, afterwards Tonna), *The Wrongs of Woman* (1843–4) bk. 4, pp. 136ff. I am grateful to Angela John for bringing this book to my attention.
89. *North Staffordshire Mercury*, 24 November 1839.
90. Ibid., 1 December 1839.
91. Ibid., 15 December 1839.

92. Ibid., 22 December 1839.
93. Revd F. Close, *The Female Chartists' Visit to the Parish Church: A Sermon Addressed to the Female Chartists of Cheltenham, Sunday, August 25th, 1839, on the Occasion of their Attending the Parish Church in a Body* (1839) pp. 2, 13, 17.
94. *The Weekly True Sun*, 8 September 1839, p. 2. I am grateful to Greg Claeys for bringing this reference to my attention.
95. *The Western Vindicator*, 23 March 1839, p. 2.
96. S. Lewis, *Woman's Mission*, 2nd edn (1839) pp. 11, 45–6.
97. *The Northern Star*, 17 June 1848, p. 1.
98. Ibid., 10 September 1842, p. 5.
99. *The Operative*, 13 January 1839, p. 6. For a similar statement from Harney, see *The Northern Star*, 13 October 1838, p. 8.
100. *The Western Vindicator*, 9 March 1839, p. 1.
101. Ibid., 23 March 1839, p. 2.
102. T. C. Salt, *To the Women of Birmingham*, 16 August 1838.
103. *The English Chartist Circular*, no. 13, p. 50.
104. For example, *The Northern Star*, 8 September 1838, p. 4.
105. *The Times*, 22 October 1842, p. 4.
106. *The English Chartist Circular*, no. 90, p. 152.
107. For example, *The Northern Star*, 8 June 1839, p. 5.
108. *HO* 40/48, p. 699.
109. *The Northern Star*, 8 September 1838, p. 4.
110. *The English Chartist Circular*, no. 90, p. 152.
111. A. Jameson, *Characteristics of Women, Moral, Poetical, and Historical* (1832) pp. x/viiff.
112. 'Woman' (1840) pp. 275, 277.
113. *The English Chartist Circular*, no. 90, p. 152.
114. Ibid., no. 13, p. 49.
115. *The Western Vindicator*, 28 September 1839, p. 1.
116. *The Charter*, 15 September 1839, p. 536.
117. W. Lovett, *Proceedings of Working Men's Associations* (Birmingham Public Library) pt. 2, p. 263.
118. Salt (1838).

Chapter 5 Chartist Women in the Family

1. For example, *The Northern Star*, 9 April 1842, p. 1.
2. *The Western Vindicator*, 28 September 1839, p. 1.
3. *The English Chartist Circular*, no. 19, p. 76.
4. For example, *The Northern Star*, 22 December 1838, p. 3.
5. Ibid., 20 June 1840, p. 2.
6. Ibid., 13 March 1841, quoted in D. Thompson, *The Chartists* (1984) p. 378.
7. *The Northern Star*, 22 December 1838, p. 3.
8. For Leno, see his autobiography: *The Aftermath: With Autobiography of the Author John Bedford Leno* (1892).
9. For Watson, see W. J. Linton, *A Memoir of James Watson* (Manchester, 1880).
10. B. Wilson, 'The Struggles of an Old Chartist', in D. Vincent, *Testaments*

of Radicalism: Memoirs of Working Class Politicians, 1790–1885 (1977) pp. 195–7.

11. W. E. Adams, *Memoirs of a Social Atom* (1903) pp. 163–4.
12. *North Staffordshire Mercury*, 3 November 1838, p. 3.
13. *The Republican*, vol. 5, p. 603, quoted in E. and R. Frow, 'Women in the Early Radical and Labour Movement', *Marxism Today*, XII (1968) p. 108.
14. G. T. Wilkinson, *The Cato-Street Conspiracy* (1820) pp. 73–4; E. P. Thompson, *The Making of the English Working Class*, 3rd edn (Harmondsworth, 1972) p. 775.
15. S. Bamford, *Passages in the Life of a Radical* (repr. Oxford, 1984) pp. 161ff.
16. In the winter of 1840–1, the government arranged for a systematic investigation into Chartist prisoners. For this purpose, Home Office prison inspectors administered a set of standardised interviews to seventy-three male prisoners. The material gained from this investigation is preserved in *HO* 20/10. Although focusing on the men's motives for becoming Chartists and on the nature of their offences, the answers elicited by these interviews do yield some statistical information on male Chartists' private lives. For the representativeness of the sample, see C. Godfrey, 'The Chartist Prisoners, 1839–41', *International Review of Social History*, XXXIX (1979).
17. D. Read and E. Glasgow, *Feargus O'Connor, Irishman and Chartist* (1961) p. 142 just mention 'several', one of whom, Edward O'Connor Terry, was born in London to a painter's wife and later became an actor, see entry in *Chambers's Biographical Dictionary*. W. H. G. Armytage, 'The Chartist Land Colonies, 1846–1848', *Agricultural History*, XXXII (1958) p. 96, referring to information he received from a local, reports two sons born to a local girl at O'Connorville.
18. Adams (1903) pp. 208–9, see also Read and Glasgow (1961) p. 142.
19. J. Watkins in *The English Chartist Circular*, no. 13, p. 49.
20. Letter from Thomas Cooper to Susanna 21 October 1879, quoted in R. J. Conklin, *Thomas Cooper the Chartist, 1805–1892* (Manila, 1935) p. 448.
21. Letter from John Frost to Mary, quoted in *The Northern Star*, 7 March 1840, p. 1; letter from William Sherratt Ellis to his wife, quoted in *The English Chartist Circular*, no. 148, p. 1.
22. Letter from John Frost to Mary, quoted in *The Northern Star*, 7 March 1840, p. 1.
23. Cooper in *The English Chartist Circular*, no. 145, p. 1; *HO* 20/10; for Lowery, see *Newcastle Chronicle*, 17 May 1856, p. 56; 24 May 1856, p. 68.
24. *Newcastle Chronicle*, 24 May 1856, p. 68.
25. Leno (1892) p. 30.
26. Cooper in *The English Chartist Circular*, no. 145, p. 1.
27. *Newcastle Chronicle*, 17 May 1856, p. 56.
28. Leno (1892) p. 30.
29. Ibid.
30. Linton (1880) p. 37.
31. W. Dorling, *Henry Vincent: A Biographical Sketch* (1879) p. 30.
32. *HO* 20/10.
33. For Harney, see F. G. and R. M. Black, *The Harney Papers* (Assen, 1969);

see also A. R. Schoyen, *The Chartist Challenge: A Portrait of George Julian Harney* (1958).

34. T. Cooper, *The Life of Thomas Cooper, Written by Himself* (repr. Leicester, 1971) pp. 93–4.
35. *The Western Vindicator*, 29 June 1839, p. 4.
36. R. G. Gammage, *History of the Chartist Movement, 1837–1854* (repr. 1976) p. 78.
37. *The Northern Star*, 11 September 1847, p. 8.
38. Ibid., 27 April 1839, p. 4; see also D. Jones, 'Women and Chartism', *History*, LXVIII (1983) p. 9, which lists active Chartist couples.
39. *The Northern Star*, 30 March 1839, p. 3.
40. A. J. Peacock, *Bradford Chartism, 1838–40* (York, 1969) p. 52.
41. See entry on Samuel Holberry in J. Saville and J. Bellamy, *Dictionary of Labour Biography*, vols 1–7 (1970–82).
42. Godfrey (1979) p. 206.
43. J. L. Baxter, 'The Origins of the Social War in South Yorkshire: A Study of Capitalist Evolution and Labour Class Realization in One Industrial Region, c. 1750–1855', Ph.D. Sheffield (1976) p. 681.
44. *The Northern Star*, 14 April 1838, p. 8.
45. Ibid., 6 April 1850, p. 4.
46. Ibid., 14 April 1838, p. 8.
47. *The Operative*, 14 April 1839, p. 9.
48. *The Northern Star*, 21 August 1841, p. 7.
49. Ibid., 13 March 1841, p. 1.
50. Ibid., 19 January 1839, p. 5.
51. J. Epstein, *The Lion of Freedom: Feargus O'Connor and the Chartist Movement, 1832–1842* (1982) p. 232.
52. See entry on James Sweet in *Dictionary of Labour Biography*.
53. *The Northern Star*, 5 October 1839, p. 4.
54 Ibid., 3 June 1848, p. 5.
55. See entry on John Goodwyn Barmby in *Dictionary of Labour Biography*; see also B. Taylor, *Eve and the New Jerusalem* (1983) p. 75.
56. For Charles Neesom, see *The National Reformer*, 20 July 1861, p. 6; E. H. Haraszti, *Chartism* (Budapest, 1978) p. 92; D. Thompson, *The Chartists* (1984) p. 192. For Elizabeth Neesom, see *The Operative*, 14 April 1839, p. 92; *The Charter*, 13 October 1839, p. 608; *The Northern Star*, 30 January 1841, p. 1.
57. Letter from Vincent to Minikin, 25 July 1841; letter from Lucy Vincent to Minikin, 6 June 1841; presumably also letter 14 July 1842, although it does not become clear from the contents of this letter how the debt mentioned was incurred.
58. *The Northern Star*, 1 May 1841, p. 8; for Ernest Jones, see F. Leary, *The Life of Ernest Jones* (1887); for O'Brien, see A. Plummer, *Bronterre: A Political Biography of Bronterre O'Brien, 1804–1864* (1971).
59. In Dorling (1879) p. ix.
60. For Cooper, see R. J. Conklin, *Thomas Cooper the Chartist, 1805–1892* (Manila, 1935) p. 445.
61. *The Midland Counties Illuminator*, 27 March 1841, pp. 26–7; 8 May 1841, p. 50; *The Northern Star*, 8 May 1841, p. 4.

62. *The Northern Star*, 3 June 1840, p. 4.
63. *The Northern Liberator*, no. 125, p. 3; see also *The Northern Star*, 29 February 1840, p. 5; see also *The Charter*, 1 March 1840, p. 9.
64. Quoted in Linton (1880) p. 76.
65. *The English Chartist Circular*, no. 149, p. 1.
66. T. Cooper, *The Purgatory of Suicides. A Prison-Rhyme* (1851) p. 251.
67. Quoted in Linton (1880) pp. 76, 78.
68. *The English Chartist Circular*, no. 149, p. 1.
69. Ibid.
70. See entry on William Cuffay in *Dictionary of Labour Biography*.
71. Letter from John Frost to Mary, quoted in *The Northern Star*, 7 March 1840, p. 1.
72. J. McCabe, *George Jacob Holyoake* (1922) p. 20.
73. *The Northern Star*, 14 March 1840, p. 5; see letter from John Frost to Mary, quoted in *The Northern Star*, 7 March 1840, p. 1.
74. Letter from Jane Jones to Ernest, quoted in D. Thompson (1984) p. 144.
75. Plummer (1971) p. 71.
76. Ibid.
77. *The Northern Liberator*, no. 136, p. 1; no. 137, p. 5; no. 138, p. 5; see also *The Northern Star*, 16 May 1840, p. 4; 30 May 1840, p. 4.
78. Letter from Ernest Jones, 18 December 1848.
79. Letter from Jane Jones to Ernest, 20 August 1848.
80. Letter from Jane Jones to Ernest, 2 September 1848.
81. Wilson (1977) p. 213. The weekly allowance of £1, to which Ernest's half salary amounted, was reduced to half that sum paid over to Jane by the Victim Fund. This amount she found utterly inadequate, see letter to Ernest Jones, 18 December 1848.
82. Letter from Jane Jones to Ernest, 2 September 1848, and letter from Ernest Jones, 18 December 1848.
83. Undated fragment of a letter from Jane Jones to Ernest.
84. Linton (1880) pp. 74–5.
85. Letter from Thomas Cooper to Susanna, 12 August 1842, in *Treasury Solicitor's Papers* 11/602 (PRO).
86. *The People*, no. 28, p. 216.
87. *The English Chartist Circular*, no. 149, p. 1.
88. In Dorling (1879) pp. vii–viii. And Jane Jones wrote to her husband on 19 March 1849: 'I do not ask you, would *not wish* you to bend, or swerve from your principles . . . so long as you conscientiously believe them to be just.'
89. Dorling (1879) p. 30.
90. *The English Chartist Circular*, no. 120, p. 270. For a historical example of a woman entirely devoting herself to her imprisoned husband, see *The English Chartist Circular*, no. 136, p. 336.
91. *The Northern Star*, 10 June 1848, p. 5.
92. *The English Chartist Circular*, no. 118, p. 262; Gammage (1969) p. 173.
93. McCabe (1922) p. 99.
94. Compare their 'dearest love, my own dearest, sweetest, my precious love, dearest and best, darling dove, darling, my own sweetest and dearest, my own darling', see Conklin (1935) pp. 446ff., with the 'dear

husband' and 'dear wife' that predominate in the Richardsons' correspondence, see *HO* 40/53, pp. 927ff.

95. This and the following quotes in Conklin (1935) pp. 450ff.
96. *The National Reformer*, 27 July 1861, p. 6.
97. Thomas Cooper, *Thoughts at Fourscore*, quoted in Conklin (1935) p. 457.
98. Cooper (1971) p. 101.
99. Leno (1892) p. 30.
100. *The English Chartist Circular*, no. 76, p. 96.
101. For example, the appeal in support of Mary Frost and family in *The Northern Liberator*, no. 162, p. 5.
102. For example, *The Northern Star*, 6 September 1845, p. 1; 15 September 1849, p. 1.
103. Ibid., 28 January 1843, p. 7; 23 March 1844, p. 5.
104. For example, *The Northern Liberator*, no. 114, p. 6.
105. Cf. Peter Hoey's and Joseph Crabtree's families, who carried on weaving during the men's imprisonment, in D. Thompson (1984) p. 221.
106. A public concert arranged at Andeston for the relief of the 'imprisoned patriots' wives', for instance, yielded a profit of £15. 15s. ½d.; see *The Northern Liberator*, no. 109, p. 106.
107. *The Northern Star*, 27 June 1840, p. 8.
108. Ibid., 31 July 1841, p. 8; see also address of Bradford FCA, in *The Northern Star*, 19 February 1842, p. 7.
109. Ibid., 30 November 1844, p. 4.
110. Ibid., 25 July 1846, p. 8.
111. Ibid., 19 February 1842, p. 7; 12 January 1850, p. 1.
112. *Proceedings of WMAs*, pt. 4, p. 189.
113. Ibid., pt. 4, pp. 191–2.
114. *The Northern Star*, 16 November 1839, p. 6.
115. *HO* 40/53, pp. 927ff; they are dated 16 February 1839, 25 February 1839, 26 February 1839, 9 March 1839, 14 March 1839, undated (presumably 29 March 1839) and 1 April 1839.
116. Cf. W. Lovett, *The Life and Struggles of William Lovett* (1876) pp. 3–4.
117. W. Lovett, *Proceedings of Working Men's Associations* (Birmingham Public Library) pt. 4, p. 242.
118. Cf. W. Lovett, *Woman's Mission* (1856). The poem had been written in 1842.
119. Lovett (1876) pp. 23, 27.
120. Place Collection. Reform 1836–47, 29 vols, set 55, Working Men. Reform – Case of Lovett and Collins, 1839–40 (British Library) p. 38.
121. Lovett (1876) p. 366.
122. Place Collection, set 55, p. 71.
123. Lovett (1876) p. 37.
124. For a discussion of the mode in which private matters were dealt with in these autobiographies, see D. Vincent, 'Love and Death and the Nineteenth-century Working Class', *Social History*, V (1980) pp. 42–3.
125. Lovett (1876) p. 37.
126. Place Collection, set 55, p. 220; see also a similar passage on pp. 72–3
127. Ibid., pp. 516, 522.

128. Ibid., p. 524.
129. W. Lovett, *Social and Political Morality* (1853) pp. 84–5.
130. Lovett (1876) pp. 37–8.
131. *Address and Rules of the Working Men's Association, for benefiting Politically, Socially and Morally, The Useful Classes* (n.d.) p. 6.
132. Lovett (1853) p. 90.
133. See letters to Mary Lovett in Place Collection, set 55.
134. Lovett (1876) p. 39.
135. Place Collection, set 55, p. 39.
136. Lovett (1876) p. 39.
137. W. Lovett and J. Collins, *Chartism: A New Organisation of the People* (1840, repr. Leicester, 1969) p. 68.
138. Lovett (1876) p. 442.
139. Lovett (1853) p. 39; see also Lovett (1856) pp. 16ff.
140. Place Collection, set 55.
141. *PP* 1840. XXXVIII. pp. 756ff.
142. Place Collection, set 55, p. 70. The prisoner in Montgomeryshire Gaol alluded to in this letter may have been Henry Vincent, since Mary was in touch with his mother (see p. 299).
143. Ibid., p. 356.
144. Ibid., p. 39.
145. Ibid., p. 192.
146. *The Northern Star*, 29 June 1839, p. 7.
147. *The Charter*, 13 October 1839, p. 607.
148. Place Collection, set 55, p. 39.
149. Ibid., p. 27.
150. Ibid., p. 497.
151. Lovett (1853) p. 85.
152. Lovett (1876) pp. 40, 242.
153. *Proceedings of WMAs*, pt. 4, p. 241.
154. Lovett (1853) pp. 89–90; see also Lovett (1856) pp. 8–9.
155. Place Collection, set 55, p. 524.
156. Lovett (1856) p. 15.
157. Place Collection, set 55, p. 74.
158. Lovett (1853) p. 93; see also Lovett (1856) p. 15.
159. Lovett (1876) pp. 430–1
160. *The National Association Gazette*, no. 1, p. 4.
161. Lovett (1853) p. 15.
162. Ibid., p. 14.

Chapter 6 Chartist Women in Public Politics

1. W. Lovett, *Proceedings of Working Men's Associations* (Birmingham Public Library) pt. 2, p. 277.
2. *The Northern Star*, 11 September 1841, p. 7.
3. For example, *Proceedings of WMAs*, pt. 2, p. 202; *The Northern Liberator*, no. 71, no. 86.
4. See, for example, *The Northern Star*, 9 March 1839, p. 1, for a subscription in favour of J. R. Stephens got up by the women of Reform Street, Bradford.

5. C. E. Martin, 'Female Chartism', University of Wales (1973) pp. 147ff, has given the following average percentages of contributions that can be identified as female: 0.4 per cent for the Land Plan Fund, 1.9 per cent for the National Rent (including an outstanding 27 per cent in July 1839), 3 per cent for the Frost Defence Fund, 8.5 per cent for the J. R. Stephens Defence Fund, 13 per cent for the fund in support of the 'Welsh widows' (including an unequalled 28 per cent in September 1840).

6. Ibid.

7. *The Northern Star*, 23 July 1842, p. 7.

8. Ibid., 2 December 1848, p. 1.

9. R. Lowery, *Address to the Fathers and Mothers, Sons and Daughters, of the Working Classes, on the System of Exclusive Dealing, and the Formation of Joint Stock Provision Companies, Shewing How the People May Free Themelves from Oppression* (Newcastle upon Tyne, 1839) p. 5. I am grateful to Logie Barrow for bringing this pamphlet to my attention.

10. *The Carlisle Journal*, 3 August 1839, p. 2.

11. *The Northern Star*, 8 July 1848, p. 1.

12. *The Western Vindicator*, 28 September 1839, p. 1.

13. See, for example, *The Northern Star*, 20 February 1841, p. 1, for a tea party for the members and friends of the Christian Chartist Church in Birmingham.

14. For example, *The Northern Liberator*, no. 160, p. 7.

15. For example, *The Northern Star*, 14 January 1843, p. 1.

16. *The Northern Liberator*, no. 160, p. 7.

17. For example, *The Northern Star*, 5 February 1842, p. 7.

18. *The Northern Star*, 30 May 1840, p. 5.

19. For example, ibid., 24 January 1843, p. 3.

20. For seventeenth-century women's petitions see E. A. McArthur, 'Women Petitioners and the Long Parliament', *English Historical Review*, XXIV (1909) pp. 698ff. I am grateful to Eileen Yeo for bringing this reference to my attention.

21. For example, *The Northern Star*, 3 February 1838, p. 5.

22. Ibid., 10 February 1838, p. 7.

23. For example, *Appendix to the Reports of the Select Committee of the House of Commons on Public Petitions* (House of Lords Record Office) App. 269, 1847, p. 132; App. 1, 511, 1847–8, pp. 810–11.

24. *The Northern Liberator*, July 1839. The first National Petition was said to have been signed by 50,000 women in the first fortnight of its existence, which induced *The Northern Star*, 25 August 1838, to entertain the sanguine hope for a total of 500,000 female signatures. The third National Petition was estimated to contain 8200 female signatures for every 100,000 male ones, see P. W. Slosson, *The Decline of the Chartist Movement* (repr. New York, 1968) p. 207.

25. See, for example, *Proceedings of WMAs*, pt. 4, p. 171 for a memorial from the women of London.

26. *The Northern Liberator*, no. 47.

27. For example, *The Northern Star*, 29 September 1838, p. 8; 4 January 1840, p. 4; 4 July 1840, p. 1; 11 July 1840, p. 1.

28. Ibid., 14 August 1841, p. 4.
29. E. Yeo, 'Culture and Constraint in Working-class Movements, 1830–1855', in E. and S. Yeo (eds), *Popular Culture and Class Conflict* (Brighton, 1981) p. 168.
30. For example, *The Northern Liberator*, no. 137, p. 7; no. 163, p. 7.
31. This was due to *The Northern Star*'s relocation from Leeds to London, which removed the paper from the centres of Chartist activity in the north. This was reflected in the number of reports sent in.
32. For example, *The Operative*, 4 November 1838, p. 5.
33. For example, *The Charter*, 23 June 1839, p. 348.
34. *The Northern Star*, 14 May 1841, p. 2.
35. Ibid., 2 July 1842, p. 1.
36. Ibid., 8 December 1838, p. 6; 2 February 1839, p. 3
37. Ibid., 4 June 1842, p. 8.
38. Ibid., 8 April 1848, p. 5.
39. *The English Chartist Circular*, no. 127, p. 298; no. 142, p. 359; see *The Friend of the People*, no. 6, p. 47.
40. *The English Chartist Circular*, no. 143, pp. 361–2; no. 144, pp. 369–70; no. 145, pp. 373–4; no. 147, pp. 378, 380–1; no. 148, p. 384.
41. For example, ibid., no. 113, p. 244.
42. For example, *The Northern Star*, 31 August 1839, p. 3.
43. *The Northern Liberator*, no 97, p. 5.
44. *Leeds Mercury*, 16 September 1848, quoted in H. Weisser, *April 10: Challenge and Response in England in 1848* (Lanham, New York, London, 1983) p. 10.
45. M. I. Thomis and J. Grimmett, *Women in Protest, 1800–1850* (1982) pp. 51–2; HO 40/42, pp. 744–5.
46. *The Union*, 1843, p. 424.
47. Ibid., 1843, pp. 423–4.
48. *The Northern Star*, 20 August 1842, p. 4; *The Union*, 1843, p. 424.
49. For example, HO 40/50, p. 642.
50. For example, *The Northern Star*, 27 July 1839, p. 8; 26 October 1839, p. 3.
51. HO 40/41, p. 576.
52. For example, HO 40/42, p. 538.
53. For example, Harney in *The Northern Star*, 27 November 1847, p. 6.
54. *The Labourer*, vol. 1, pp. 44–8.
55. *The Northern Star*, 8 May 1847, p. 1.
56. PP 1847–8. pp. 189–90.
57. *The Northern Star*, 8 May 1847, p. 1.
58. Ibid., 16 September 1848, p. 5.
59. For example, ibid., 3 July 1847, p. 1.
60. G. J. Barnsby, *The Working Class Movement in the Black Country, 1750–1867* (Wolverhampton, 1977) p. 137.
61. *The Northern Star*, 4 December 1847, p. 1.
62. See, for example, A. M. Hadfield, *The Chartist Land Company* (Newton Abbott, 1970) pp. 105, 118–19 for O'Connorville.
63. PP 1847–8. pp. 242 *passim*.
64. For example, *The Northern Star*, 20 May 1848, p. 6.

65. W. Lovett and J. Collins, *Chartism: A New Organisation of the People* (1840, repr. Leicester, 1969) p. 70.
66. *The Labourer*, vol. 4, p. 253.
67. For example, *The National Association Gazette*, no. 9, p. 71.
68. *The English Chartist Circular*, no. 22, p. 87.
69. Ibid., no. 16, p. 63.
70. T. Gisborne, *Enquiry into the Duties of the Female Sex* (1797) pp. 21–2; 'A Woman' (Mrs Richard Napier), *Women's Rights and Duties* (1840) vol. 1, pp. 211, 283–4.
71. Gisborne (1797) pp. 22, 33–5; 'Woman' (1840) pp. 283–4.
72. For example, S. Stickney Ellis, *The Women of England, Their Social Duties and Domestic Habits*, 2nd edn (1839) p. 68; S. Lewis, *Woman's Mission*, 2nd edn (1839) pp. 65–6; H. G. Clark, *The English Maiden: Her Moral and Domestic Duties* (1841) pp. 46ff.
73. *The English Chartist Circular*, no. 22, p. 88. By the time of 'Sophia's' writing, the Birmingham Mechanics' Institute was already notorious for its preservation of male exclusiveness. In 1840, a group of women had petitioned for classes, and, on refusal, turned to the Owenities, who promptly complied with their request; see B. Taylor, *Eve and the New Jerusalem* (1983) p. 233.
74. *The National Association Gazette*, no. 9, p. 72.
75. *The English Chartist Circular*, no. 16, p. 63; for a similar opinion, see *The Northern Star*, 28 August 1841, p. 1.
76. W. E. Adams, *Memoirs of a Social Atom* (1903) pp. 165ff.
77. *The Labourer*, vol. 1, p. 48; Lovett and Collins (1840) p. 49.
78. For example, *The Northern Star*, 26 June 1841, p. 2.
79. Lovett and Collins (1840) pp. 45, 101.
80. *The People*, no. 129, pp. 197–8; repeated in no. 145–6, p. 335.
81. For example, lecture by William Hollis, the Cheltenham Chartist educationalist, in *The Cheltenham Free Press*, 23 November 1839, p. 7.
82. Lovett and Collins (1840) p. 71.
83. For example, C. R. Pemberton quoted in *The National Association Gazette*, no. 17, p. 138.
84. *The English Chartist Circular*, no. 22, p. 88.
85. For example, *The Northern Star*, 20 April 1844, p. 1.
86. M. A. Cruickshank, 'A Lancashire Handloom Weavers' School', *Journal of Educational Administration and History*, XI (1979) p. 17.
87. *The Northern Star*, 14 March 1838, p. 4.
88. See address of the ELFPA in *The Northern Star*, 30 January 1841, p. 1; *Proceedings of WMAs*, pt. 3, p. 104.
89. *The Northern Star*, 6 May 1843, p. 1.
90. Ibid., 30 April 1842, p. 4.
91. D. Thompson, *The Chartists* (1984) p. 147.
92. For example, point 8 of the *Rules and Objects of the LWMA*, p. 6.
93. R. F. Wearmouth, *Some Working-class Movements of the Nineteenth Century* (1948) p. 143.
94. *The National Association Gazette*, no. 19, p. 148.
95. This was first suggested by A. R. Schoyen, *The Chartist Challenge: A Portrait of George Julian Harney* (1958) pp. 203–4. Despite the

inconclusive evidence, Saville has found this hypothesis not unreasonable, see introduction to *The Red Republican* (1966) p. XII.

96. For Helen Macfarlane, see *Quarterly Bulletin of the Marx Memorial Library* (1975) pp. 4ff.; see K. Marx and F. Engels, *Werke* (Berlin, DDR) Bd. 8, p. 75; Bd. 27, p. 196.
97. *The Democratic Review*, April–June 1850; *The Red Republican*, no. 1, 4, 5, 7, 9, 13, 14, 17, 20, 21; *The Friend of the People*, no. 2, 3.
98. *The English Chartist Circular*, no. 24, pp. 97–8; no. 27, p. 108; no. 33, p. 129; no. 41, p. 161; no. 51, p. 204; *The National Association Gazette*, no. 17, 21.
99. For example, *The Charter*, 19 May 1839, p. 264; *The Northern Star*, 9 May 1846, p. 5.
100. For example, *The Charter*, 14 April 1839, p. 184.
101. For example, *The Northern Star*, 21 April 1838, p. 7.
102. For example, *The Charter*, 12 May 1839, p. 248.
103. D. Thompson (1984) pp. 342ff.
104. *The Northern Star*, 1 September 1838, p. 6.
105. Ibid., 20 May 1843, p. 4.
106. *The Operative*, 14 April 1839, p. 9; *The Northern Star*, 21 August 1841, p. 7.
107. For example, *The Northern Liberator*, no. 47.
108. *The Charter*, 27 October 1839, p. 640; *The Northern Liberator*, no. 72.
109. *The Charter*, 27 October 1839, p. 640.
110. For example, *The Northern Star*, 4 May 1839, p. 4; 17 September 1842, p. 1.
111. For example, *The Operative*, 28 April 1839, p. 7.
112. *The Charter*, 18 November 1838, p. 371; *The Northern Star*, 10 November 1838, p. 6; 29 April 1848, p. 7; *The Northern Liberator*, no. 85; no. 163, p. 6.
113. *Proceedings of WMAs*, pt. 2, p. 279.
114. *The Northern Star*, 14 December 1839, p. 1.
115. For example, *The Northern Liberator*, no. 48.
116. For example, *The Western Vindicator*, 29 June 1839, p. 4; 17 August 1839, p. 4; *The Northern Star*, 19 October 1839, p. 7; 14 March 1840, p. 4.
117. For example, *The Northern Star*, 24 March 1838, p. 5.
118. *The Western Vindicator*, 28 September 1839, p. 1.
119. *The Northern Star*, 14 April 1838, p. 8.
120. For example, ibid., 22 December 1838, p. 3.
121. Ibid., 26 January 1839, p. 8.
122. For example, ibid., 1 June 1839, p. 5. Not merely similar in reasoning, the Bristol address was in part identical in wording to that of the women of Newcastle; see ibid., 9 February 1839, p. 6; 2 August 1839, p. 6.
123. For example, ibid., 10 October 1840, p. 5.
124. *The Western Vindicator*, 15 June 1839, p. 2.
125. Taylor (1983) p. 94.
126. S. Lewenhak, *Women and Trade Unions: An Outline History of Women in the British Trade Union Movement* (1977) p. 39.
127. *Leeds Mercury*, 4 May 1833, quoted in J. Wade, *History of the Middle and Working Classes* (1833) pp. 570–1.
128. Teesside is a case in point. According to M. S. Chase, 'Chartism, 1838–1858', *Northern History*, XXIV (1988) p. 160, this region boasted a

considerable number of female Friendly Societies. Their tradition was continued by women Chartists.

129. S. Bamford, *Passages in the Life of a Radical* (repr. Oxford, 1984) p. 123.
130. Taylor (1983) p. 93.
131. *Manchester Observer*, 31 July 1819, quoted in K. A. Corfield, 'Some Social and Radical Organizations among Working-class Women in Manchester and District, 1790–1820', BA Birmingham University (1970) p. 17.
132. Thomis and Grimmett (1982) p. 96.
133. *Black Dwarf*, 7 October 1818, quoted in ibid., p. 98.
134. Ibid., p. 105.
135. *The Northern Star*, 25 May 1838, p. 3.
136. *The Birmingham Journal*, 7 April 1838, p. 1.
137. *The Northern Star*, 25 May 1838, p. 3.
138. *The Birmingham Journal*, 14 July 1838, p. 3.
139. T. C. Salt, *To the Women of Birmingham*, 16 August 1838.
140. *The Northern Star*, 8 September 1838, p. 4.
141. *The Northern Liberator*, no. 65.
142. For example, *The Charter*, 24 November 1839, p. 701; *The Northern Liberator*, no. 63; Harney in *The Northern Liberator*, no. 106.
143. For example, *The Operative*, 9 June 1839, p. 8; *The Northern Star*, 22 June 1839, p. 3.
144. For example, *The Northern Star*, 12 February 1842, p. 2.
145. For example, ibid., 30 March 1839, p. 7.
146. For example, ibid., 7 August 1841, p. 7.
147. For example, Martin (1973) pp. 54–5.
148. For example, *The Charter*, 28 April 1839, p. 215.
149. For example, *The North Staffordshire Mercury*, 13 November 1838, p. 3.
150. For example, *The Operative*, 14 April 1839, p. 9; *The Northern Star*, 4 May 1839, p. 4; *The Charter*, 13 October 1839, p. 608.
151. J. E. B. Lowe, 'Women in the Chartist Movement', Birmingham University (1985) p. 180.
152. *The Operative*, 14 April 1839, p. 9.
153. Ibid.; *The Charter*, 13 October 1839, p. 608.
154. *The Charter*, 27 October 1839, p. 640.
155. *New Moral World*, 27 November 1841, quoted in Taylor (1983) p. 350.
156. *The Northern Star*, 27 April 1839, p. 4.
157. Ibid., 7 May 1842, p. 1.
158. Ibid., 10 September 1842, p. 4; 6 May 1843, p. 5.
159. Ibid., 8 July 1848, p. 1.
160. Ibid., 17 December 1842, p. 4.
161. Ibid., 20 May 1843, p. 4.
162. Ibid., 7 January 1843, p. 4.
163. D. Jones, 'Women and Chartism', *History*, LXVIII (1983) pp. 11–12.
164. For Mary Grassby of Elland FCA, see *The Northern Star*, 13 July 1839, p. 4; for Miss Jones of Hampton, see *The Charter*, 20 October 1839, p. 617; 17 November 1839, p. 685; for Anna Pepper of Leeds FCA, see *The Northern Liberator*, no. 114, p. 7; *The Northern Star*, 14 December 1839, p. 5; for Mrs Jocelyn, see *The Northern Star*, 9 April 1842, p. 1; for

Susanna Inge of the City of London FCA, see *The Northern Star*, 5 November 1842, p. 1; 29 July 1843, p. 2; for Mary Ann Walker of the City of London FCA, see *The Northern Star*, 10 December 1842, p. 7; 21 January 1843; for Mrs Fields (or Fildes) of Manchester, see Corfield (1970) p. 19; *The Northern Star*, 14 January 1843, p. 5; 21 January 1843, p. 8; I. McCalman, 'Females, Feminism and Free Love in an Early Nineteenth Century Radical Movement', *Labour History*, no. 38 (1980) p. 21; for Eliza Blatherwick of Nottingham, see *The Northern Star*, 27 May 1843, p. 4; for Mrs Bessell, see *The Northern Star*, 12 August 1843, p. 1; for Mrs Mathews, see *The Northern Star*, 1 December 1849, p. 8; 13 April 1850, p. 1.

165. *The Sheffield Times*, 14 October 1848, p. 5.
166. *The Northern Star*, 27 January 1849, p. 5; 10 February 1849, p. 1.
167. *The Times*, 20 October 1842, p. 3.
168. *The Northern Star*, 28 January 1843, p. 5.
169. For example, report on Mary Ann Walker's lecture in ibid., 10 December 1842, p. 7.
170. E. Nicholson, 'Working-class Women in Nineteenth-century Nottingham, 1815–1850', BA Birmingham (1973) p. 46 has listed female Chartists who had previously served as itinerant preachers of Methodism.
171. McCalman (1980) p. 11, for instance, argues that there would have been no need for women in the Reform movement to form separate societies merely in order to sew caps of liberty.

Chapter 7 Gender Relations within the Chartist Movement

1. For example, *The Northern Star*, 26 January 1839, p. 6.
2. Ibid., 29 June 1839, p. 1.
3. Ibid., 14 July 1849, p. 1.
4. Ibid., 8 July 1843, p. 4; 15 July 1843, p. 5; 29 July 1843, p. 4.
5. For example, *The Northern Liberator*, no. 163, p. 7.
6. *The Western Vindicator*, 7 December 1839, p. 1.
7. Ibid., 31 August 1839, p. 3.
8. *The Northern Star*, 2 July 1842, p. 7.
9. *The Western Vindicator*, 7 December 1839, p. 1.
10. Ibid., 31 August 1839, p. 3.
11. *The Northern Star*, 10 October 1846, p. 5.
12. For example, *The Western Vindicator*, 29 June 1839, p. 3.
13. For example, *The Charter*, 17 March 1839, p. 126.
14. *The Western Vindicator*, 11 May 1839, p. 1.
15. For example, R. B. Pugh, 'Chartism in Somerset and Wiltshire', in A. Briggs (ed.), *Chartist Studies* (1959) p. 180.
16. For example, *The Northern Star*, 26 January 1839, p. 3.
17. *The Western Vindicator*, 6 April 1839, p. 3.
18. Ibid., 2 March 1839, p. 2.
19. W. Lovett, *Proceedings of Working Men's Associations* (Birmingham Public Library) pt. 2, p. 282a.
20. R. G. Gammage, *History of the Chartist Movement, 1837–1854* (repr. 1976) p. 78.

21. Ibid., pp. 11, 77–8.
22. *The Northern Liberator*, no. 50.
23. *The Northern Star*, 25 September 1841, p. 1.
24. *The Operative*, 10 March 1839, p. 5.
25. *The Northern Star*, 8 December 1838, p. 6.
26. *The English Chartist Circular*, no. 94, p. 165.
27. *The Northern Star*, 29 January 1842, p. 8.
28. *HO* 40/42, p. 279.
29. Ibid., p. 259.
30. Ibid. 40/44, p. 545.
31. *The Northern Liberator*, no. 12.
32. *Weekly Record of the Temperance Movement*, 22 November 1856, p. 281.
33. M. Jenkins, *The General Strike of 1842* (1980) pp. 122–3.
34. *The Northern Liberator*, no. 160, p. 5.
35. *The Northern Star*, 20 October 1839, p. 6–7.
36. For example, ibid., 8 June 1839, p. 5.
37. For example, ibid., 24 July 1841, p. 1.
38. Ibid., 1 June 1839, p. 5.
39. Ibid., 23 July 1842, p. 7.
40. Ibid., 24 June 1848, p. 6.
41. *The North Staffordshire Mercury*, 3 November 1838, p. 3.
42. For example, *The Northern Star*, 6 July 1839, p. 8.
43. *The Northern Liberator*, no. 55.
44. *The Northern Star*, 6 July 1839, p. 5.
45. Ibid., 13 March 1841, p. 1.
46. *The National Association Gazette*, no. 6, p. 45.
47. *The Northern Star*, 15 May 1841, p. 2.
48. Ibid., 22 December 1838, p. 3.
49. *The English Chartist Circular*, no. 86, p. 136.
50. Ibid., no. 13, p. 50.
51. *The Northern Star*, 2 February 1839, p. 3.
52. For example, *The Northern Liberator*, no. 85.
53. Ibid., no. 65.
54. *The Northern Star*, 27 October 1838, p. 8.
55. *Weekly Record of the Temperance Movement*, 8 November 1856, p. 266.
56. *The Northern Star*, 8 September 1838, p. 4.
57. For example, ibid., 12 September 1840, p. 1.
58. *The Sheffield and Rotherham Independent* in *HO* 40/57, p. 248.
59. *HO* 45/249C, p. 280.
60. *The Northern Star*, 2 October 1841, p. 8.
61. Ibid., 12 September 1840, p. 1.
62. Ibid., 5 November 1842, p. 1.
63. For example, ibid., 5 October 1839, p. 1; 29 May 1847, p. 1; 25 March 1848, p. 1.
64. For example, ibid., 22 November 1845, p. 3.
65. *Notes to the People*, p. 632.
66. *The Northern Star*, 28 August 1847, p. 8.
67. For example, *The Sheffield and Rotherham Independent*, 18 January 1840, p. 8 in *HO* 40/57, p. 250.

68. For example, *The Northern Star*, 13 March 1841, p. 1; 26 November 1842, p. 6.
69. For example, ibid., 25 May 1839, p. 5.
70. For example, ibid., 5 July 1845, p. 6; 1 February 1851, p. 1.
71. For example, *Proceedings of WMAs*, pt. 2, p. 262.
72. Cf. both versions of NCA rules in *The Northern Star*, 1 August 1840 and 23 July 1842, p. 4.
73. Ibid., 14 August 1841, p. 8; 21 August 1841, p. 8.
74. Ibid., 5 March 1842, p. 8.
75. Ibid., 24 June 1843, p. 1 for Oldham; see ibid., 6 May 1843, p. 2 and 8 July 1843, p. 7 for Nottingham.
76. Ibid., 4 September 1841, p. 6; 25 September 1841, p. 8.
77. Report on the founding meeting of Hanley FCA in *The North Staffordshire Mercury*, 3 November 1838, p. 3.
78. F. Tristan, *London Journal* (1980) p. 49; *The Northern Star*, 14 August 1841, p. 7.
79. For example, *The Northern Liberator*, no. 65; *The Northern Star*, 8 June 1839, p. 5.
80. For example, *The Northern Liberator*, no. 163, p. 6.
81. *The Northern Star*, 22 December 1838, p. 3; Pugh (1959) p. 191; *The Northern Star*, 29 June 1839, p. 1, where Mrs Campbell is mentioned as the president of the local FCA, and cf. *The Charter*, 15 September 1839, p. 5, where she is described as its treasurer.
82. D. Jones, 'Women and Chartism', *History*, LXVIII (1983) p. 12.
83. *The Northern Star*, 3 June 1848, p. 5.
84. For example, *The Charter*, 2 February 1840, p. 9.
85. *The Northern Star*, 26 August 1842, p. 1; 10 December 1842, p. 7.
86. Ibid., 6 July 1839, p. 8.
87. Ibid., 6 March 1841, p. 2.
88. Ibid., 5 November 1842, p. 1.
89. Ibid., 3 February 1849, p. 7.
90. *The Western Vindicator*, 29 June 1839, p. 3.
91. *The North Staffordshire Mercury*, 3 November 1838, p. 3.
92. *The Western Vindicator*, 20 April 1839, p. 4.
93. *The Birmingham Journal*, 1 September 1838, quoted in J. E. B. Lowe, 'Women in the Chartist Movement', Birmingham University (1985) p. 170.
94. *The Northern Star*, 8 June 1839, p. 5.
95. Ibid., 6 July 1839, p. 8.
96. For example, *The Charter*, 8 September 1839, p. 527.
97. *The Operative*, 14 April 1839, p. 9.
98. *The Northern Star*, 20 October 1839, pp. 6–7.
99. *Address and Rules of the LWMA*, especially p. 2.

Chapter 8 Working-class Women's Post-Chartist Activities

1. *The Friend of the People*, no. 17, pp. 158–9; no. 18, p. 166.
2. See, for example, G. J. Barnsby, *The Working Class Movement in the Black Country, 1750–1867* (Wolverhampton, 1977) pp. 194, 201 for the Black

Country; see *The People's Paper*, 20 February 1858, p. 5; 22 May 1858, p. 1 for London.

3. *The Northern Star*, 15 June 1839, p. 5.
4. H. Blackburn, *Women's Suffrage. A Record of the Women's Suffrage Movement in the British Isles* (1902) p. 19.
5. Letter to Mrs Rooke, Sheffield, and dealing with women's suffrage, and O'Connor's land purchase scheme, by Anne Knight (York Public Library) 20 January 1851.
6. *The Charter*, 27 October 1839, p. 629.
7. *The Sheffield and Rotherham Independent*, 16 November 1850, p. 8.
8. Letter from Anne Knight to Mrs Rooke, 20 January 1851.
9. *The Northern Star*, 21 October 1843, p. 5.
10. *The People*, no. 92, p. 315.
11. *The Friend of the People*, no. 13, p. 102; no. 25, p. 216.
12. *The Sheffield Free Press*, 8 February 1851, p. 8.
13. Ibid., 15 February 1851, p. 8.
14. Ibid., 1 March 1851, p. 8.
15. *The Northern Star*, 29 March 1851, p. 8.
16. J. Salt, 'English Radicalism: a Neglected Document ("An Address to the People of France") Compiled by the Sheffield Chartists in 1848', *Notes and Queries*, CCXI (1966) p. 332.
17. *The Sheffield Free Press*, 14 June 1851, p. 8.
18. Ibid., 21 June 1851, p. 8.
19. *The Democratic Review*, June 1849, p. 391.
20. *The Northern Star*, 9 August 1851, p. 1.
21. Concern among Sheffield Chartists with women's condition can be traced back at least to 1842. In that year, the local Chartists sent the Irish Universal Suffrage Association a parcel of the movement's propaganda material, including 1000 copies of Watkins's *Address to the Women of England*, introduced in Chapter 2; see D. Jones, *Chartism and and the Chartists* (1975) p. 96. Unfortunately, Jones's book has not been footnoted throughout. Nevertheless it has apparently been found valuable by many scholars of Chartism.
22. *The Northern Star*, 15 November 1851, p. 1.
23. *The Sheffield Free Press*, 29 November 1851, p. 8.
24. *The Northern Star*, 28 June 1851, p. 1.
25. Ibid., 15 November 1851, p. 1; 6 March 1852, p. 1.
26. Ibid., 8 May 1852, p. 5.
27. *The Sheffield Free Press*, 10 May 1851, p. 8.
28. Abiah Higginbottom, its energetic corresponding secretary, had been an active Chartist in the period 1845–50 together with her husband Aaron, a spring knife cutler – at least according to J. L. Baxter, 'The Origins of the Social War in South Yorkshire: A Study of Capitalist Evolution and Labour Class Realization in One Industrial Region, c. 1750–1855', Ph.D. Sheffield (1976) p. 684. However, a check of *The Sheffield Iris* has not yielded any references for the years 1845–8. In November 1850, Aaron had been the chairman of the local NCA council; see *The Sheffield and Rotherham Independent*, 16 November 1850, p. 8. Moreover, out of the seven female Chartists eager to take action

over female suffrage, four are known to have continued as members of the Women's Political Association. Apart from Abiah Higginbottom, this was true of Mrs Stephenson, see *The Sheffield Free Press*, 19 July 1851, p. 8, where her name is spelt Stevenson; Mrs Mary Brook, once elected financial secretary, see *The Northern Star*, 6 March 1852, p. 1; and Mrs Ash, see *The Sheffield Free Press*, 19 April 1851, p. 8. See also *The Sheffield Free Press*, 1 March 1851, p. 810; May 1851, p. 8.

29. D. Thompson, 'Women and Nineteenth-century Radical Politics: A Lost Dimension', in J. Mitchell and A. Oakley (eds), *The Rights and Wrongs of Women* (Harmondsworth, 1976) pp. 134ff.; *The Chartists* (1984) pp. 122ff.

30. *Notes to the People*, p. 624.

31. Ibid., p. 709.

32. For example, *The Western Vindicator*, 2 March 1839, p. 3.

33. For example, *The Northern Star*, 17 October 1840, p. 1.

34. Ibid., 30 January 1841, p. 1.

35. *Address and Rules of the LWMA*, pp. 2–4.

36. *The English Chartist Circular*, no. 64, p. 47.

37. E. Yeo, 'Culture and Constraint in Working-class Movements, 1830–1855', in E. and S. Yeo (eds), *Popular Culture and Class Conflict* (Brighton, 1981) p. 138.

38. E. Ross, 'Survival Networks: Women's Neighbourhood Sharing in London Before World War I', *History Workshop*, no. 15 (1983) pp. 10–11.

39. D. Thompson (1976) p. 137; (1984) p. 122. The argument has been applied – successfully or not – to Owenism by B. Taylor, *Eve and the New Jerusalem* (1983) p. 220, and has been reiterated by J. Rendall, *The Origins of Modern Feminism: Women in Britain, France and the United States, 1780–1860* (1985) p. 205.

40. D. Thompson (1976) pp. 137–8; (1984) p. 131.

Chapter 9 Gender and Class in Chartism

1. *The Northern Star*, 6 October 1849, p. 3.

2. Ibid.

3. Ibid., 5 January 1850, p. 3.

4. Ibid., 13 October 1849, p. 3.

5. Ibid., 20 October 1849, p. 3.

6. Ibid., 13 October 1849, p. 3.

7. Ibid., 6 October 1849, p. 3.

8. Ibid., 20 October 1849, p. 3.

9. *The English Chartist Circular*, no. 13, p. 50.

10. *The Northern Star*, 20 October 1849, p. 3.

11. Ibid.

12. E. Ross, '"Not the Sort that Would Sit on the Doorstep": Respectability in Pre-World War I London Neighborhoods', *International Labour and Working Class History*, no. 27 (1985) p. 39.

13. E. P. Thompson, *The Making of the English Working Class*, 3rd edn (Harmondsworth, 1972) p. 820.

14. Cf. W. Cobbett, *Advice to Young Men, and (Incidentally) to Young Women,*

in the Middle and Higher Ranks of Life (1829) letter 3, § 90; letter 4, § 182, § 186, § 189, § 200, § 207; letter 6, § 336.

15. An explicit reference to Cobbett's view of gender relations is to be found in *The English Chartist Circular*, no. 142, p. 360. The journal quoted a passage from the *Advice to Young Men* in which the author emphasised wives' duties towards their husbands and stated their willingness and ability to render the latter active support to be of greater value than any amount of goods.
16. *Notes to the People*, pp. 612, 689, 692, 891, 892.
17. *The Northern Star*, 1 September 1849, p. 3.
18. *Notes to the People*, p. 711.
19. Ibid., p. 1011.
20. *The Northern Star*, 14 April 1849, p. 3; for floral morality, see also ch. 4 of N. Scourse, *The Victorians and their Flowers* (1983).
21. *The Northern Star*, 14 July 1849, p. 3.
22. *The National Instructor*, p. 36.
23. *The Northern Star*, 30 June 1849, p. 3.
24. *The National Instructor*, p. 85.
25. *The Northern Star*, 1 December 1849, p. 3.
26. Ibid., 5 January 1850, p. 3.
27. For example, J. J. Hillocks, *Life Story* (n.d.) pp. 69–70.
28. For example, *The National Instructor*, 13 July 1850, p. 128.
29. J. R. Stephens, *The Political Pulpit: A Selection of Sermons* (1839) p. 21.
30. *The Western Vindicator*, 17 August 1839, p. 2.
31. S. Stickney Ellis, *The Wives of England, Their Relative Duties, Domestic Influence, and Social Obligations* (1843) p. 18.
32. For example, *The Charter*, 20 October 1839, p. 621; cf. *The Northern Star*, 16 October 1841, p. 3; cf. *The Northern Liberator*, no. 137, p. 3; *The English Chartist Circular*, no. 123, p. 284; *The National Reformer*, no. 11, pp. 8–9; *The People*, no. 65, p. 98.
33. See, for example, *The English Chartist Circular*, no. 106, p. 216 for Lady Morgan and *The English Chartist Circular*, no. 58, p. 24 for Harriet Martineau.
34. *The Northern Star*, 22 November 1851, p. 1.
35. Marion Reid (Mrs Hugo Reid), *A Plea for Woman* (Edinburgh, 1843) pp. 7ff.
36. Ibid., pp. 10ff, 51ff.
37. For example, ibid., p. 74.
38. J. H. Murray, *Strongminded Women* (New York, 1982) p. 20.
39. *The Western Vindicator*, 24 August 1839, p. 2.
40. *The Northern Star*, 8 July 1848, p. 1.
41. Charlotte Elizabeth (i.e. Charlotte Elizabeth Phelan, afterwards Tonna), *The Wrongs of Woman* (1843–4) bk. 4, p. 34; cf. *Notes to the People*, pp. 592, 913.
42. Charlotte Elizabeth (1843–4) bk. 2, p. 97.
43. *Notes to the People*, p. 515.
44. B. Taylor, 'The Feminist Theory and Practice of the Owenites', D.Phil. Sussex (1981) p. 83. This argument has curiously been omitted in the published version of 1983.

Index

Female Friendly Societies – *continued*
  and community support networks,
    206
  rules of, 205–6
  significance of, 206
Female Reform Societies
  history of, 103, 206–7
  hostility encountered by, 208
  justification of women's political
    involvement by, 103
  political attitude of members of,
    207
  sexual division of labour and
    power in, 207
femininity
  Chartist notion of, 268–71, 280,
    283: Chartist novelists on,
    271–5; similarity with middle-
    class notion, 270, 278, 279
  Lady Morgan's view of, 276
  Martineau's view of, 276
  middle-class, 3
  Reid's view of, 276
  working-class, 4
feminism, 63
  definition of, 5
  early Victorian, 277
  Owenite, 281
  resulting from female waged
    labour, 282
  socialist in *The Appeal* . . ., 66
Flower, Mr (Barnsley Chartist), 132
Flower, Mrs (Barnsley FCA member), 132
Flynn, Mr (Bradford Chartist), 132
Flynn, Mrs (Bradford Chartist), 132
Foden, Peter (Sheffield Chartist),
  132
Foden, Sarah (Sheffield FCA member), 132
food riots, 11
Fox, Charles James
  against female suffrage, 58
franchise
  see under suffrage
Friends of the Oppressed, The, 175
Frost, John (Newport Chartist), 129,
  137

Frost, Mary (wife of John), 136, 137–8
Frost, Thomas (socialist and Chartist), 36
  on domestic service, 40
  on female vulnerability to exter-
    nal circumstances, 275
  on marriage, 46–7
  on prostitution, 54, 55–6

Galpin, William (Owenite), 60–1
Gammage, Robert George (Chartist
  historian), 38
  anti-feminism of, 226
  on Vincent, 225–6
Gandy, G. N., 9
Garrard, William (Ipswich Chartist),
  61
Gaskell, T. W. (Chartist), 116–17
gender, 2
gender relations
  as a result of social set-up: in
    *Labour's Wrongs and Labour's
    Remedy*, 66–7; in *The Appeal*,
    65
  Chartism's impact on, 4, 62–3, 77
  Chartist aims concerning, 4, 227
  Chartist view of, 50–1, 77, 227–8,
    276: affinity to capitalism,
    285; as a result of social set-
    up, 76–7; attraction for
    women, 287; Jones, 51–2; le-
    gacy to working class, 284;
    Richardson, 69–70, 73–5;
    Stephens, 50; variation in
    Chartist leaders' views, 280;
    Wheeler, 52–3
  Evangelical view of, 105, 276
  impact of Industrial Revolution
    on, 77
  in domestic industry, 10–11, 75
  in peasant society, 11
  in working-class marriage, 33–4
  men's need for dominance, 281,
    287
  of Chartist couples, 126–73:
    wives of active Chartists,
    154, 161–3, 167–9, 172–3
  Owenite concept of, 3, 281
  renegotiation of, 3

infanticide
Chartist view of, 56, 57
'Marcus' on, 93
women Chartists' view of, 93
Inge, Susanna (City of London FCA
member) 101–2, 241, 242, 242
criticising O'Connor, 221–2
on female suffrage, 102
on gender solidarity, 102
on sexual division of labour, 102
on sexual equality, 102
on women as political agents,
102, 223
organising FCAs nationally, 215–
16
political address by, 101–2, 216–
17
political self-confidence of, 217
Ireland, Mary (London FCA member), 132
Ireland, Mr (London Chartist), 132
Ironside, Isaac (Sheffield Chartist
and Owenite), 248–9, 252

Jones, Ernest, 36, 40, 51, 137, 139–40,
143, 187, 237, 256–7, 278–9
on femininity, 271–2, 273
on gender relations, 51–2
on marriage, 47, 48
on motherhood, 56–7, 271–2
on prostitution, 48, 55, 56
on woman's love, 48–9, 271
on women's waged work, 41
Jones, Gareth Stedman, 38, 39
Jones, Jane (wife of Ernest), 135, 137,
139–40, 143

kinship, 223–4, 226
Knight, Anne (Chelmsford Quaker
feminist), 249–51, 251–2, 254
for female suffrage, 248, 249, 250

Labour's Wrongs and Labour's Remedy
(Bray)
on gender relations, 66–7
McDouall on, 67
reviewed in *The Northern Star*, 67
Lambertz, Jan, 45–6

LaMont, John (editor of *Dundee
Chronicle*), 59
Land Company, Chartist, 81, 132
agitating women, 187–8
dissolution of, 190
membership of, 189: female, 82–
4, 262, 287 (employed in
domestic service, 83; em-
ployed in textile trades, 83,
84; geographical distribution
of, 84; social composition of,
84–6, 88); in rural areas, 82;
social composition of, 79–81
women's satisfaction with settlements, 189–90
Land Plan, Chartist, 186–7
restoration of proper family life,
188–9
women's response to, 189
Langston, Mr (Bilston Chartist), 133
Langston, Mrs (Bilston Chartist),
133, 242
Lapworth, Mr (Birmingham Chartist), 133
Lapworth, Mrs (Birmingham Chartist), 133, 231, 240, 244
leisure pursuits, working-class, 25
Leno, John Bedford (Uxbridge Chartist), 125–6, 130, 131, 146
Lewenhak, Sheila, 205
Lewis, Sarah (Evangelical writer),
117
Lilley, Mr (Nottingham Chartist),
133
Lilley, Mrs (Nottingham FCA member), 133
Lingard, Mr (Barnsley Chartist), 132
Lingard, Mrs (Barnsley Chartist), 132
Linton, William James (London
Radical), 134, 140
on prostitution, 54
Livesey, John (Manchester Chartist),
132
London Working Men's Association, 54, 59, 126, 131, 157, 166,
208, 245
for temperance, 259
on education, 64

Wollestonecraft, Mary – *continued*
on female suffrage, 63
on gender relations, 73
on marriage, 63
on prostitution, 63
on sexual division of labour, 64
on women as their own liberators, 63
on women's education, 64, 65
on women's oppression, 65
women Chartists' view of, 100
woman's character
Chartist view of, 235, 272–6:
Chartist novelists, 271–5
Evangelical view of, 106, 192
Woman's Elevation League, 254
Woman's Mission (Lovett), 151
on separate spheres, 169–70
on sexual equality, 171–2
on women as primary educators,
158
Woman's Wrongs (Jones), 40, 47–9,
51–2, 55, 237, 278–9
plot, 36–7
women
as historical agents, 1, 4
as their own liberators, 63, 66,
102
earnings of, 7, 13–14
subordinate in factories, 14
women Chartists: activities
arranging socials, 177–8
as male Chartists' adjuncts, 89,
99
as political agents, 89
attending meetings: Chartist sermons, 181; lectures, 181;
political meetings, 180; socials, 180
collecting money, 178
collecting signatures, 178
contributing to Chartist funds,
174–5
contributing to family economy,
131
educating children, 124–6
housework of politics, 124–6,
146–7
lecturing, 217–19

making banners, 181
memorialising the Queen, 180
middle-class women's difficulties,
138–40
performing in a male domain,
99, 101
politically active couples, 132–3
rioting, 182–6
scale of increasing visibility of
involvement, 123
seeking legal advice, 198
sending delegates, 239–40
showing gender solidarity, 101
signing petitions, 178
specific forms of involvement,
123, 174–8
subordination in movement, 178,
219, 246
supporting politically active husbands, 126–7, 140, 151: suffering from husband's imprison
ment, 137–8, 160–1; supporting imprisoned husbands,
135–6, 167
teaching, 195–6
timing of support for the movement, 248
turning everyday tasks political,
177
venerating Chartist leaders, 220–1
see also Female Chartist Associations
women Chartists: beliefs
against factory system, 91–2
against infanticide, 93
against New Poor Law, 92, 104–5
against Owenism, 215
against political oppression, 93,
95, 101
concern for family well-being,
91–2
concerning Chartist prisoners,
222–3
concerning female slavery, 95
concerning historical predecessors, 100
concerning patriotism, 99
concerning sexual division of
labour, 92